SUPERFICIAL OVERVIEW OF

# DATA MINING TOOL

# SUPERFICIAL OVERVIEW OF
# DATA MINING TOOL

*M. Usha Rani*
&
*R.J. Rama Sree*

GRP
GLOBAL RESEARCH PUBLICATIONS
NEW DELHI (INDIA)

First Published - 2008

ISBN: 81-89630-02-4



*Published by*

**GLOBAL RESEARCH PUBLICATIONS**
4800/24, 1st Floor, Ansari Road
Darya Ganj, New Delhi-110002 (India)
Phone : 23245225. Fax : 91-11-23272135
E-mail: serials@satyam.net.in

***Dedicated to***

***The Students of***

*2005-2008 Batch of MCA*

*Department of Computer Science*

*Sri Padmavathi Women's University,*

*Tirupati–517502 (A.P.)*

# Contents

## Preface

Data Mining is a set of processes related to analyzing and discovering useful, actionable knowledge buried deep beneath large volumes of data stores or data sets. This knowledge discovery involves finding patterns or behaviors within the data that lead to some profitable business action. Data Mining requires generally large volumes of data including history data as well as current data to explore the knowledge. There are a number of initiatives for the development of a formal/ documented data mining process both in Europe and North America.

An increasingly competitive business environment drives the need for Data Mining. For the first 25 years of computing the emphasis was on automating existing business processes. During the last 10 years much of the emphasis has been on managing these automated processes better. Executive Information Systems(EIS), management reporting tools and more recently On Line Analytical Processing(OLAP) tools have allowed management to observe the performance of the business. Data Mining is the extension of EIS. It can be used to find patterns in data that optimize existing processes and better conduct of the business.

If Data Mining is understood and applied properly, it can generate new revenue, increased profits and have significant cost savings. Gartner Group Advanced Technology Research note listed Data Mining and Artificial Intelligence at the top of 5 key technology areas. Data Mining is emerging as a major solution to solve a series of critical and fast growing issues. In particular with the effects of globalization and deregulation, major corporations are facing new pressure from increased competition on a world wide basis. Effectively responding to this challenge requires faster marketing cycles to produce a greater number of campaigns to attract and retain the best customers.

Data Mining Tools are automatic collection and integration of data from a variety of internal data sources and of content from any web site. Many Data Mining tools, vendors, and service providers are now available to service the Data Mining market.

Fundamental Aims of Data Mining Tools are to make measurable increase of marketing ROI, to make free data mining resource.

Software that allows you to analyze large volumes of raw data from business systems, applications, databases, web sites, and text based mediums. Data mining software extracts and manipulates information that is hidden in the raw data and is then reported back to you. The data mining software can help in improving the business processes and increase of business performance.

The Data Mining Software benefits are raw data can be quickly analyzed, prospect areas in a given domain of customers can be identified, business decisions can be fastened, and future demand can be predicted and segment markets can be identified, evaluated and strengthened.

Data Mining tools can enhance inference process, speed up design cycle and it can not substitute for statistical and domain expertise. Users are advised to get training on tools, and be alert for product upgrades. The illustrated different tools in this book are all free tools. And an attempt is made to list number of tools that are available, and their availability(links).

**M. Usha Rani**

# 1

# Introduction to Data Mining

## Introduction

Data Mining is a set of processes related to analyzing and discovering useful, actionable knowledge buried deep beneath large volumes of data stores or data sets. This knowledge discovery involves finding patterns or behaviors within the data that lead to some profitable business action. Data Mining requires generally large volumes of data including history data as well as current data to explore the knowledge.

*Crucial Concepts in Data Mining*

- Bagging (Voting, Averaging)
- Boosting
- RISP
- Data Preparation (in Data Mining)
- Data Reduction (for Data Mining)
- Deployment
- Drill-Down Analysis
- Feature Selection
- Machine Learning
- Meta-Learning

### Data Mining is a Process

There is increased interest in a process or methodology for data mining. It is argued that such a formalized process will widen the exploitation of data mining as an enabling technology for solving business problems. It will allow people with varying expertise in data mining and from different business sectors to carry out successful data mining projects with a high degree of consistency.

There are a number of initiatives for the development of a formal/documented data mining process both in Europe and North America. It is reassuring to the data mining community that the processes emerging from all of these initiatives reveal a large degree of similarity. There is widespread agreement on the main steps (stages) involved in such a process and any differences relate only to the detailed tasks within each stage.

A summary of the major stages of a data mining process is:

- *Goal definition:* This involves defining the goal or objective for the data-mining project. This should be a business goal or objective, which normally relates to a business event such as arrears in mortgage repayment, customer attrition (churn), energy consumption in a process, etc. This stage also involves the design of how the discovered patterns would be utilized as part of the overall business solution.
- *Data selection:* This is the process of identifying the data needed for the data-mining project and the sources of this data.
- *Data preparation:* This involves cleansing the data, joining/merging data sources and the derivation of new columns (fields) in the data through aggregation, calculations or text manipulation of existing data fields. The end result is normally a flat table ready for the application of the data mining itself (*i.e.* the discovery algorithms to generate patterns). Such a table is normally split into two data sets; one set for pattern discovery and one set for pattern verification.

- *Data exploration:* This involves the exploration of the prepared data to get a better feel prior to pattern discovery and also to validate the results of the data preparation. Typically, this involves examining the statistics (minimum, maximum, average, etc.) and the frequency distribution of individual data fields. It also involves field versus field graphs to understand the dependency between fields.
- *Pattern Discovery:* This is the stage of applying the pattern discovery algorithm to generate patterns. The process of pattern discovery is most effective when applied as an exploration process assisted by the discovery algorithm. This allows business users to interact with and to impart their business knowledge to the discovery process. In the case of inducing a tree, users can at any point in the tree construction examine/ explore the data filtering to that path, examine the recommendation of the algorithm regarding the next data field to use for the next branch then use their business judgment to decide on the data field for branching. The pattern discovery stage also involves analyzing the ability of the discovered patterns to predict the propensity of the business event, and for verification against an independent data set.
- Pattern Validity monitoring: As a process changes over time, the validity of patterns discovered from historic data will deteriorate. It is therefore important to detect these changes at the earliest possible time by monitoring patterns with new data. Significant changes to the patterns will point to the need to discover new patterns from more recent data.

**Definition of Data Mining**

Data Mining is a useful tool, a new approach that combines discovery with analysis. It become an important tool for competitive business. Data Mining tools predict future trends and behaviors allowing business to make proactive, knowledge driven decision. Data mining tools can answer business questions that traditionally were too time consuming to resolve. They search Data bases for hidden patterns, finding predictive information that experts may miss because it lies outside their expectations. Data Mining is a new interdisciplinary field merging ideas from statistics, machine learning, Data bases and parallel computing.

Researchers have defined the term "Data Mining" in many ways.

1. Data Mining or Knowledge Discovery in Data bases (KDD) is non-trivial extraction of implicit, previously unknown and potentially useful information from data.
2. Data Mining is the search for relationships and global patterns that exist in large Data bases but are hidden among vast amounts of data.
3. Data Mining is a combination of powerful methods that help reducing costs and risks as well as increasing revenues by extracting information from the available data.
4. Data Mining is the exploration and analysis by automatic and semiautomatic means of large quantities of data in order to discover meaningful patterns and rules.

**The Need of Data Mining**

An increasingly competitive business environment drives the need for Data Mining. For the first 25 years of computing the emphasis was on automating existing business processes. During the last 10 years much of the emphasis has been on managing these automated processes better. Executive Information Systems(EIS), management reporting tools and more recently On Line Analytical Processing(OLAP) tools have allowed management to observe the performance of the business. Data Mining is the extension of EIS. It can be used to find patterns in data that optimize existing processes and better conduct of the business.

If Data Mining is understood and applied properly, it can generate new revenue, increased profits and have significant cost savings. Gartner Group Advanced Technology Research note listed Data Mining and Artificial Intelligence at the top of 5 key technology areas. Data Mining is emerging as a major solution to solve a series of critical and fast growing issues. In particular with the effects of globalization and deregulation, major corporations are facing new pressure from increased competition on a world wide basis. Effectively responding to this challenge requires faster marketing cycles to produce a greater number of campaigns to attract and retain the best customers.

Data Mining offers a rich capability for modeling historical performance and then using this model to predict likely future outcomes. The only real prerequisite for Data Mining is a business problem plus relevant data. Collecting this data is the most time consuming part of Data Mining. Successful Data Mining requires both business knowledge and some analytical ability. The result of Data Mining is one or more decision models. Once tested these models can be deployed in many different places throughout the enterprise. For example, a model may be trained to recognize cases of bad credit risk and this would be deployed at sales transaction process.

The overall approach of Data Mining is first define a business goal, then deploy the Data Mining technology on the data and test models, then deploy the models to reap the benefit.

## Data Mining Technologies

The first name for Data Mining, beginning in 1960s was statistical analysis. The pioneers of statistical analysis were SAS, SPSS and IBM. All three of these companies are very active in Data Mining field today. Originally statistical analysis consisted of classical statistical routines such as correlation, regression, chi-square and cross tabulation. In late 1980s, classical statistical analysis was augmented with fuzzy logic, heuristic reasoning and neural networks. In late 1990s these statistical techniques were packaged with Decision Trees, Neural Networks, Rule Induction, Genetic Algorithms and other powerful techniques.

### *Decision Trees*

A tree shaped structure that represents a set of decisions. From a business perspective decision trees can be viewed as creating segmentation of original data sets. Each branch of a tree is a classification question and leaves of the tree are partitions of the data set with their classification i.e., segmentation of customers, products, sales regions etc. Segmentation is done for the prediction of some important piece of information.

The decision trees and algorithms that create predictive segments may be complex but the results are easy to understand and are useful to business user.

Decision tree algorithms are ID3, C4.5, Cart (Classification And Regression Trees), CHAID(Chi-Square Automatic Interaction Detector).

*Advantages of Decision trees*

- Ability to easily generate rules.
- Clarity
- Can build complex and understandable models.
- Able to handle numerical and categorical data.
- Can indicate which fields are most important.
- Used for both exploration and prediction.

Decision trees can identify which variables should be used as inputs to Neural networks. Because they are very fast and can deal with thousands of independent variables. (Neural networks in general do not perform well with large number of inputs).

### Neural Networks

Neural networks has an ability to deal with complicated or imprecise data and can be used to extract patterns and detect trends that are complex to be noticed by either humans or other techniques.

Neural networks are highly accurate, predictive models that can be applied to different types of problems like customer response prediction, sales forecasting, risk management, target marketing and fraud detection. Artificial neural networks can learn to detect the patterns in Data Bases and make better predictions similar to human beings. Neural networks can learn and improve over time while other techniques are static. A trained Neural network can be thought of as an expert and is used to provide projections given new situation and answers "what if" questions. But there are many important design decisions that need to be made in order to effectively use a Neural network such as number of nodes, connection of nodes, flow of information.

*Advantages of Neural networks*

- Adaptive learning
- Self organization
- Real time operation
- Fault tolerance

One of the key benefits of Neural network solutions is their capacity to save time, an important consideration in today's business world. Because of the adaptive nature of learning algorithms they are faster than traditional techniques. But understanding the data and clear definition of business problem to be solved are essential to ensure success.

***Rule Induction***

The extraction of useful if-then rules from data based on statistical significance. A Data Mining System has to infer a model from a Data base. When classes are defined, the system should be able to infer the rules that govern classification. Production rules have been widely used to represent knowledge in expert systems and can be easily interpreted by human experts.

Rules induced by Data Mining tools are descriptions of patterns found in the data. They may be "explanations" which suggest some causal dependency.

***Genetic Algorithms***

Genetic algorithms initiated and developed in early 1970s by John Holland. They are unorthodox search and optimization algorithms. Genetic algorithms are relatively new software paradigm inspired by Darwin's theory of evolution. A population of individuals, each representing a possible solution to a problem is initially created at random. Then pairs of individuals combine to produce offspring for next generation. A mutation process is also used randomly to modify genetic structure of some members of each new generation. Genetic algorithms are good at taking larger, potentially huge search spaces looking for optimal combinations of things and solutions.

**KDD vs Data Mining**

Data mining is a process to search for relationships and patterns that exist in data but are 'hidden' among the vast amount of data. These hidden patterns and relationships represent valuable knowledge about the database and the objects in the database Data mining, or Knowledge Discovery in Databases (KDD) is extraction of implicit, previously unknown, and potentially useful information from data. This includes a number of different technical approaches, such as clustering, data summarization, learning classification rules, finding dependency net works, analyzing changes, and detecting anomalies. Knowledge discovery in databases (KDD) is the process of identifying a valid, potentially, useful and ultimately understandable structure in data. This involves sampling data from a data warehouse, cleaning or preprocessing it, transforming or reducing it (if needed), applying a data mining component to produce a structure, and then evaluating the derived structure.

**Trends in Data Mining**

***Phenomenal Data Mining***

Data Mining involves computer programs that infer relations in different kinds of data in large databases. Data amounts to observations of the world, and it is possible to infer relations among entities in the world from the data. Such relations are likely to be as useful to know about, as are relations among the entities directly represented in the data. Phenomenal Data

Mining finds relations between the data and the phenomena that give to rise to data rather than just relations among the data. One example of phenomenal data mining is that, using receipts from cash super market purchases, it is possible to identify various aspects of the customers who are marketing these purchases. Some of these phenomena include age, income, ethnicity and purchasing habits.

### *Constraint Based and Multidimensional Data Mining*

Integrating both constraint-based and multidimensional mining into one framework provides an interactive, exploratory environment for effective and efficient data analysis and mining. By constraint-based Data Mining we mean, Data Mining process in which the user provides constraints that guide the mining in the databases. Constraint based Data Mining techniques can provide a more adhoc query-driven process that exploits the semantics of data, more efficiently than current stand-alone Data Mining system.

### *Multi–Relational Data Mining*

Multi relational Data Mining is the multi disciplinary fields dealing with knowledge discovery from relational databases consisting of multiple tables. Mining data which consists of complex/structured object also falls with in the scope of the field, since the normalized representation of such objects in a relational database requires multiple tasks.

### *Spatial Data Mining*

Spatial data mining, i.e., mining knowledge from large amounts of spatial data, is important because huge amounts of spatial data have been collected in various applications, ranging from remote sensing, to geographical information systems (GIS), computer cartography, environmental assessment and planning, etc. Recent studies on data mining have extended the scope of data mining from relational and transactional databases to spatial databases. A spatial database stores spatial objects represented by spatial data types and spatial relationships among such objects. Spatial data carries topological and/or distance information and it is often organized by spatial indexing structures and accessed by spatial access methods. These distinct features of a spatial database pose challenges and bring opportunities for mining information from spatial data. Spatial data mining, or knowledge discovery in spatial database, refers to the extraction of implicit knowledge, spatial relations, or other patterns not explicitly stored in spatial databases. Efficient tools for extracting information from geo-spatial data sets, including NASA, the National Imaging and Mapping Agencies (NIMA), the National Cancer Institute (NCI). These organizations spread across many application domains including ecology and environmental management, Transportation, earth science, epidemiology and climatology.

*Geographical Data Mining*

The immense explosion in geographically referenced data occasioned by developments in IT, digital mapping, remote sensing and the global diffusion of GIS emphasizing the importance of developing data driven inductive approaches to geographical analysis and modeling to facilitate the creation of new knowledge and aid the processes of scientific discovery. Geographical data mining tools are useful for summarizing the essential features of large spatial data sets to create geo-demographics classifications. Analyzing spatial and geographic data include such tasks as understanding and browsing spatial data, uncovering relationships between spatial data items (and also between non-spatial and spatial items), and also analyzing using spatial databases and spatial knowledge bases. The application of these would be useful in such fields as remote sensing, medical imaging, navigation, and related issues.

*Hyper Text and Multi-media Data Mining*

Multimedia data mining is the mining and analysis of various types of data, including image, video, audio and animation. Some of the important data mining techniques used for hypertext and hyper media data mining include classification, clustering, semi-structured learning and social network analysis.

### *Ubiquitous Data Mining*

The advent of laptops, palmtops, cell phones, is making ubiquitous access to large quantity of data possible. After accessing, advanced analysis of data for extracting useful knowledge is the next step. The key issues include theories of UDM, advanced algorithms for mobile and distributed applications, data management issues, mark up language and other data representation techniques.

## Applications of Data Mining

### *Risk Analysis*

Insurance companies and banks use data mining for risk analysis. An insurance company searches in its own insurants and claims databases for relationships between personal characteristics and claim behavior. The company is especially interested in the characteristics of insurants with a highly deviating claim behavior. With data mining these so-called risk profiles can be discovered.

### *Direct Marketing*

Data mining can also be used to discover the relationships between one's personal characteristics ex: age, gender, home town and the probability that one will respond to a mailing. Such relationships can be used to select those customers from the mailing database that have the highest probability of responding to a mailing. This allows the company to mail its prospects selectively, thus maximizing the response.

### *Production Quality Control*

Data mining can also be used to determine those combinations of production factors that influence the quality of the end product.

This information allows the process engineers to explain, why certain products fail the final test and to increase the quality of the production process.

### *Healthcare*

Healthcare generates mountains of administrative data about patients hospitals, bed costs claims etc. Clinical trials, electronic patients records and computer supported disease management will increasingly produce mountains of clinical data. This data is a strategic resource for health care institutions. Clinically - based data warehouse product designed for use through out a hospital, bring the potential for specialized information production to the clinicians and manages desktop through use of clinical workstations and executive information systems (EIS) data mining products are designed to take this one stage further. It brings the facility to discover patterns and correlation hidden within data repository and assists professionals to uncover these patterns and put them to work.

### *Customer Relations*

In customer relationship management (CRM), web mining is the integration of information gathered by traditional data mining methodologies and techniques with information gathered over the world wide web.

Customer relationship management centers around customer acquisition, retention and cross selling. Data mining tools can be employed very effectively to achieve both customer acquisition, product launch campaign and cross selling. Data mining will be essential for understanding customer behavior on the web and for helping the websites of the world to create their personalized responses.

### *Financial Data Mining*

Financial data mining is used to classify and cluster the customers for targeted marketing. Financial data collected in banks and financial institutions are often relatively complete, reliable, and of high quality. Multidimensional segmentation by nearest neighbor, classification, decision trees, etc, are used to identify customer groups or associate a new customer to an appropriate customer group. It is also used to detect money laundering and other financial crimes. Data mining tools like data visualization linkage analysis, classification, clustering tools, outlier analysis and sequential pattern analysis tools are used to find unusual access sequences.

### *Retail Industry*

Retail data mining applications are used to identify customer buying behaviors, discover customer shopping patterns and trends, improve the quality of the customer service, achieve better customer retention and satisfaction and design more effective goods transportation and distribution policies.

## Data Mining Tools

Many Data Mining tools, vendors, and service providers are now available to service the Data Mining market. Data Mining Tools are automatic collection and integration of data from a variety of internal data sources and of content from any web site.

### *Fundamental Aims of Data Mining Tools*

- To make measurable increase of marketing ROI
- To make free data mining resources

## A Survey

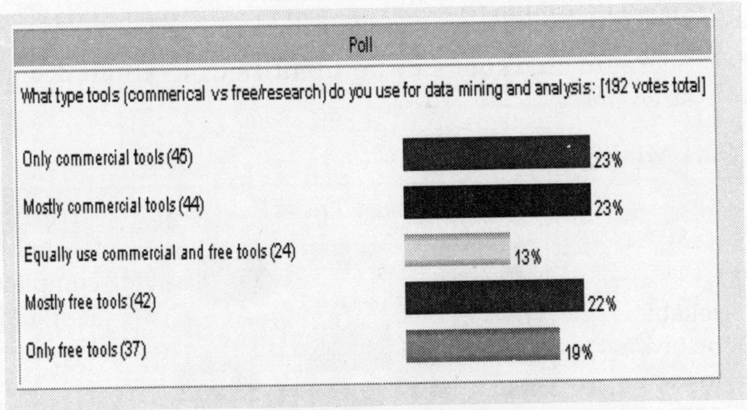


**Commercial vs. Free Data Mining Tools**

### *Caveats*

- The level of functionality of each tool is not known.
- The requirement of user is ever changing.
- The tools are not standardized in terms of their goal.
- The users are of different domains belonging to different areas.
- The availability of the tools is quite abundant.
- New versions appear regularly.

### *The Data Mining Software*

Software that allows you to analyze large volumes of raw data from business systems, applications, databases, web sites, and text based mediums. Data mining software extracts and manipulates information that is hidden in the raw data and is then reported back to you. The data mining software can help in improving the business processes and increase of business performance.

### *Benefits of Data Mining Software*

- Raw data can be quickly analyzed.
- Prospect areas in a given domain of customers can be identified.
- Business decisions can be fastened.
- Future demand can be predicted.
- Segment markets can be identified, evaluated and strengthened.

## Data Mining Products

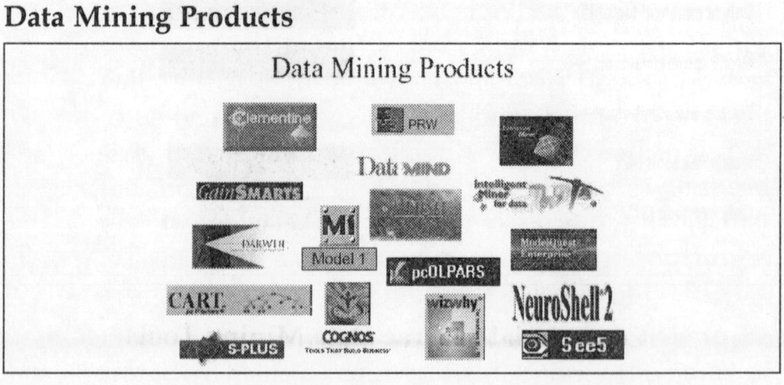

### *Parameters for Comparing Different Data Mining Products*

- Platforms Supported
- Algorithms Included
    - Decision Trees
    - Neural Networks
    - Other
- Data Input and Model Output Options
- Usability Ratings
- Visualization Capabilities
- Modeling Automation Methods

**Summary**

- Data Mining Tools Can:
    - ~ Enhance inference process
    - ~ Speed up design cycle
- Data Mining Tools Can Not:
    - ~ Substitute for statistical and domain expertise
- Users are advised to:
    - ~ Get training on tools.
    - ~ Be alert for product upgrades.

# 2

# Superficial Overview of Data Mining Tools

The following paragraphs provide a superficial overview of Data Mining Tools on the market. Links are provided to resources where more detailed information can be found.

**4Thought**

Product : 4Thought
Vendor : Cognos Inc.
URL : www.cognos.com /products/4thought
Functions : Prediction
Techniques : Neural networks (MLP)
Platform : Windows

4Thought supports decision support applications, including forecasting. A spreadsheet interface is provided. Data can be accessed as text files, Excel, Lotus, dBase, Impromptu, Powerplay, and Scenario files.

**AC²**

Product : AC²
Vendor : ISoft
URL : www.alice-soft.com/html/prod_ac2.htm
Functions : Clustering, classification, prediction, segmentation
Techniques : Decision trees
Platforms : Unix, Windows

$AC^2$ is a complete data mining toolkit designed for knowledgeable users.$AC^2$ has a graphical object oriented modeling language and C/C++ libraries. Interactive editing of trees is supported. It behaves as a multiplatform library of data mining functions.

**Affinium Model**

Products : Affinium Model
Vendor : Unica Corporation
URL : www.unicacorp.com
Functions : Classification, Segmentation
Platforms : Unix, Windows

Affinium Model provides CRM applications with segmentation capabilities.

**AI Trilogy**

Products : AI Trilogy
Vendor : Ward Systems Group, Inc.
Functions : Classifications, forecasting, prediction
Techniques : Genetic algorithms, jackknife estimation, neural networks
Platform : Windows

AI Triolgy is a suite of three products: NeuroShell Predictor, NeuroShell Classifier and GeneHunter. Ascii, CSV, and Excel files are supported. The NeuroShell Run-Time Server is also included as a utility for trained neural networks to run in Excel and user programs.

**Alice**

Product : Alice d'ISoft & Alice Server
Vendor : ISoft
URL : www.alice-soft.com/html/prod_alice.htm
Functions : Clustering, correlation, segmentation
Techniques : Decision trees
Platforms : Metaframe, TSE, Windows, Unix

Alice d'ISoft is an interactive data mining tool that covers all aspects of the KDD process. Alice can access data in many different formats, including relational databases via both

ODBC and OLE DB drivers. Alice integrates decision tree techniques with an OLAP engine. A companion tool, Amadea, supports data transformation and cleaning. The Alice Server version supports a client/server architecture.

**AnswerTree**

| | | |
|---|---|---|
| Products | : | AnswerTree 3.0 |
| Vendor | : | SPDD Inc. |
| URL | : | www.spss.com/answertree |
| Functions | : | Classification |
| Techniques | : | Decision tree [CHAID, Exhaustive CHAID, C&RT (a variation of CART), QUEST]. |
| Platforms | : | Client(Windows), Server (Solaris, Windows) |

AnswerTree is an SPSS product used to create decision trees. As a data mining tool it targets profiling groups for marketing and sales. Four basic decision tree algorithms are used. Included are two CHAID algorithms, both of which SPSS has extended to handle nominal categorical, ordinal categorical, and continuous dependent variables.

**AOM**

| | | |
|---|---|---|
| Product | : | AOM(Ace Optimizer Maintenance-3.1.0) |
| Vendor | : | Acelogix |
| URL | : | www. |
| Functions | : | Maintain PC |
| Platforms | : | Windows 98 /ME/2000/XP,Windows Server 2003/Vista |

AOM (Ace Optimizer Maintenance–Ace Utilities) is an award winning collection of tools to optimize your PC's performance. It allows you to find and remove the junk files in your PC, invalid registry entries, delete your internet usage history, provides plug-in support to erase the usage-history for over 200 third-party applications, manage your internet cookies and much more. With a detailed startup-manager you can see what all programs, services, drivers, etc start automatically with Windows and optionally disable them.

**Braincel**

| | | |
|---|---|---|
| Products | : | Braincel |
| Vendor | : | Jurik Research and Consulting |
| URL | : | www.jurikres.com/catalog/ms_bcel.htm |
| Functions | : | Forecasting |
| Techniques | : | Neural networks (back-percolation) |
| Platform | : | Windows |

Braincel is an Excel add-in that uses neural networks to perform forecasting. An improved version of backpropagation called back-percolation is used. Promised Land Technologies developed Braincel, and Jurik Research developed the back-percolation approach.

**BrainMaker**

| | | |
|---|---|---|
| Product | : | BrainMaker |
| Vendor | : | California Scientific Software |
| URL | : | www.calsci.com |
| Functions | : | Forecasting |
| Techniques | : | Neural networks |
| Platforms | : | Macintosh, Windows |

BrainMaker is neural network software that can be used with many different data sources, including Lotus, Excel, dBase, ASCII, or binary. It is one of the most popular NN software tools. A companion product, NetMaker, is included to assist in the construction of the neural networks. An optional package, Genetic Training Option (GTO), uses a genetic algorithm to create several possible neural nets. Though several iterations of training and genetic evolution, the best network can be chosen. This process also helps to choose the best training data.

**CART**

| | | |
|---|---|---|
| Product | : | CART |
| Vendor | : | salford-systems.com |
| URL | : | www.salford-systems.com |
| Functions | : | Classification |
| Techniques | : | Decision tree |
| Platforms | : | CMS, MVS, UNIX (LINUX), WINDOWS. |

CART is a Decision tree tool that uses the CART algorithm and different file formats (including excel, Informix, lotus, oracle) may be used. An optimal product, Tree coder, allows the use of CART directly in SAS. Tree viewer allows trees created on a unix platform to be viewed on windows. Boosting, Missing data are handled through specialized backup rules that do not always assume that all values for a missing attribute are the same. Seven different splitting criteria (including Gini) are used.

**CBA**

| | |
|---|---|
| Product | : CBA (Classification Based on Association) |
| Vendor | : UNESCO |
| URL | : www.comp.nus.edu.sg/~dm2 |
| Functions | : Classification and Prediction, Text Categorization and Classification, Mining Association rules with multiple minimum supports. |
| Mining Strategies | : Classification Mining, Association Mining |
| Platform | : Windows |

CBA is used for mining various forms of association rules, and for text categorization or classification. It also solves a number of problems with the existing classification techniques (e.g., decision tree, or neural networks, and many others).

CBA can be used for Classification and Prediction, Text Categorization and Classification, Mining association rules with Multiple Minimum Supports, Mining association rules from relational data or transactional data.

**Clementine**

| | |
|---|---|
| Product | : Clementine |
| Vendor | : SPSS Inc. (formerly Integral Solutions, Ltd.) |
| URL | : www. Spss.com/Clementine |
| Functions | : Association rules, classifications, clustering factor analysis, forecasting, prediction, sequence discovery. |
| Techniques | : Apriori, BIRCH, CARMA, Decision trees (C5.0, C&RT a variation of CART), K-means |

clustering, neural networks (Kohonen, MLP, RBFN), regression (linear, logistic) rule induction (C5.0, GRI).

Platforms : HP/UX, IBM AIX, Sun Solaris, Windows NT

Perhaps the most unique feature of *Clementine* is its GUI approach to data mining, which Clementine pioneered in 1994. though the use of descriptive icons, a user creates a data flow description of the functions to be performed. Each icon represents a step in the overall KDD process. Included are icons for such functions as accessing data, preparing data, visualization and modeling. By dragging and dropping the icons onto the Clementine desktop, a stream of functions is created. Through the use of predefined templates of streams, Clementine provides support for common Web usage mining applications. To assist in the creation of sequences, Clementine uses Capri.

Clementine mines large data sets using a client/server model. When applicable, the server converts data access requests into SQL queries, which can then access a relational database. Clementine supports a wide variety of data formats. Clementine solutions are exported and deployed outside of Clementine using Clementine Solution Publisher.

**CTree**

Product : CTree
Vendor : SALFORD-SYSTEMS.COM
URL : WWW.geocitiecs.COM
Functions : Predication, Classification, Clustering
Techniques : Decision tree, Classification Tree
Platforms : WINDOWS Family, LINUX, UNIX

CTree is freely downloadable, easy to use, learn and performance not too bad. A decision tree is a classification scheme, which generates a tree and a set of rules, representing a model of different classes, from a give data set. The set of records available for developing classification method is generally divided into two disjoint subsets-training dataset and test dataset. The former is used for deriving classifier and later is used to measure the accuracy.

A tool that does not require special installations to be done, does not require licences to be bought, quick and easy to distribute on students' machines, does not requires data files to be prepared in special formats and can quickly run a bunch of examples.

**Cubist**

| | | |
|---|---|---|
| Product | : | Cubist 1.10 |
| Vendor | : | RuleQuest Research Pty Ltd |
| URL | : | www.rulequest.com/cubist-info.html |
| Functions | : | Numerical modeling |
| Techniques | : | Regression, rules |
| Platforms | : | Windows, Unix (Linux, Irix, Solaris) |

As a companion product to see5/C5.0, *Cubist* generates actual prediction values with the rules. Source code in C is provided so that models generated by Cubist can be embedded in applications.

**Darwin**

| | | |
|---|---|---|
| Product | : | Darwin |
| Vendor | : | Oracle Corporation |
| URL | : | www.Oracle.com/ip/analyze/warehouse/datamining/content.html |
| Functions | : | Clustering, prediction, classification, association rules |
| Techniques | : | Decision trees (CART), K-means, K-nearest neighbors, neural net-works, regression (linear, logistic). |
| Platforms | : | Windows, Sun Solaris, HP-UX |

Darwin, or Oracle Data Mining Suite, provides a simple-to-use Windows-based GUI interface and parallel implementations of various data mining algorithms. It implements a complete KDD process model. Through OCI direct data access and ODBC, access to many relational systems is facilitated. Access to text and SAS files is also supported. Oracle Data Mining uses a client-server approach. C, C++, or Java code can be exported.

**DataEngine**

| | | |
|---|---|---|
| Product | : | DataEngine |
| Vendor | : | Management Intelligenter Technologies GmbH |
| URL | : | www.dataengine.de |
| Functions | : | Classifications, clustering, decision trees, time series analysis |
| Techniques | : | Decision trees, fuzzy rules, K-means, neural networks (MLP, Kohonen), regression (linear) |
| Platform | : | Windows |

DataEngine supports many different data mining tasks as well as statistical methods. DataEngine supports many methods for data cleansing, data transformation and handling missing data. Many types of data are supported via an import-export interface. With DataEngine ADl you can generate C code or produce DLLs, which can be incorporated in application code for subsequent use of a generated model.

**Data Mining Suite**

| | | |
|---|---|---|
| Product | : | Data Mining Suite |
| Vendor | : | Information Discovery, Inc. |
| URL | : | www.datamining.com/dmsuite.htm |
| Functions | : | Association rules, forecasting, prediction, rules |
| Techniques | : | Rule induction |
| Platform | : | Windows |

The Data Mining Suite is designed to mine large relational databases. The suite of tools actually consists of six different modules, each targeted to different data mining functions. Incremental data mining is supported, as are multidimensional mining and ROLAP. The results of all data mining are viewed as patterns or rules. The most unique feature of the Data Mining Suite is the fact that generated patterns are stored and are accessible using the Pattern Query Language (PQL).

**DataMite**

| | | |
|---|---|---|
| Product | : | DataMite |
| Vendor | : | Logic Programming Associates Ltd. |

URL : www.1pa.co.uk/ind.pro.htm
Functions : Rules
Techniques : Decision trees, rules induction
Platforms : ODBC, Windows

DataMite performs mining against relational databases, which can be accessed via ODBC. If-then rules are generated based on outcomes desired by the user.

**Data Stage**

Product : Data Stage
Vendor : Ascential
Functions : Extract, transformation and loading of data from different sources and storing in a data warehouse
Platform : Windows XP

DataStage is a tool set for designing, developing, and running applications that populate one or more tables in a data warehouse or data mart. It consists of client and server components. DataStage has four client components which are installed on any PC running Windows 95, Windows 2000, or Windows NT 4.0 with Service Pack 4 or later. There are three server components which are installed on a server: Repository: A central store that contains all the information required to build a data mart or data warehouse. DataStage Server. Runs executable jobs that extract, transform, and load data into a data warehouse. DataStage Package Installer. A user interface used to install packaged DataStage jobs and plug-ins.

**DataMite**

Product : DataMite
Vendor : Logic Programming Associates Ltd.
URL : www.1pa.co.uk/ind.pro.htm
Functions : Rules
Techniques : Decision trees, rules induction
Platforms : ODBC, Windows

DataMite performs mining against relational databases, which can be accessed via ODBC. If-then rules are generated based on outcomes desired by the user.

**DBMiner**

Product : DBMiner Analytical System
Vendor : DBMiner Technologies Inc.
URL : www.dbminer.com
Functions : Association rules, classification, clustering
Techniques : Decision trees, K-means
Platform : Windows

DBMiner accesses data from many sources, including Microsoft SQL Server, Excel, OLEDB and other relational databases through ODBC. Users can use either a DMSQL interface or a GUI interface. Interface through MS SQL server's OLAP allows a cube view of data. There actually are three different products: DBMiner AX 2000 targets association rules, DBMiner SX 2000 performs sequential mining and DBMiner GX 2000 targets OLAP mining.

**DD**

Product : Discrete Distributor
URL : www.discretedistributer.com
Functions : Distributions, ratio, hypergeometric Analysis
Platform : Windows

**Decider**

Product : Decider and Decider-online
Vendor : Neural Technologies
URL : www.neuralt.com
Functions : Classification, prediction rules
Techniques : Neural networks
Platform : Windows

*Decider* and *Decider-online* are DSS tools that incorporate data mining functionality to identify credit risks and fraud.

**DecisionTime**

Product : DecisionTime and WhatIf
Vendor : SPSS Inc.
URL : www. Spss.com/decisiontime
Functions : Time series forecasting and analysis
Techniques : ARIMA, exponential smoothing
Platform : Windows

DecisionTime is a time series forecasting tool. Through user interaction, DecisionTime chooses the best of the included models via a wizard to perform the forecasting or allows the more sophisticated user to build his or her own models. Input is accepted from many different types of files, including Excel, SPSS, ASCII and an ODBC source. The *WhatIf?* Part of the solution allows the user to change ARIMA model predictor variables to create various scenarios of the forecasts generated in DecisionTime.

**DTREG**

Product : DTREG
Vendor : Phillip H.Sherrod
URL : www.dtreg.com
Functions : Construction of Decision Tree
Techniques : Classification
Platform : Windows

DTREG accepts a dataset containing of number of rows with a column for each variable. One of the variables is the "target variable" whose value is to be modeled and predicted as a function of the "predictor variables". DTREG analyzes the data and generates a model showing how best to predict the values of the target variable based on values of the predictor variables.

DTREG can create classical, single-tree models and also TreeBoost and Decision Tree Forest models consisting of ensembles of many trees. DTREG also can generate Neural Networks, Support Vector Machine (SVM), Discriminant Analysis and Logistic Regression models.

**EDM**

Product : Estard Data Miner
Vendor : SAS Institute Inc.
URL : www.estard.com/products/miner
Functions : Statistical Analysis, Data Analysis, classification.
Techniques : Decision trees
Platform : Windows

Estard Data Miner is a comprehensive data mining application, able to discover hidden relations both in structured and unstructured data. The newest data mining techniques were incorporated into Estard Data Miner for carrying out automated data analysis. Estard Data Miner performs statistical analysis, reveals all "If-Then" (production) rules and creates decision trees. The created decision models can be easily viewed and interpretate.

**Enterprise Miner**

| | | |
|---|---|---|
| Product | : | Enterprise Miner |
| Vendor | : | SAS Institute Inc. |
| URL | : | www.sas.com/products/miner |
| Functions | : | Association rules, classification, clustering prediction, time series |
| Techniques | : | Decision trees (CART, CHAID), K nearest neighbors, regression (linear, logistic), memory-based reasoning, neural networks (kohonen, MLP RBF, SOM). |
| Platforms | : | Client (Windows), Server (Unix, Windows) |

Enterprise Miner from SAS implements the complete KDD process using their own process model called SEMMA (Sample, Explore, Modify, Model, Assess). An icon-based, joint and click GUI (not unlike Clementine) creates a process flow to be performed by the data mining task. In addition, Enterprise Miner contains many tools for bagging and boosting, sampling, visualization, imputation, filtering, transformations and model assessment. An experiment text mining feature is also available. Enterprise Miner generates the complete scoring formula for all stages of model development in the form of SAS, C and Java for subsequent model deployment and scoring.

**ERUPT**

| | | |
|---|---|---|
| Product | : | ERUPT |
| URL | : | www.rockware.com/catalog/pages/erupt.html |
| Functions | : | Interactive graphical program designed to simulate a wide range of volcanic activity and display it 2-dimensionally. |

Techniques : Temporal and Spatial Mining
Platforms : Windows 95, NT

Erupt is a user interactive graphical program designed to simulate a wide range of volcanic activity and display it 2-dimensionally. The graphical display shows the temporal and spatial evolution of particle paths for lava and pyroclasts, their deposition and the construction of a volcanic edifice in two dimensions. It simulates various volcanic eruption types, including Strombolian, Plinian, Vulcanian/Surtseyan, Hawaiian lava flows, Peléean viscous lava dome emplacement, Fumarolic/Phreatic activity, and sector collapse. Tectonic (faulting) and erosional events are also simulated.

**GainSmarts**

Product : GainSmarts
Vendor : Urban Science
URL : www.urbanscience.com/main/gainpage.htm
Functions : Classification, clustering, prediction
Techniques : Bayesian classification, decision trees (AID, CHAID), genetic algorithms, K-means, neural networks, regression (linear, logistic)
Platforms : SAS, Windows

GainSmarts is a comprehensive product that supports all steps in the KDD process. It is flexible in the data sources that are supported, including any supported by SAS or ACCESS. Collaborative filtering and survival analysis are also supported.

**GEOTRIG**

Product : GEOTRIG
Vendor : UNESCO
URL : www.rockware.com
Functions : Height, 3-point problem, true dip, apparent dip, vertical exaggeration, map thickness (from dist), drilled thickness, map thickness (from xyz)
Platform : Windows

GEOTRIG is a collection of geologically-related geometric and trigonometric problem solvers for windows.

**HNC Risk Suite**

| | | |
|---|---|---|
| Product | : | HNC Risk Suite |
| Vendor | : | HNC Software |
| URL | : | www.hnc.com |
| Functions | : | Prediction |
| Techniques | : | Neural networks, rules |
| Platform | : | Windows |

HNC's Risk Suite actually is a set of tools targeting risk analysis and prediction. The Falcon Fraud Manager is an integral part of this suite.

**Intelligent Miner**

| | | |
|---|---|---|
| Product | : | Intelligent Miner |
| Vendor | : | IBM Corporation |
| URL | : | www.software.ibm.com/data/iminer |
| Functions | : | Association rules, clustering, classifications, prediction, sequential patterns, time series |
| Techniques | : | Decision trees (modified CART), K-means, neural networks (MLP, back-propagation, RBF), regression (linear) |
| Platforms | : | Windows, Solaris, AIX, OS/390, OS/400 |

DB2 Intelligent Miner for Data performs mining functions against traditional DB2 databases or flat files. It also has capabilities to access data in other relational DBMSs using ODBC. However to do this IBM's DataJoiner must be used. It is implemented using a client-server approach with a straightforward GUI interface provided to assist the user in choosing data mining functions. Several visualization techniques are used.

There are two other products in the IBM Intelligent Miner family. Intelligent Miner for Text performs mining activities against textual data, including e-mail and Web pages. It consists of text analysis tools, a search engine, NetQuestion Solution, Web crawler package. The text analysis tools include the ability to cluster, classify, summarize and extract important features from a document. NetQuestion Solution is a set of tools to facilitate indexing and searching Web documents. DB2 Intelligent Miner Scoring allows SQL applications the ability to request data mining applications against a DB2 or Oracle database. It is a user-defined extension to DB2. it can be used to determine the actual score that a record has with respect to user-defined ranking criteria.

**JDA Intellect**

| | | |
|---|---|---|
| Product | : | JDA Intellect (formerly Decision Series) |
| Vendor | : | JDA Software Group, Inc. |
| URL | : | www.jda.com/jdad/ProductsServices/Intellect.facts.htm |
| Functions | : | Association rules, classification, clustering, prediction |
| Techniques | : | Naive Bayes, decision trees, K-means, K nearest neighbors, neural networks (back-propagation, RBF) |
| Platforms | : | Solaris, Windows |

JDA purchased NeoVista in June 2001. The new JDA Intellect product is based on NeoVista's Decision Series data mining suite. JDA intellect actually is a set of KDD and data mining tools. Seasonal Profiling Intellect can be used to extract and describe profiles reflecting seasonal sales trends. Channel Clustering Intellect is targeted to the clustering of retail stores based on products sold. The decision Series consists of many different data mining engines, including DecisionNet, DecisionCubist, DecisionTree, DecisionBayes, DecisionCluster, DecisionKmean and DecisionAR. Each of these engines implements one or more of the data mining techniques. A GUI interface facilitates creation of data flow designs by naïve users. More experienced users can use a command line and programming interface.

**JDBC Mine**

| | | |
|---|---|---|
| Product | : | JDBCMine |
| Vendor | : | Intelligent Systems Research |
| URL | : | www.intsysr.com/JDBCMine.htm |
| Functions | : | Classification |
| Techniques | : | Decision trees (C4.5) |
| Platforms | : | Windows, Java |

JDBCMine performs classification against JDBC and ODBC databases using C4. 5. The decision trees created can be visually browsed, printed, or saved as JPEG files.

**Kaidara Advisor**

| | | |
|---|---|---|
| Product | : | Kaidara Advisor (formerly KATE) |
| Vendor | : | Kaidara |
| URL | : | www.kaidara.com |
| Functions | : | Classification, clustering, prediction |
| Techniques | : | Case-based reasoning, decision trees |
| Platform | : | Windows |

Kaidara Advisor (formerly KATE) is a data mining tool targeted to support CRM applications. Kaidara Advisor supports sales automation and intelligent catalogs.

**KnowledgeSTUDIO**

| | | |
|---|---|---|
| Product | : | KnowledgeSTUDIO |
| Vendor | : | ANGOSS Software Corporation |
| URL | : | www.angoss.com/ProdServ/AnalyticalTools/index.html |
| Functions | : | Classification, clustering, prediction, rules |
| Techniques | : | Decision trees (CHAID, expectation-maximization, K-means, neural networks (MLP, RBF), regression (linear, logistic) |
| Platforms | : | Windows, Server (Solaris, Windows). |

KnowledgeSTUDIO is a complete data mining workbench that performs many different tasks. It reads data from all major statistical packages and can import data from relational databases using ODBC. The optional KnowledgeSTUDIO Software Development Kit can be used to create in-house data mining applications. Application cade can be generated for Visual Basic, PowerBuilder, Delphi, C++ and Java and then embedded into user code. KnowledgeSERVER can be used to create a client-server architecture. It also can be used to access data directly in relational databases.

KnowledgeSEEKER has a graphically based GUI and supports decision tree classification algorithms.

**KnowledgeSEEKER**

| | | |
|---|---|---|
| Product | : | KnowledgeSEEKER |
| Vendor | : | ANGOSS Sofware Corporation |
| URL | : | www.angoss.com/ProdServ/Analytical Tools/index.html |
| Functions | : | Classification |
| Techniques | : | Decision trees (CHAID, XAID, entropy-based algorithms) |
| Platforms | : | Windows, Unix (AIX, HP-UX, IRIX, Digital Alpha, Sinux, Solaris, SCO, Linux) |

**LOGIT**

| | | |
|---|---|---|
| Product | : | LOGIT |
| Vendor | : | Salford Systems |
| URL | : | www.salford-systems.com |
| Functions | : | Forecasting, hypothesis testing |
| Techniques | : | Regression (logistic) |
| Platforms | : | DOS, MacOS, Unix |

LOGIT is a logistic regression tool. As with MARS, DBMS/copy allows the use of many different data formats.

**MAGNETIC**

| | | |
|---|---|---|
| Product | : | MAGNETIC.EXE (8.0.10) |
| URL | : | http://www.rockware.com (rdetenbe@uvm.edu) |
| Techniques | : | Spatial Mining |
| Platform | : | Windows 3.1/95/98 |

The Magnetic.EXE program permits students to compare the predictions of their own models, for magnetic anomalies over mid-ocean spreading ridges, with real experimental data. The geophysical situation is fascinating. Magnetic stripes on the ocean floor serve as a tape recorder of the reversals of the earth's magnetic field.

The physics and geology are not hard to explain to students. However, calculations of the predictions of models are tedious without the help of a programmable computer, and discourage students from making models of their own and playing "what if ..." games. Even a modest PC makes short work of the calculations, permitting students to test models and tinker with their details.

**MA**

Product : Mortality Analysis
URL : www.mortalityanalysis.com
Functions : Prediction
Platform : Windows

Mortality Analysis predicts and presents life table, PGLE, YPLL, SMR, and CMF.

**Magnify**

Product : Magnify
Vendor : Magnify
URL : www.magnify.com
Functions : Prediction
Platform : Unix

Magnify offers complete solutions (technology suite, consulting) for customer related prediction problems. Magnify targets the insurance, direct marketing and government industries. The technology used is designed to be scalable to any size dataset.

**Magnum Opus**

Product : Magnum Opus 1.3
Vendor : RuleQuest Research Pty Ltd
URL : www.rulequest.com/MagnumOpus-info.html
Functions : Association Rules
Techniques : Opus
Platforms : Windows, Unix (Solaris, Linux)

Magnum Opus generates association rules using the measures of leverage, lift, strength, coverage and support. Only rules that satisfy the desired measurement constraints are generated. Filtering of rules is also performed. Association rules can be generated for market basket-type data as well as other attribute values. Numeric attributes are automatically partitioned into subranges.

**Mantas**

Product : Mantas
Vendor : Mantas, Inc.
URL : www.mantas.com
Functions : Association rules, classification, clustering, link analysis, prediction, sequence analysis, time series
Techniques : Decision trees, neural networks
Platforms : Unix, Windows

Mantas, Inc., a spin-off from SRA International in May 2001, provides knowledge discovery solutions for the global financial services industry. The Mantas Knowledge Discovery Platform provides an extensible foundation that proactively collects, analyzes, highlights and disseminates relevant, actionable information. The Mantas product suite includes five products. Mantas Best Execution is used to analyze brokerage trading and identify opportunities to improve execution quality. Mantas Equities Trading Compliance monitors trading behaviors to ensure adherence to industry rules and regulations. Mantas Brokerage Fraud and Anti-Money Laundering monitors security and monetary transaction for potential fraud and money laundering activities. Mantas Brokerage and Investor Protection monitors broker and investor behavior and trading activity to identify potential risks to both the investor and the firm. Mantas Enterprise Anti-Money Laundering is used to identify potential money laundering risks relating to enterprise products and transaction services.

**MarketMiner**

Product : MarketMiner
Vendor : MarketMiner Inc.
URL : www.marketminer.com
Functions : Classification, pattern recognition, prediction, segmentation
Techniques : Decision trees (C4.5), KNN, regression (linear, logistic), statistical techniques.
Platform : Windows

MarketMiner is a set of marketing analysis tools designed to automate the data mining and analysis process for a business user without advanced statistics knowledge.

**MARS**

Product : MARS
Vendor : Salford Systems
URL : www.salford-systems.com
Functions : Forecasting
Techniques : Regression
Platforms : Unix (Linux, Solaris), Windows

MARS performs forecasting via the Multivariate Adaptive Regression Spliners technique. It fits separate splines to different intervals for the predictor variables. Automatic selection of predictor variables is performed. As with CART, DBMS/COPY allows access to many diccerent formats of data. A graphical GUI is provided.

**Minotaur**

Product : Minotaur and Minotaur Transcure
Vendor : Neural Technologies
URL : www.neuralt.com
Functions : Classification, prediction, rules
Techniques : Neural networks
Platform : Windows

Minotaur and Minotaur Transcure and neural network products targeted to support financial applications. Minotaur is aimed at fraud detection analysis in the telecommunications industry. Minotaur Transcure targets improving the efficiency of credit card transaction processing.

**Multinomial**

Product : Multinomial
Vendor : Quantitative Skills Research and Statistical Consultancy
Function : Statistical Mining
Platform : Windows

The multinomial program is the exact solution to the Chi-square Goodness of fit test of testing for a difference between an observed and an expected distribution in a one-dimensional array. In a two-category array the multinomial test provides a two-sided solution for the Binomial test.

**Net Perceptions Retail Analyst**

Product : Net Perception Retail Analyst (formerly KDI)
Vendor : Net Perceptions, Inc.
URL : www.netperceptions.com
Functions : Association rules, clustering
Platform : Windows

Net Perceptions Retail Analyst is a retail analysis and report tool targeted toward retail sales applications. It supports OLAP functions.

**NLREG**

Product : Non Linear Regression Analysis
URL : www.nlreg.com
Functions : Regression Analysis
Platform : Windows

The goal of regression analysis is to determine the values of parameters for a function that cause the function to best fit a set of data observations that you provide.

**Oracle9i Database**

Product : Oracle9i Database
Vendor : Oracle Corporation
URL : www.oracle.com/ip/deploy/database/oracle9i/bi-dm.html
Functions : Association rules, classification, prediction
Techniques : Naive Bayes
Platforms : All platforms on which Oracle9i runs

Oracle9i Database has a data mining component embedded within it. The API used is based on a Java data mining approach called Java Data Mining (JDM).

**Partek**

Product : Partek
Vendor : Partek Incorporated
URL : www.partek.com
Functions : Clustering, prediction
Techniques : Genetic algorithms, neural networks, regression
Platforms : Unix, Windows

Partek actually consists of several companion products designed to perform pattern recognition, exploratory data analysis, statistical inference and predictive modeling. The pattern recognition product, Partek Pro, contains over 20 predefined similarity measures. Partek can access data imported from flat files. ODBC databases and Web servers. Many normalization and scaling transformation techniques are supported. The Pattern Visualization System contains many tools to graphically view the data mining results.

**PNC2**

Product : PNC2
Vendor : MSITStore
URL : www.Pnc2Gui.com
Function : Clustering
Platform : Windows

The PNC2 Rule Induction System induces rules from data using the newly invented PNC2 Cluster Algorithm. The PNC2 Rule Induction System has a clean and useful user interface projects are set up within a few minutes.

**Poly Analyst**

Product : Poly Analyst 4.4
Vendor : Megaputer Intelligence Inc.
URL : www.megaputer.com/products/pa/index.php3
Functions : Association rules, classification, clustering, prediction
Techniques : Decision trees, neural networks
Platforms : Windows, Unix

PolyAnalyst can access data stored in relational databases using the ODBC interface. In addition, it can process flat files, MS Excel and DBF files. A point and click object-oriented GUI is provided to facilitate use. Many different visualization tools are included.

**Quadstone**

Product : Quadstone System
Vendor : Quadstone
URL : www.quadstone.com
Functions : Prediction, Profiling, segmentation
Techniques : Decision trees, regression
Platforms : Unix (Solaris, HP, IBM AIX) and Windows NT

Quadstone System is a comprehensive analytical CRM software tool that includes tools to create customer-oriented datasets; segment, profile and model customer data with advanced data mining algorithms; and deploy customer selections, models and scores in real-time or batch modes. A sophisticated GUI interface and graphical visualization tools are provided.

**Re:order**

Product : Reorder (formerly Capri)
Vendor : Lumio Limited
URL : www.lumio.com/products.reorder
Functions : Sequential patterns
Platform : Windows

The Reorder software product targets the efficient discovery of sequences. Sequences may or may not be required to be contiguous in time. Through the use of templates, users indicate the type of sequences to be detected. Templates may include temporal constraints as well as information about required or optional items to appear in the sequence. Capri uses the *Predictive Modeling Mark-Up Language (PMML)*to represent sequences.

**SC**

Product : Statistic calculator
URL : www.statcalc.com

Functions : Basic Statistical Calculations
Platform : Works on all platform

Statistics Calculator is an easy-to-use program designed to perform a series of basic statistical procedures related to distributions and probabilities. Most of the procedures are called inferential because data from a sample is used to infer to a population.

**Scenario**

Product : Scenario
Vendor : Cognos Inc.
URL : www.cognos.com/products/scenario
Functions : Classification, clustering, outlier detection
Techniques : Decision trees
Platform : Windows

Scenario provides support for clustering and classification applications. Data may be input from various sources, including Excel, Lotus 1-2-3, and from relational databases using ODBC.

**See5**

Product : See5/C5.0 1.15
Vendor : RuleQuest Research Pty Ltd
URL : www.rulequest.com/see5-info.html
Functions : Classification
Techniques : Decision trees, rules
Platforms : Windows, Unix (Linux, Solaris, Irix)

The classification algorithm C5.0 is implemented in these two products: *See 5* runs on Windows machines and C5.0 runs on Unix. Source code in C is provided so that classifiers generated by See5/C5.0 can be embedded in applications.

**S-Plus**

Product : S-Plus
Vendor : Insightful Corporation
URL : www.insightful.com
Functions : Classification, clustering, hypothesis testing, prediction, time series analysis

Techniques : ARIMA, correlation (Pearson), decision trees, hierarchical clustering (agglomerative, divisive), K-means, regression (linear, logistic, nonlinear, polynomial), statistical techniques (Jackknife, Monte Carlo).

Platforms : Unix, Windows

The *S-Plus* data mining tool has versions for Unix (including Linux) and Windows, as well as client-server versions. S-PLUS can import or export data from ASCII, SAS, SPSS, Matlab, Excel and Lotus spreadsheets and other formats. S-PLUS can also import data from databases via ODBC or directly from Oracle on Solaris. S-PLUS is extensible: analytics are created using the object-oriented "S" language, and user-defined C, C++, Fortran, or Java code can be incorporated into S routines. A GUI is provided on both Windows and Unix and S-PLUS supports over 80 different charting types. Techniques are provided to handle missing data and for analysis of data with outliers.

**SSC**

Product : SSC(Sample size calculator)

Vendor : Macorr Research Solutions Online

URL : www.Macorr.com/ss_calculator.htm

Functions : Calculates sample size required for a given confidence interval for a given sample size and can handle finite populations.

Mining Strategies : Statistical mining

Platform : Windows

It calculate sample size required for a given confidence interval for a given sample size. It can handle all finite populations. This sample size calculator is used for performing sample size calculations. This is used for studies of opinions and behavior of groups. Sampling is the foundation of all research. Reliable sampling helps you make business decisions with confidence.

**STATISTICA Data Miner**

Product : STATASTICA Data Miner

Vendor : StatSoft, Inc.

URL : www.statsoft.com/dataminer.html
Functions : Classifications, clustering, prediction
Techniques : ARIMA, decision trees (CART, CHAID), exponential smoothing, neural networks (Back-propagation, MLP, RBF, SOM), regression.
Platform : Windows

STATISTICA Data Miner provides a comprehensive set of statistical methods to solve data mining problems. It offers a point and click iconic-based GUI to create a workflow description of the KDD and data mining tasks to be performed. Created Visual Basic code can be used to update or modify the tasks at a later date. Extended versions of traditional neural network techniques, association rule algorithms, CART and CHAID and a wide variety of other techniques are included. The application offers options to process remote databases "in place" (without creating local copies), which greatly increases the performance when data repositories are very large.

**SuperQuery**

Product : SuperQuery
Vendor : AZMY Thinkware, Inc.
URL : www.azmy.com
Functions : Rules
Techniques : Rule induction
Platform : Windows

There are two main versions of SuperQuery. The office edition is designed to work with Excel and Access data files, whereas the Discovery edition can be used to access many different types of data sources, including Access, xBASE, Borland Paradox, Excel, text files and ODBC databases.

**SurfAid Analytics**

Product : SurfAid Analytics
Vendor : IBM Corporation
URL : www.ibm.com/surfaid
Functions : Web mining
Platform : Windows

SurfAid Analytics is an IBM e-business service offering that provides Business Intelligence for Web sites. SurfAid identifies visitor attributes that directly relate to customer retention, navigation patterns and buying habits. SurfAid is compatible across all servers and platforms, requires no software installation or prerequisite hardware and is serviced entirely on SurfAid machines by SurfAid consultants. Customers send their Web logs to the IBM SurfAid facility for processing.

**TABLES**

| | | |
|---|---|---|
| Product | : | TABLES |
| URL | : | http://www.free statistical software.com |
| Functions | : | Statistics Calculations |
| Techniques | : | Analysis of Tables |
| Platform | : | Windows |

A windows program for the analysis of tables with up to 2*7 and 3*3 cells. The program allows for exact and approximate statistics to be calculated for traditional, ordinal and agreement tables. Fisher exact, Number Needed to Treat (NNT)proportional reduction in error statistics, Normal approximations, Four different chi-squares, Gamma, odds

**TANAGRA**

| | | |
|---|---|---|
| Product | : | Tanagra (1.4.18) |
| URL | : | eric.univ-lyon2.fr/~ricco/tanagra/en/tanagra.html. |
| Functions | : | Data analysis, statistical learning, machine learning, clustering, factorial analysis, parametric and nonparametric statistics, association rule, feature selection and construction algorithms. |
| Platform | : | Windows |

TANAGRA is free DATA MINING software for academic and research purposes. It proposes several data mining methods from exploratory data analysis, statistical learning, machine learning and databases area, it contains some supervised learning but also other paradigms such as clustering, factorial analysis, parametric and nonparametric statistics, association rule, feature selection and construction algorithms.

The main purpose of Tanagra project is to give researchers and students an easy-to-use data mining software, conforming to the present norms of the software development in this domain (especially in the design of its GUI and the way to use it), and allowing to analyze either real or synthetic data.

**Visualizer Workstation**

| | | |
|---|---|---|
| Product | : | Visualizer Workstation |
| Vendor | : | Computer Science Innovations, Inc. |
| URL | : | www.csi-inc.com |
| Functions | : | Classifications, clustering correlations, prediction, rules |
| Techniques | : | Neural networks (RBF) |
| Platform | : | Windows |

Visualizer Workstation facilities the process of identifying trends and correlations in data, as well as outliers and exceptions thereto. It is a module of CSI's Advisor Toolkit, which includes software to build predictive models and perform additional data mining functions. CSI supports its own KDD development process called the Cognitive Engineering Methodology, which closely matches the CRISP-DM, with an extension to address ROI analysis.

**WebAnalyst**

| | | |
|---|---|---|
| Product | : | WebAnalyst |
| Vendor | : | Megaputer Intelligence Inc. |
| URL | : | www.megaputer.com/products/wa/index.php3 |
| Functions | : | Web mining (prediction, patterns) |
| Platform | : | Windows |

WebAnalyst provides Web usage mining functions in a client-server architecture. WebAnalyst not only analyzes Web usage logs, but also can be used to make real-time predictions as to the future behavior of a web site visitor. These can then be used to dynamically personalize pages for the user.

**WebMiner ASP**

| | | |
|---|---|---|
| Product | : | WebMiner ASP |
| Vendor | : | Webminer |
| URL | : | www.webminer.com |
| Functions | : | Prediction, web mining |
| Platform | : | Windows |

WebMiner ASP is a subscriber-based data mining tool for e-commerce Web sites. By evaluating both customer databases and click stream data, rules are generated that are used to segment users allowing customization for future Web site visitors.

**winIDAMS**

| | | |
|---|---|---|
| Product | : | winIDAMS |
| Vendor | : | UNESCO |
| URL | : | http://freestatistics.altervista.org/stat.php |
| Functions | : | Validation, Manipulation and statistical analysis |
| Techniques | : | Cluster Analysis, Linear Regression, Factor Analysis etc. |
| Platform | : | Windows |

IDAMS performs classical techniques such as table building, regression analysis, one-way analysis of variance, discriminant and cluster analysis and also some more advanced techniques such as principal components factor analysis and analysis of correspondences, partial order scoring, rank ordering of alternatives, segmentation and iterative typology. In addition, WinIDAMS provides for interactive construction of multidimensional tables, interactive graphical Data Analysis Facilities.

**WizWhy**

| | | |
|---|---|---|
| Product | : | WizWhy |
| Vendor | : | WizSoft |
| URL | : | www.wizsoft.com/Why.html |
| Functions | : | Prediction, rules (if-then and if-and-only-if) |
| Techniques | : | Rule induction |
| Platform | : | Windows |

WizWhy is a rule induction data mining tool that can be used for (1) analyzing the data. (2) issuing predictions, and (3) revealing unexpected cases that deviate from the rules. WizWhy accesses many different types of data, including dBase, MS Access, MS SQL, Oracle, OLE databases, ODBC and ASCII.

**XpertRule Miner**

| | | |
|---|---|---|
| Product | : | XpertRule Miner |
| Vendor | : | Attar Software Ltd. |
| URL | : | www.attar.com |
| Functions | : | Association rules, classifications, clustering |
| Techniques | : | Decision trees, rules |
| Platform | : | ODBC, Windows |

XpertRule Miner supports the complete KDD process through the use of an iconic click an drag GUI interface. It supports the CRISP DM KDD development process. Visualization of results includes various 2D and 3D graphs and figures. XpertRule Miners supports a multitier client-server architecture. Access to any database supported by an ODBC connection is allowed.

Attar provides a companion product to XpertRule Miner. XpertRule Knowledge Builder provides a data flow development environment for KDD applications. The output from XpertRule Miner can be exported to a knowledge Builder application.

# 3

# AOM (Ace Optimizer Maintenance)

**Introduction**

AOM(Ace Optimizer Maintenance–Ace Utilities) is an award winning collection of tools to optimize your PC's performance. It allows you to find and remove the junk files in your PC, invalid registry entries, delete your internet usage history, provides plug-in support to erase the usage-history for over 200 third-party applications, manage your internet cookies and much more. With a detailed startup-manager you can see what all programs, services, drivers, etc start automatically with Windows and optionally disable them.

**Features**

- Clean junk, temporary and obsolete files from your disks using a swift disk cleaner.
- The most advanced registry cleaner to clean the Windows registry.
- Clean browser and application history, cache, temp files, cookies etc.
- Control the applications that start automatically with Windows using a startup manager.
- Fix broken Start Menu and Desktop shortcuts.
- Remove true duplicate files.

- Uninstall applications easily and correctly.
- Two modes-expert and normal.
- User friendly, stable and safe.

**Benefits**

- Optimize, clean and boost the speed of your Windows.
- Run applications smoothly and reduces crashes.
- Load Windows faster.
- Protect your privacy and security.
- Regain disk space.
- Block spyware, trojans, adware, etc.
- Fix certain application errors.
- No need to spend too much time; do it ultra fast.
- Runs much more quickly than others in its class and is very safe.

**Ace Utilities**

**Clean Up**

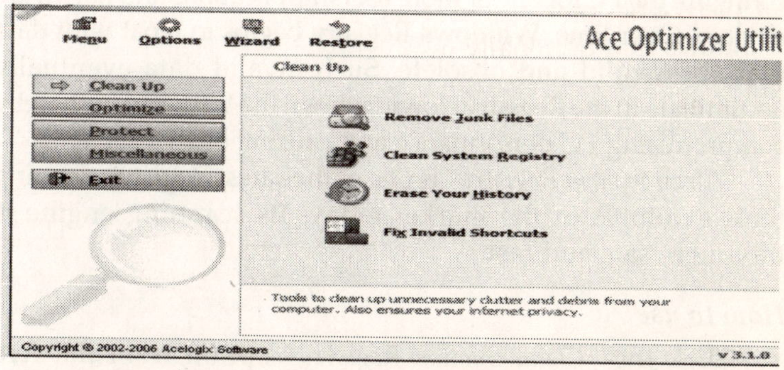


***Remove Junk Files***

Junk files are created by almost all of the Windows applications you use. Junk files left behind will reside in your hard disk and accumulate over time unless you manually find and remove them. Some of the results of having a substantial amount of such junk files are dramatic reduction in system performance, consumption of hard disk space, system crashes etc. *"Remove Junk Files"* tool can spot out these miscreant files and help you get rid of them very fast and effectively.

***How to use***

- Click the *"Remove Junk Files"* option from the Ace Utilities 'Clean Up' page.
- Now, on the next window, go to the *"Select Drives"* bar on the right side. Choose the drives you want to scan.
- To set more options for this tool, click *"Options"* button located on the top of this window. After changing the options, click 'Ok' to save the preferences. *Note:* Some of these options are for the advanced users.
- After selecting the necessary settings, it is now time to start scanning for junk files. Click *"Scan"*.

***System Registry Clean***

The Registry, the central hierarchical database used in the Microsoft Windows, is used to store information necessary to configure the PC for one or more users, applications and hardware devices. Over time, Windows Registry begins to bloat with data that are invalid and obsolete. Such invalid data eventually accumulate in the Registry slowing down the Windows, whereby compromising PC performance and causing other problems.

*"Clean System Registry"* is one of the safest Registry cleaning tools available in the market today. Its scanning engine is thorough, safe and fast.

***How to use***

- Click the *"Clean System Registry"* option from the Ace Utilities 'Clean Up' page.
- Now, on the next window, go to the *"Select the options to scan"* bar on the right side. Here you will be presented with a list of sections where this tool will check for errors.
- To set more options for this tool, click *"Options"* button located on the top of this window.

- After selecting the necessary settings, it is now time to start scanning for erroneous Registry entries. Click *"Scan"*.
- After scanning is completed, a list of invalid and erroneous entries found will be shown. 'Check mark' those items which you want to remove from the Registry.

***Erase your History***

Your Windows operating system keeps tracks of many things that you do with your computer, like the websites you visit using Internet browsers, the pictures you view using image viewers, the movies you watch using Media player etc. Owing to the fact that such information is stored at different places by different programs, it is impossible, or rather tedious and time-consuming, to maintain your privacy by manually searching for such entries and eliminating them.

***How to use***

*"Erase History"* tool makes the job much easier by taking care of everything at the click of a button: freeing up wasted hard-drive space and getting rid of your past activity records from the PC.

***Fix Invalid Shortcuts***

*"Fix Invalid Shortcuts"* tool provides you with an easy and convenient way to address these invalid shortcuts. It scans your system, finds all the invalid shortcuts and reports back to you so that you can remove it from your system.

***How to use***

- Click the *"Fix Invalid Shortcuts"'* option from the Ace Utilities 'Clean Up' page.
- Now, on the next window, click the *"Options"* button on the top. Here you can select the drives/folders to scan for invalid shortcuts.
- After applying the necessary settings, it is now time to start scanning for invalid shortcuts. Click *"Scan"*.
- After scanning is completed, a list of invalid shortcuts found will be displayed. 'Check mark' those entries which you want to remove from your system.

## Optimize

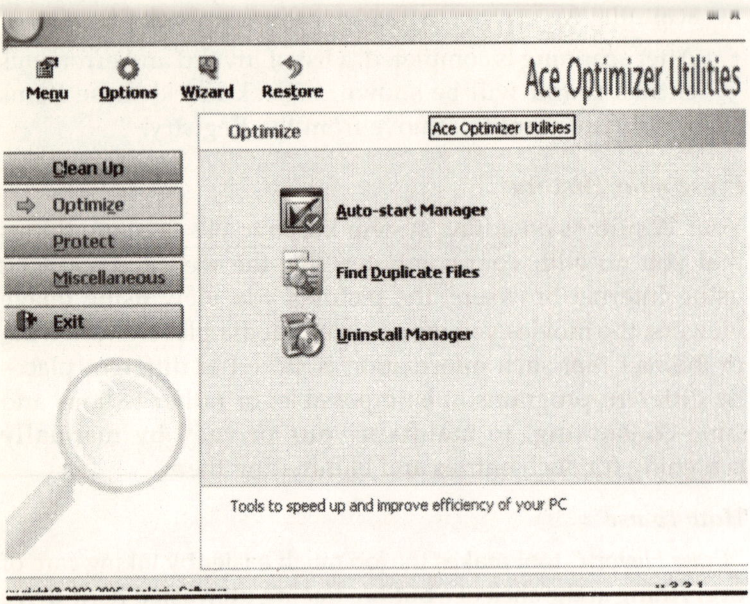


### *Auto-Start Manager*

*"Auto-Start Manager"* allows you to manage all such applications which start automatically. This tool can organize programs that run automatically using the Registry, the 'Startup' folder.

### *How to use*

- Click the *"Optimize"* tab option from the Ace Utilities main page. Then, click the *"Auto-Start Manager"*.
- The next window shows the various entries - Logon, Services, DLLs, Scheduled tasks, drivers and more - as instructed by you. The different categories to be shown here are set through the main 'Options' page. Click *"Options"* to do so.

### *Find Duplicate File*

"Find Duplicate Files" tool can easily find and remove duplicates of the same file.

*Note:* The files that you delete using this tool are entirely your selection. Ace Utilities can only find duplicate copies of files; it can't tell which one is the duplicate or the unneeded one.

***How to use***

- Click the *"Optimize"* tab option from the Ace Utilities main page. Then, click the *"Find Duplicate Files"*.
- Now, on the next window, you can select the drive(s) and/or folder(s) you want to scan. Click the *"Folders"* button on the right to see the list of selected drive(s)/folder(s) for scanning. To set more options for this tool, click the *"Options"* button at the top.
- After selecting the necessary settings, it is now time to start scanning for duplicate files. Click *"Scan"*.
- After scanning is completed, all the duplicate files will be listed after grouping appropriately.

***Uninstall Manager***

Sometimes, by either manually deleting applications or from untidy un installation, the file that these entries refer may no longer exist and this results in an error when the corresponding entry is tried to uninstall. It is impossible to remove these orphaned entries manually. Using this tool, you can easily remove these invalid entries.

***How to use***

- Click the *"Optimize"* tab option from the Ace Utilities main page. Then, click the *"Uninstall Manager"*.
- To uninstall an entry, click the *"Uninstall"* button on the top.
- *Uninstall*: Uninstalls the selected program from your system, double-click on it, you will be taken to the un installation window for the program related to the entry.

  *Repair/Update*: To repair or update a particular installed software. These features will be available only for programs installed using the 'Windows Installer'.

*Support/About*: Will try to get more information about the selected software. This may require an internet connection to work.

*Remove Entry*: To delete a particular entry from the list. This will also remove the entry from the Windows Registry. This option is useful for deleting uninstall entries for non-existent programs.

*Edit Entry*: To edit the uninstall command for a particular program.

*View*: To change the display of the list: as a list of large icons, a simple list, etc.

*Report:* Saves the whole list as a text file.

**Protect**

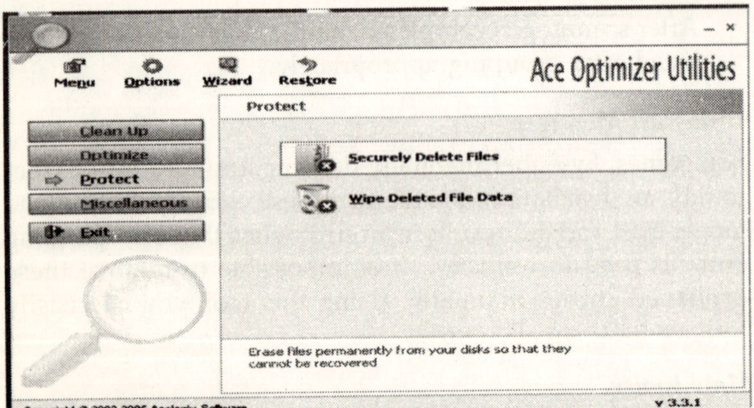


***Securely Delete Files***

The standard Windows Recycle Bin allows you to delete files and folders, presumably removing them from prying eyes. However, there are many ways to retrieve and view files and folders which have been removed in this manner–even months after they have been deleted. The reason items can be so easily retrieved intact even long after being supposedly deleted is because Windows does not actually erase the physical data on your drive. This option is used to delete the files permanently from your system.

### *How to use*

- Click the *"Protect"* tab option from the Ace Utilities main page. Then, click the *"Securely Delete Files"*.
- Click the *"Add File(s)"* button to find and insert the files from your hard drive. You can add folders by clicking the *"Add Folder"* button. If you click the *"Add Folder and subfolder(s)"* option, all subfolders inside the selected folder will also be added for the secure delete process.
- After adding the files and folders to the delete-list, click *"Start Wipe"* to permanently delete them.

### *Wipe Deleted File Data*

Wiping a disk's free space ensures any such data currently stored will be destroyed. Save all documents and close all running programs that may write to the disk, before using this tool.

### *How to use*

- Click the *"Protect"* tab option from the Ace Utilities main page. Then, click the *"Wipe Deleted File Data"*.
- Now, on the next window, you have two options: *"Wipe Free Space"* and *"Shred Files in the Recycle Bin"*.

### Miscellaneous

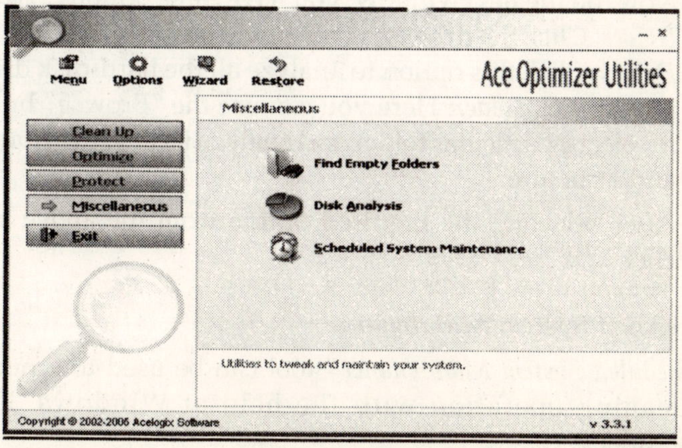

***Find Empty Folders***

*"Find Empty Folders"* tool can be used to find the empty folders in your hard drive.

***How to use***

- Click the *"Miscellaneous"* tab option from the Ace Utilities main page. Then, click the *"Find Empty Folders"*.
- Now, on the next window, go to the *"Select Drives"* bar on the right side. Select the drives you want to scan.
- After selecting the necessary settings, it is now time to start scanning for duplicate files. Click *"Scan"*.
- After scanning is completed, a list of empty folders found will be displayed.

***Disk Analysis***

*"Disk Analysis"* tool shows the disk usage of your drives. Use it when your hard disk is almost full, and you don't know where the big files are residing, what all files occupy how much space, etc. They may well be hidden in sub-sub-directories.

***How to use***

- Click the *"Miscellaneous"* tab option from the Ace Utilities main page. Then, click the *"Disk Analysis"*.
- Now, on the next window, you have three options: *Selected Drives*: Click the drive(s) you want to be analyzed. *All Local Drives*: Click this option to analyze all the hard-disk drives in your PC. *Folder*: Here you can use the "Browse" button to select a particular folder and analyze its data distribution and structure.
- After selecting the required option from the above step, click *"Ok"*.

***Scheduled System Maintenance***

*"Scheduled System Maintenance"* tool can be used to schedule a cleaning operation with the help of Windows 'Task Scheduler'.

***How to use***

- Click the *"Miscellaneous"* tab option from the Ace Utilities main page. Then, click the *"Schedule System Maintenance"*.
- In the "Schedule System Maintenance" window that pops up, check-mark the tools you want to run (like Junk File Cleaner).
- Now, select a time schedule to run the selected tasks from the set of options available.
- After choosing the time, click *"Set Schedule"*.

# 4

# Cart

## Introduction

CART uses an intuitive, Windows-based interface, making it accessible to both technical and non-technical users. Underlying the "easy" interface, however, is a mature theoretical foundation that distinguishes CART from other methodologies and other decision trees.

Salford Systems' CART is the only decision-tree system based on the original CART code developed by world-renowned Stanford University and University of California at Berkeley statisticians Breiman, Friedman, Olshen and Stone; this code now includes enhancements co-developed by Salford Systems and CART's originators.

## Features

Based on a decade of machine learning and statistical research, CART provides stable performance and accurate results. Its market-proven methodology is characterized by.

### *A Reliable Pruning Strategy*

CART's developers determined definitively that no stopping rule could be relied on to discover the optimal tree, so they introduced the notion of over-growing trees and then pruning back; this idea, fundamental to CART, ensures that important structure is not overlooked by stopping too soon. Other decision-tree techniques use problematic stopping rules.

### *A Powerful Binary-split Search Approach*

CART's binary decision trees are more sparing with data and detect more structure before too few data are left for learning. Other decision-tree approaches use multi-way splits that fragment the data rapidly, making it difficult to detect rules that require broad ranges of data to discover.

### *Automatic Self-validation Procedures*

When searching for patterns in databases it is essential to avoid the trap of "over fitting," that is, of finding patterns that applies only to the training data. CART's embedded test disciplines ensure that the patterns found will hold up when applied to new data. Further, the testing and selection of the optimal tree are an integral part of the CART algorithm. In other decision-tree techniques, testing is conducted after the fact and tree selection is left up to the user.

CART accommodates many different types of real-world modeling problems by providing a unique combination of automated solutions.

### *Surrogate Splitters Intelligently Handle Missing Values*

CART handles missing values in the database by substituting "surrogate splitters," back-up rules that closely mimic the action of primary splitting rules. The surrogate splitter contains information that typically is similar to what would be found in the primary splitter.

Other products treat all records with missing values as if the records all had the same unknown value; with that approach all such "missings" are assigned to the same bin. In CART, each record is processed using data specific to that record, allowing records with different data patterns to be handled differently and resulting in a better characterization of the data.

### *Adjustable Misclassification Penalties Help Avoid the most Costly Errors*

CART can accommodate situations in which some misclassifications, or cases that have been incorrectly classified, are more serious than others. CART users can specify a higher penalty for misclassifying certain data, causing the software to steer the tree away from that type of error.

Further, when CART cannot guarantee a correct classification, it will try to ensure that the errors are less costly. If credit risks were classified as low, moderate, or high, for example, it would be more costly to classify a high-risk person as low-risk than as moderate-risk. Traditional data mining tools cannot distinguish between these types of misclassification errors.

### *Alternative Splitting Criteria Make Progress when other Criteria Fail*

CART includes seven single-variable splitting criteria, Gini, Symgini, Twoing, Ordered Twoing, Entropy and Class Probability for classification trees, and Least Squares and Least Absolute Deviation for regression trees, and, in addition, one multi-variable splitting criterion, Linear Combinations.

The default Gini method typically performs best, but in specific circumstances, other methods can generate more accurate models. CART's unique "twoing" procedure, for example, is tuned for classification problems with many classes, such as modeling which of 170 products would be chosen by a given consumer. To deal more effectively with select data patterns, CART also offers splits on linear combinations of continuous predictor variables.

Salford Systems' latest release, CART 5.0, incorporates many new user-requested enhancements and features. The most intuitive decision-tree interface is now even easier to use and the underlying algorithm is more versatile and powerful than ever.

**New CART 5 Features**

- Discrete Variables
- Ability to Automatically Detect Distinct Classes
- Fractional Values Can Be Specified as Categorical

- Character Data
- Native Support for Text Data
- Data Information
- Auxiliary Variables
- Groves Files
- Exporting CART Model Information
- Missing Value Summary Report
- Entropy Splitting Rule
- 32-Character Variable Names
- Path Length Extended to Windows Maximum
- Improved Navigator Window
- New and Improved Summary Reports
- Additional Tree Details for Viewing and Printing
- Improved Model Setup
- Easy Data Access
- Improved Printing

**Interactive Walkabout**

To experience a walkabout through the key features an *http://www.salfordsystems.com/walkaboutcart1.phpd* functionality of CART, click on the product below.

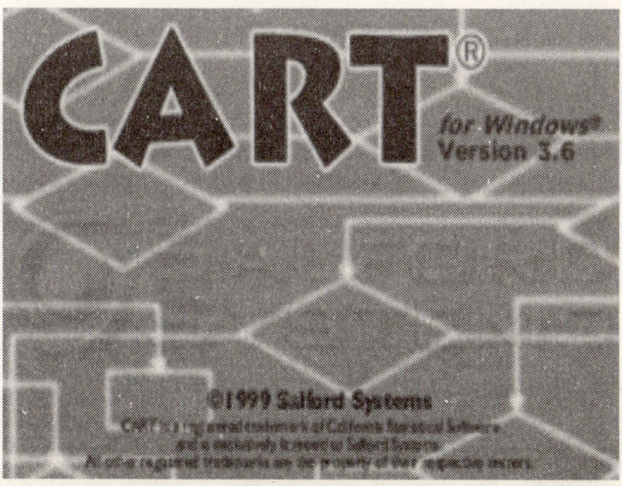

Financial Services data mining example Identifying risky borrowers: To introduce you to data mining with the CART decision tree software we are going to walk through a real world example drawn from the Financial Services industry. The database is an extract from a group of customers who selected a financial loan product, some of whom went "BAD". The information we will make use of comes from standard credit reports provided by all the major credit bureaus, including variables such as:

- Number of credit reports requested for this person in last 6 months
- Number of credit cards with balances greater than 80% of available credit
- Number of new credit accounts opened in last 12 months
- How long ago was oldest account opened?
- How long ago was newest account opened?

Such measures are well known in the industry although the terminology used to refer these measures is somewhat obscure.

Our goal is to see if we can predict who goes BAD (stops making payments) using standard credit bureau information. We'll use this example to display he look and feel of CART and to show you how much you can learn quickly from a CART analysis.

First let's read in our data which sits in an Excel spreadsheet called DEFAULT.XLS. We click on the File Menu, select **[Open]** and see a display like.

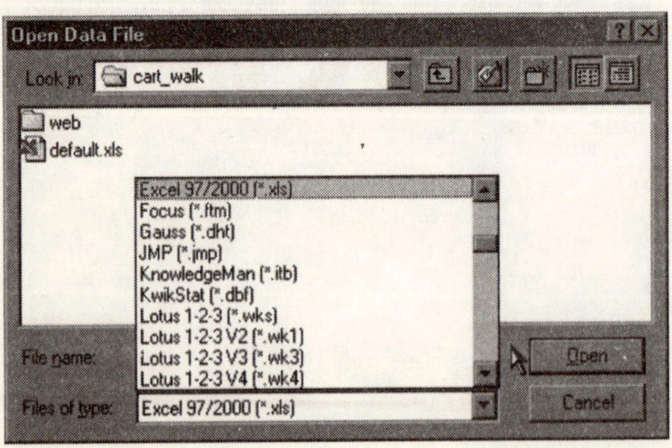

Note that CART will recognize a broad range of file formats, a few of which are visible in the selector box. Altogether there are about 85 formats to choose from including all the major databases, statistical packages, and spreadsheets. ODBC connectivity is also supported as is plain ASCII.

Since our data was provided to us as an Office 2000 document we select the **[Excel 97/2000]** format and then click on our data file.

After you open a data file, the Model Setup dialog automatically appears. This is the control center housing all model setup and refinement options in one convenient location.

To run an analysis all you have to do is:

- Select your target variable, in this case "BAD"
- Specify that this is a "Classification" problem
- State that BAD has two levels starting with 0

That's it! All you need to do now is—click **[Grow Tree]**!

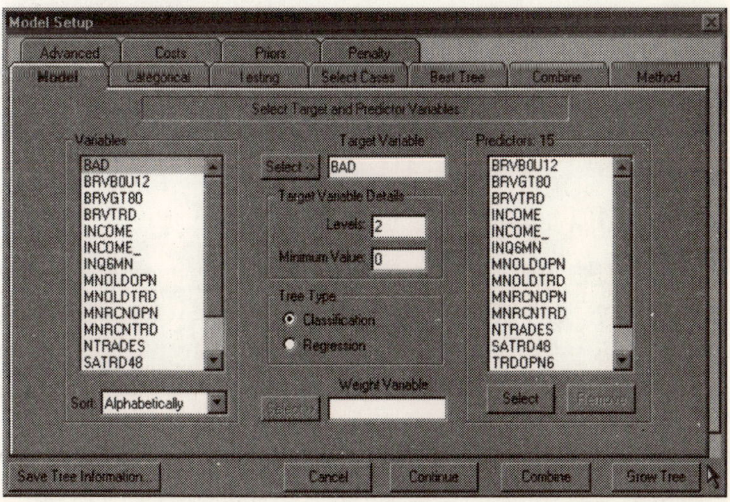


You don't have to select predictors if it is OK for CART to use all available columns. In this case we didn't want CART to use ID or similar information so we opted to list predictors explicitly. Note the running count kept of the number of predictors selected so far—15.

Eventually you will want to learn how to take advantage of the controls and options available on each of the Model Setup tabs. The good news is that all the options are set to intelligent defaults so you can get started without worrying about them.

The tree **Navigator** is the first report CART presents when the analysis is done. It displays a high-level picture of what has been accomplished but underneath it contains complete details on every aspect of the analysis. The tree diagram shows you how complex the best model is, how accurately it predicts, and where the interesting segments are located. Let's take a closer look at some of the specifics.

In the lower right hand corner we see that our tree has 13 terminal nodes. The two bright red nodes are where the highest concentrations of BADs are to be found; the pink nodes are a little less concentrated, the white nodes are typical of the overall population and the blue nodes contain very few BADs. Later we will drill down into our data by double-clicking on the nodes that interset on the nodes that interest us the most.

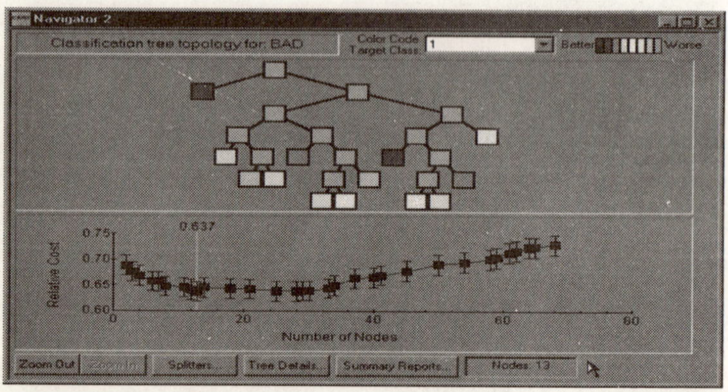


The curve under the tree diagram reports on the overall accuracy of the tree and tells us how we might trade off accuracy for a smaller simpler tree. The most accurate tree flagged by the horizontal green bar has a error rate that is 63.7% of that experienced without a mode.

By clicking on another box on the error curve you will bring up a tree of different size, in this case ranging anywhere from

2 terminal nodes to over 70. We'll discuss why you might want to look at these other trees later.

Let's prepare for some drill down. Positioning your mouse anywhere in the gray area surrounding the tree diagram click and hold down the Right mouse button. The pop-up menu, shown below, illustrates your options regarding the amount of detail you will see when you hover the mouse pointer over a node. The choices are:

- Column used to split the node
- Column and split value
- Simple tabulation of target variable
- Complete tabulation of target variable

For a quick succint overview of the entire tree click on the **[Splitters...]** button at the bottom of Navigator window. This displays the variables used in every split in the tree. We like this view because it is an easy way to check for the main themes of the analysis and to make sure that no unwanted variables or major errors have crept into the analysis. This display also packs the entire tree into the smallest possible window.

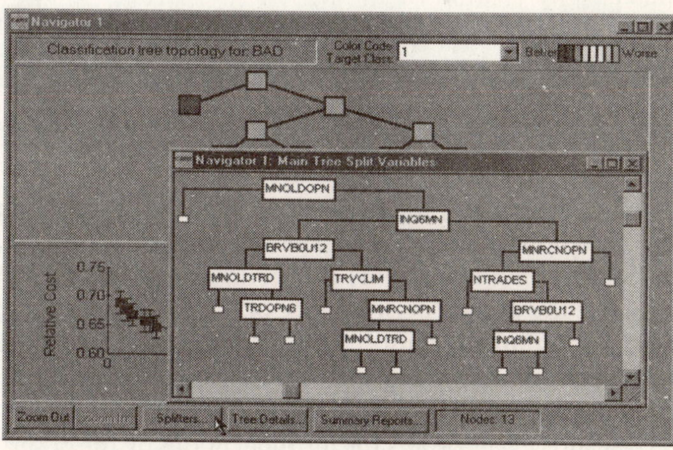


As we will see later, any of these displays can be printed, sent to a formatted report window, saved as a windows metafile (wmf) or copied to clipboard for later processing of your choosing.

You can see the whole tree in full detail by clicking the **[Tree Details...]** button at the bottom of the navigator. You have considerable control over exactly what is displayed in each node from the **[View] [NodeDetail...]** menu. The miniature Tree Map window help you keep track of your current position by showing you where you are relative to the overall tree. You can also click on a location in the miniature window and the larger window will reposition to reflect the clicked-on location.

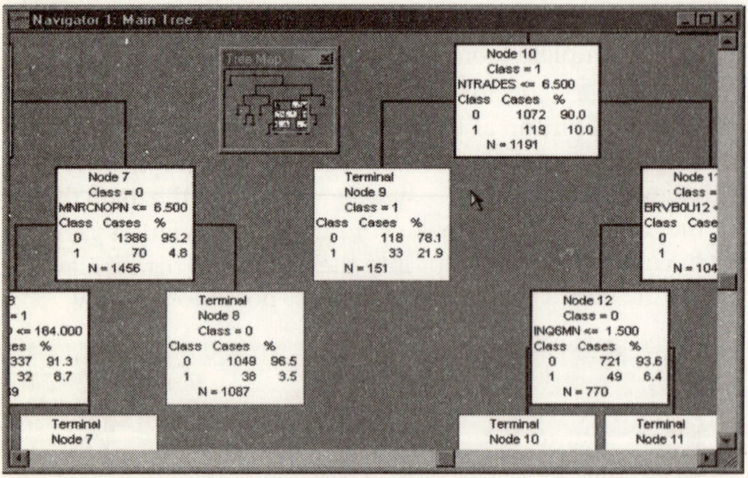


Right clicking and then selecting **[Export...]** allows you to save the whole tree in any of several graphics formats for inclusion in other documents or publication to the Web. We can review the overall performance of the tree by clicking the **[SummaryReports...]** button in the Navigator window. The tabs in this window all provide summary information pertaining to the entire tree.

The Gains Chart orders the terminal nodes by the observed lift. Terminal node 9 displays a bad rate 2.988 times that of the sample as a whole and has the highest concentration of bads in the tree. By common industry experience this tree is a reasonably strong performer.The top four nodes represent 24% of the total population but capture 61% of the bad accounts.

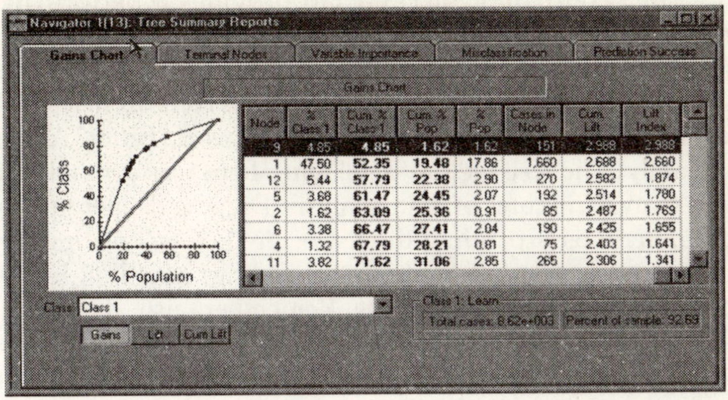

More useful information is provided in the **[Variable-Importance]** tab. This ranking tells us which variables do most of the work in separating well from bad accounts. Two variables related to the age of the customer's oldest account stand at the top of the list followed by the number of satisfactory accounts. Total credit limit from revolving accounts comes next along with an income related variable.

This report is meant to highlight any outstandingly important variables and to allow you to separate the wheat from the chaff. Several different ways of computing importance are offered for the expert but usually the standard report is all you need to look at.

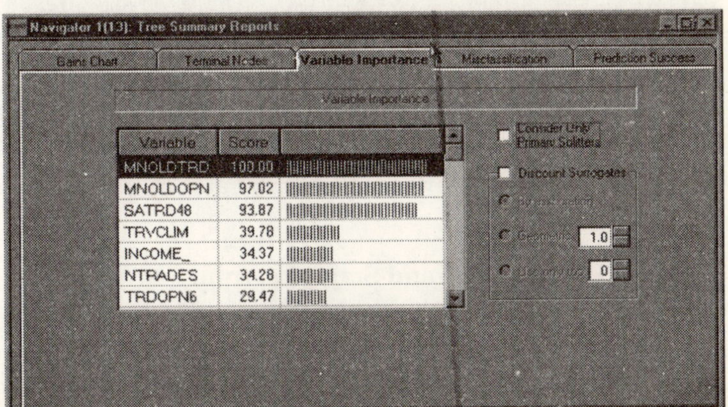

The **[Prediction Success]** tab provides a performance report. Of the 8,617 cases in the test file the CART tree gets 70.5% classified correctly. Among the 680 bad accounts the tree gets 65.9% correct. Remember these results come from test data which was not used to grow the tree. Can we do better? Almost certainly! The tree we are displaying here was arrived at in less than 30 minutes of data analysis. Digging deeper into the data, perhaps expanding the list of predictors, creating new measures, trying different control settings could all lead to substantially improved results. Remember, also, that the lift in our top nodes was quite satisfactory. We decided to use this set of results because they are typical of difficult to predict outcomes and are a refreshing change from artificial examples permitting 99% accurate classifications.

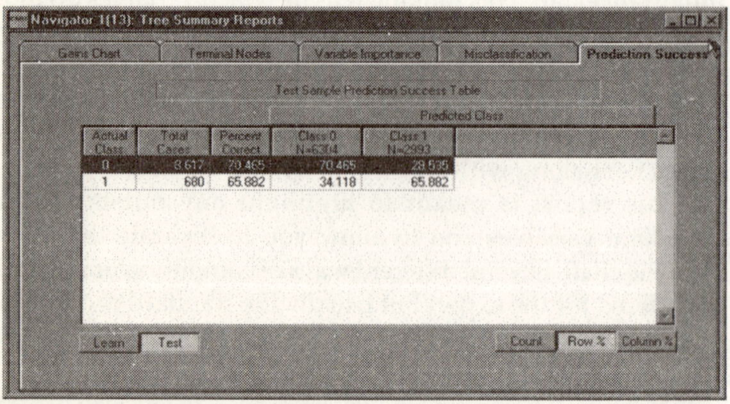


The **[Misclassification]** tab gives you another view of performance with other class. We usually see a slightly worse performance on the test sample but in most cases CART is able to deliver a tree with very similar error rates in the learn and test samples.

### The CART Audit Trail and Script Learning

CART keeps a record of every step you take in your analyses and makes it available for replay in another session or on another platform. The record serves as an audit trail documenting how you arrived at your conclusions. To access this record click on **[View] [Open Command Log...]** or select the "L" icon from the toolbar.

The scripting language is quite simple and makes it easy to run multiple experiments in batch mode. We know of a CART user who needs to run thousands of trees almost daily; their work is fully automated with scripts (called command files) that look something like what you see below. The command log is plain text; you can save its contents, edit it, and cut and paste to other applications.

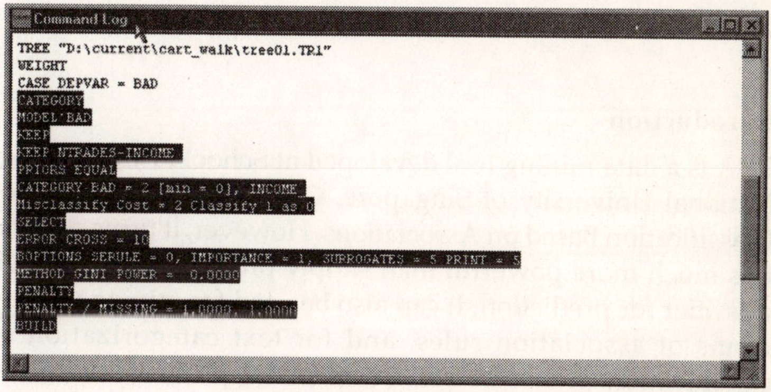

# 5

# CBA (Classification Based on Associations)

## Introduction

CBA is a data mining tool developed at School of Computing, National University of Singapore. CBA originally stands for Classification Based on Associations. However, it turns out that it is much more powerful than simply producing an accurate classifier for prediction. It can also be used for mining various forms of association rules, and for text categorization or classification. It also solves a number of problems with the existing classification techniques (e.g., decision tree, or neural networks, and many others).

## Unique features of CBA

1. *Classification and Prediction*

   Build accurate classifiers from relational data, where each record is described with a fixed number of attributes. This type of data is what traditional classification techniques use, e.g., decision tree, neural networks, and many others.

2. *Text Categorization and Classification*

   Build accurate classifiers from transactional data, where each data record has a variable number of items, e.g., items bought in a supermarket by a customer, or the keywords in a text document.

3. *Mining association rules from relational data or transactional data*
   4. *Mining association rules with Multiple Minimum Supports.*
4. *Cross-Validation* for evaluating classifiers, and allows the user to view and to query the discovered rules.

**Mining Methods**

CBA has two types of mining strategies.

1. Classification Mining
2. Association Mining

These two mining strategies use two types of data.

1. Relational Database Table
2. Transaction Data

***Classification Mining***

Classification is a way to classify data according to a classification model, in our case is set of rules. One can use this set of rules do prediction on the testing cases.

***Table Classification***

Classification techniques can be applied to the relational database table which has a set of attributes. Each attribute has a set of attribute values.

*Transaction Classification*

This method is close to the transaction association. The difference is that it has a class item at the end of each transaction (i.e. education, government, arts).A set of classification rules will be generated.

*Rules Generated from Classification Mining*

Classification mining produces a classifier (a set of rules) with file extension rul. This classifier is selected from a larger set of rules. We call it all rules. One can use both set of rules to do prediction. However, the number of rules in the classifier is normally much smaller compare to all rules. In terms of prediction accuracy, classifier is normally better than all rules. This is mainly due to rule conflicting and overfitting in all rules. However, all rules are still useful in understanding the data.

### *Association Mining*

Association Mining based on the Apriori algorithm (Agrawal and Srikant 1994) is an efficient way of discovering a set of association patterns in the transaction data (Transaction Association). It's also possible to adapt this algorithm to work with a relational table (Table Association).

#### *Transaction Association*

This type of data does not have a fixed number of attribute. Each row of the data is a transaction. The number of items in each transaction can vary. You could think this type of data as items bought from a super market whereas each transaction records the items that purchased by a custom. In association rules, there's no fixed class, and any attribute might appear at the right hand side of a rule.

#### *Table Association*

You could also use the relational table format for association rule mining purpose. In table association there is no class attribute &all attributes must be discrete attributes.

### *Item Sets & Rules Generated from Association Rule Mining*

The association rule mining follows the Apriori algorithm (Agrawal and Srikant 1994) works in two steps.

1. Generating candidate sets.
2. Pruning the generated candidate sets.

Generating frequent item sets that satisfy the Minimum Support and Minimum Confidence The item sets produced by the system can be saved in a file, we use the extension .itm for item sets file. The association rules produced by the system can be saved in a file, we use the extension .arl for association rule file.

**Data File Format**

| | *Classification* | *Association* |
|---|---|---|
| Table | Table Classification (*.data,*.names) | Table Association (*.data,*.names) |
| Transaction | Transaction Classification (*.trc) | Transaction Association (*.tra) |

***Relational Database Table***

Relational Database Table has set of attributes. Each attribute can be continue or discrete. For examples, the following table has three attributes (A, B, C). Attribute A has 3 attribute values (A1, A2, A3).

| A | B | C |
|---|---|---|
| A1 | -1 | good |
| A2 | 3.5 | bad |
| A1 | 800 | good |
| A3 | 3.5 | good |

**.data File:* The data file is just the rest of the table without the first row (the attribute names). The separator is comma. For example:

```
A1, -1, good
A2, 3.5, bad
A1, 800, good
A3, 3.5, good
```

**.names File for Table Classification:* The names file is the attribute description. There are 2 types of names file (TableClsType1 & TableClsType2).

*TableClsType1*

If you think the attribute B is a continuous attribute, you have to specify it to "continuous" in your names file. If an attribute is a discrete attribute, you can write "discrete" in all the values of the discrete attribute in the names file. A sample TableClsType1 names file.

```
-1
A: discrete.
B: continuous
C: discrete.
```

*TableClsType2*

The main difference between TableClsType1 & TableClsType2 is that the first line has all possible class values All possible discrete attribute values must be specified in attribute description. The class attribute is always the last attribute in the data file. If an attribute is a continuous attribute, you can put keyword "continuous". A sample TableClsType2names file.

---

Good bad.
A: A2, A1, A3.
B: continuous

---

**.names for Table Association*

In TableAssocType file:

(1) There's no class attribute in TableAssocType names file.

(2) All attributes must be discrete attribute in TableAssocType names file.

(3) Use-2 in the first line to indicate running table association.

*For example:*

---

-2
A: discrete.
B: discrete.
C: discrete.

---

**Transaction Data**

This type of data does not have a fixed number of attributes. Each row of the data is a transaction. The number of items in each transaction can vary. You could think that this type of data as items bought from a super market whereas each transaction records the items that purchased by a custom. The following is a sample:

(1) Ketchup, orange juice, tomato sauce, potato chips, sugar
(2) Onion rings, sugar, pamper, roses, soya sauce, cd.

There are two types of data format, one for association (.tra) and one for classification (.trc). There is no name file for the transaction type of data.

**.trc for Transaction Classification*

A class attribute (or item) should be present at the end of each transaction. For example:

0 military, politics, law, taxes, government

1 book, text, dictionary, education

**.tra for Transaction Association:*

This is a normal type of data used in the association rule mining. With extension .tra, CBA will know you are running this data in transaction association.

**Main Window of CBA**

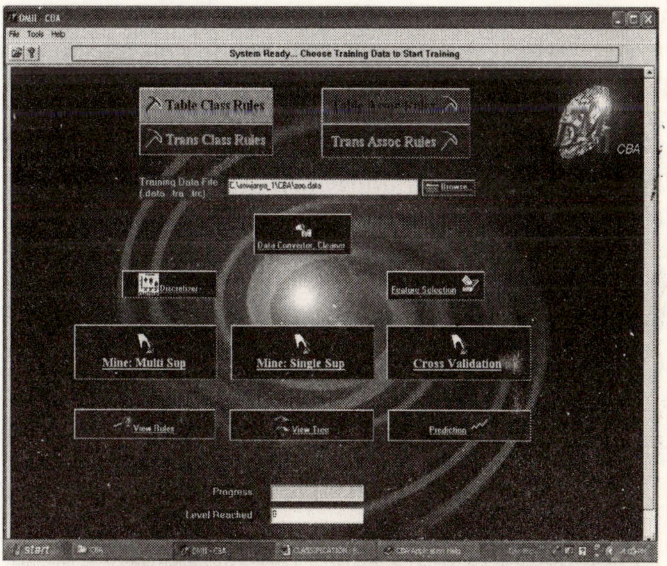


***Data Converter & Cleaner***

CBA uses different data file format for the different types of mining. Data converter & cleaner is mainly used in the table classification and association. During this process, system will check the data consistency and try to clean data. Data cleaner will detect and clean the following errors:

(1) Number of Attributes in a data tuple is different from the number of attributes specified in the names file.

(2) A non-numeric value appears in a continuous attribute.

(3) Missing Class item in the table classification data file.

(4) Class Attribute having "continuous" description in the names file.

(5) There are reserved characters in the names and data file. They need to be replaced with a non-reserved character. The set of reserve characters are: () {}: = > < + .

***Discretizer***

CBA cannot directly use a data file with continuous attributes in mining. Pass your data file with continuous attributes to this system, which will discretize the continuous attributes and output a file that contains the discretized data. Upon return, discretized data can then be used in the mining.

In this discretizer, you can choose automatic discretization to discretize all the continuous attributes in the data file. You can also do manual Discretization by giving your discretization specifications (cut points) for a set of selected continuous attributes.

To automatically discretize a data file:

(1) Enter the path of data file to be discretized.

(2) Enter the path of output data file.

(3) Press "Load" button to load in the data.

(4) Press "Automatically Discretize" button to start discretization.

To manually discretize a data file:

(1) Enter the path of data file to be discretized.

(2) Enter the path of output data file

(3) Press "Process Data" button to do pre-discretization data process.

(4) Select a continuous attribute from the list of continuous attributes. Enter cutting points for this attribute in the format of "point1, point2, ..., pointN". Press "Add" button to add the new discretization specification to the list of specifications.

(5) Repeat step 4 for continuous attributes you want to discretize.

(6) Press "Manually Discretize" button to start discretization.

***Feature Selection***

The number of features (attributes) and number of instances in the raw dataset can be enormously large. The objective of Feature selection is to select a minimal subset of features according to some reasonable criteria so that the original task can be achieved equally well, if not better. By choosing a minimal subset of features, irrelevant and redundant features are removed according to the criterion. Simpler data can lead to more concise results and their better comprehensibility.

***Run With Single Support***

This is the main learning engine for all the mining methods. Single Support means that there will be only one minimum support during learning. This techniques can be applied to the normal association rule mining, and also classification mining.

In this option window, you can specify the CBA's running parameters:

Common options (classification & association mining):

(1) *MinSupport, MinConfidence:* In this release, MinConfidence can be computed automatically if running classification mode.

(2) *Rule Limit (a memory limit):* Association rule generating algorithm has exponential grow in nature. A hard memory limit is necessary to prevent the program runs beyond the machine limit. Rule limit has direct connection with a machine's physical memory. In general, if one set rule limit to 50,000, 4-5 MB memory will be allocated.

(3) *Num Conds:* To constrain the length of generating rules. Long rules with 5 or 6 conditions are generally difficult to be interpreted.

Options only apply to Classification mining:

(4) *Pruning Control:* The number of rules generated from CBA algorithm can be subjected to a pruning operation. CBA can use some pruning techniques to reduce the number of rules without lose the prediction accuracy.

(5) *Rule Usage Control:* During the CBA rule generating stage, some rules with low support but good confidence will be selected when this option is enabled.

(6) *Random Testing on Training Data:* After a classifier (model) has been generated, system can perform testing on a random portion of training data. By default, the entire training file will be used.

## Multiple Min Support

### *Overview*

User will have to first enter the options (Upper Limit, Lower Limit and Steps Level) desired for the particular analysis in the General Options section. Then users can select the appropriate attribute values, which support level need to be modified, in the Attribute Tree View. Finally, the new support level is captured in the Enter Support section.

## Detailed Description

### *General Options*

In this area, the user is allowed to specify the upper limit, lower limit and step levels. What values the user set is largely dependent on the application involved. After the new values are entered, the user can press the update button to refresh all the values. The program will then recalculate all the attribute items based on the new setting and display it to the Attribute Tree View.

### *Attribute Tree View*

The Attribute Tee View present two kinds of object, Attribute (represented by the symbol "A") and Attribute Value Name (represented by the symbol "V"). Each Attribute Value Name belongs to an Attribute and user can only modify the support level of this item. When the attribute value name which support level the user would like to modify is selected, its info will be displayed in the Enter Support area.

***Enter Support***

Once the user selects an attribute value name on the Attribute Tree View, the corresponding info on that particular item will be displayed in this view. From here, the user can modify the existing minimum support for that item and update it by pressing the Update button.

***Other operations***

If the user wants to discard all changes during the process of modification and revert back to the default values, they can do so by pressing the Restore Default button. Once they are happy with the results, users are allowed to save their work into a save file (the save file will have an extension of .mus) and load it in for use later. One point to note about loading of saved support file is that the main data file selected in the CBA view need to be the same as the saved file. Else the program will reject loading the saved values.

**Multiple Support Window**

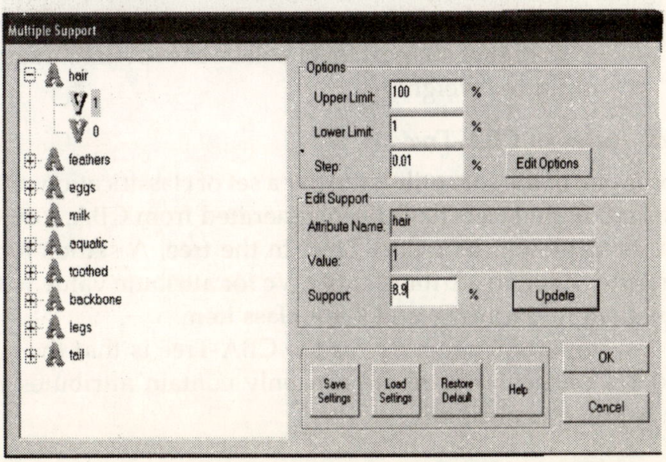

### *Cross Validation*

Cross Validation is a way to test how accurate a classification algorithm is. The system bases on the number of folds (number of times system should run) splitting data to training case and testing case. Get the average error rate after it's done. This test is only available for the table classification method.

In each fold of cross validation, the training data is first discretized (the discretiser does not see the test data). After the classifier has been built, it will test on the unseen test data. All these are done automatically.

### *View Rules*

This is one of the rule utilities. After a set of rules are generated from CBA. You can choose to view it in a edit window. You can also manipulate the rules by using the sorting utilities. Three types of sorting are available:

(1) *Sort by Confidence-Support*: If rule A's confidence level is higher than rule B's, A will be displayed first. If they have the same confidence level, the one has a higher support level will be displayed first.

(2) *Sort by Support-Confidence*: This will consider support level first. If two have same support, the one with higher confidence level will be shown first.

(3) *Sort by Support-Confidence Weight*: Linear combination function (Support + (Weight) * Confidence) is used to sort the rules. If 2 rules have the same value, the one with higher support level will be shown first. User can input the weight.

### *View Rules in CBA-Tree*

This is one of the rule utilities. After a set of classification rules/ association item sets have been generated from CBA. You can choose to view it in a CBA-Tree. In the tree, A stands for an attribute, V for an attribute value, Vc for attribute value with a class item underneath, and C for class item.

An important property for the CBA-Tree is that the rules under a particular attribute can only contain attributes that are below this attribute.

### *Prediction*

This is one of the rule utilities. After a set of rules are generated from CBA. You can use them to do predictions. Prediction can be done in a case by case basis, or a batch manner.

You can only use the rules generated from classification mining to perform prediction. Item sets or association rules generated from association mining cannot be used in prediction.

### *Batch Testing*

You can predict number of testing cases in one goal by putting all the testing cases in one file with extension .test. You can use this test in 2 ways:

(1) You can give a comparing class label in each testing case, the testing engine will compare the predicted class outcome with the stated class outcome and give error rate after comparison.

(2) Ignore comparing class label, the testing engine will simply give the predicted class for each case.

*Test file format:* The test file will be the same format as table classification data file data.

### *Input Files*

**.names file*

```
    | 1. Title: Animals database
    |
    | 2. Relevant Information:
    | - A simple database containing 10 Boolean-valued
attributes. The "type" attribute appears to be the
class attribute.
    |
    | 3. Number of Instances: 49
    |
    | 4. Number of Attributes: 11 (animal name, 8 Boolean
attributes, 2 numeric)
    | 5. Attribute Information: (name of attribute and
type of value domain)
    | 1. Animal name: Unique for each instance
    | 2. Hair         Boolean
    | 3. Feathers     Boolean
```

```
| 4. Eggs          Boolean
| 5. Milk          Boolean
| 6. Aquatic       Boolean
| 7. Toothed       Boolean
| 8. Backbone      Boolean
| 9. Legs          Numeric (set of values:
                   {0,2,4,5,6,8})
| 10. Tail         Boolean
| 11. Type         Numeric (integer values in range
                   [1,7])
|
| 6. Missing Attribute Values: None
1, 2, 3, 4, 5, 6, 7.

Hair:        0, 1.
Feathers:    0, 1.
Eggs:        0, 1.
Milk:        0, 1.
Aquatic:     0, 1.
Toothed:     0, 1.
Backbone:    0, 1.
Legs:        0, 2, 4, 5, 6, 8.
Tail:        0, 1.
```

**.data file*

```
1,0,1,0,0,0,0,6,0,6.
1,0,0,1,0,1,1,2,0,1.
1,0,1,1,1,1,1,2,1,1.
1,0,1,1,0,1,1,4,1,1.
1,0,1,1,0,0,1,4,1,1.
0,1,1,0,1,1,0,2,1,2.
0,1,1,0,0,1,0,2,1,2.
0,1,1,0,1,1,1,0,1,4.
1,0,1,0,1,1,1,0,1,4.
0,0,1,0,0,0,0,4,1,3.
0,0,1,0,1,1,0,0,0,7.
1,0,1,0,0,0,0,6,0,6.
1,0,0,1,0,1,1,4,1,1.
1,0,0,1,1,0,1,4,1,1.
1,0,0,1,1,1,1,4,1,1.
1,0,0,1,0,1,1,4,1,1.
0,1,1,0,0,1,0,2,1,2.
0,1,1,0,0,0,0,2,1,2.
0,0,1,0,1,1,1,0,1,4.
```

**Table Class Rules**

- *.data file is given as input file.
- Data converter & Cleaner is then clicked which will clean the input data and save result in the file with .data.
- Discritizer is then clicked in order to make the continuous attributes as discrete attributes.
- Now click on Feature Selection, which will allow you to select the specific attributes based on some criteria.
- When Multi support is clicked, user have to first enter the options (Upper Limit, Lower Limit and Steps Level) desired for the particular analysis in the General Options section.
- A confusion matrix will be displayed based on the training sets.
- Now a window will be opened where the Classifier rules are displayed. Save this file with .rul extension.
- Cross Validation is made on the system based on the number of folds (number of times system should run) splitting data to training case and testing case.
- The rules generated can then be viewed by clicking on view rules.
- The tree can be viewed by clicking on view tree.
- After a set of rules are generated from CBA. You can use them to do predictions. Prediction can be done in a case by case basis.

**Table Association Rules**

- Same as the Table class rules except that discretizer, feature selection, cross validation will be inactive.
- When Multi support is clicked, a window will be opened where the Association rules are displayed

***.trc Input File**

```
University, college, education
Military, politics, law, taxes, government
Book, text, dictionary, education
```

```
School, university, arts
Literature, events, museums, arts
Body art, drawing, fashion, arts
University, technology policy, countries, ethics,
government
Taxes, government
University, college, education
Military, politics, law, taxes, government
Book, text, dictionary, education
School, university, arts
Literature, events, museums, arts
Body art, drawing, fashion, arts
School, university, arts
Literature, events, museums, arts
Body art, drawing, fashion, arts
University, technology policy, countries, ethics,
government
Taxes, government
University, college, education
Military, politics, law, taxes, government
University, college, education
Military, politics, law, taxes, government
Book, text, dictionary, education
```

### Transaction Class Rules

- *.trc file is given as input file.
- Data Converter & Cleaner is then clicked which will clean the input data and save result in the file with .data.
- When Multi support is clicked, user have to first enter the options (Upper Limit, Lower Limit and Steps Level) desired for the particular analysis in the General Options section.
- Now a window will be opened where the Classifier rules are displayed. Save this file with .rul extension.
- The rules generated can then be viewed by clicking on view rules.
- The tree can be viewed by clicking on view tree.
- After a set of rules are generated from CBA. You can use them to do predictions. Prediction can be done in a case by case basis.

*.tra Input File

```
Onion, sugar, roses, soya sauce, cd
Rice, sugar, tomato sauce, apple
Orange juice, tomato sauce, potato chips, sugar
Onion rings, sugar, roses, soya sauce
Newspaper, cd, battery, sweets, soya sauce, rice
Rice, sugar, tomato sauce, apple, bananas
Newspaper, cd, battery, sweets, soya sauce, rice
Rice, sugar, tomato sauce, apple, flowers
Newspaper, cd, battery, sweets, soya sauce, rice
Onion rings, sugar, roses, soya sauce, cd
Sugar, orange juice, vase, oven, rice cooker
Newspaper, cd, battery, sweets, soya sauce, rice
Pulses, sugar, tomato sauce, apple
Rice, sugar, tomato sauce, apple, lamp
Newspaper, cd, battery, sweets, soya sauce, rice
Orange juice, tomato sauce, potato chips, sugar
Newspaper, cd, battery, sweets, soya sauce, rice
Rice, sugar, tomato sauce, apple, brinjal
Newspaper, cd, battery, sweets, soya sauce, rice
Rice, sugar, tomato sauce, apple, floppy
Onion rings, sugar, roses, soya sauce, cd
Rice, sugar, tomato sauce, apple, salt
Newspaper, cd, battery, sweets, soya sauce, rice
Rice, sugar, tomato sauce, apple
Orange juice, tomato sauce, potato chips, sugar
```

**Transaction Association Rules**

- *.tra file is given as input file.
- Same as the Transaction class rules.
- When Multi support is clicked, a window will be opened where the Association rules are displayed.

**References**

Jiawei Han and Michiline Kamber (2000), "Data Mining-Concepts and Techniques", Morgan Kaufmman Publishers.

John Wang, "Encyclopedia of Data Warehousing and Data Mining".

# 6

# CTree (Classification Tree in Excel)

## Introduction

CTree is freely downloadable, easy to use, learn and performance not too bad. A decision tree is a classification scheme, which generates a tree and a set of rules, representing a model of different classes, from a give data set. The set of records available for developing classification method is generally divided into two disjoint subsets-training dataset and test dataset. The former is used for deriving classifier and later is used to measure the accuracy.

We categorize the attributes of the records into two different types. Attributes whose domain is numerical is called numerical attributes and whose domain is categorical is called categorical attributes.

A tool that does not require special installations to be done, does not require licences to be bought, quick and easy to distribute on students' machines, does not requires data files to be prepared in special formats and can quickly run a bunch of examples.

## Features of the Application

- The columns for input and output variables in our data need not reside in contiguous columns. Assume that we have ten columns in our data set. We can tell the application that columns 2,3, 5 and 10 are our predictors, column 8 is the Class variable and the rest of the columns we don't want to use This comes in very handy if we want to try out various models on the same data set keeping and droping different predictors for different models.

- We can break up our data set into training and test set. We can build our model on the training set and test its performance on test set. We can either randomly select a portion of our data as test set or we can specify that the last few rows of our data should be treated as the test set.
- Application has some limited capability of handling missing data. For continuous variable, any non-number in any of our data column will be treated as missing value. Application will replace all the missing values in a column by respective column medians. For categorical variables, any blank cell or any cell containing an Excel error will be treated as missing value and application will replace it with the most frequently occuring category.
- Application has capability of growing a large tree and then pruning it back to generate a stable tree.
- After the model is built, application reports Confusion Matrices on your training/test data.
- The application has a viewer sheet which lets us to see graphically the class distribution in each node of the tree.
- The application generates a set of decision rules. These are IF-THEN rules to describe the classes. The rules give us insight about the structure of the classification problem. For each rule, three performance measures (support, confidence, capture) are reported. These measures can be used to assess the presents the quality of the rules. The plot also tells us how effective the rules in separating out the classes are.
- Application also generates a rule plot. Rule plot visually once we have built the tree, we have the option of saving the model in a separate workbook. Using this option we save the output in a separate work book. Thus we can have a clear idea about the output.

- Once you save the final tree in a new workbook, we can set it up to classify new observations using the tree you have just built.

When we save the tree in a new workbook, along with the tree following things are also saved.

- The Training and Test data use to build and validate the tree.
- The predicted classes for the Training/Test data.
- The different settings that were used to build the tree.
- Graphical representation of the class distributions in various nodes of the tree.

**Characteristics**

***Algorithm***

Application uses C4.5 algorithm by Ross Quinlan.

***Node Splitting Criterion:***

Application uses Entropy based criterion to select the split. While growing the tree, at any point a predictor is chosen to split a node such that the InformationGain is maximized after the split. As specified in C4.5, it actually uses the *Gain Ratio (= Gain / Split Info)* to choose the split. We have the option of using Gain instead to Gain Ratio, in which case the Split Info is forcibly set to 1.

***Stopping Criteria***

Application stops splitting a node and declares it, as a leaf node is any one of the following ctirerion is met.

- Number of records in the node is less than some pre-specified limit.
- Purity of the node is more than some pre-specified limit *p*. This means that the proportion of records in the node with class equal to the majority class is *p* or more.
- Depth of the node is more than some pre-specified limit.
- Predictor values for all records are identical.

### *Tree Pruning*

It is based on the *pessimistic error* rate at the node. At the node a 50% confidence interval of the error rate is computed and its upper limit is taken as the pessimistic error rate. If the pessimistic error rate of a node is less than that of the sub tree rooted at that node, the node is pruned. If we fail to prune a node-none of its predecessors is pruned.

### *Rule Generation*

It is according to the methods mentioned in C4.5. For each leaf node in the tree, the path from root to that node gives a rule. Thus if we have *k* nodes in the tree we start with a set of *k* rules. Then individual rules are pruned by dropping clauses one by one from that rule. The decision on whether or not to drop a clause is taken based on the outcome of a statistical independence test. The test tries to see whether keeping or dropping a clause is independent of the final decision of the rule. If it is independent, then that shows that the clause is NOT contributing towards the final decision and hence we drop the clause to simplify the rule. The independence tests used are Chi-square test and Fisher's exact test.

## Instructions on Using this Tool

### *Step 1: Enter Your Data*

(A) Enter your data in The Data worksheet, starting from the cell L24. Number of rows in your data should be between 10 and 10,000.

(B) The observations should be in rows and the variables should be in columns.

(C) Above each column, choose appropriate Type (Omit, Class, Cont, Cat).

- To drop a column from model-set the type=Omit
- To treat a column as categorical predictor, set type =Cat
- To treat a column as continuous Predictor, set type= Cont
- To treat a column as Class variable, set type = Output

You can have at most 50 predictor variables. You should have exactly one Class variable. Application will treat the Class variable as categorical. Each of your Categorical predictors should have at most 20 categories.

(D) Please make sure that your data does not have blank rows or blank columns.

(E) Your Class variable should not have any missing values.

*Continuous Predictors*

- Any non-number in Cont column will be treated as missing value. Aplication is replacing it by the column median.

*Categorical Predictors*

- Any blank cell or cells containing Excel error in Cat column will be treated as a missing value. Application will replace it by the most frequently occurring category.
- Category labels are case sensitive.
- There should be at least 2 observations in each category of a Cat column.

***Step 2: Fill up Model Inputs***

(A) Fill up the model inputs in the User Input Page.

(B) Make sure that your inputs are within the range of values allowed by the application.

(C) Click the 'Build Tree' button to start modeling.

***Step 3: Results of Modeling***

(A) When the run is over, the classification tree can be seen in Tree sheet. You can enter the values of predictors.

(B) You can select a cell in any of the nodes and click the View Node button to see the details information on that node in NodeView Sheet.

(C) In cell F7 of NodeView sheet you can enter any node number to see the class distribution and other information about that node.

### *Step 4: Rule Generation*

After the tree is grown, tree is further processed to generate Rules. Rule sets generated here are for viewing ONLY. The tool does NOT have the capability of using these rules to classify new data points. Rule Summary Table tells you the quality of the individual rules.

Quality is measured by 3 different metrics explained below.

*For example, consider a rule:*

IF Petal Width > 7 and Petal Length <= 70 THEN Species = Setosa.

*Support:* % of training data for which the Left Hand Side (LHS) of the Rule (I.e. Petal Width > 7 PetalLength <=70) is true If for a observation the LHS of the rule is true, we say that the rule APPLIES for that observation. This measures how widely applicable is the rule.

*Confidence:* Out of the training records for which the (LHS) of the Rule is true, % of records for which the Right Hand side is also true. In other words, for what % of the observations on which the rule applies, the rule is true. This measures the accuracy of the rule.

*Capture:* What % of Setosa records is correctly captured by this rule? This is more of a reflection of the structure of the problem. If there is a rule with capture close to 100%, that means, in the predictor space, all observations with this class sit closely to each other and the rule has been able to capture that part of the predictor space very well.

Suppose there are 150 observations in the training data, out of which 50 is Setosa.

Also assume that the above rule applies to 70 records and out of which 30 is Setosa Then,

*Support:* 47% (=70/150), Confidence: 43% (=30/70), Capture: 60% (= 30/50).

**Classification Tree Inputs**

- Minimum Node Size (Default = 5 records)
- Maximum Purity (Default = 100% purity)
- Maximum Depth (Default = Maximum Depth 20)

- Minimum Confidence (Default = 50%)
- Minimum Support (Default = 0%)

**Enter Your Data in this Sheet**

***Instructions***

- Start entering your data from cell G24.
- Specify variable type in row 22.
- Class–Class variable Cat–Categorical Predictor Cont–Continuous Predictor. Omit–If you don't want to use the variable in the model.

| *Var Type* | *Omit* | *Class* | *Cont* | *Cont* | *Omit* | *Omit* | *Omit* |
|---|---|---|---|---|---|---|---|
| *Var Name* | *Species No.* | *Species name* | *Petal width* | *Petal length* | *Sepal width* | *Sepal length* | *My Stuff* |
| | | Setosa | 2 | 14 | 33 | 50 | b |
| | 1 | Setosa | 2 | 10 | 36 | 46 | c |
| | 1 | Setosa | 2 | 16 | 31 | 48 | b |
| | 1 | Setosa | 1 | 14 | 36 | 49 | c |
| | 1 | Setosa | 2 | 13 | 32 | 44 | b |
| | 1 | Setosa | 1 | 11 | 33 | 49 | c |
| | 1 | Setosa | 2 | 19 | 22 | 44 | b |
| | 2 | Versicolor | 13 | 42 | 27 | 56 | a |
| | 2 | Versicolor | 16 | 45 | 34 | 60 | a |
| | 2 | Versicolor | 13 | 45 | 27 | 56 | a |
| | 2 | Versicolor | 16 | 33 | 34 | 60 | a |
| | 2 | Versicolor | 13 | 54 | 29 | 62 | a |
| | 2 | Versicolor | 10 | 35 | 26 | 57 | a |
| | 2 | Versicolor | 13 | 42 | 27 | 56 | a |
| | 3 | Verginica | 17 | 33 | 22 | 49 | b |
| | 3 | Verginica | 24 | 56 | 31 | 67 | b |
| | 3 | Verginica | 23 | 51 | 33 | 69 | c |
| | 3 | Verginica | 20 | 52 | 30 | 65 | b |
| | 3 | Verginica | 19 | 44 | 27 | 58 | c |
| | 3 | Verginica | 23 | 55 | 35 | 69 | c |
| | 3 | Verginica | 20 | 49 | 30 | 65 | b |

After entering the data in the Data sheet Click on Build Tree in the UserInput Sheet then we can generate output work sheet with six sheets. That is Result sheet, Tree sheet, NodeView sheet, Rules sheet, UserInput sheet, and Data sheet.

**Result Sheet**

Result Sheet gives the information about Tree, Tree nodes, Tree depth, Confusion Matrix for training set and test set and time taken for tree drawing, tree generation, rule generation. The resultant output of the Result Sheet is as follows.

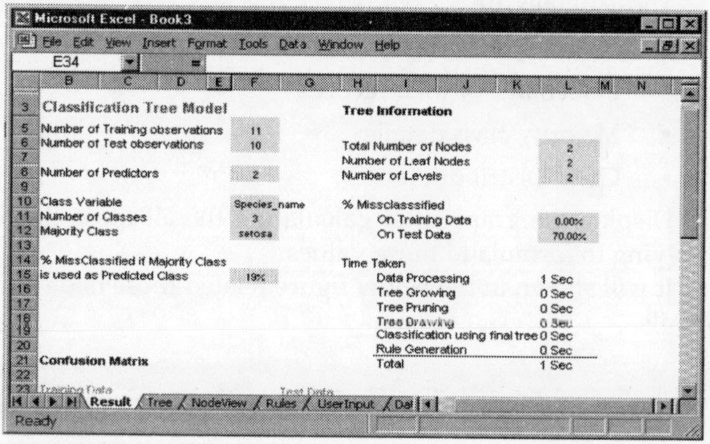


**Tree Sheet**

Tree Sheet displays the information we entered in the data sheet in the form of tree. It generates the tree for test data according to the rules.It also generates the support and confidence of each node in the tree. The TreeSheet is as follows.

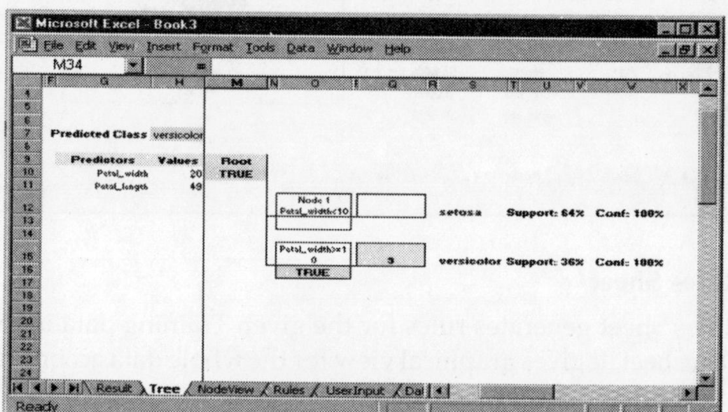

## Node View Sheet

- Node View Sheet contains the information about nodes in the Tree. In this Sheet we can view the details of the each node.
- Node ID shows that particular details view.

  Those details are

  - Number of Records
  - Percentage of total records
  - Majority class details
  - Class Distribution

Display the graph after calculating the all those details applying to formula to those values.

It will shown in the below figure related those node view details.

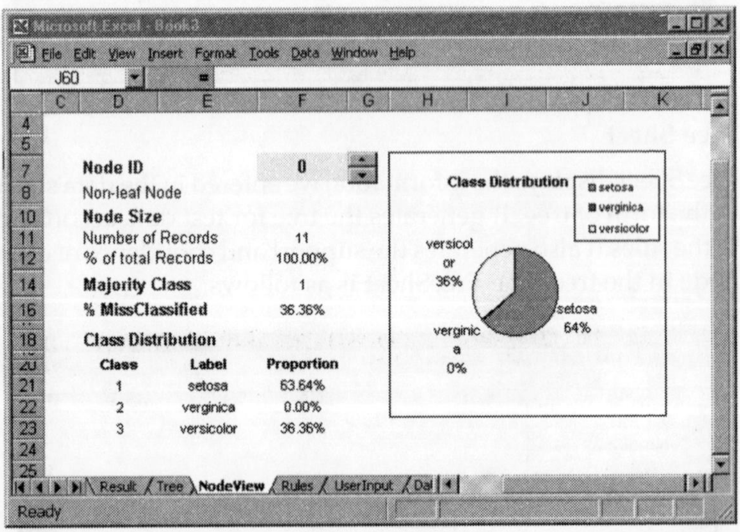


## Rules Sheet

Rules Sheet generates rules for the given Training data in the Datasheet. It gives graphical view for the whole data according to the rules. It displays the Summary Table. This table contains,

- Rule Id for Class
- Class
- Length
- Support
- Confidence
- Capture

The rules for the given data in the DataSheet are as follows.

**Rule Text**

**Rule 0:** species_name=setosa

**Rule 1:** IF petal_width<10
THEN species_name=setosa

**Rule 2:** IF petal_width>=10
THEN specis_name=versicolor

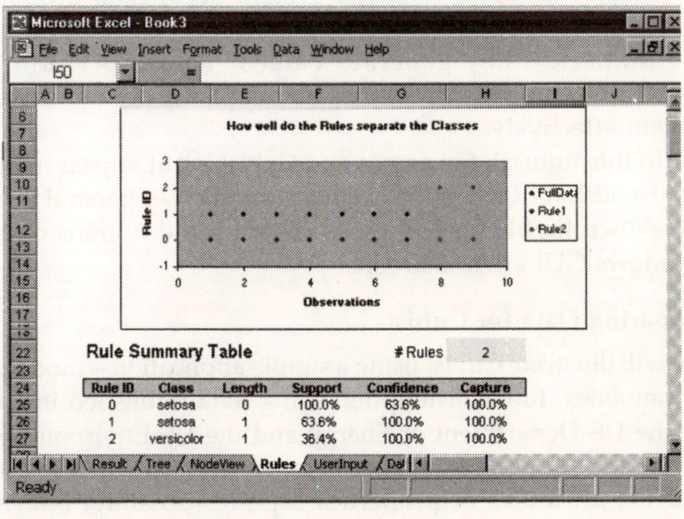


**Note**

CTree is highly secured tool. First, we have to minimize the security by from Tools/Macro/low.

To unprotect every sheet in this tool, from Tool / Unprotect Sheet, enter PassWord. The PassWord is: CTree.

# 7

# Cubist

## Introduction

Cubist is a tool for generating rule-based predictive models from data. Whereas its sister system See5/C5.0 produces classification models that predict categories, Cubist's models are numeric—they generate values. This short tutorial introduces Cubist's capabilities and explains how to use the system effectively.

In this tutorial, file names and Cubist input appear in blue fixed-width font while file extensions and other general forms are shown highlighted in green. Buttons and options on the Windows GUI are in maroon.

## Preparing Data for Cubist

We will illustrate Cubist using a simple application—modeling automobiles' fuel consumption using data published in 2002 by the US Department of Energy and the US Environmental Protection Agency. Each data point concerns one automobile and the attributes or properties capture (possibly) relevant information as follows.

Each case has a target attribute or dependent variable—here the city miles per gallon achieved by the automobile—and the other attributes provide information that may help to predict this value, although some automobiles may have unknown values for some attributes. There are only thirteen attributes in this example including the target attribute, but Cubist can deal with any number of attributes (well, up to two billion or so).

| *Attribute* | *Case 1* | *Case 2* | *Case 3* |
|---|---|---|---|
| Class | Subcompact | Midsz Wag | Midsz Car |
| Manufacturer | Pontiac | Ford | Linc-merc |
| Model | Sunfire | Focus | Wag Ls |
| Displacement (1) | 2.2 | 2.0 | 3.9 |
| Cylinders | 4 | 4 | 8 |
| Drive | Auto | Manual | Auto |
| Gears | 4 | 5 | 5 |
| Transmission | FWD | FWD | RWD |
| Fuel | Regular | Regular | Premium |
| Charger (super- or turbo-) | None | None | None |
| Valves/cylinder | 2 | 2 | 4 |
| Displacement/cylinder | 0.55 | 0.5 | 0.49 |
| City mpg | 26.1 | 31.5 | 18.6 |

Cubist's job is to find how to estimate a case's target value in terms of its attribute values—here, to relate *miles per gallon* to the other information provided for the automobile. Cubist does this by building a *model* containing one or more *rules*, where each rule is a conjunction of conditions associated with a linear expression. The meaning of a rule is that, if a case satisfies all the conditions, then the linear expression is appropriate for predicting the target value. A Cubist model thus resembles a *piecewise linear model*, except that the rules can overlap. As we will see, Cubist can also construct multiple models and can combine rule-based models with instance-based (nearest neighbor) models.

## Application Files

Every Cubist application has a short name called a filestem; we will use the filestem mpg2001 for this illustration. All files read or written by Cubist for an application look like filestem.extension, where filestem identifies the application and extension describes the contents of the file.

Here is a summary table of the extensions used by Cubist.

| | | |
|---|---|---|
| names | description of the application's attributes | [required] |
| data | cases used to generate a model | [required] |
| test | unseen cases used to test a model | [optional] |
| cases | cases to be modeled subsequently | [optional] |
| model | rule-based model produced by Cubist | [output] |
| pred | actual and predicted target values for any test cases | [output] |
| out | report produced when a model is generated | [output] |
| set | settings used for the last model | [output] |

The case of letters in both the filestem and extension is important—file names APP.DATA, app.data, and App.Data, are all different. It is important that the extensions are written exactly as shown below, otherwise Cubist will not recognize the files for your application.

If Cubist cannot seem to find your files even though the filestem and extensions are correct, please check that file extensions are not hidden on your computer. (If extensions are hidden and you write a text file from wordpad, it automatically adds an extension .txt that makes the file invisible to Cubist.) Here's what to do:

Double click "My Computer", select "Tools" (or "View" for Windows 98), then "Folder Options" and then the "View" tab. The box "Hide file extensions for known file types" should not be checked. If it is, uncheck it and click "Apply". All files for an application must be kept together in one folder but several applications can share the same folder.

**Names File**

The first essential file is the names file (e.g. mpg2001.names) that defines the attributes used to describe each case. There are two important subgroups of attributes:

The value of an explicitly-defined attribute is given directly in the data. A *discrete* attribute has a value drawn from a set of nominal values, a *continuous* attribute has a numeric value, a *date* attribute holds a calendar date, a *time* attribute holds a clock time, a *timestamp* attribute holds a date and time, and a *label* attribute serves only to identify a particular case.

### *What's in a Name?*

Names, labels, and discrete values are represented by arbitrary strings of characters, with some fine print:

- Tabs and spaces are permitted inside a name or value, but Cubist collapses every sequence of these characters to a single space.
- Special characters (comma, colon, period, vertical bar '|') can appear in names and values, but must be prefixed by the escape character '\'. For example, the name "Filch, Grabbit, and Co." would be written as 'Filch\, Grabbit\, and Co\.'. (However, it is not necessary to escape colons in times and periods in numbers.)

Whitespace (blank lines, spaces, and tab characters) is ignored except inside a name or value and can be used to improve legibility. Unless it is escaped as above, the vertical bar '|' causes the remainder of the line to be ignored and is handy for including comments. When used in this way, '|' should not occur inside a value.

The first important entry of the names file identifies the attribute that contains the target value—the value to be modeled in terms of the other attributes—here, city mpg. This attribute must be of type continuous or an implicitly-defined attribute that has numeric values (see below).

Following this entry, all attributes are defined in the order that they will be given for each case.

### Explicitly-defined Attributes

The name of each explicitly-defined attribute is followed by a colon ':' and a description of the values taken by the attribute. The attribute name is arbitrary, except that each attribute must have a distinct name, and case weight is reserved for setting weights for individual cases. There are eight possibilities:

#### *Continuous*

The attribute takes numeric values.

*Date*

The attribute's values are dates in the form YYYY/MM/DD or YYYY-MM-DD, e.g. 1999/09/30 or 1999-09-30. Valid dates range from the year 1601 to the year 4000.

*Time*

The attribute's values are times in the form HH:MM:SS with values between 00:00:00 and 23:59:59.

*Timestamp*

The attribute's values are times in the form YYYY/MM/DD HH:MM:SS or YYYY-MM-DD HH:MM:SS, e.g. 1999-09-30 15:04:00. (Note that there is a space separating the date and time).

The attribute takes discrete values, and these are the allowable values. The values may be prefaced by [ordered] to indicate that they are listed in a meaningful order, otherwise they will be taken as unordered. For instance, the values low, medium, high are ordered, while meat, poultry, fish, vegetables are not. If the attribute values have a natural order, it is better to declare them as ordered so that this information can be exploited by Cubist.

*Discrete*

N for some integer *N*
The attribute also takes discrete values, but the values are assembled from the data itself; *N* is the maximum number of such values. (This is not recommended, since the data cannot be checked, but it can be handy for discrete attributes with many values.)

*Ignore*

The values of the attribute should be ignored.

*Label*

This attribute contains an identifying label for each case, such as an account number or an order code. The value of the attribute is ignored when models are constructed, but is used when referring to individual cases. A label attribute can make it easier to locate errors in the data and also helps with cross-referencing of results to individual cases. If there are two or more label attributes, only the last is used.

### *Attributes Defined by Formulas*

The name of each implicitly-defined attribute is followed by ':=' and then a formula defining the attribute value. The formula is written in the usual way, using parentheses where needed, and may refer to any attribute that has been defined before this one. Constants in the formula can be '?' (meaning unknown), 'N/A' (meaning not applicable), numbers (written in decimal notation), dates, times, and discrete attribute values enclosed in string quotes '""'. The operators and functions available for use in the formula are:

- +, -, *, /, % (mod), ^ (meaning 'raised to the power')
- >, >=, <, <=, =, <> or != (the last two both meaning 'not equal')
- and, or
- sin(...), cos(...), tan(...), log(...), exp(...), int(...) (meaning 'integer part of')

The value of an implicitly-defined attribute is either numeric or true/false depending on the formula. This example includes one implicitly-defined attribute, engine displacement per cylinder. This is a numeric attribute since its value is a ratio of two explicitly-defined numeric attributes. The value of a hypothetical attribute

small := cylinders = 4 and class = "COMPACT CARS"

would be either t or f since the value given by the formula is either true or false.

If the value of the formula cannot be determined for a particular case, the value of the implicitly-defined attribute is unknown. For example, consider a car with a value '?' for the attribute cylinders. It is then impossible to find the value of engine displacement per cylinder so this attribute would also have an unknown value.

***Dates, Times, and Timestamps***

Dates are stored by Cubist as the number of days since a particular starting point so some operations on dates make sense. Thus, if we have attributes,

d1:date.

d2: date.

We could define

interval := d2 - d1.

gap := d1 <= d2 - 7.

d1-day-of-week := (d1 + 1) % 7 + 1.

interval then represents the number of days from d1 to d2 (non-inclusive) and gap would have a true/false value signaling whether d1 is at least a week before d2. The last definition is a slightly non-obvious way of determining the day of the week on which d1 falls, with values ranging from 1 (Monday) to 7 (Sunday).

Similarly, times are stored as the number of seconds since midnight. If the names file includes,

Start: time.

Finish: time.

Elapsed: = finish - start.

the value of elapsed is the number of seconds from start to finish.

Timestamps are a little more complex. A timestamp is rounded to the nearest minute, but limitations on the precision of floating-point numbers mean that the values stored for timestamps from more than thirty years ago are approximate. If the names file includes,

departure: timestamp.

arrival: timestamp.

flight time := arrival - departure.

the value of flight time is the number of minutes from departure to arrival.

*Selecting the Attributes that can Appear in Models*

An optional final entry in the names file affects the way that Cubist constructs models. This entry takes one of the forms attributes included: followed by a comma-separated list of attribute names. The first form restricts the attributes used in models to those specifically named; the second form specifies that models must not use any of the named attributes.

Excluding an attribute from models is not the same as ignoring the attribute (see 'ignore' above). As an example, suppose that a numeric attribute A is defined in the data, but background knowledge suggests that only the logarithm of A should appear in models. The names file might then contain the following entries:

A: continuous.

LogA := log(A).

attributes excluded: A.

In this example the attribute A could not be defined as ignore because the definition of LogA would then be invalid.

The same pattern could be used if the goal was to model the log of A rather than the value of A itself. In this case the target attribute would be given as LogA and the exclusion of A would be necessary to prevent the value of A being used in the model for LogA.

### *Data File*

The second essential file, the application's data file (here mpg2001.data), provides information on the *training* cases that Cubist will use to construct a model. The entry for each case consists of one or more lines that give the values for all explicitly-defined attributes. Values are separated by commas and the entry for each case is optionally terminated by a period. Once again, anything on a line after a vertical bar is ignored. (If the information for a case occupies more than one line, make sure that the line breaks occur after commas.)

### *Test and Cases Files (optional)*

Of course, the value of predictive models lies in their ability to make accurate predictions! It is difficult to judge the accuracy of a model by measuring how well it does on the cases used in its construction; the performance of the model on new cases is much more informative.

The third kind of file used by Cubist is a test file of new cases (here mpg2001.test) on which the model can be evaluated. This file is optional and has exactly the same format as the data file. In this application the 852 cases have been split randomly 70%:30% into data and test files containing 596 and 256 cases respectively.

Another optional file, the cases file (e.g. mpg2001.cases), has the same format as the data and test files. The cases file is used primarily with the cross-referencing procedure and public source code, both of which are described later on.

***User Interface***

It is difficult to see what is going on in an interface without actually using it. As a simple illustration, here is the main window of Cubist after the mpg2001 application has been selected:

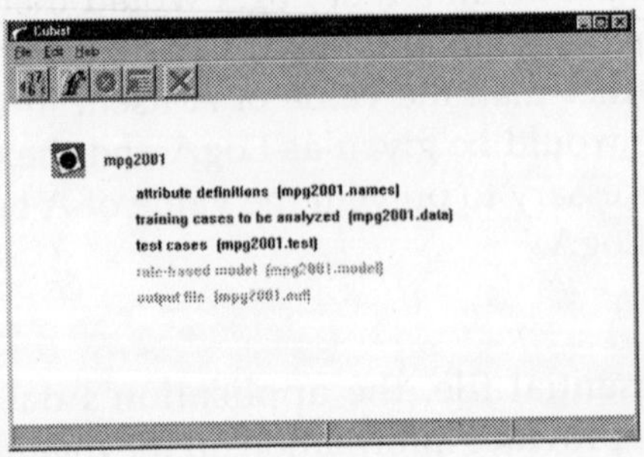


The main window of Cubist has five buttons on its toolbar. From left to right, they are:

*Locate Data*

Invokes a browse dialog to find the files for your application, or to change the current application;

*Build Model*

Selects the type of model to be constructed and sets other options;

*Stop*

Interrupts the model-generating process;

*Review Output*

Re-displays the output from the last model construction (if any);

*Cross-Reference*

Maps between data and models.

These functions can also be initiated from the File menu.

The Edit menu facilities changes to the names file after an application has been located. On-line help is available through the Help menu.

**Constructing Models**

Once the names, data, and optional files have been set up, everything is ready to use Cubist. The first step is to locate the date using the Locate Data button on the toolbar (or the corresponding selection from the File menu). We will assume that the mpg2001.data file above has been located in this manner.

There are several options that affect the type of model that Cubist produces and the way that it is constructed. The Construct Model button on the toolbar (or selection from the File menu) displays a dialog box that sets out these model construction options:

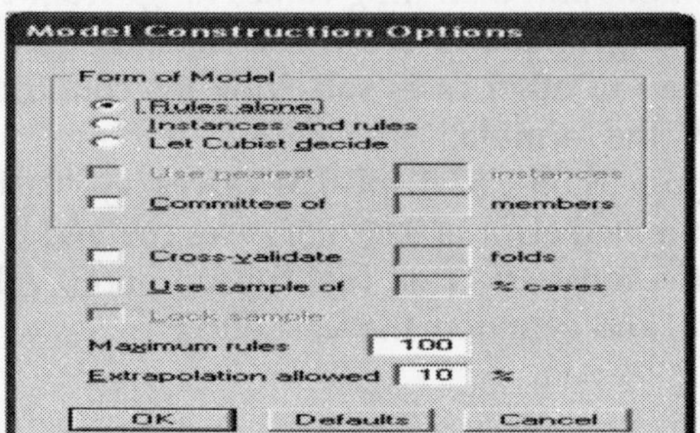


**Rule-based Models**

When Cubist is invoked with the default values of all options, it constructs a rule-based model and produces output.

The first part identifies the version of Cubist, the run date, and the attribute that contains the target value.

Now we come to the training data. Some attribute values might be missing; if so, Cubist replaces them by the most probable values. Missing values of continuous attributes are replaced by the mean of the known values for that attribute, while the replacement for missing discrete values is the most frequent attribute value.

Cubist constructs a model from the 596 training cases in the file mpg2001.data, and this appears next. A model consists of an unordered collection of rules, each of the form: If condition then linear model.

A rule indicates that, whenever a case satisfies all the conditions, the linear model is appropriate for predicting the value of the target attribute. (If two or more rules apply to a case, then the values are averaged to arrive at a final prediction.) Each rule also carries some descriptive information: the number of training cases that satisfy the rule's conditions, their target values' mean and range, and a (rather erratic) estimate of the expected error magnitude of predictions made by the rule. Within the linear model, the attributes are ordered in decreasing relevance to the result.

Among the 596 training cases there are 56 that satisfy all three conditions and their mpg values range from 12.4 to 19.8 with an average value of 15.74. Cubist finds that the target value of these or other cases satisfying the conditions can be modeled by the formula:

City mpg=31.66-2.87 displ–0.54 valves/cyl–0.04 cylinders with an estimated error of 0.66. For cases covered by this rule, displ has the most effect on fuel consumption, valves/cyl a lesser effect, and cylinders the least effect.

**Evaluation**

Models constructed by Cubist are evaluated on the training data from which they were generated, and also on a separate file of unseen test cases if this is present.

Evaluation on training data (596 cases):

| | |
|---|---|
| Average (error) | 1.03 |
| Relative (error) | 0.26 |
| Correlation coefficient | 0.97 |

The average error magnitude is straightforward enough. The relative error magnitude is the ratio of the average error magnitude to the error magnitude that would result from always predicting the mean value; for useful models, this should be less than 1! The correlation coefficient measures the agreement between the cases' actual values of the target attribute and those values predicted by the model.

If a test file is present, Cubist produces a summary similar to that for the training cases:

Evaluation on test data (256 cases):

| | |
|---|---|
| Average \| error \| | 1.16 |
| Relative \| error \| | 0.32 |
| Correlation coefficient | 0.94 |

Cubist also generates a file filestem.pred (here mpg2001.pred) that shows the actual and predicted value for each test case.

Another way of assessing the accuracy of the predictions is through a visual inspection of a *scatter plot* that graphs the real target values of new cases against the values predicted by the model. When a file filestem.test of test cases is present, Cubist also provides a scatter plot window. In this example, it looks like this:

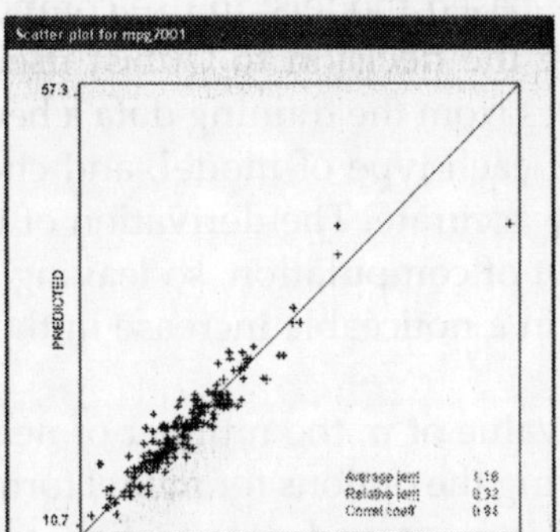

### *Composite Models*

For some applications, the predictive accuracy of a rule-based model can be improved by combining it with an instance-based or nearest-neighbor model. The latter predicts the target value of a new case by finding the **n** most similar cases in the training data, and averaging their target values.

Cubist employs an unusual method for combining rule-based and instance-based models. Cubist finds the **n** training cases that are "nearest" (most similar) to the case in question. Then, rather than averaging their target values directly, Cubist first adjusts these values using the rule-based model. Here's how it works:

Suppose that **x** is the case whose unknown target value is to be predicted, and **y** is one of **x**'s nearest neighbors in the training data. The target value of **y** is known: let us call it **T(y)**. The rule-based model can be used to predict target values for any case, so let its predictions for **x** and **y** be **M(x)** and **M(y)** respectively. The model then predicts that the difference between the target values of **x** and **y** is **M(x)-M(y)**. The value of **x** predicted by neighbor **y** is adjusted to reflect this difference, so that Cubist uses **T(y)+M(x)-M(y)** instead of **y**'s raw target value. (This is described in more detail in the paper "Combining instance-based and model-based learning", Proceedings of the Tenth International Conference on Machine Learning, pages 236-243, Morgan Kaufmann Publishers, San Francisco, 1993).

The model construction dialog box contains three options: to use purely rule-based models, to use composite models as above, or to leave the decision to Cubist itself. In the latter case, Cubist derives from the training data a heuristic estimate of the accuracy of each type of model, and chooses the form that appears more accurate. The derivation of these estimates requires quite a lot of computation, so leaving the decision to Cubist can result in a noticeable increase in the time required to build a model.

Now for the value of **n**, the number of nearest neighbors to be used. Following the options for model form in the options dialog box above is a (grayed-out) section covering nearest neighbors. If composite models are selected or Cubist is allowed to decide whether to use them, this option becomes active and, when selected, allows the number of nearest neighbors to be entered directly; the allowable range is from 1 to 9. If the value is not specified in this way, Cubist will choose an appropriate value in the range.

To continue the illustration: when Cubist is allowed to choose a model on the basis of the 596 training cases and the number of nearest neighbors is not specified, it opts for a composite model using a single nearest neighbor. The rule-based model itself is unchanged, but the composite model gives different results on the training and test cases, the latter being

Evaluation on test data (256 cases):

| | |
|---|---|
| Average \| error \| | 0.88 |
| Relative \| error \| | 0.25 |
| Correlation coefficient | 0.95 |

The performance of the composite model on the test cases in mpg2001.test thus improves upon that of the rule-based model alone, average error magnitude falling from 1.16 to 0.88.

Nearest neighbor models are adversely affected by the presence of irrelevant attributes. All attributes are taken into account when evaluating the similarity of two cases and irrelevant attributes introduce a random factor into this measurement. As a result, composite models are most effective when the number of attributes is relatively small and all attributes are relevant to the prediction task.

### *Committee Models*

In addition to the composite rule-based/nearest neighbor models discussed above, Cubist can also generate *committee models* made up of several rule-based models. Each member of the committee predicts the target value for a case and the members' predictions are averaged to give a final prediction.

The first member of a committee model is always exactly the same as the model generated without the committee option. The second member is a rule-based model designed to correct the predictions of the first member; if the first member's prediction is too low for a case, the second member will attempt to compensate by predicting a higher value. The third member tries to correct the predictions of the second member, and so on. The recommended number of members is five, a value that balances the benefits of the committee approach against the cost of generating extra models. The dialog box has a checkbox for selecting committee models and a field for specifying the number of committee members. When this option is invoked with the default five members, the results show a smaller improvement than that obtained with composite models:

Evaluation on test data (256 cases):

| | |
|---|---|
| Average \| error \| | 1.06 |
| Relative \| error \| | 0.30 |
| Correlation coefficient | 0.92 |

Committee models are of most benefit when single models are reasonably accurate, so they are more useful for fine-tuning good models than for overcoming the deficiencies of poor models. Finally, committee models can be used in conjunction with composite models if desired.

***Simplicity-accuracy Trade-off***

Cubist employs heuristics that try to simplify models without substantially reducing their predictive accuracy. In some applications, however, it might be desirable to generate simpler models—for instance, when the models must be very easy to understand. Of course, over-simplified models usually have lower predictive accuracy so there is a trade-off between simplicity and utility.

***Extrapolation***

The extrapolation parameter controls the extent to which predictions made by Cubist's linear models can fall outside the range of values seen in the training data. Extrapolation is inherently more risky than interpolation, where predictions must lie between the lowest and highest observed value.

The dialog box contains a field for this extrapolation factor in the form of a percentage. Each rule records the highest and lowest target value of the training cases satisfying that rule's conditions. When the target value of a new case is predicted using the rule, the value computed from the linear model may fall outside this range. The extrapolation parameter limits the degree to which new values can lie above or below the values seen in the training data, expressed as a percentage of the range (default 10%).

For example, the lowest target value among the 89 training cases covered by Rule 1 above is 13.2 and the highest is 30.1. The range is therefore 16.9 and, under the default extrapolation limit of 10%, the value predicted by this rule for a new case cannot be lower than 11.5 (13.2 - 1.7) or higher than 31.8 (30.1 + 1.7). Any computed value that lies outside these bounds is changed to the nearer bound. If the linear model associated with Rule 1 were to predict a value of 10, say, then this would be adjusted to 11.5.

Extrapolation may be constrained even further in two situations. When all the training cases covered by a rule have target values greater than or equal to zero, the rule will never predict a value less than zero. (This restriction prevents Cubist from making silly predictions such as negative miles per-gallon values.) Similarly, when a rule covers cases whose target values are all less than or equal to zero, the predicted value from the rule will never be positive.

### *Sampling from Large Datasets*

Even though Cubist is relatively fast, building models from a large number of cases can take an inconveniently long time. Cubist incorporates a facility to extract a random sample from a dataset, construct a model from the sample, and then test the model on a disjoint collection of cases. By using a smaller set of training cases in this way, the process of generating a model is expedited, but at the cost of a possible reduction in the model's predictive performance.

The Sample option with x% has two consequences. Firstly, a random sample containing x% of the cases in the application's data file is used to construct the model. Secondly, the model is evaluated on a non-overlapping set of test cases consisting of another (disjoint) sample of the same size as the training set (if

$x$ is less than 50%), or all cases that were not used in the training set (if $x$ is greater than or equal to 50%).

As an example, suppose that the application's data file contains 100,000 cases. If a sample of 10% is used, the model will be constructed from a sample of 10,000 cases and tested on a disjoint sample of 10,000 cases. Alternatively, selecting sampling with 60% will cause the model to be constructed from 60,000 cases and tested on the remaining 40,000 cases.

By default, the random sample changes every time that a model is constructed, so that successive runs of Cubist with sampling will usually produce different results. This re-sampling can be avoided by selecting the Lock sample option that uses the current sample for constructing subsequent models. If this option is selected, the sample will change only when another application is loaded, the sample percentage is altered, the option is unselected, or Cubist is restarted.

***Cross-validation Trials***

As we saw earlier, the performance of a model on the training cases from which it was constructed gives a poor estimate of its accuracy on new cases. The true predictive accuracy of the model can be estimated by sampling, as above, or by using a separate test file; either way, the classifier is evaluated on cases that were not used to build it. However, this estimate can be unreliable unless the numbers of cases used to build and evaluate the model are both large. If the cases in mpg2001.data and mpg2001.test were to be shuffled and divided into new training and test sets, Cubist would probably construct a different model whose accuracy on the test cases might vary considerably.

One way to get a more reliable estimate of predictive accuracy is by *f-fold cross-validation*. The cases in the data file are divided into f blocks of roughly the same size and target value distribution. For each block in turn, a model is constructed from the cases in the remaining blocks and tested on the cases in the hold-out block. In this way, each case is used just once as a test case. The accuracy of a model produced from all the cases is estimated by averaging results on the hold-out cases.

Running a 10-fold cross-validation using the composite model option gives results on the hold-out cases similar to these:

*Summary*

| | |
|---|---|
| Average \| error \| | 1.14 |
| Relative \| error \| | 0.29 |
| Correlation coefficient | 0.90 |

The file mpg2001.out contains the results of each cross-validation fold and the file mpg2001.pred shows a case-by-case summary of the performance of the Cubist models on unseen cases. A scatter plot of performance on the unseen cases is also provided.

A different random partition of the training cases is used every time a cross-validation is run. The whole cross-validation can be repeated a few times and results averaged to give a more reliable estimate.

Since a single cross-validation fold uses only part of the application's data, running a cross-validation does not cause a model to be saved. To save a model for later use, simply run Cubist without employing cross-validation.

### *Weighting Individual Cases*

By default, all training cases are treated equally when a model is constructed. In some applications, however, it may be desirable to assign different importance to the cases. Cubist achieves this by recognizing an optional attribute that gives the weight of each case. The attribute name must be case weight and it must be of type continuous. The relative weight assigned to each case is its value of this attribute divided by the average value; if the value is undefined ("?"), not applicable ("N/A"), or is less than or equal to zero, the case's relative weight is set to 1.

*The case weight attribute itself is not used in the model!*

To illustrate the idea, we will apply case weights to our example by adding an implicitly-defined attribute to mpg2001.names as follows:

case weight := displ.

This means that the importance of a training case varies as the total displacement of that case. Cubist will now attempt to minimize weighted error, so cars with higher displacements should have more influence on the new model. The following table shows the results from the case-weighted and original (un weighted) models for the seven vehicles in the unseen test cases that have the highest displacement:

| *Vehicle* | *Displacement* | *MPG* | *Predicted weighted* | *MPG Un weighted* |
|---|---|---|---|---|
| Viper Coupe | 8.0 | 12.5 | 12.52 | 14.51 |
| Rolls Royce Corniche | 6.8 | 12.6 | 12.48 | 12.73 |
| Bentley Continental T | 6.8 | 12.4 | 12.48 | 12.73 |
| Bentley Azure | 6.8 | 12.6 | 12.48 | 12.73 |
| Dakota Pickup 4WD | 5.9 | 15.7 | 16.71 | 16.57 |
| Ram Wagon 2500 2WD | 5.9 | 13.3 | 13.30 | 13.23 |
| Ram Van 1500 2WD | 5.9 | 13.4 | 13.30 | 13.23 |

The average error of the case-weighted model is 0.21, somewhat lower than the average error of 0.53 given by the original model.

A cautionary note: The use of case weighting does not guarantee that the model will be more accurate for unseen cases with higher weights. Predictive accuracy on more important cases is likely to be improved only when cases with similar values of the predictor attributes also have similar values of the case weight attribute, i.e. when relatively important cases "clump together." Without this property, case weighting can introduce an unhelpful element of randomness into the model generation process.

**Cross-Referencing Models and Data**

Cubist incorporates a helpful facility that links data and the relevant model rules. We will illustrate this facility using the first run with the mpg2001 application.

The Cross-Reference button brings up a dialog asking the user to choose a set of cases from among filestem.data, filestem.test, and filestem.cases. (This dialog is skipped if only one of these files is present.) For this example we have used the data file from which the model was generated.

Cubist then shows a window containing the most recent model for the current application and a list of the selected cases. Each case listing has an identifying label or index number, the case's actual target value, and, in blue, the target value predicted for it by the most recent model.

Clicking on a case number or label shows the model rules relevant to that case. Clicking on the first case shows that it is covered by Rule 5:

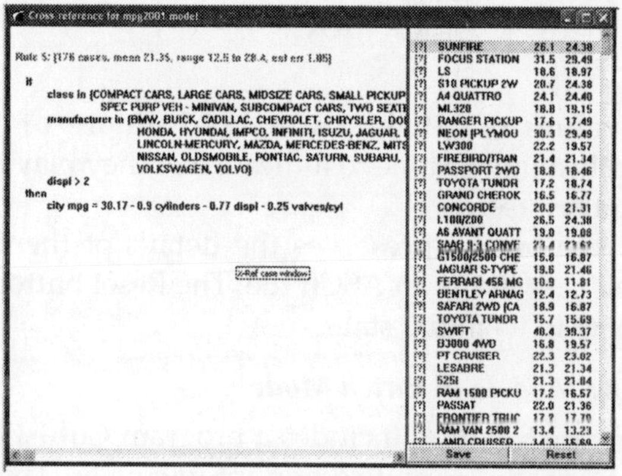

Click on any rule to show all the cases covered by that rule. For instance, clicking on Rule 5 shows the 176 training cases that satisfy the conditions of that rule:

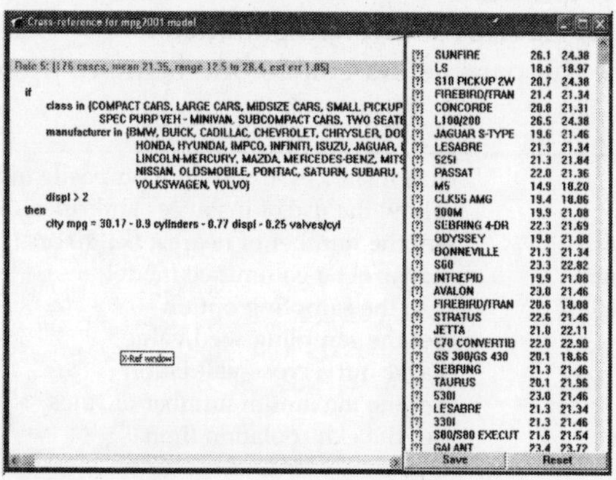

Finally, clicking on the text [?] in front of a case number or label displays that case:

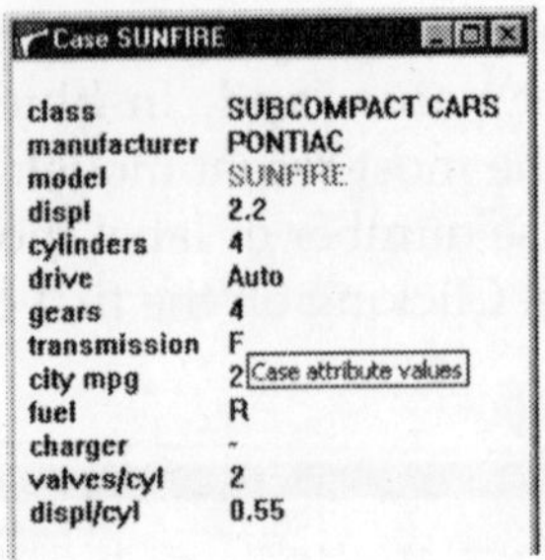


The values of attributes marked ignore or label are displayed in a lighter tone to indicate that they play no part in modeling the case.

The Save button preserves the details of the displayed model and case list as an ASCII file. The Reset button restores the window to its initial state.

### *Generating Models in Batch Mode*

The Cubist distribution includes a program **CubistX** that can be used to produce models non-interactively. This console application resides in the same folder as Cubist (usually C:\Program Files\Cubist for single-computer licensees or the Cubist folder on your desktop for network licences) and is invoked from an MS-DOS Prompt window. The command to run the program is:

start /B CubistX -f filestem parameters.

Where the parameters enable one or more options to be selected:

| | |
|---|---|
| `-i` | use instances and rules (composite models) |
| `-a` | allow the use of instances and rules |
| `-n` neighbors | set the number of nearest neighbors (1 to 9) |
| `-C` members | construct a committee model |
| `-S` percent | use the sampling option |
| `-I` seed | set the sampling seed value |
| `-X` folds | carry out a cross-validation |
| `-r` rules | set the maximum number of rules |
| `-e` percent | set the extrapolation limit |

For a more detailed discussion of these options, please see the Unix tutorial.

If desired, output from Cubist can be diverted to a file in the usual way.

As an example (for a single-computer licensee), typing the commands

cd "C:\Program Files\Cubist"

Start /B CubistX -f Samples\boston -S 80 -a >save.txt

from a MS-DOS Prompt window focuses on the boston application in the Samples directory, uses a sample of 80% of the cases for constructing the model (and tests it on the remaining 20%), allows Cubist to build composite models, and leaves the output in file save.txt.

# 8

# DATAStage—Data Ware Housing Tool

## Introduction

### *About Data Warehousing*

The aim of data warehousing is to make more effective use of the data available in an organization and to aid decision-making processes. A data warehouse is a central integrated database containing data from all the operational sources and archive systems in an organization. It contains a copy of transaction data specifically structured for query analysis. This database can be accessed by all users, ensuring that each group in an organization is accessing valuable, stable data.

A data warehouse is a "snapshot" of the operational databases combined with data from archives systems. The data warehouse can be created or updated at any time, with minimum disruption to operational systems. Any number of analyses can be performed on the data, which would otherwise be impractical on the operational sources.

### *Operational Databases versus Data Warehouses*

Operational databases are usually accessed by many concurrent users. The data in the database changes quickly and often. It is very difficult trying to obtain an accurate picture of the contents of the database at any one time. Because operational databases are task oriented, for example, stock inventory systems, they are likely to contain "dirty" data. The high throughput of data into operational databases makes it difficult to trap mistakes or incomplete entries. However, you can cleanse data before loading it into a data warehouse, ensuring that you store only "good" complete records.

### *Constructing the Data Warehouse*

A data warehouse is created by extracting data from one or more operational databases. The data is transformed to eliminate inconsistencies, aggregated to summarize data, and loaded into the data warehouse. The end result is a dedicated database which contains stable, nonvolatile, integrated data. This data also represents a number of time variants (for example, daily, weekly, or monthly values), allowing the user to analyze trends in the data.

The data in a data warehouse is classified based on the subjects of interest to the organization. For a bank, these subjects may be customer, account number, and transaction details. For a retailer, these may include product, price, quantity sold, and order number.

Each data warehouse includes detailed data. However, where only a portion of this detailed data is required, a data mart may be more suitable. A *data mart* contains focused data that is frequently accessed or summarized, for example, sales or marketing data.

The person who constructs the data warehouse must know the needs of all the users who will use the data warehouse or data marts. This means knowing the data contained in each operational database and how each database is related (if at all).

### *Advantages of Data Warehousing*

Capitalizes on the potential value of the organization's information.

- Improves the quality and accessibility of data.
- Combines valuable archive data with the latest data in operational sources.

- Increases the amount of information available to users
- Reduces the requirement of users to access operational data.
- Reduces the strain on IT departments, as they can produce one database to serve all user groups.
- Allows new reports and studies to be introduced without disrupting operational systems.
- Promotes users to be self sufficient.

### *Defining the Data Warehouse*

The definition of the warehouse is one of the first steps in the creation of a data warehouse. The definition describes the content of the data warehouse by specifying the data elements and any transforms (conversions) required before the data is stored. The definition of the data warehouse is described in terms of meta data (data about data) or table definitions.Meta data can be created using the schemas or subschemas that are used to define the operational databases. Although meta data can be difficult to define and be a time-consuming process, it holds the key to a successful data warehouse.

### About DataStage

DataStage is a tool set for designing, developing, and running applications that populate one or more tables in a data warehouse or data mart. It consists of client and server components.

### *Client Components*

DataStage has four client components which are installed on any PC running Windows 95, Windows 2000, or Windows NT 4.0 with Service Pack 4 or later:

- *DataStage Designer:* A design interface used to create DataStage applications (known as jobs). Each job specifies the data sources, the transforms required, and the destination of the data. Jobs are compiled to create executables that are scheduled by the Director and run by the Server.

- *DataStage Director:* A user interface used to validate, schedule, run, and monitor DataStage jobs.
- *DataStage Manager:* A user interface used to view and edit the contents of the Repository.
- *DataStage Administrator:* A user interface used to configure DataStage projects and users.

This online help file describes both the DataStage Designer and the DataStage Manager. Many DataStage tasks can be performed from either client. Generally, you use the DataStage Designer when working on specific jobs, and will access the Repository through the Designer to modify elements of those jobs. You use the DataStage Manager in more of an administrative way, for example, when setting up items in the Repository that are available to all jobs in one or more projects. This help file distinguishes between descriptions of Designer-only, Manager-only or common features using the graphics in the topic title bars:

### *Server Components*

There are three server components which are installed on a server:

- *Repository:* A central store that contains all the information required to build a data mart or data warehouse.
- *DataStage Server:* Runs executable jobs that extract, transform, and load data into a data warehouse.
- *DataStage Package Installer:* A user interface used to install packaged DataStage jobs and plug-ins.

### *DataStage Features*

DataStage has the following features to aid the design and processing required to build a data warehouse:

- Uses graphical design tools. With simple point-and-click techniques you can draw a scheme to represent your processing requirements.
- Extracts data from any number or types of database.

- Handles all the meta data definitions required to define your data warehouse. You can view and modify the table definitions at any point during the design of your application.
- Aggregates data. You can modify SQL SELECT statements used to extract data.
- Transforms data. DataStage has a set of predefined transforms and functions you can use to convert your data. You can easily extend the functionality by defining your own transforms to use.
- Loads the data warehouse.

***DataStage Projects***

You always enter DataStage through a DataStage project. When you start a DataStage client you are prompted to connect to a project. Each project contains:

- DataStage jobs.
- Built-in components. These are predefined components used in a job.
- User-defined components. These are customized components created using the DataStage Manager or Data Stage Designer.

A complete project may contain several jobs and user-defined components. There is a special class of project called a protected project. Normally nothing can be added, deleted, or changed in a protected project. Users can view objects in the project, and perform tasks that affect the way a job runs rather than the job's design. Users with Production Manager status can import existing DataStage components into a protected project and manipulate projects in other ways.

***DataStage Jobs***

A DataStage job populates one or more tables in the target database. There is no limit to the number of jobs you can create in a DataStage project. DataStage jobs are defined using DataStage Designer, but you can view and edit some job properties using the DataStage Manager. The job design contains:

- Stages to represent the processing steps required.
- Links between the stages to represent the flow of data.

There are three basic types of DataStage job:

*Server jobs:* These are compiled and run on the DataStage server. A server job will connect to databases on other machines as necessary, extract data, process it, then write the data to the target data warehouse.

*Parallel jobs:* These are available only if you have Enterprise Edition installed. Parallel jobs are compiled and run on a DataStage UNIX server, and can be run in parallel on SMP, MPP, and cluster systems.

*Mainframe jobs:* These are available only if you have Enterprise MVS Edition installed. A mainframe job is compiled and run on the mainframe. Data extracted by such jobs is then loaded into the data warehouse.

There are two other entities that are similar to jobs in the way they appear in the DataStage Designer, and are handled by it. These are:

- *Shared containers:* These are reusable job elements. They typically comprise a number of stages and links. Copies of shared containers can be used in any number of server jobs and edited as required.
- *Job Sequences:* A job sequence allows you to specify a sequence of DataStage jobs to be executed, and actions to take depending on results.

Server and Mainframe jobs consist of individual stages. Each stage describes a data source, a particular process, or a data mart. For example, one stage may extract data from a data source, while another transforms it. Stages are added to a job and linked together using the Designer. There are two types of stage:

- Built-in stages. Supplied with DataStage. Used for extracting, aggregating, transforming, or writing data.
- Plug-in stages. Additional stages separately installed to perform specialized tasks that the built-in stages do not support.

- Job Sequence Stages. Special built-in stages which allow you to define sequences of activities to run.

The following diagram represents the simplest job you could have: a data source, a Transformer stage, and the final database. The links between the stages represent the flow of data into or out of a stage.

You must specify the data you want at each stage, and how it is handled. For example, do you want all the columns in the source data, or only a select few? Should the data be aggregated or converted before being passed on to the next stage? You can use DataStage with MetaBrokers in order to exchange meta data with other data warehousing tools. You might, for example, import table definitions from a data modelling tool.

**The DataStage Manager–Overview**

The DataStage Manager is used to view and edit the contents of the Repository. Some of these tasks can also be performed from the DataStage Designer. You can use the DataStage Manager to:

- Import table or stored procedure definitions.
- Create table or stored procedure definitions, data elements, custom transforms, server job routines, mainframe routines, machine profiles, and plug-ins.

There are also more specialized tasks that can only be performed from the DataStage Manager. These include:

- Perform usage analysis queries.
- Report on Repository contents.
- Importing, exporting and packaging DataStage jobs.

**Starting the Manager**

To start the Manager, choose Start > Programs > Ascential DataStage > DataStage Manager. The Attach to Project dialog box appears. To connect to a project:

1. Enter the name of your host in the **Host system** field. This is the name of the system where the DataStage Server components are installed.

2. Enter your user name in the **User name** field. This is your user name on the server system.
3. Enter your password in the **Password** field.
4. Choose the project to connect to from the **Project** drop-down list box. This list displays the projects installed on your DataStage server.
5. Select the **Save settings** check box to save your logon settings.
6. Click OK. The DataStage Manager window appears.

**The DataStage Manager Window**

The DataStage Manager window appears when you start the DataStage Manager. Use it to access the Repository and all DataStage Manager tasks. The DataStage Manager operates in two modes, Host View or Project View. Follow the links to see examples of the window types. By default, the DataStage Manager opens in Project View the first time, showing the contents of the project that you opened. If you switch to Host View, the server hosting DataStage is shown at the top of the tree in the left pane, with all the DataStage projects currently defined beneath it. You can switch to the other projects in the tree as required. The next time you open DataStage Manager, it will reopen in whichever mode you left it.You can also specify whether the Manager will show you an Extended Job View or not. With Extended Job View enabled, you can see the individual elements of a job design (for example, links and stages) as stored in the Repository.The right mouse button provides access to various shortcut menus in the DataStage Manager window.If you connect to a protected project, (Protected) appears in the Manager title bar after the project name. You cannot edit the objects within a protected project.

**Using the DataStage Manager**

The DataStage Manager is a means of viewing and managing the contents of the Repository. You can use the DataStage Manager to: Create items,

- Rename items.
- Select multiple items.
- View or edit item properties.
- Delete items.
- Delete a category.
- Copy items.
- Move items between categories.
- Create empty categories.

### *Choosing an Alternative Project*

When you start the DataStage Manager, the project specified in the **Attach to Project** dialog box is opened. You can choose to view any DataStage project in the DataStage Manager. To choose an alternative project when using the Host View, choose an alternative project from the tree in left pane.To choose an alternative project when using Project View:

1. Choose **File > Open Project...** . The **Open Project** dialog box appears:

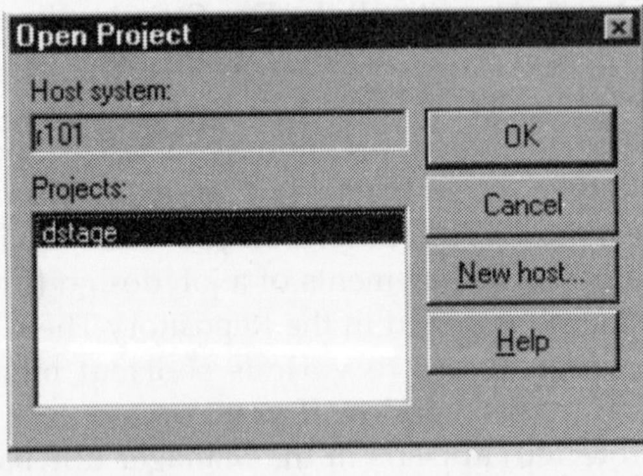


2. Choose the project you want to open from the **Projects** list. This list contains all the DataStage projects on the DataStage server (specified in the **Host system** field).
3. Click **OK** to open the chosen project. The updated DataStage Manager window displays the contents of the new project.

To open a project on a different DataStage server from this dialog box:

1. Click **New host....** The **Attach to Project** dialog box appears.
2. Enter the name of the DataStage server and your logon details.
3. Choose the project from the Project drop-down list box.
4. Click **OK** to open the chosen project. The updated DataStage Manager window displays the contents of the new project.

***Starting the Designer***

To start the Designer, choose **Start > Programs > Ascential DataStage > DataStage Designer**. The **Attach to Project** dialog box appears. You can also start the Designer from the shortcut icon on the desktop, or from the DataStage Suite applications bar if you have DataStage XE installed. You can connect to a project as follows: Enter the name of your host in the **Host system** field. This is the name of the system where the DataStage Server components are installed.

1. Enter your user name in the **User name** field. This is your user name on the server system.
2. Enter your password in the **Password** field. If you are connecting to the server via LAN Manager, you can select the **Omit** check box. The **User name** and **Password** fields gray out and you log on to the server using your Windows NT Domain account details.
3. Choose the project to connect to from the **Project** drop-down list box. This list box displays all the projects installed on your DataStage server.
4. Click **OK**. The DataStage Designer window appears, by default with the New dialog box open, allowing you to choose the type of job (you can set an option to specify that the Designer opens with an empty job of the chosen type, or with nothing open).

### *DataStage Designer Window*

The DataStage Designer window appears when you start the Designer. The DataStage Designer is a graphical design tool used by developers to design and develop a DataStage job.By default, DataStage initially starts with no jobs open. You can choose to create a new job as follows:

- *Server job:* These run on the DataStage Server, connecting to other data sources as necessary.
- *Parallel job:* These are compiled and run on the DataStage server in a similar way to server jobs, but support parallel processing on SMP, MPP, and cluster systems.
- *Mainframe job:* These are available only if you have installed Enterprise MVS Edition. Mainframe jobs are uploaded to a mainframe, where they are compiled and run.
- *Server shared containers:* These are reusable job elements. Copies of shared containers can be used in any number of server jobs and edited as required. They can also be used in parallel jobs to make server job functionality available.
- *Parallel shared containers:* These are reusable job elements. Copies of shared containers can be used in any number of parallel jobs and edited as required.
- *Job sequences:* A job sequence allows you to specify a sequence of DataStage server and parallel jobs to be executed, and actions to take depending on results.

You can also choose to create a new job from a template, create a new template, or create a data migration job. Selecting one of these starts the Intelligent Assistant to guide you through the process.You can choose to open an existing job of any of the above types. You can use the DataStage options to specify that the Designer always opens a new server, parallel, or mainframe job, server or parallel shared container, or job sequence when its starts.The right mouse button accesses various shortcut menus in the DataStage Designer window. The example below shows a DataStage Designer window with a Server Job open.

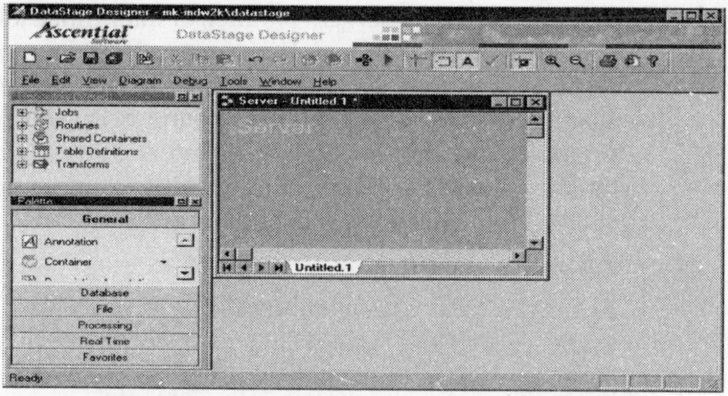


### *Developing a Job*

A DataStage job populates one or more tables in the target database. There is no limit to the number of jobs you can create in a DataStage project. Jobs are designed and developed using the DataStage Designer. The DataStage Designer is a graphical design tool used by developers to design and develop a DataStage job. A job design contains:

- Stages to represent the data sources, data mart, and processing steps required
- Links between the stages to represent the flow of data There are three different types of job within DataStage:
- *Server jobs*: These are available if you have installed DataStage Server. They run on the DataStage Server, connecting to other data sources as necessary.
- *Parallel jobs:* These are only available if you have installed Enterprise Edition. These run on DataStage servers that are SMP, MPP, or cluster systems. They can also run on a separate z/OS (USS) machine if required.
- *Mainframe jobs:* These are only available if you have installed Enterprise MVS Edition. Mainframe jobs are uploaded to a mainframe, where they are compiled and run.
- Stages are linked together using the tool palette. The stages that appear in the tool palette depend on

whether you have a server, parallel, or mainframe job open, and on whether you have customized the tool palette.This on-line help tells you about the individual stage types that each type of job supports, and is designed to provide you with quick information when you are actually working on a job. Note that before you start to develop your job, you must:

- First assess your data.
- Then create your data warehouse.
- Then define table or stored procedures definitions.
- Optionally create and assign data elements.

### *Creating a Job*

By default the DataStage Designer opens with no jobs open. You can set options to specify that an empty server, parallel, or mainframe job is created or that the New dialog box appears and allows you to specify the type of job (or job sequence or shared container) to create.If you are displaying an existing job design and you want to create a new one, do one of the following: Choose File > New.

- Click the **New** button on the toolbar. An adjacent drop-down menu allows you to specify the job type.

A Diagram window appears, in the right pane of the Designer, along with the Toolbox for the chosen type of job. You can now save the job and give it a name.

### *Deleting a Job*

To delete a job, job sequence, or shared container from the DataStage Designer:

1. Select the icon in the tree in the Repository window.
2. Choose **Delete** from the shortcut menu.

To delete a job, job sequence, or server or parallel shared container from the DataStage Manager:

1. Select the icon in the Display area.
2. Choose **Edit > Delete** from the main menu.

### *Opening a Job*

If you have previously worked on the job, job sequence, or server or parallel shared container you want to open, then you can select it from the list of most recently used items in the **File** menu. Otherwise, to open one:

1. Do one of the following from the DataStage Designer window:
   - Choose **File > Open**.
   - Click the **Open** button on the toolbar.

   The Open dialog box appears.

2. Choose the item you want to open from the tree, then click **OK**.

Alternatively you can find the job in the tree in the Repository window and double-click it, or select it and choose **Edit** from its shortcut menu,or drag it onto the background to open it.

The updated DataStage Designer window displays the chosen job, job sequence, or server or parallel shared container in a Diagram window.

### *Saving a Job*

To save a job, job sequence, or server or parallel shared container:

1. Choose **File** > **Save** . If this is the first time you have saved the job, the Save as New dialog box appears.
2. Enter the required name in the **Job name** field.
3. Type in a category or select a category from the existing categories shown in the tree structure by clicking on it. It appears in the **Category** box. (If you have already specified a category in the **Properties** dialog box, this will be displayed in the **Category** box when you open the **Save As New** dialog box.)
4. Click **OK**. If the **Job name** is unique, the job, job sequence, or shared container is created and saved in the Repository. If the **Job name** is not unique, a message box appears. You must acknowledge this message before you can enter an alternative name.

To save an existing job with a different name choose **File > Save As...** and fill in the **Save As New** dialog box, specifying the new name and the category the job is to be saved in.

### Stages

A job consists of stages linked together which describe the flow of data from a data source to a final data warehouse. A stage usually has at least one data input and one data output. However, some stages can accept more than one data input, and output to more than one stage. Server jobs,parallel jobs and mainframe jobs have different types of stages. The stages that are available in the DataStage Designer depend on the type of job that is currently open in the Designer.

#### *Built-In Stages–Server Jobs*

There are a number of built-in stage types:

- **Aggregator:** Classifies incoming data into groups, computes totals and other summary functions, and passes them to another stage in the job.
- **Hashed File:** Extracts data from or loads data into databases that contain hashed files. Also acts as an intermediate stage for quick lookups.
- **UniVerse:** Extracts data from or loads data into UniVerse databases.
- **UniData:** Extracts data from or loads data into UniData databases.
- **ODBC:** Extracts data from or loads data into databases that support the industry standard Open Database Connectivity API. This stage is also used as an intermediate stage for aggregating data.
- **Sequential File :** Extracts data from or loads data into "flat files" in the Windows NT file system.
- **Folder :** Folder stages are used to read or write data as files in a directory located on the DataStage server.
- **Transformer :** Receives incoming data, transforms it in a variety of ways, and outputs it to another stage in the job.

- **Container:** Represents a group of stages and links. The group is replaced by a single Container stage in the Diagram window.
- **IPC Stager:** Provides a communication channel between DataStage processes running simultaneously in the same job. It allows you to design jobs that run on SMP systems with great performance benefits
- **Link Collector Stage:** Takes up to 64 inputs and allows you to collect data from these links and route it along a single output link.
- **Link Partitioner Stage:** Takes one input and allows you to distribute partitioned rows to up to 64 output links.
- **Container Input** and **Container Output**. Represent the interface that links a container stage to the rest of the job design

### Server Job Stages

#### *Aggregator Stages*

Aggregator stages are active stages that classify data rows from a single input link into groups and compute totals or other aggregate functions for each group. The summed totals for each group are output from the stage via an output link. If you want to aggregate the input data in a number of different ways, you can have several output links, each specifying a different set of properties to define how the input data is grouped and summarized.

#### *BCPLoad Plug-in Definition*

The BCPLoad stage is a passive plug-in stage supplied by Ascential. It bulk loads data into a single table in a Microsoft SQL Server (Release 6.0 or 6.5) or Sybase (System 10 or 11) database. The files are loaded into the target database using the bulk copy API. By default, the BCPLoad stage is configured to bulk load data into a Microsoft SQL Server. You can configure the BCPLoad stage properties to bulk load data into a Sybase

SQL Server table using the Sybase DBLIB or CTLIB client libraries. There is one input link to this stage which provides a sequence of rows to load into the SQL Server or Sybase database table. The meta data for each input column determines how it is loaded. There are no output links from this stage type.

***ODBC Stages***

ODBC stages are used to represent a database that supports the industry standard Open Database Connectivity API. You can use an ODBC stage to extract, write, or aggregate data. Each ODBC stage can have any number of inputs or outputs. Input links specify the data you are writing. Output links specify the data you are extracting and any aggregations required.You can specify the data on an input link using an SQL statement constructed by DataStage, a user-defined query, or a stored procedure.You can specify the data on an output link using an SQL statement processed by ODBC, or one that is passed thrust ODBC and processed by the underlying database, or by a stored procedure.

***Orabulk Stages***

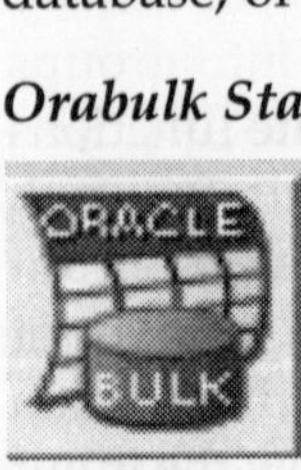


The Orabulk stage is a plug-in stage supplied by Ascential. It generates control and data files for bulk loading into a single table on an Oracle target database. The files are suitable for loading into the target database using the Oracle command *sqlldr*.One input pin provides a sequence of rows to load into an Oracle table. The meta data for each input column determines how it is loaded. One optional output pin provides a copy of all input rows to allow easy combination of this stage with other stages.

***Sequential File Stages***

Sequential File stages are used to extract data from, or write data to, a text file in the server file system. The text file can be created or exist on any drive that is either local or mapped to the server. Each

Sequential File stage can have any number of inputs or outputs.

**Debugger Overview**

The DataStage debugger provides you with basic facilities for testing and debugging your job designs. The debugger is run from the DataStage Designer. It can be used from many places in the Designer:

- Debug menu
- Debug toolbar
- Shortcut menu (selected items)

The debugger enables you to set breakpoints on the links in your job. When you run the job in debug mode, the job will stop when it reaches a breakpoint. You can then step to the next action (reading or writing) on that link, or step to the processing of the next row of data (which may be on the same link or another link). Any breakpoints you have set remain if the job is closed and reopened. Breakpoints are validated when the job is compiled. If a link is deleted, or either end moved, the breakpoint is deleted. If a link is deleted and another of the same name created, the new link does not inherit the breakpoint. Breakpoints are not inherited when a job is saved under a different name, exported, or upgraded.You can debug instances of shared containers where they appear in a job design. The Debug window allows you to view variables in a watch list and any in-context variables when you stop at a breakpoint. Another useful aid for monitoring and debugging jobs once they have been developed is the graphical performance monitor.

**Compiling a Job**

When you have edited all the stages in a server or parallel job design, you can create an executable version of the job. Executable jobs are created by compiling a job design. Jobs are compiled using the DataStage Designer. To compile a job, open the job in the Designer and do one of the following:

- Choose **File > Compile**.
- Click the **Compile** button on the toolbar.

If the job has unsaved changes, you may be prompted to save the job by clicking **OK**. The Compile Job window appears.The job is compiled as soon as this window appears. You must check the display area for any compilation messages or errors that are generated.If there have been breakpoints set for links that no longer exist, a message appears during compilation warning you of this. The breakpoints are then automatically removed.

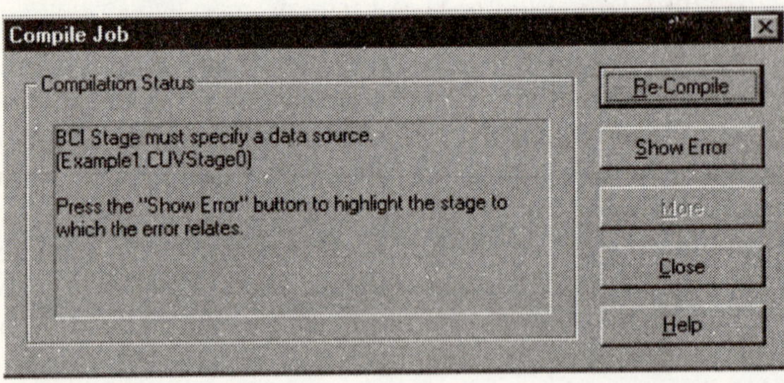


For parallel jobs there is also a force compile option. The compilation of parallel jobs is by default optimized such that transformer stages only get recompiled if they have changed since the last compilation. The force compile option overrides this and causes all transformer stages in the job to be compiled. To select this option: Choose **File > Force Compile.** You can also compile DataStage jobs from the command line on the DataStage client. A wizard interface is also available, which lets you compile multiple jobs. You can open the wizard from the Tools menu of the DataStage Designer, Manager, or Director client, or from the Ascential DataStage start menu.

**Successful Compilation**

If the Compile Job window displays the message `Job successfully compiled with no errors`, you can:

- Validate the job.
- Run or schedule the job.
- Release the job.
- Package (or export) the job for deployment on other DataStage systems.

Jobs are validated and run using the DataStage Director.

**Troubleshooting Compilation Errors**

If the Compile Job window displays an error, you can use the **Show Error** button to troubleshoot your job design. When you click the **Show Error** button, the stage that contains the first error is highlighted in the Diagram window. You must edit the stage to change any incorrect settings and recompile. The process of troubleshooting compilation errors is an iterative process. You must refine each "problem" stage until the job compiles successfully.

**Releasing a Job**

If you are developing a job for users on another DataStage system, you must label the job as ready for deployment before you can package it. To label a job for deployment, you must release it. A job can be released when it has been compiled and validated successfully at least once in its life. Jobs are released using the DataStage Manager. To release a job:

1. From the DataStage Manager, browse to the required category in the **Jobs** branch in the project tree.
2. Select the job you want to release in the display area.
3. Choose **Tools > Release job**. The **Job Release** dialog box appears.
4. Select the job that you want to release.
5. Click **Release Job** to release the selected job, or **Release All** to release all the jobs in the tree.

A physical copy of the chosen job is made (along with all the routines and code required to run the job) and it is recompiled. The Releasing Job dialog box appears and shows the progress of the release process.The released job is automatically assigned a name and version number using the format *jobname*%rel*n.n.n*, where *jobname* is the name of the job you chose to release and *n.n.n* is the job version number. When you refer to a job by its released name, this is known as a "fixed job release", and always equates to that particular version of the job. You can use the DataStage Designer to view the design of a released job. However, if you edit the job design you cannot save the changes. The meta data and settings displayed in the job design are stored as part of the released job and these may not match the information currently held in the Repository. This is especially true if you developed the table definitions, transforms, routines, or job design after the job was released. If you want to develop and enhance a job design, you must edit the original job. To use the changes you have made, you must release the job again.

**References**

John Wang, "Encyclopedia of Data warehousing and Data Mining".

# 9

# DD (Discrete Distribution)

## Accident Analysis

### *Negative Binomial (For rare events)*

The Negative Binomial Distribution for rare events is produced if the program detects that the input is for a Poisson distribution because the user gives only an expected value and an observation value. Both the expected value and the observed value can be any positive value. A variance value also has to be given in the (co-)variance -bottom right- box and this value will mostly be larger in size than the value for the expectation. If the mean and variance are exactly the same the program will give you the Poisson distribution.

This version of the negative binomial is a generalization of the Poisson, as used to study the distribution of accidents and events at the individual level. For the Poisson it is assumed that the chance of having an accident or a disease is randomly distributed: all individuals have an equal chance, of having one, two or more accidents. However, this assumption may be incorrect; you may observe that relatively more people have a higher number of accidents than the Poisson predicts. Mathematically the correctness of the assumption can be checked by seeing if in the Poisson the variance and the mean are equal. If the variance is larger than the mean, the assumption is incorrect.

The negative binomial does not assume randomness: there is a possibility of 'proneness', i.e. certain groups of individuals in the population have a higher chance of having accidents or diseases than others. A third parameter is now included, the variance of the distribution. The variance can be interpreted as a factor that expresses the level of proneness. The larger the variance is relative to the mean, the higher the level of proneness in the population. Note that the variance is an expectation value, it is related to the expected value. The variance is the square of the standard deviation. Lastly, the mean to which the variance is related is in this case always a mean, even if the value of the mean is between zero and one. There is therefore no mathematical relationship between the variance and the mean, as is the case with proportions.

One of the problems with the negative binomial is that there does not seem to be a clear meaning which can be easily given to the variance (Arbous AG, Kerrich JE, 1951). Thus, after fitting the empirical distribution to the Negative Binomial, and estimating the variance, as a measure of accident or disease proneness in the population, you are confronted with the question of what this measure means fpr individuals or groups in the population, or the development of policy or decisions.

An exact Negative Binomial confidence interval for the observed value cannot be given.

**Poisson**

Poison analysis is done if the user gives an expected value and an observation value and checks the 'exact' box. Both the expected value and the observation value can be type real, positive numbers with decimals.

The Poisson distribution has two applications:

(1) It can be used as an alternative to the Binomial distribution in the case of very large samples. Your hypothesis was that you would find 'x' (the top cell) occurrences of a phenomenon, whereas in fact you found 'n' (the second input cell). The phenomenon might be the number of cases of a rare disease, the number of accidents on a busy junction, the number

of stoppages on a production line, or the number of ethnic children at a football match. You want to test the assumption that environmental and other factors influencing the phenomenon were constant between observation periods.

The main difference between the Poisson and the binomial distribution is that in the binomial all eligible phenomena are studied, whereas in the Poisson only the cases with a particular outcome are studied. For example: in the binomial all cars are studied to see whether they have had an accident or not, whereas in the Poisson only the cars which have had an accidents are studied.

(2) The Poisson can also be used to study how 'accidents' or 'malfunctions' or the chance of winning the lottery never, once or more than once, are distributed on the level of a population. It gives you the chance of an individual person or object meeting with one, two or more accidents or winning the lottery once, twice or more often. People may have one, two, three, or more accidents during a certain period of time. The Poisson distribution tells you how these chances are distributed if having one 'accident' has no influence on the chance of having another accident, i.e. the victim is `put back into the population' immediately after an 'event'. Mean or incidence is the number of accidents divided by the size of the population and is given to the program in the top expectation box.

**Binomial**

A table of binomial values is produced if the program detects that the input is for a binomial distribution, i.e. if an expected value, an observation value and a number of cases studied are given by the user, and the 'exact' box is checked. The expected value will usually be a proportion between zero and one, the number of positive observations and the number of cases will be integers, whole positive numbers. They can be type real, in which case these values will be rounded to the nearest integer. When the expected value is above one it will be divided by the sample size.

The binomial is probably the best known of the discrete distributions and a discussion of its properties can be found in most introductory statistics books (Blalock HM, 1960; Wonnacott TH, Wonnacott RJ, 1977). The distribution gives you the likelihood of finding 'x' failures (or white or female or large or tail or accidents, only your imagination limits you), as opposed to success (or black or male or small or heads or cars coming by which didn't have an accident). Your findings are the results of having done 'n' experiments, having made 'n' observations, or having studied a sample of size 'n'. You expected to find that an average of 'u' in your sample would have been failure, for example `white' or `large'. 'x', the number observed as positive, is what changes in the output box. 'u', the expected proportion of occurrences, is given in the top box, and 'n' , the sample size or number of experiments, is given in the third box.

The normal distribution, or z-distribution, is often used to approximate the binomial and data for this statistic is presented if you check the 'approximation' box. However, if the sample size is very large the Poisson distribution is a philosophically more correct alternative for the Binomial than the normal distribution. One of the main differences between the Poisson distribution and the binomial distribution is that in the binomial all eligible phenomena are studied, whereas in the Poisson only the cases with a particular outcome are studied. For example: in the binomial all cars are studied to see whether they have had an accident or not, whereas in the Poisson only the cars which have had an accidents are studied.

If you know the number of outcomes and the number of expected outcomes, and you would like to determine how likely it is that a particular size of a sample, or a particular number of experiments, would have produced this result, you can use the Negative Binomial. In the case of samples drawn without replication from small populations the Hyper geometric distribution should be used.

An exact binomial confidence interval for the observed number (the value in the second box) is given if the C.I. box is checked. There is no point in giving an expected value for this exact procedure; only the observed value and the sample size are taken into consideration and only these should be given.

A number of items based on the normal approximation of the binomial can be obtained by checking the approximation box. It is then possible to construct a confidence interval around the difference in proportions, or numbers, which is tested. If the confidence interval is small we are very sure that there is an important difference; if the confidence interval is large then we are not very sure. If the value zero is between the upper and the lower value of the confidence interval, this means that the difference between the two numbers is not statistically significant.

The normal deviation, the standardized difference, can be used to estimate p-values as a direct alternative to using a binomial procedure. However, remember that exact tests are superior to normal approximations.

One assumption in this application of the Poisson is that the chance of having an accident is randomly distributed: every individual has an equal chance. Mathematically this is expressed in the fact that the variance and the mean for the Poisson are equal. A good way to check if this assumption that individuals have an equal chance of having the trait is correct is to compare the variance of an (accident) distribution with its mean. If the variance is larger, then the assumption was not correct. The Negative Binomial has been implemented to provide an alternative for the Poisson in the case of a non-random distribution.

Exact and normal approximations of the Poisson distributed confidence interval of the observed number are given. The exact Poisson confidence interval for the observed number (the value in the second box) is given if the C.I. box is checked. There is no point in giving an expected value for this exact procedure; only the observed value is taken into consideration. The normal approximation of the confidence interval is given if the 'approximation' box is checked. If you divide the observed number by the expected number, you will get the Rate Ratio. A full analysis of the rate ratio is also provided if a Poisson approximation is requested.

**Catch Recatch**

Catch-Recatch is used to estimate the size of a population 'in the wild'. First a number of animals or individuals are caught and marked. These individuals are then put back into the population and given the chance to mix in again. Then a random sample is drawn from the population and the number of marked individuals is counted. By comparing the number of marked individuals (i.e. positive observations) in relation to the sample size and the number of marked individuals in the population as a whole, the size of the population can be estimated.

Input the number of marked individuals in the top box (expectations), the number of positive observations in the second box (observations) and the sample size in the third box (sample size). The number in the expectations box should be larger than the number in the observations box. If you check the Negative Binomial/CRC box and the CI box the program will calculate the most likely population size and the Exact Hypergeometric Confidence Interval around the population size.

Note that this procedure is based on inverting the Hypergeometric Distribution, a complex process which is very computing-intensive. It may not always work successfully. Therefore, if you check the Negative Binomial/CRC box and the approximation box, the program will calculate the most likely population size, its variance, and the estimated Hypergeometric Confidence Interval around the population size. This procedure will work more reliably but less precisely.

**Fieller**

Fieller confidence intervals around a rate ratio are produced if an expected value and an observation value are given to the program, and the 'approximation' box is checked. Both the expected value and the observation value can be type real, positive numbers with decimals.

The Fieller Confidence Interval has two applications:

(1) The Fieller estimate is a method to estimate the approximate confidence interval around a rate ratio when there is error in both the observed and the expected value and the number of cases is relatively large. For very large numbers, the Fieller provides a good method to approximate the results of the exact Binomial/Incomplete Beta method, which is also presented in the module. The Incomplete Beta method is the more suitable exact method for estimating the confidence interval around a rate ratio with error in both the observed and the expected values, but the method may not work well for a very large number of observations.

(2) The Fieller method makes it possible to take covariance between the observation and the expectation into account. This would be relevant if the observations are a subset of the data on the basis of which the expectation was calculated. For example, the Standardize Mortality Ratio is often calculated by applying data of the national population to the local population.

The mortality in Hampshire could be compared with the national mortality by using an expectation calculated by applying the national age-specific death rates (the standard) to the population of Hampshire (the index). A major crash on the motorway in Hampshire would show up in both the observation of the number of deaths in Hampshire and in the national death rates, which are used to calculate the expectation. Silcocks. (1994) proposes the covariance 'q' parameter for the Fieller in such a case to be: q=Sum(d(i)*n(i)/N(i))/d-tot whereby, d(i) number of deaths in the index population in the i-th age band, n(i) number of individuals in the i-th age band of the index population which are part of the standard population, N(i) number of individuals in the i-th age band in the standard population, d-tot, total number of deaths in the index population. The q-covariance parameter is entered in the program in the right bottom `(Co-)Variance' box. The default setting of this parameter is zero.

The Fieller will give an estimate only if the expected value is larger than one. Thus, real cases or a mean of real cases is considered and not a proportion.

**Rate Ratio**

The rate ratio analysis is produced if the input consists of an expected and an observation value, and the 'approximation' box is checked. Both the expected value and the observation value can be type real, positive numbers with decimals.

This module was inspired by two papers, one by Liddell and one by Silcocks. It concerns estimating the confidence interval for a rate-ratio, in practice this will often be the Standardized Mortality Ratio. It concerns the estimation of events in a constant domain while the denominator is very large. Often it will concern phenomena in demography, epidemiology or biology. For those who work with events in smaller samples this module is less interesting and the risk-ratio or odds-ratio will probably be more appropriate. The risk-ratio and the odds-ratio are implemented on the SISA website by the procedures t-test and two by two tables, and in the SISA-tables program.

In making comparisons our instinct is to use subtraction. For example, in comparing the number of pairs of breeding rare birds between years, we say that the number this year is 20 more than last year. It is a good year.

A good thing about doing it this way is that it is easy to understand, you can easily imagine the breeding birds. The disadvantage is that it doesn't consider the scale problem; it makes a big difference to have 20 more pairs of breeding birds if the usual number is 50, compared with a usual number of 500. That is why we prefer the use of ratio's, or division. We take the number of birds we observe, this years birds, and compare this with our expectations on the grounds of previous experience.

Thus, if we expect 500 breeding pairs, and 520 pairs are observed this year, than we have an increase of 4%, 520/

500=1.04 (*100). However, if we expect 50 breeding pairs, and observe 70 pairs, the increase is about 40%, 70/50=1.40. The next step is to use the generalizing statistical approach. This year, the number of breeding pairs of rare birds is 40% as large compared with the average in the 'usual' years, within a certain margin of confidence. The confidence interval given in the output gives you an impression of the precision of the estimate.

The module presents various approximations for the confidence interval for the rate ratio. First, the exact confidence interval by way of a Chi-square transformation of the Poisson is given. Liddell discusses this method. The way this is implemented results in an exact estimation of the Poisson confidence interval of about four significant digits precision. In case the number of events comes above 80 the precision will rapidly decrease and it might be a better idea to use the Poisson process approximation, also discussed by Liddell. The program issues a warning when that is required.

Silcocks pointed out that an important assumption, that the expectation is theoretical and error free, is not met when calculating the SMR in epidemiology and demography. The age specific rates in the standard population on which the calculation of the expectation is based are empirical observations, which will show random fluctuation. Also, in the breeding bird example, it is correct to use the Poisson to compare this years breeding birds with "the usual number", a theoretical concept.

SISA's usual Chi-square distribution is used to do the exact Poisson confidence interval. SMR-Exact is a demanding procedure. Precision is limited to four digits for expectations under about 80 and should not be used above that number. SISA's usual Binomial procedure is used for the exact Binomial confidence interval. Here the choice is between precision and speed, the precision can be set using the ExactCI option. Both procedures require the observed number to be an integer.

If it's not an integer the procedures will echo the values for the nearest integer less than the observed value. You can use real observations if you want, most of the approximations will handle those. Real value expectations are treated as such with high precision in all modules, exact and approximations. Lastly, the Walds approximation is discussed by Rothman and Greenland, the square root, the normal deviate and the Poisson process by Liddell.

**Hypergeometric**

User input is recognized as a request for a hypergeometric analysis if all four input boxes are used, with the highest number in the population box at the bottom. Input in the top expectation box should be a proportional value, between zero and one. If a larger number is given, it will be divided by the number of cases in the sample, as given in the third box. There is a preference for the result of this division to be an integer value. If this is not the case, the program will suggest a correction.

The hypergeometric distribution is used for calculating probabilities for samples drawn from relatively small populations and without replication. This means that an item's chance of being selected increases on each trial. This distribution is often used in zoology to study small animal or plant populations. Your hypothesis was that you would find a proportion of 'u' (fill in the population proportion in the top box) occurrences of a phenomenon in a sample sized 'n' (third box). In fact what you found was 'x' occurrences of the phenomenon (second box). Lastly you give the size of the population, 'n', in the bottom (fourth) box. The program gives you the probability for a number of values of 'x'.

For sampling with replication (i.e. sampling whereby an individual or item which is 'drawn' and studied is then put back into the population or 'pool' so that it has an equal chance of being 'drawn' and studied again), the Binomial should be used. If the population size is relatively large the binomial should also be used; calculating the Hypergeometric with a large population is very computing intensive and may not produce satisfactory results. If the population is infinitely large, there is no difference between the hypergeometric distribution and the binomial.

A number of items based on the normal approximation of the hypergeometric have been added and will be produced if the user checks the 'approximation' box. It is then possible to construct a confidence interval around the difference in proportions, or numbers, which is tested. If the confidence interval is small we are very sure that there is an important difference, if the confidence interval is large then we are not very sure. If the value zero is between the upper and the lower values of the confidence interval this means that the difference between the two numbers is not statistically significant.

The normal deviation, the standardized difference, can be used to estimate p-values as a direct alternative to using a hypergeometric procedure. It is not really relevant in our case because we already have the superior hypergeometric estimate itself. The standard error in the estimates provided is based on the main hypergeometric assumption, i.e. that there was a sampling procedure without replication in a relatively small population. If sampling was with replication or if the population was large, use the binomial, as explained above.

An exact hypergeometric confidence interval for the observed number (the value in the second box) is given if the C.I. box is checked. There is no point in giving an expected value for this exact procedure. Only the observed value, the sample and population size are used in the calculations. An exact hypergeometric population size is given if the C.I. and the CRC.

**Input box**

The input boxes are the four fill-in boxes on the left of the form. They will accept real type data. This data should always be positive. The boxes should only contain numbers and the associated notation, so decimal dots and the letter E for a mantissa are accepted, but no other characters.

Using extended real type numbers allows for numbers up to 1.0E+4932 to be input. However, if you input such a large number, you should not expect to get a meaningful output. See the discussion on the Limitations page. The input will not always be treated as a real type. The expectation will be used as a real type in all procedures. The observed number, sample size and population size will often, but not always, be treated as an integer, usually the largest integer smaller than the real number given. To be sure, give preference to observed numbers, sample size and population size in the form of integers.

The input boxes support editing operations such Ctrl-C=Copy, Ctrl-V=Paste and Ctrl-X=Cut-and-Copy. Beware of leading or trailing spaces and other characters when pastingdata into an input box. The continental European decimal comma is not accepted as a valid character. It must be a dot.

**PASCAL -Negative Binomial (marginal binomial)**

The Negative Binomial Distribution as the marginal of the binomial is produced if an expected value, an observation value and a number of cases are given by the user, and if the 'Negative Binomial' and the exact box are checked. The expected value must be a proportional value between zero and one. The observation value can be type real. The number of cases value can also be type real, but then it will be truncated to the value of the nearest integer smaller than the given real number.

The distribution is also known as the Pascal Distribution or the Polya Distribution. The Geometric Distribution is a special case of the Negative Binomial with the number positive, in the second blue box, being '1' (one).The negative binomial does basically the same thing as the Binomial, except that now we are asking about the probability of a particular sample size, given that we have found 'x' results to be positive (or `white', or `car crashes'), whereas we had expected to find 'u' results to be positive.

Input is the same as for the binomial, but now the output expresses a change in the number of cases and not, as in the binomial, the number found positive. It is not possible to fill in a number in the first (expected value) box; it has to be a proportion. The reason is that the bottom box (the number of cases) is not fixed and there is therefore no fixed relationship between the expected proportion and the expected number (the expected number will increase with the sample size, if the expected proportion stays the same).

If you are used to other discrete distributions, the output may come as a surprise. Usually there is a probability for a zero value: a phenomenon not being observed. This time the counting does not start at the '0' (zero) value but at the first meaningful value. The first meaningful value is that in which the sample size and the observed number of positive responses are equal. This is because you must have a sample size of at least as large as the number of positive responses observed.

An exact Negative Binomial confidence interval for the sample size (the value in the third box) based on the number of positive responses observed, is given if the C.I. box is checked. There is no point in giving an expected value for this exact procedure; only the observed value and the sample size are taken into consideration. The usual estimate for the confidence interval for the sample size is produced if the negative binomial and the estimate box are checked.

Because this confidence interval is not very good, SISA's own estimate is also given. This estimate is based on inverting the well-known normal approximation of the Binomial. For the estimation procedures you can give an expected proportion for the likelihood of a positive observation on each trial; this proportion would normally be estimated from the data but an 'extraneous' expectation can also be considered. However, beware, this is not a tried and tested procedure.

**Variance**

Checking the descriptives box will produce descriptive statistics for the Poisson, Binomial or Hypergeometric distribution. The program will determine which distribution to use on the basis of the input provided. The Poisson distribution will be chosen if only the top two boxes contain values, the Binomial if the top three boxes contain values and the Hypergeometric if all four boxes contain values. If the negative binomial box is also checked the Negative Binomial are given instead the Binomial. If the 'all' box is checked, data is shown for all possible distributions given the input.

Descriptives presented depend on the selected distribution. Possible descriptives are the mean, the variance, the skewness and the kurtosis of distributions. The statistics are given by default for the observed distribution, in which case you do not have to give an expectation value. Under the options menu you can select using the expected instead of the observed distribution.

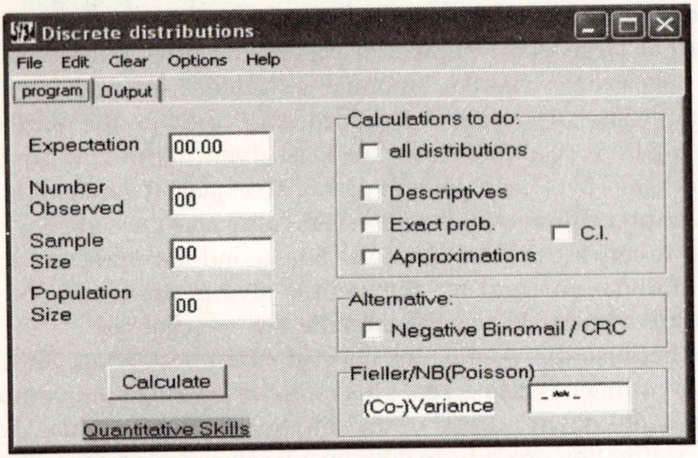


**Output**

Expectation: 5400
Number observed: 3

***Descriptives for Poisson***
***for the Observed Distribution***

Mean= 3
Variance= 3
Standard Deviation= 1.73205080756888
Mode= 2 and 3
Skewness= 0.577350269189626
Kurtosis= 3.33333333333333
**********************

*******POISSON*******

single prob(0): 0.00000000; cumulative prob(> 0): 1.00000000
single prob(1): 0.00000000; cumulative prob(> 1): 1.00000000
single prob(2): 0.00000000; cumulative prob(> 2): 1.00000000
single prob(3): 0.00000000; cumulative prob(> 3): 1.00000000

*** summary ***

Probability Observed= 3: 0.00000000
(note, all probabilties based on an expected value of 5400)

Single sided probabilities:
observed>=3: 1.00000000; observed<3: 0.00000000
observed>3: 1.00000000; observed<=3: 0.00000000
Mid-p: 1.00000000; left: 0.00000000
Double mid-p: 0.00000000
Two sided probabilities: difference (exp-obs)>=5397: 0.00001637

**References**

Arbous A.G., Kerrich J.E., "Accident Statistics and the Concept of Accident-Proneness", Part I: A Critical Evaluation. Part II. The Mathematical Background. Biometrics 1951;341-433.

Blalock H.M. (1960), "Social Statistics", New York, McGraw-Hill.

Wonnacott T.H. (1977), Wonnacott R.J., "Introductory Statistics", New York, John Willey.

Uitenbroek D.G. (1995), "The Mathematical Relationship Between the Number of events in which People are Injured and the Number of People Injured", *British Journal of Sports Medicine*, 126-128.

Silcocks P. (1994), "Estimating Confidence Limits on a Standardized Mortality Ratio when the Expected Number is not Error Free", *Journal of Epidemiology and Community Health*, 48:313-317.

# 10

# Dtreg

## Introduction

DTREG provides the best, state-of-the-art modeling methods including neural networks, decision trees, TreeBoost, decision tree forests, support vector machines (SVM), discriminant analysis and logistic regression. By applying the right method to the problem, the analyst using DTREG should be able to match or exceed the predictive ability of any other modeling program.

## Classes of Variables

The "target variable" is the variable whose values are to be modeled and predicted by other variables. You can specify three classes of variables when performing analyses:

*Target variable:* The "target variable" is the variable whose values are to be modeled and predicted by other variables. It is analogous to the dependent variable (i.e., the variable on the left of the equal sign) in linear regression. There must be one and only one target variable.

*Predictor variable:* A "predictor variable" is a variable whose values will be used to predict the value of the target variable. It is analogous to the independent variables (i.e., the variables on the right side of the equal sign) in linear regression. There must be at least one predictor variable specified, and there may be many predictor variables. If more than one predictor variable is specified, DTREG will determine how the predictor variables can be combined to best predict the values of the target variable.

*Weight variable:* Optionally, you can specify a "weight variable". If a weight variable is specified, it must a numeric (continuous) variable whose values are greater than or equal to 0 (zero). The value of the weight variable specifies the weight given to a row in the dataset. For example, a weight value of 2 would cause DTREG to give twice as much weight to a row as it would to rows with a weight of 1; the effect is the same as two occurrences of the row in the dataset. Weight values may be real (non-integer) values such as 2.5. A weight value of 0 (zero) causes the row to be ignored. If you do not specify a weight variable, all rows are given equal weight.

## Demonstration–Using DTREG

Once you understand the concept of decision trees, it is very easy to use DTREG to analyze data and build decision trees to model data.

### *Installing DTREG*

To install DTREG, run the installation program named **DTREGsetup.exe**. A "wizard" screen will guide you through the installation process. You can accept the default installation location (C:\Program files\DTREG) or select a different folder location. When the installation finishes, you should see this icon for DTREG on your desktop: To launch DTREG, double-click the Shortcut to DTREG icon on your desktop.

### *DTREG's Main Screen*

When you launch DTREG, its main screen displays as follows:

From this screen, you can

- Open an existing decision tree project by clicking
- Create a new project to build a decision tree by clicking
- Set options and enter your registration key.

***Setting DTREG Preferences***

To set DTREG preferences, click "Tools" on the menu bar and select "Preferences" from the dropdown menu.

***Max. Execution Threads***

Specify how many execution threads you want DTREG to use during its computations. If you have a multi-CPU system, you can increase the speed of calculation by allowing DTREG to use more than one CPU, but this will place a heavier load on your system.

*Note:* Currently, multiple execution threads are only used for cross validation.

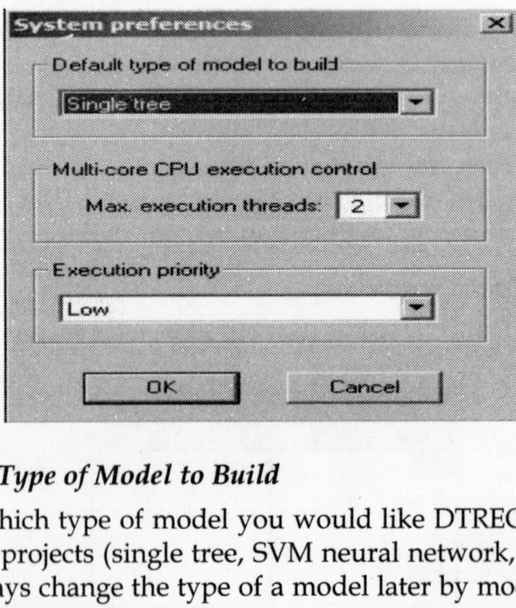


***Default Type of Model to Build***

Select which type of model you would like DTREG to create for new projects (single tree, SVM neural network, etc.). You can always change the type of a model later by modifying its property.

### *Execution Priority*

Specify the preferred execution for DTREG to use during an analysis. Currently the execution priority is only applied to neural network training process.

### *Creating a New Project*

To create a new project, click the leftmost icon on the toolbar that looks like this:

Project "wizard" screens will guide you through setting up the project. The first screen looks like this:

There are several fields on this page

- **Title of project**—This is an optional field. If you wish, you can specify a title to be displayed for this project.
- **Input data file**—This is a required field. Specify the device, folder and name of the file containing the input (learning) dataset to be used to build the tree. The data must be in a comma separated value (CSV) file with the names of the variables on the first line. Please see page 29 for detailed information about the format of input data files. You can click the "Browse files" button to browse for the file rather than typing it in.
- **Character used for a decimal point in the input data file**—Select whether a period or a comma will be used to indicate the decimal point in numeric values in the input data file. The American standard decimal point marker is a period while the European standard is a comma. This setting affects only data read from the input file; a period always is used as the decimal point marker in the generated report.
- **Character used to separate columns**—Select the character that will be used to separate columns in the input file. The default separator is a comma, but you may select any character you wish to use.
- **Data sub setting**—If you wish, you can tell DTREG to use only a subset of the records in the data file for the analysis. This speeds up the analysis and is useful when experimenting with different model settings. If

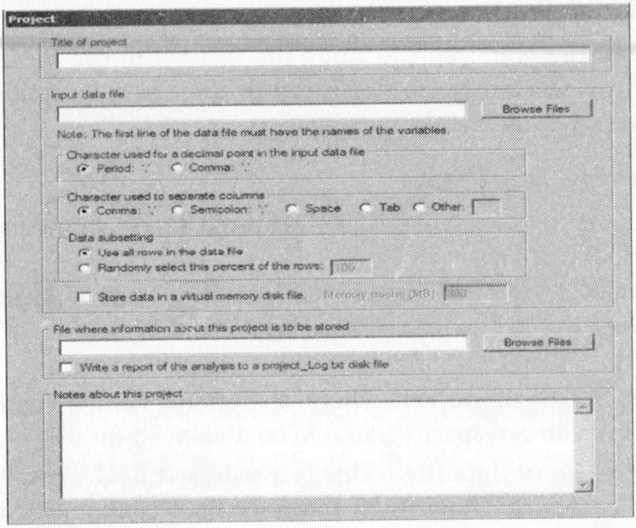


you tell DTREG to use a subset of the data, specify the percentage of the rows that you want it to use. Since random selection is used to select the rows, the actual number of rows used may be slightly different than the percent you specify.

- **Store data in a virtual memory file**—If you check this box, News Rover will store part of the training data in a disk file during the analysis rather than storing all of it in RAM memory. This option allows DTREG to handle analyses where the training data is too large to fit in memory, but it also significantly slows down the training time. The associated "**Memory cache**" value specifies the amount of memory (in mega-bytes) to be held in RAM; if the training data exceeds that size, the remaining portion will be stored in a disk file. Increasing the size of the memory cache will speed up the analysis, but it will make it more likely that DTREG will run out of memory. This option is available only in the Enterprise Version of DTREG.
- **File where information about this project is to be stored**—This is a required field. Specify the name of

the project file where DTREG will store parameters and computed values for the project. DTREG project files are stored with the type "**.dtr**" (for example, "Iris.dtr"). You can click the "Browse file" button to browse for the directory where you want to store the file.

- **Notes about this project**—This is an optional field. You can enter any notes that you want to store with the project data.

### *Opening an Existing Project*

All of the information about a DTREG project is stored in a project database. This includes parameters that control the analysis, information about variables, the name of the data input file, the generated report, and information required to construct and display the generated decision tree. These project files have the file type ".dtr". You can open project files, examine the report and tree, modify parameters and rerun the analysis. The actual input data is not stored in the project file but remains in the original comma separated value (CSV) file. The project file stores only the name of the input data file. To open an existing project file, click the icon on the toolbar. If you are reopening a project that was opened recently, you can click the "File" entry on the main menu line, and select the project from the list of recent projects. Once you open a project, the last report generated for it will be displayed in the right panel, and the left panel will show a list of property pages you can select to review and change option settings.

### *Running an Analysis to Build a Decision Tree*

Once you have created a new project or opened an existing project, you can tell DTREG to perform an analysis and build a decision tree. To do this, click the icon on the toolbar. You can also click "Run-analysis" on the main menu. While an analysis is running, a progress screen similar to this will be displayed: When the analysis finishes, the new report will be displayed in the main right panel.

### *Viewing the Generated Decision Tree*

Once an analysis has been completed, you can view the generated decision tree by clicking the toolbar icon or by clicking "View-tree" on the main menu. To save the decision tree in a jpg, png or bmp disk file, click the disk icon. To print the decision tree, click the printer icon.

### *Single Tree Model Property Page*

The Single Tree property page is used to specify parameters for single tree models.

- **Type of model to build**–Select the type of model that DTREG should build. The controls on this screen are disabled for any type of model other than single tree.
- **Minimum size node to split**–This specifies that a node (group) should never be split if it contains fewer rows than the specified value.
- **Maximum tree levels**–Specify the maximum number of levels in the tree that you want DTREG to construct when it is building the tree. It is best to let DTREG initially build a large tree with many levels and then allow the pruning phase of the analysis to remove levels. See page 246 for information about how pruning is done.
- **Generate report of tree splits**–If you check this box DTREG will write a report of each node split to the analysis log. If the tree is large, this report will be large.

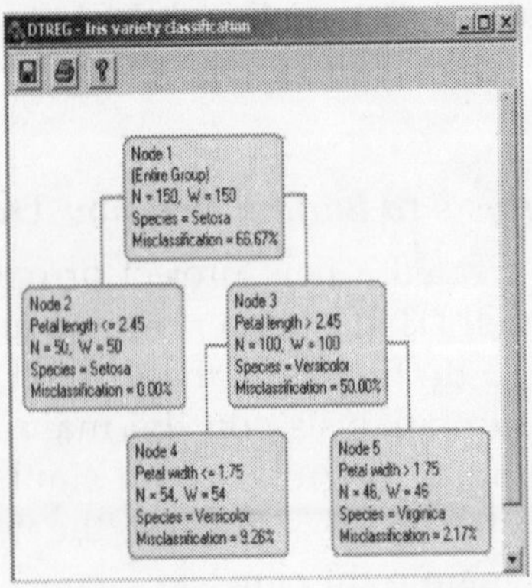

## Example of Hospital Data

An emergency room treats patients with chest pain. Based on factors such as blood pressure, age, gender, severity of pain, location of pain, and other measurements, the care giver must decide whether the pain indicates a heart attack or some less critical problem. A decision tree can be generated to decide which patients require immediate attention.

**The Data will be as Shown in the given following Table**

| *Patient Name* | *B.P* | *Age* | *Gender* | *Severity of pain* | *location of pain* |
|---|---|---|---|---|---|
| A | 90 | 59 | M | High | chest |
| B | 110 | 30 | F | medium | liver |
| D | 60 | 60 | F | low | lungs |
| C | 70 | 55 | M | low | lungs |
| E | 120 | 38 | F | high | heart |
| F | 115 | 40 | M | high | chest |
| G | 67 | 25 | m | low | chest |
| H | 89 | 45 | m | high | lungs |
| I | 90 | 56 | f | medium | liver |
| J | 60 | 67 | m | High | heart |
| K | 129 | 78 | f | low | chest |
| L | 89 | 23 | f | medium | chest |
| M | 150 | 43 | f | medium | chest |
| N | 80 | 54 | f | medium | chest |
| O | 97 | 65 | m | High | heart |
| P | 68 | 76 | m | low | chest |
| Q | 189 | 32 | m | medium | liver |
| R | 56 | 34 | f | low | lungs |
| S | 110 | 76 | f | High | heart |
| T | 150 | 80 | m | medium | lungs |
| U | 160 | 74 | f | High | heart |
| V | 190 | 72 | f | High | heart |
| W | 67 | 27 | m | medium | liver |
| X | 89 | 90 | m | low | lungs |
| Y | 90 | 87 | f | low | lungs |
| Z | 70 | 78 | f | medium | chest |

This Data will be classified based on the classification of data mining technique.

Here is the first screen we set up for this project

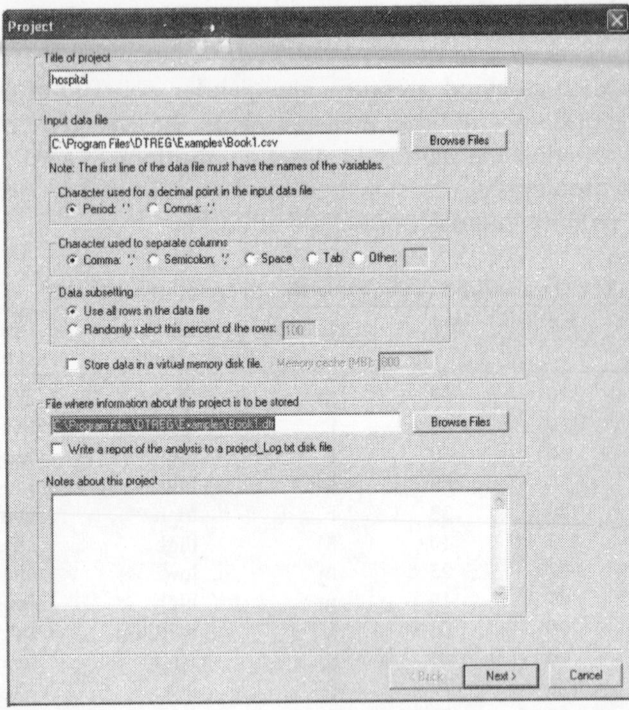


On the second screen, specify information about the variables:

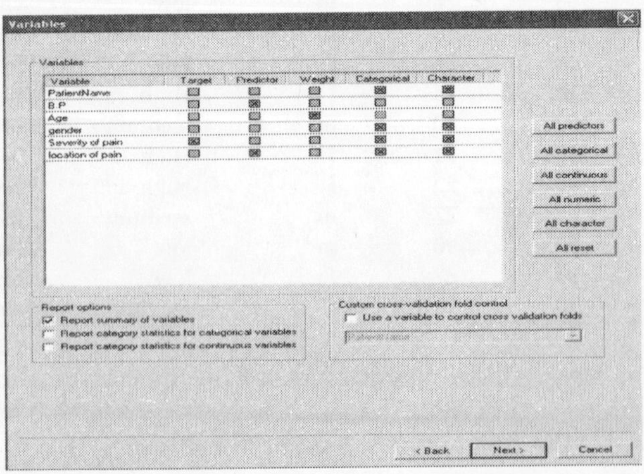

Here severity of pain as variable, location of pain & B.P as predictor variables and age is treated as weight variable.

The variable Location of pain is treated as initial split variable The screen would be after setting information about

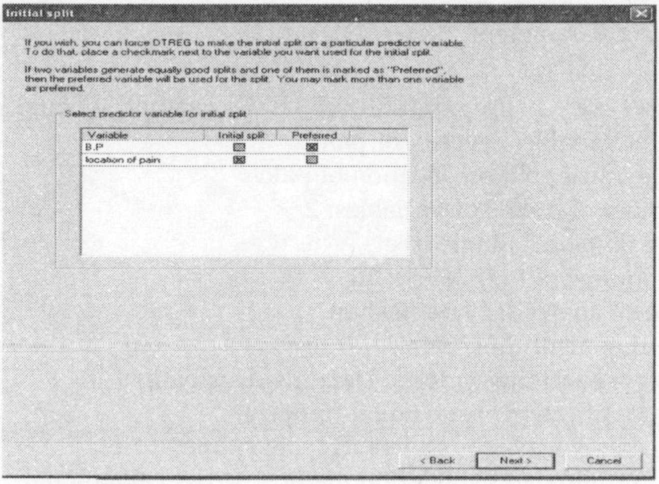


variables, click the "Next" button to advance through the setup screens.

After you finish the last setup screen for the project, DTREG asks if you want to save the settings for the project:

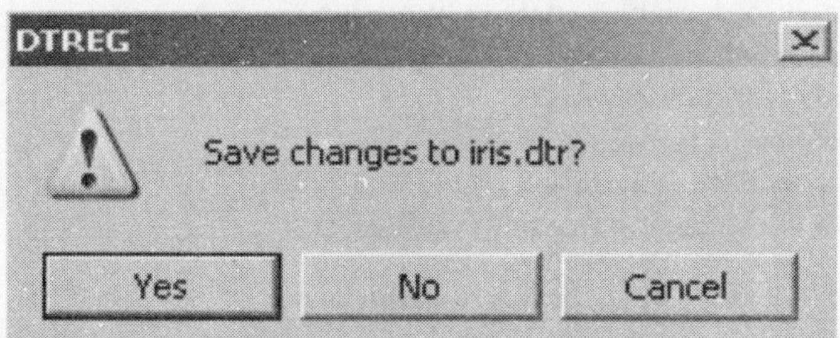


After running the analysis the code will be generated as follows:

weights: Equal
Minimum size node to split: 10

Max. categories for continuous predictors: 200
Use surrogate splitters for missing values: Yes
Starting analysis at 24-Aug-2007 17:04:54
DTREG version 6.5 (Demonstration Version)
http://www.dtreg.com

**Project Parameters**

Project title: ref
Project file: C:\Program Files\DTREG\Examples\Book1.dtr
Target variable: Severity of pain
Force initial split on: location of pain
Number of predictor variables: 2
Type of model: Single tree
Maximum splitting levels: 10
Type of analysis: Classification
Splitting algorithm: Gini
Category weights (priors): Data file distribution
Misclassification costs: Equal (unitary)
Variable Always compute surrogate splitters: No
Tree pruning and validation method: Cross validation
Number of cross-validation folds: 10
Tree pruning criterion: Minimum cost complexity (0.00 S.E.)

**Input Data**

Input data file: C:\Program Files\DTREG\Examples\Book1.csv
Number of variables (data columns): 6
Data subsetting: Use all data rows
Number of data rows: 26
Total weight for all rows: 1464
Rows with missing target or weight values: 0
Rows with missing predictor values: 0

**Summary of Variables**

| *Variable* | *Class* | *Type* | *Missing rows* | *Categories* |
|---|---|---|---|---|
| Patient Name | Unused | Categorical | 0 | |
| B.P | Predictor | Continuous | 0 | 17 |
| Age | Weight | Continuous | 0 | |
| Gender | Unused | Categorical | 0 | |
| Severity of pain | Target | Categorical | 0 | 3 |
| Location of pain | Predictor | Categorical | 0 | 4 |

## Model Size Summary Report

Maximum depth of the tree = 6
Total number of group splits = 5
The full tree has 6 terminal (leaf) nodes.
The minimum validation relative error occurs with 6 nodes.
The relative error value is 0.5701 with a standard error of 0.0176
The tree will be pruned from 6 to 4 nodes.

**Validation Statistics**

| *Nodes* | *Val cost* | *Val std. err.* | *RS cost* | *Complexity* | |
|---|---|---|---|---|---|
| 6 | 0.5701 | 0.0176 | 0.1843 | 0.000000 | <– Min. validation error |
| 5 | 0.5701 | 0.0176 | 0.2640 | 0.050546 | |
| 4 | 0.5701 | 0.0176 | 0.3481 | 0.053279 | <– Pruned size |
| 3 | 0.5701 | 0.0176 | 0.4440 | 0.060792 | |
| 2 | 0.6346 | 0.0181 | 0.6110 | 0.105874 | |
| 1 | 1.0000 | 0.0000 | 1.0000 | 0.246585 | |

## Misclassification Tables

**Training Data**

| | *Actual* | | *Misclassified* | | | |
|---|---|---|---|---|---|---|
| *Category* | *Count* | *Weight* | *Count* | *Weight* | *Per cent* | *Cost* |
| High | 9 | 536 | 3 | 144 | 26.866 | 0.269 |
| low | 8 | 505 | 3 | 179 | 35.446 | 0.354 |
| medium | 9 | 423 | 0 | 0 | 0.000 | 0.000 |
| Total | 26 | 1464 | 6 | 323 | 22.063 | 0.221 |

**Validation Data**

| | *Actual* | | *Misclassified* | | | |
|---|---|---|---|---|---|---|
| *Category* | *Count* | *Weight* | *Count* | *Weight* | *Per cent* | *Cost* |
| High | 9 | 536 | 3 | 144 | 26.866 | 0.269 |
| low | 8 | 505 | 1 | 78 | 15.446 | 0.154 |
| medium | 9 | 423 | 6 | 318 | 75.177 | 0.752 |
| Total | 26 | 1464 | 10 | 540 | 36.885 | 0.369 |

## Confusion Matrix

**Training Data**

| *Actual* | *Predicted* | | *Category* |
|---|---|---|---|
| *Category* | *High* | *low* | *medium* |
| High | 392 | 45 | 99 |
| low | 0 | 326 | 179 |
| medium | 0 | 0 | 423 |

**Validation Data**

| *Actual* | *Predicted* | *Category* | |
|---|---|---|---|
| *Category* | *High* | *low* | *medium* |
| High | 392 | 104 | 40 |
| low | 0 | 427 | 78 |
| medium | 0 | 318 | 105 |

**Lift and Gain**

*Lift and Gain for training data*
*Lift/Gain for Severity of pain = High*

| *Tree Node* | *Class % of bin* | *Cum % Population* | *Cum % of class* | *Cum Gain* | *% of Population* | *% of Class* | *Lift* |
|---|---|---|---|---|---|---|---|
| 3 | 100.00 | 26.78 | 73.13 | 2.73 | 26.78 | 73.13 | 2.73 |
| 6 | 18.13 | 64.07 | 91.60 | 1.43 | 37.30 | 18.47 | 0.50 |
| 7 | 12.13 | 89.41 | 100.00 | 1.12 | 25.34 | 8.40 | 0.33 |
| 5 | 0.00 | 100.00 | 100.00 | 1.00 | 10.59 | 0.00 | 0.00 |

*Average gain = 1.570*
*Percent of cases with Severity of pain = High: 36.61%*
*Lift/Gain for Severity of pain = low*

| *Tree Node* | *Class % of bin* | *Cum % Population* | *Cum % of class* | *Cum Gain* | *% of Population* | *% of Class* | *Lift* |
|---|---|---|---|---|---|---|---|
| 7 | 87.87 | 25.34 | 64.55 | 2.55 | 25.34 | 64.55 | 2.55 |
| 6 | 32.78 | 62.64 | 100.00 | 1.60 | 37.30 | 35.45 | 0.95 |
| 5 | 0.00 | 73.22 | 100.00 | 1.37 | 10.59 | 0.00 | 0.00 |
| 3 | 0.00 | 100.00 | 100.00 | 1.00 | 26.78 | 0.00 | 0.00 |

*Average gain = 1.627*
*Percent of cases with Severity of pain = low: 34.49%*

| *Tree Node* | *Class % of bin* | *Cum % Population* | *Cum % of class* | *Cum Gain* | *% of Population* | *% of Class* | *Lift* |
|---|---|---|---|---|---|---|---|
| 5 | 100.00 | 10.59 | 36.64 | 3.46 | 10.59 | 36.64 | 3.46 |
| 6 | 49.08 | 47.88 | 100.00 | 2.09 | 37.30 | 63.36 | 1.70 |
| 3 | 0.00 | 74.66 | 1 00.00 | 1.34 | 26.78 | 0.00 | 0.00 |
| 7 | 0.00 | 100.00 | 100.00 | 1.00 | 25.34 | 0.00 | 0.00 |

*Average gain = 1.972*
*Percent of cases with Severity of pain = medium: 28.89%*

**Overall Importance of Variables**

| *Variable* | *Importance* |
|---|---|
| location of pain | 100.000 |
| B.P | 24.721 |

Finished the analysis at 24-Aug-2007 17:04:54
Analysis run time: 00:00.09

Now the tree will be generated as follows:

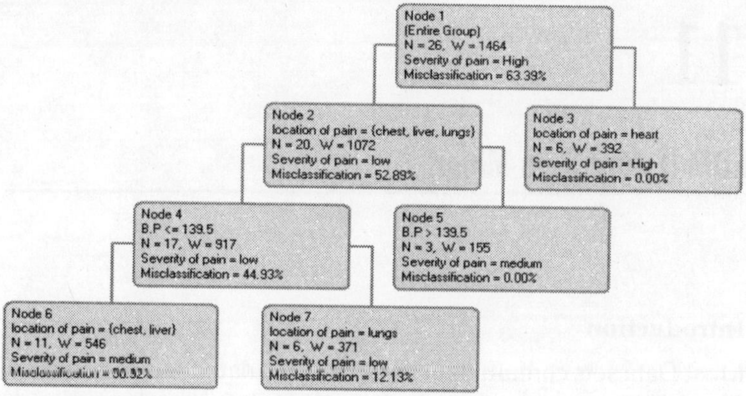


## References

Agresti, Alan (2002), "*Categorical Data Analysis*", *Second Edition*, Wiley Series in Probability and Statistics.

Aldenderfer, Mark S. and Roger K. Blashfield, "*Cluster Analysis*", Sage Publications.

# 11

# EDM (Estard Data Miner)

## Introduction

Most Data sets contain data that is accumulated for many years. These Data sets (databases, also called data warehouses) can become not only a data storage, but a source of new knowledge.

Estard Data Miner is a comprehensive data mining application, able to discover hidden relations both in structured and unstructured data. The newest data mining techniques were incorporated into Estard Data Miner for carrying out automated data analysis.

The program is a powerful end-to-end analytical solution, some of it's functions are: importing data from databases, Excel and Text files, data editing, sorting, manipulation, visualization and reporting.

Estard Data Miner performs statistical analysis, reveals all "If-Then" (production) rules and creates decision trees. The created decision models can be easily viewed and interpretate.

The unique feature of Estard Data Miner is the analysis flexibility. The newest data mining algorithms allow to perform knowledge discovery with no limits. Another special feature of the program is that the discovered knowledge can be easily used for prediction and searching for data patterns in databases.

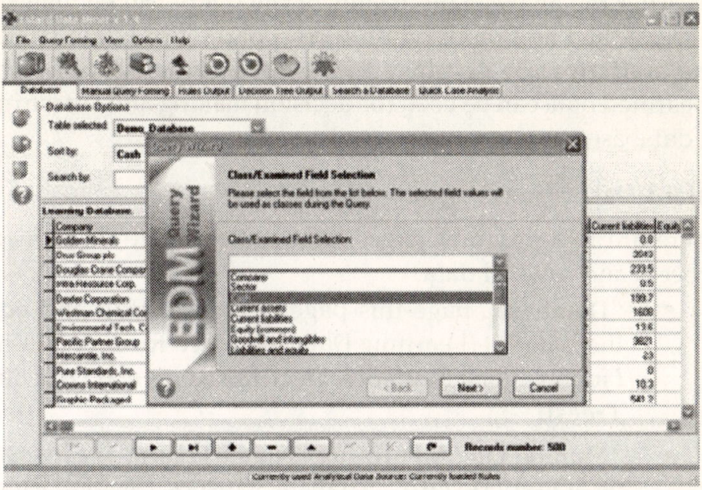


**Fields of Application**

Fields of Estard Data Miner application vary from data mining in Insurance industry, Banking and Marketing to Medicine and Education. Estard Data Miner can improve processes in any field, related to decision making. Between applications of the program is analysis of clients databases. Data mining clients databases allows to detect loyal and fraudulent customers, decreasing marketing costs and improving the campaigns response.

**Getting Started**

The first step for the Data Mining process is selecting the database to be analysed. It can be either customers database, or any other database containing information to be analysed.

To start the analysis select the database and a table with the help of Estard Data Miner. The database selecting is simple and easy thanks to a special **wizard.** The wizard can be started from the **text menu** (File) or with the help of buttons, available on the corresponding **program pages.**

The next step is to start the data mining query. The easiest way is to start the "**Query Wizard**". The query can also be manually formed and started on the "**Manual Query Forming**" page.

After the analysis the results of the query can be viewed, saved, edited and reported on corresponding program pages. The **statistics** are displayed in a special dialog. Now the unearhted data can be used for decision making and **searching** in databases.

**Estard Data Miner Pages**

There are five program pages, that contain controls to load, process and save all data.

- **"Database"** page-this page is used to load and edit the Data Set (Learning Database) used for data mining ( for obtaining **Statistics, Decision Rules** and **Decision Trees).**
- **"Manual Query Forming"** page-use this page instead of **"Query Wizard"** to create Statistics, Decision Rules and Decision Trees manually. Manual Query creation and processing is faster and more convenient for experienced users.
- **"Rules Output"** page-use this page to view, load and edit **Decision Rules.**
- **"Decision Tree Output"** page-this page contains controls for viewing and working with **Decision Trees.**
- **"Search a Database"** page-contains additional controls for using the **Analytical Data.**

***"Database" Page***

The "Database" page is designed for convenient working with Data Sets, used as Learning Databases.

Controls, placed on this page, allow to:

- Load Data Sets for data mining
- Easily switch between tables
- View and sort table records
- Edit table records
- Search for values in tables
- Export Data Sets to various file formats

### *Manual Query Forming Page*

The "Manual Query Forming" page is used for manual setting and processing data mining Queries (Manual Query).

The controls allow to obtain Statistics, Decision Trees and Decision (If-Then) Rules.

Main functions of the "Manual Query Forming" page are:

- Class/Examined Field Selection
- Classes information viewing
- Manual Classes Creation
- Selection of the fields for analysis
- Editing Queries settings
- Starting queries

### *Page Controls*

"Manual Query Forming" program page contains such controls:

- "General Query Settings" group - contains main query managing controls.
- "Rules Query Settings" group-allows to change the probabilities and settings of the Rules for the Decision Rules Query.
- "Decision Tree Query Settings" group-used to edit settings for the Decision Tree Query.

### *Main buttons*

- "Process Query" button-Data pre processing. The button is always enabled. Pressing the button starts the pre processing Query. The result of the Query are Statistics. After the pre processing Decision Rules and Decision Trees can be created.
- "Create Rules" button-starts the Decision Rules Query. Is not enabled in case if Data pre processing ("Process Query" button) is needed.
- "Create Decision Tree" button-starts the Decision Tree Query. Is not enabled in case if Data pre processing ("Process Query" button) is needed.
- "Query Settings" button-opens the "Query Settings" dialog.

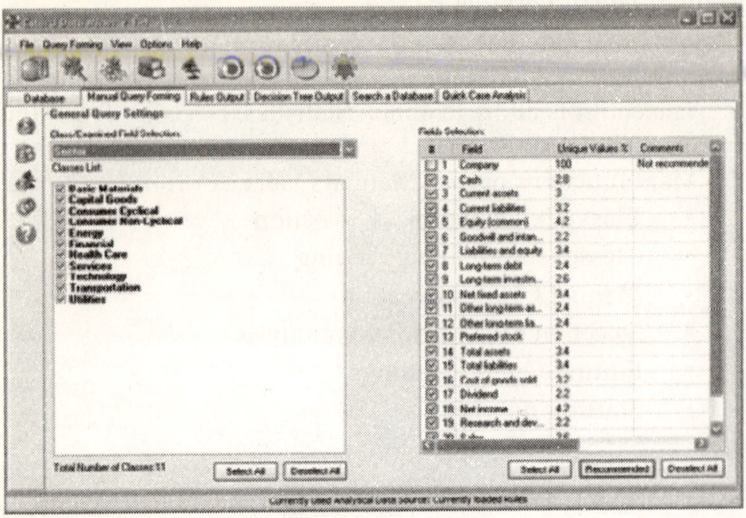

### *Rules Output Page*

The Rules Output page is used to:

- View the results of Decision Rules Query
- Load previously saved Decision Rules
- View, print and save Rules reports
- Edit Created or Loaded Decision Rules

### *Page Controls*

- **"Load Rules..."** button-opens the Load dialog. Use it to load previously saved files of "*.ltr" type.
- **"Save Rules..."** button - press to save the Decision Rules as a "*.ltr" file.
- **"Edit Rules..."** button-press it to open "Edit Rules" dialog.
- **"Report on Rules..."** button-shows the "Report" dialog.
- **"Clear Rules"** button-clears the results of Decision Rules query, after asking for a confirmation.

**Rules Output"** page contains such buttons.

### *Decision Tree Output Page*

The Decision Tree page is used to:

- View the decision models, obtained as a result of Decision Tree Query.
- Load previously saved Decision Trees.
- View brief reports.

**Page Controls:** "Decision Tree Output" page contains such controls.

- "Expand Trees" button-press it to expand all Decision Tree nodes.
- "Collapse Trees" button-press to collapse all Decision Tree nodes.
- "Save Tree As..." button-opens "Save as" dialog. Decision Tree can be saved as "*.ltt" file, structured Text "*.txt" file or as a Bitmap "*.bmp" file.
- **"Load Tree"** button-opens "Load from" dialog. The program can open decision models from "*.ltt" file, or from a structured Text "*.txt" file. *Note: ".txt" files can only be previewed.*
- "Clear Tree" button-clears the obtained decision trees and brief report.
- A brief report is shown in the "Brief Decision Tree Report" control. If all Classes could be defined, it will contain such information:

  –*"All Classes Were Defined."*

  –All defined Classes are listed under *"Defined Classes:"* title.

  –If some Classes were not defined, their list will be placed under *"Undefined Classes:"* title.

  –*"Number of Decision Trees Built:"* displays the number of Trees that were built during the Query.
- **"Processed Decision Tree"** control-displays structured Decision Trees. Each Tree is been marked with a number, for example *"Decision Tree #1"*.

### *"Search a Database" Page*

This page is designed to provide convenient using of Analytical Data.

Controls, placed on this page, allow to:

- Load the Database (Analysed Database)
- Form SQL Queries for searching data in tables with the use of Decision Rules and Decision Trees, created during the process of data mining
- Change SQL Queries settings
- Easily switch between Database tables
- View and sort table records
- Edit table records
- Search for values in tables

### *"Search a Database" Page Controls*

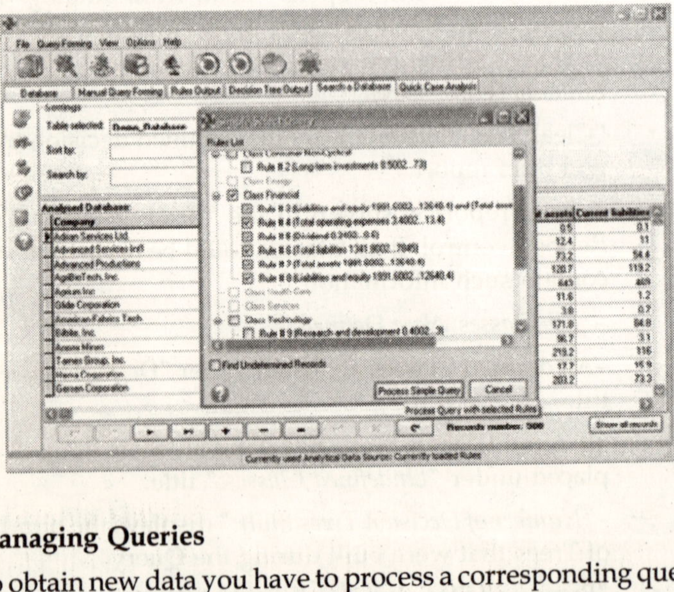

### Managing Queries

To obtain new data you have to process a corresponding query.

If you are just getting started with the program, it is recommended to use the "Query Wizard". In other case use the "Manual Query Forming" page for faster calculations.

### Query Processing

Here, a Query is a kind of data processing, used for knowledge discovery with Estard Data Miner. There are two main query types in Estard Data Miner:

- Data mining queries for obtaining Analytical Data, like Decision Rules, Decision Trees and Statistics.
- Queries to use Decision Rules and Decision Trees for searching in databases.

#### *Queries to Obtain Analytical Data*

To obtain Analytical Data you can use either Query Wizard or the "Manual Query Creation" page.

Using Query Wizard is recommended for starting users. With it's help you will easily create Decision Rules, Decision Trees and Statistics in a few steps.

Manual Query Creation is faster and more convenient for experts, acknowledged with program structure.

The main difference between using Query Wizard and Manual Query Creation is that Manual Query Creation is more flexible, allows to create Statistics separately from Decision Rules and Decision Trees. As a result, the whole Analysis is been speed up:

#### *Query to Use Obtained Analytical Data*

After obtaining the Analytical Data can be used for calculations, reports, statistics, or for data searching in databases with the help of Estard Data Miner.

*For example: After obtaining Decision Rules describing loyal customers, you can search for loyal customers in other databases.*

#### *Types of Analysed Fields*

Processing Queries, Estard Data Miner can use Field of such types:

- Text (TStringField)
- Integer (TIntegerField)
- Small Integer (TSmallIntField)
- rational (TrationalField)
- Logical (TBooleanField)

### *Simple Select Query*

The Simple Select Query is an easy and a fast way to use the Analytical Data obtained as a result of data mining. The Query allows to search for records in a database, correlating to the Decision Rules or Decision Trees. With the help of this Query you can detect Classes in a database, without performing additional analysis.

*For example:* after creating Decision Rules, describing loyal clients in the customers database, Rules can be used for detecting loyal clients in other databases. Even if there is a difference in databases structures, Decision Rules and Decision Trees can be applied after setting an Analogy between databases fields.

The set of controls for the Query is placed on the "Search a Database" page.

Simple Select Query uses the source of Analytical Data (Decision Rules or Decision Trees), determined in the "Query Forming".

## Query Settings

### *Rules Query Settings*

The "Rules Query Settings" group box contains the following controls:

- "Element belongs to class(%)"-input the probability for Decision Rules.
- "Minimum number of cases for a Rule" - the rules, describing less than minimum number of cases, will be ignored by the program.
- "Rational fields minimum value"-determines minimum rational values that Estard Data Miner will use for the analysis.
- "Create full Rules" control - marking this control will make Estard Data Miner to find all Decision Rules, without cutting off unnecessary elements.
- "Create minimized Rules" control-marking the control will allow to create minimized Rules, enough for

Classes analysis. The overall number of Rules might be less than with "Create full Rules" option marked.

- "Maximum Rules number for a Class"-this control allows to limit the number of created Rules. For example, if setting controls value to 10, the program will create no more than 10 Rules for each Class.

*Decision Tree Query Settings*

The Decision Tree can be created in various ways.

- "Build Automatically" control-mark it if you want the program to decide how to create the Decision Tree.
- "Build Tree for Each Field" control-mark it if you want to receive a Decision Tree for each Field, marked in the "Selection of Fields" control. Time, necessary to obtain Decision Trees is proportional to number of Fields used in analysis processing.
- "Build starting with Field" control-mark it to create a concrete Decision Tree, starting with the Field selected in the list below the control.
- "Build a Single Tree"-in case if some Classes were not defined after building the first Tree, Estard Data Miner will try to build a new Tree. Marking this control will make Estard Data Miner to create a single Decision Tree.
- "Stop After defining All Classes" control-will stop Decision Trees creation in case if all Classes were defined.

*Decision Tree Output Settings*

- "Clear previous Trees before adding new ones" option-clears up the displayed Decision Trees before adding new Decision Trees.
- "Add new Decision Trees to previously created"-if some Decision Trees are displayed in the control on the "Decision Tree Output" page, they won't be removed when creating a new Tree.

Exceptions SettingsExceptions settings allow to set the program to search for exceptions from dependencies in data. You also can make the program to search for exceptions only for classes met in some number of cases.

"Search for exceptions" control-allows to turn on and off exceptions searching.

"Minimum number of Class cases" control-Classes, met in less number of cases than set in this control, will not be searched for exceptions.

"Minimum exception difference (%)" control-allows to set the program sensitivity to exceptions.

**Analytical Data**

***Analytical Data Description***

Analytical Data (also called Analytical Information) is all the Data you obtain while working with Estard Data Miner, including created Decision Rules and Decision Trees. The Data can be used not only to create reports, but to analyse databases with the "Simple Select Query" and "Quick Case Analysis".

***Analytical Data Destination and Application***

All the Data you receive while working with Estard Data Miner can be reported, saved and stored in various files, loaded from files and used for "Simple Select Query".

Current source of Data is shown in the status bar, for example: *"Currently used Analytical Data: Currently Loaded Rules"*. The source of Analytical Data for Queries is set in the "Analytic Data Source" dialog.

The Analytical Data Source is **empty** if no Decision Rules or Decision Trees (depending on the selected Data source, "Analytic Data Source") where loaded or created. The "Simple Select Query" can not be processed while the source of Analytical Data is **empty.**

***Editing Obtained Analytical Data***

Estard Data Miner is an Expert System. In some cases it might be necessary to edit the results of the analysis. That's why Decision Rules can be edited, if necessary.

## Decision Rules (IF-THEN)

Decision Rules, also called Production Rules or If-then Rules are a basic structure in data mining and expert systems. This method of knowledge representation is simple and easy to use for data analysis. Each Rule defines a piece of overall knowledge. The Rules can be edited, removed or added independently from each other.

### *Rule Structure*

The Rule consists of condition and conclusion. In case if there are many conditions, they are separated by "and". *For example:*

*IF condition1 and condition2 THEN conclusion*

As a conclusion, Estard Data Miner represents so-called **Classes-values**, obtained from database or created manually by the user. During the Query, the program reveals all Rules for Classes, structurizes them and outputs in a special control.

## Decision Trees

Decision Tree is a data mining method that allows to create easy to understand and use decision models. The decisions are represented as the nodes of the tree model. The results of the decisions are outputted as the final "leafs" of the tree.

### *Decision Tree Advantages*

Amongst other data mining methods, decision tree is the method that has several advantages:

- Intuitively comprehensible classification model. People are able to understand decision tree models after a brief explanation.
- Data preparation for a decision tree is basic or unnecessary. Other techniques often require data normalization, dummy variables need to be created and blank values to be removed.
- Rules generation in the fields where experts have difficulties with formalizing their knowledge.

- Is a white box model. If a given situation is observable in a model the explanation for the condition is easily explained by a simple Boolean logic.
- It is easy to validate a model using statistical tests and other data mining methods. That makes it possible to account for the reliability of the model.
- Is robust, perform well with large data in a short time. Large amounts of data can be analyzed using personal computers in a time short enough to enable stakeholders to take decisions based on its analysis.

Because of these and many other reasons, methodology of decision trees is an important tool for any scientist dealing with data analysis, no matter if he is theorist or practician.

***Areas of Decision Trees Application***

Decision trees are an excellent tool in decision-making and data mining systems. They can be of good service to any analyst, manager or scientist. Decision trees are successfully used to solve real-world problems in the following fields:

- Banking. Estimation of clients creditworthiness when giving credits.
- Insurance Industry. Detecting possibly fraudulent clients in customers databases.
- Medicine. Diagnostics of various diseases.
- Molecular biology. Analysis of amino acids composition.

**Estard Data Miner Files**

All Data obtained with the help of Estard Data Miner can be stored in three kinds of files:

- "*.ltf"-files of this type store information about statistics. They can be loaded from the "Statistics" dialog. You can also create reports on previously saved data.
- "*.ltr"-files store all necessary data to work with Decision Rules. To save or load them you have to switch to the "Rules Output" program page and press

the corresponding button. They can also be chosen as a source of Analytical Data.

- "*.ltt"-files store all necessary data to work with Decision Trees. You can save or load files of this type on the "Decision Tree Output" program page. Just as the "*.ltr" files, "*.ltt" fiels can also be chosen as a source of Analytical Data.

Files can be loaded to Estard Data Miner any time and in any order, without inflicting each other.

# 12

## Erupt

Volcanic Eruption is an opening, or rupture in a planet's surface or crust, which allows hot, molten rock, ash and gases to escape from below the earth's surface. In other words, it is a sudden occurrence of violent discharge of steam and volcanic material.

**Why Eruption:** An eruption begins when pressure on a magma chamber forces magma up through the conduit and out the volcano's vents. When the magma chamber has been completely filled, the type of eruption partly depends on the amount of gases and silica in the magma. The amount of silica determines how **sticky** (level of viscosity) the magma is and **water** provides the explosive potential of **steam**.

Obstacles also influence the type of eruption. When the pipe is blocked by a stopple or an accumulation of pumice, the pressure in the pipe will build up very high resulting in an explosion. When magma reaches earth's surface it is called **lava**. It may pour out in gentle streams called **lava flows** or erupt violently into the air. Rocks ripped loose from the inside of the volcano or torn apart by the gas may be shot into the air with the lava. These rocks blown out of a volcano are called **pyroclastic** rocks. The rock fragments fall back to earth in many different shapes and sizes:

**1.** ***low water, low silica-runny lava flows (not viscous)***

**2.** ***low water, high silica (very viscous)-pasty lava-****often building domes*

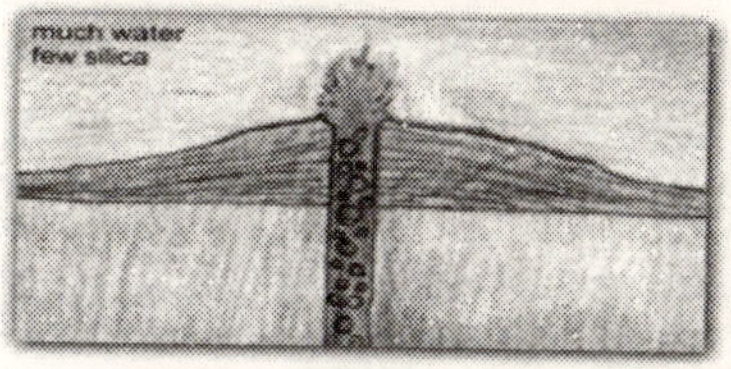


**3.** ***high water, low silica (not viscous)-fountain of runny lava***

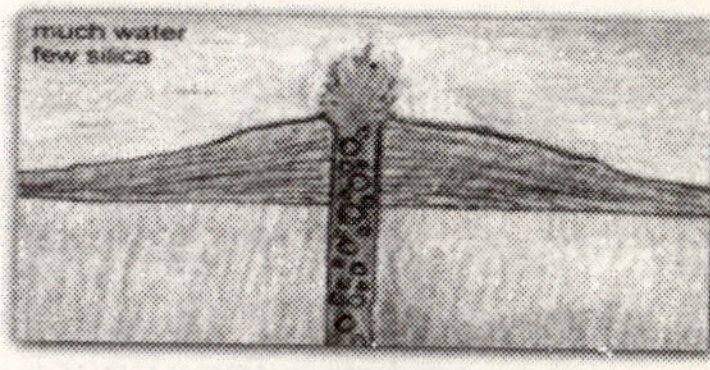


**4.** ***high water, high silica (very viscous)-explosion***

- **Dust**—particles less than 1/100 inch in diameter
  Dust particles may be carried great distances. In a powerful eruption they may be carried around the earth several times.
- **Ash**–fragments less than 1/5 inch in diameter
  Most volcanic ash falls to the surface and cemented together by water to form a rock called **volcanic tuff**.
- **Bomb**–A rounded piece of newly hardened lava which takes shape while flying through the air.
- **Block**–A piece of lava that has sharp corners.
- **Cinder**–Bubbly rock formed by liquid lava cooling in the air.
- **Pumice-Cinder** so bubbly that it floats in water.

Volcanic activity is classified by **how often** a volcano erupts. A volcano may be **active, intermittent, dormant**, or **extinct**. Active volcanoes erupt **constantly**. Intermittent volcanoes erupt fairly **regularly**. Dormant volcanoes are inactive, but not long enough to determine whether they will erupt again or not. Extinct volcanoes have been inactive **since the beginning of recorded history**.

**Why Erupt**

Although we are having many optimal models, because of the complexity involved in the computations we had gone for erupt.

Erupt is a user interactive graphical program designed to simulate a wide range of volcanic activity and display it 2-dimensionally. The graphical display shows the temporal and spatial evolution of particle paths for lava and pyroclasts, their deposition and the construction of a volcanic edifice in two dimensions.It simulates various volcanic eruption types, including Strombolian, Plinian, Vulcanian/Surtseyan, Hawaiian lava flows, Peléean viscous lava dome emplacement, Fumarolic/Phreatic activity, and sector collapse. Tectonic (faulting) and erosional events are also simulated.

Parameter selection allows a manual and automatic mode for setting the eruption parameters. The manual mode allows the user to specify eruption type, magnitude, and vent location, and will continue in that mode until the user presses any key to stop the current eruptive phase and start a new one. The automatic mode of this program runs simulations that follows semi-random eruption scenarios of silicic, intermediate, or mafic trends with time.

Each eruptive phase produces a color-coded stratigraphic representation of the erupted products, such that complex volcanic stratigraphies can be created. Current program memory allocations allow up to 100 eruptive phases to be superimposed, after which only static (no deposition) eruptions may be specified. The user has the option to switch between manual and automatic mode of operation at any time after completion of an eruptive phase.

The horizontal (vertical with no exaggeration) scale is calibrated to kilometers, but if larger screen portrayals of Strombolian bursts are desired, the eruptive strength can be increased beyond the limit of 1.0, which results in scoria dispersal that is beyond that of typical Strombolian ranges.

**Start an Eruption Simulation:** To run erupt after starting the program, select an eruption type from the parameters menu, then proceed to the parameters panel and select "ok." Now the "Erupt" button will be activated so that you can start the eruption by pressing it. To stop the eruption at any point, simply press the "Pause/Stop" button twice.

**Using Erupt3**

Upon startup, the user generally selects an eruption type from the Parameter menu and then proceeds with adjusting (changing) the parameters for the selected event in the parameters panel. Then by pressing the "OK" button in the change window, ERUPT is ready to start by pressing the "ERUPT" button. Status bars at the top and bottom of the ERUPT window provide information about current settings and activities. Alternatively, the user may wish to open a saved stratigraphic file or record file first before choosing new ERUPT parameters. Also the user may wish first to change ERUPT options (such as speed, enable maps, scale, etc.).

From the File menu, the user can open and save files as well as print them. Erupt file formats include stratigraphic files, eruption record files, and digital elevation model files (DEM). After creating a volcano or volcanic fields, the user can save a file in one of the above formats.

Options can be changed during the course of simulations. The user can disable sound, change the speed of the simulation, set the gravity to simulate conditions on other planets, enable and set the precision of mapping, and change the scale of the erupt window (note this feature will truncate data). After completing an eruptive phase the user can use the View menu to see maps, topography, Erupt-3D, and detailed stratigraphy to see alternate portrayals of the evolving volcano or volcanic field. In addition, if the recorder is active, the simulation can be played back from the point at which the recorder was activated, and then after playback, the user can continue recording more eruptive phases.

The user may wish to make an image file of and eruption in progress, the stratigraphy, or maps. To do this use "Capture" in the view menu to activate the screen capture and then copy the screen image to the Windows clipboard.

There are many techniques that can be applied in simulations that make Erupt more realistic. Basically these techniques require some knowledge of volcanoes and their properties, morphology, and characteristic eruption history.

During an eruption, the extruded volume and volcanic explosivity index (VEI) is shown below the Erupt button. These values give an indication of how large a given eruptive phase is.

*Parameters Menu*

The parameter menu allows manual selection of different eruption event types and their parameters as well as an auto mode. Upon selection of an eruption type, a parameters panel will open below the simulation window. Using this panel, the user may change various parameters that determine the nature of each eruption type. Then the program is ready to simulate.

**Principal Eruption Type Parameters**

**Hawaiian (Basaltic Lava Flow/Flood):** Fluid type lava flows of basaltic lava that tends to pond and form shield volcanoes best typified by current eruptions in Hawaii.

**Peléean (Silicic Lava Flow/Dome):** Viscous lava that tends to pile up and build dome volcanoes.

**Strombolian (Ballistic Fountain/Scoria Cone):** Ballistic ejections of scoria and ash that form scoria (cinder) cones and ash deposits on larger composite cones. This parameter allows formation of diatremes when the strength parameter is 0.3 or less.

**Plinian (Pumice and Ash Column):** Plinian eruptions produce vertically driven jets and buoyant plumes of pumice and ash that rise several tens of km into the stratosphere and deposit ash over wide spread areas by simple fallout. Calderas can be formed by this eruption type when the power parameter is 0.5 or greater.

**Vulcanian/Surtseyan (Pyroclastic Flow/Surge):** This eruption type produces cannon-like bursts that generally form laterally moving clouds of tephra moving at hurricane speeds downslope from the vent (known as pyroclastic flows or pyroclastic surges). These eruptions build up ash and pumice deposits during explosive eruptions, often the most hazardous type of volcanic activity. Calderas can be formed by this eruption type when the power parameter is 0.6 or greater. This parameter allows formation of diatremes when the strength parameter is 0.3 or less.

**Fumarolic/Phreatic (Gas Plume/No Magma):** Associated with pre/post eruption activity, this eruption type involves passive steaming to infrequent steam explosions, caused by boiling groundwater near a cooling magma body (after eruption) or by the thermal increased caused by new rising magma. This activity though does not erupt magma, only pieces of older volcanic rock that is generally altered to clay-like material by the action of steam.

**Tectonic Parameters**

**Sector Collapse (Debris Avalanche):** Sector collapse eruptions involve slope failure a high-standing volcanic edifice with debris avalanche removing part of the cone and leaving an open amphitheatre-like crater. Often accompanied by Plinian activity, this activity will produce a truncated volcano.

**Tectonic (Faulting/Erosion):** Parameters that control tectonic events with options allowing user to simulate faulting and erosional interludes.

**Eruption Parameters Panel**

To proceed with an eruption and activate the Erupt button, the user must press the "OK" button in the eruption parameter panel.

- Primary Parameters
- Secondary Parameters

***Primary Parameters***

**Location**: Position in km along the horizontal scale for the new vent that will be created. As this parameter is changed, a gray cursor will move across the screen above the horizontal scale to show the position. A simple method for changing this parameter involves clicking on the desired position in the simulation window or, if the "Enable Maps" option is checked, by using the Erupt 3D Vent Position window.

**Strength:** Scale (0.1 to 1) of relative strength or energy hence column height for Plinian and Strombolian type eruptions. For some explosive eruptions, setting this parameter will change the default mass flux simulated. For Vulcanian/Surtseyan eruptions, the strength value is used by Erupt to compute a "Heim Coefficient", which is a measure of run out mobility for pyroclastic flow/surge and sector collapse eruptions. Higher the values produce shorter the run out and smaller craters.

**Wind**: Wind velocity in m/s to the right (positive) or left (negative) directions.

**Mass Flux:** The eruption discharge rate is proportional to the number of representative marker particles for Plinian, Strombolian, Vulcanian/Surtseyan, and Fumarolic/Phreatic eruptions. A default value will be assigned based on the strength selected, but this number can be changed to suit the user's needs.

*Secondary Parameters*

**Directed Blast:** A check box to designate whether a pyroclastic flow/surge will dominantly run out in the direction of lowest topography around the vent.

**Explosive Bursts:** A check box for specifying that Fumarolic/Phreatic eruptions are punctuated by explosions.

**Caldera:** A check box that determines whether a Vulcanian/Surtseyan or Plinian eruption forms a caldera collapse event. This parameter is only available for eruptions of sufficient strength.

**Diatreme:** A special option for Strombolian and Vulcanian/Surtseyan type eruptions of strength less than 0.3, respectively, which simulates the emplacement of a diatreme below the vent.

**Caldera Type:** Select either "Mazama" or "Valles" type; the former type is that associated with composite cones and the latter to volcanic fields.

**Scarp Top and Base:** For sector collapse eruptions only, select the locations of the collapse scarp top and the base of the volcanic edifice in the direction of desired run out. Note that the top and/or base location must be different in order for the 'OK' to be enabled. As this parameter is changed, a gray cursor will move across the screen above the horizontal scale to show the position. Clicking the simulation window at a desired location will alternatively set the scarp top or base.

*Advanced Parameters*

**Advanced Parameter Options:** Allows specification of lava flow length, crater diameter, strength growth, speed adjustment, and if Maps enabled, allows specification of 3d position of the vent.

**Erupt3 Simulation Window**

The Erupt window (the main window) shows simulation controls and the simulation window. The size of the window chosen determines the size of the stratigraphy, map, and topography windows when they are displayed. Upon exiting Erupt, the size and position will be saved for future sessions.

When the cursor is passed over the simulation window, a cross-hair appears showing the horizontal location and elevation. The Erupt window consists of the simulation area, a status bar showing current simulation events just above the simulation area, panels showing a Legend (pictured below) or eruption/tectonic parameters, the Erupt and Halt buttons, current simulation phase volume and VEI, an optional and customizable ToolBar at the base, and a second status bar at the very base of the window, which shows current date and time, options selected, and file opened.

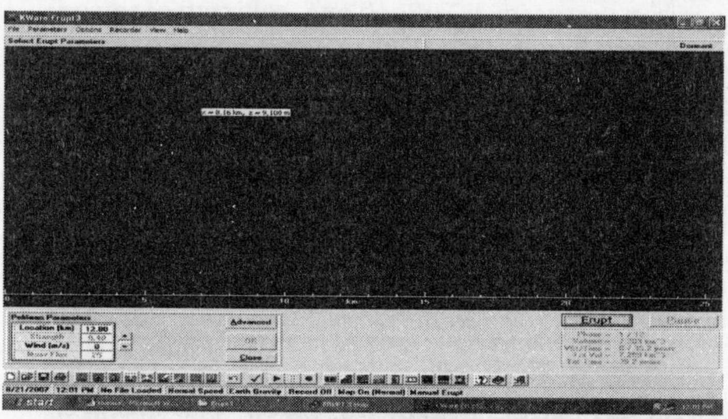

### *Detailed Stratigraphy*

When the option "stratigraphy" is chosen from the view menu, a columnar window will appear with a "zoomed" view of the stratigraphy at any position. To change the view position, the scroll bar must be used. The various colors shown in the detailed stratigraphy window are keyed to the legend. This view allows the user to see the nature of contacts among the various strata that may not be readily apparent in the main erupt window. In addition the "Copy" button allows copying the topographic image to the Windows clipboard, and the Print button will display the print panel for the detailed stratigraphy.

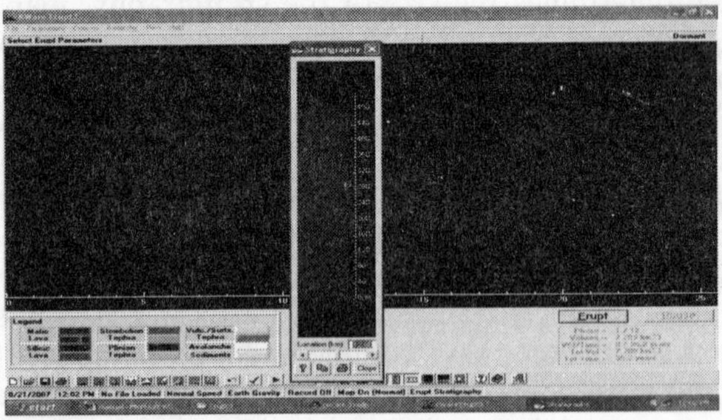

### Map Window

The Map window is displayed when View/Map is chosen from the menu. The map window displays buttons for showing the

topographic map, copying the map image to the Windows clipboard, saving a bitmap image of the map , printing , or closing the map window. The cursor displays the horizontal (x) and 3D (y) position for any point it passes over.

**Topography Window**

The Topography window is displayed when View/Topography is chosen from the menu or the topography button is pressed when viewing the geological map. The topography window displays buttons for showing the geologic map, copying the topographic image to the Windows clipboard, saving a bitmap

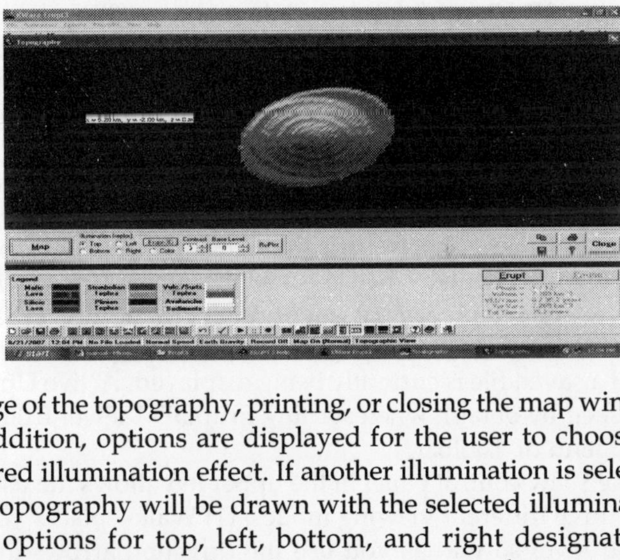

image of the topography, printing, or closing the map window. In addition, options are displayed for the user to choose the desired illumination effect. If another illumination is selected, the topography will be drawn with the selected illumination. The options for top, left, bottom, and right designate the direction of lighting. The color option portrays the topographic map with elevations shown by a color scheme where warmer colors are used for higher elevations. The contrast adjustment can be changed to suit the users preferences. The base level setting determines the elevation above which the topography is displayed—a kind of "water level." After selecting another contrast or base level, simply press the replot button to redraw the screen. The cursor shows the horizontal (x), 3D position (y), and elevation (z) for any point it passes over. Finally the Erupt-3D button opens the Erupt3D Viewer application.

**Erupt3D Viewer**

An added feature for Erupt3 is the Erupt3D Viewer, which utilizes DirectX 3D rendering in hardware or in software emulation.The veiwer allows the user to view topography from any angle and to "fly" or "walk" over it, revealing much of the intricate details simulated by Erupt3. The picture below shows the viewer window. It consists of control panels, a map or plan view of the topography, and the 3D view. This viewer can be one of the funnest parts of Erupt3, providing an action arcade game-like environment (but no shooting, monsters, or alien craft).

Start the Erupt3D Viewer from Erupt either by choosing (1) "Erupt 3D Viewer" from the File menu or (2) by selecting "Erupt-3D" from the View menu or from the Erupt Toolbar (only enabled after a map has been created). When started from the File menu, the user may open any saved Erupt topographic image (or for that matter any "BMP" format graphics file which has dimensions less than 180x180 pixels) to view a 3D rendering. When started from the View menu or Toolbar, the viewer will immediately load the current topogrphic image that erupt has created When checked the Active Update check box will check every 10 seconds for a newly created topographic image from Erupt and update the view display, even if a saved file is currently being displayed. Active Update is checked by default when starting Erupt3D Viewer from the View menu or Toolbar.

The View control panel in the upper left allows the user to select three different viewing modes: (1) Walk—places you at ground level so that as you use the direction arrows at the bottom, you experience climbing up, down, and across the topography; (2) Fly—simulates movement across a volcanic field in an aircraft; and (3) Pan—rotates the view around an axis. The speed, height above ground(except for Walk), and the vertical view angle can all be adjusted.

The Mesh control panel in the upper right controls the 3D rendering of the topography. Software rendering is the default, but hardware rendering may be a bit faster but it may not be supported well by your graphics board. The height and Light values determine the topographic exaggeration and brightness of the view. These options can only be selected if the rendering is stopped (the start button is showing at the bottom). The user must reload the topography by either using the "Open" button in the lower right corner or by simply double-clicking the small map view picture. The color button instantly changes the color of shading in the 3D view, and the "Points", "Solid" (Default), and "Mesh" options will instantly change the display mode.

At the bottom of the display is the Navigation Control in light blue, showing navigation "direction" arrows that can be pressed by the mouse to start movement. These buttons only are active if the "Start" button is pressed and has become the "Stop" button. If the Erupt3D Viewer has been opened from Erupt3, it will automatically load the topography created in Erupt3 and the start button will be activated. Also, when opened from Erupt3, Erupt3D veiwer will automatically update its view every 10 seconds as new eruptions happen in Erupt3. The "Reset" button returns the view to it initial home in case you get lost in the hills and valleys. The "Auto" button places the movement arrows in a continuous mode, such that pressing them once starts motion that continues until they are pressed again or the "Stop" button is pressed. The navigation arrow functions can also be operated by the keyboard arrows.

**Other Controls**

During movement around the 3D view, a red circle displays the users location on the small plan view map at the top. While movement is started with the Start button, clicking anywhere on the small map will instantly move your view to that location.

While movement is stopped stopped with the "Stop" button, users may use the "Open" button to load another topography file that was previously saved from Erupt3D Viewer by the "Save" button. Likewise the "Printer" button will open a print-preview window for setting up a printed copy.

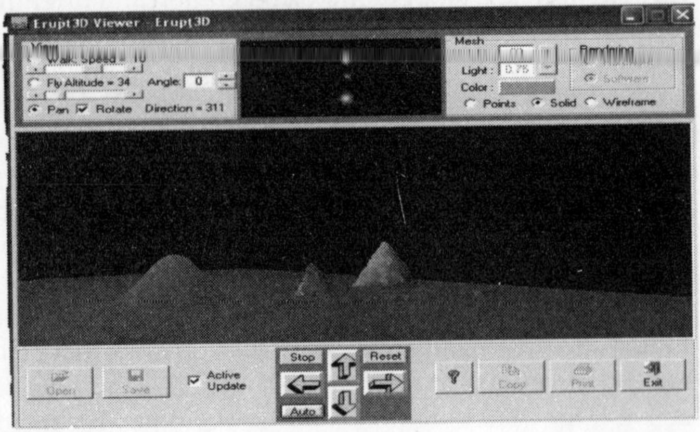


## References

Dobran F., Neri A., and Macedonio G. (1993), Numerical Simulation of Collapsing Volcanic Columns, J.Geophys res., 98:4231-4259.

MacDonald G. (1972), Volcanoes, Prentice hall inc., Englewood Cliffs, NewJersy, 51. opp.

# 13

# Fisher

The Fisher's exact procedure calculates an exact probability value for the relationship between two dichotomous variables, as found in a two by two table. The program calculates the difference between the data observed and the data expected, considering the given marginal and the assumptions of the model of independence. It works in exactly the same way as the Chi-square test for independence; however, the Chi-square gives only an estimate of the true probability value, an estimate which might not be very accurate if the marginal is very uneven or if there is a small value (less then five) in one of the cells. In such cases the Fisher is a better choice than the Chi-square. However, in many cases the Chi-square is preferred because the Fisher is difficult to calculate.

The one-sided probability for the Fisher is calculated by generating all tables that are more extreme than the table given by the user, in one direction. The p-values of these tables are added up, including the p-value of the table itself. The single-sided p-value is the summed probability of all more extreme or similar tables compared with the given table (notation p(Observed >=Expected)). There is also a p-value of the relationship going in the other direction. This is calculated by taking all the tables which are less extreme or more extreme in the opposite direction (notation: O<=E). Do not take too much notice of this p-value; it is not so important. However, it is mentioned in the textbooks and SISA does not want to deprive you of this information.

There are a number of theories about how to present double-sided p-values (Agresti, 1992). Data on the basis of two of these theories are presented. First, the sum of small p-values. For the sum of small p-values all tables are generated which are possible given the margins. All p-values of the same size or smaller than the point probability are added up to form the cumulative p-value. The result is relevant to the notation p(O>=E | O<=E). Statisticians usually recommend this method. Another method of estimating the double-sided p-value is to take twice the single-sided probability. The notation for this method is the same as for the method of small p-values. Simulations show that the p-value for the method of small p-values not including the point probability {p(O>E | O<E)} is often closer to the Chi-square. You can compare the relevant p-values and the Chi-squares yourself. Lastly, note that the difference between p(O>=E | O<=E) and p(O>E | O<E) and the problem of which p-value to compare with the Chi-square is dependent on the amount of continuity inherent in the table.

### Chi-Squares

#### *For all Tables*

In all tables the Chi-square test tests for the model of independence between the row and the column marginal. They ask the question if knowledge of the row variable predicts someone's score on the column variable, and vice versa. For example, does someone's sex 'predict' his or her income, or does someone's schooling 'predict' his or her occupation? Independence is the situation that sex does not predict income, and that schooling does not predict occupation.

The following chi-square tests are available:

Pearson's Goodness-of-Fit (in all tables) (preferred)

Maximum Likelihood (in all tables) (second best)

Mantel-Haenszel(in 2 by 2 table) (not often used)

Yates (in 2 by 2 table) (Pearson with continuity correction)

Empty rows are ignored and the table is reduced before analysis. An empty-zero-cell is not ignored if it is located beside a valid cell.

### *Lambda*

Goodman and Kruskal's Lambda is an example of a Proportional Reduction in Error (PRE) measure. PRE measures work by taking the ratio of: (1) an error score in predicting someone's most likely position (in a table) using relatively little information; with: (2) the error score after collecting more information. In the case of Lambda we compare the error made when we only have knowledge of the marginal with the reduced error after we have collected information regarding the inside of the table. Two Lambda's are produced. First, how much better are we able to predict someone's position on the row marginal if we also know the distribution of individuals in the table compared with only having knowledge of the row marginal, or in causal terms, how likely is it that the column scores 'cause' the row scores via the inside of the table (Lambda A). Second, how much better are we able to predict someone's position on the column marginal if we also know the distribution of individuals in the table compared with only having knowledge of the column marginal, or in causal terms, how likely is it that the row scores 'cause' the column scores via the inside of the table (Lambda B). The program gives the proportional improvement.

## Odds Ratio

### *For Two by Two Table*

The odds ratio takes values between zero ('0') and infinity. One ('1') is the neutral value and means that there is no difference between the groups compared; close to zero or infinity means a large difference. An odds ratio larger than one means that group one has a larger proportion than group two, if the opposite is true the odds ratio will be smaller than one. If you swap the two proportions, the odds ratio will take on its inverse (1/OR).

The odds ratio gives the ratio of the odds of suffering some fate. The odds themselves are also a ratio. To explain this we will take the example of traditional versus alternative surgery. If 10% of operations results in complications, then the odds of having complications if traditional surgery is used equals 0.11 (0.1/0.9, you have a 0.11 times higher chance of getting complications than of not getting complications). 12.5% of the operations using the alternative method result in complications, giving odds of 0.143 (0.125/0.875). The odds ratio equals 0.778 (0.11/0.143). You have a 0.778 times higher chance of getting complications than of not getting complications, in traditional as compared with alternative surgery. The inverse of the odds ratio equals 1.286. You have a 1.286 times higher chance of getting complications than of not getting complications, in alternative as compared with traditional surgery. This takes some getting used to, we admit, but it has its advantages.

The odds ratio can be compared with the Risk Ratio. The risk ratio is easier to interpret than the odds ratio. However, in practice the odds ratio is used more often. This has to do with the fact that the odds ratio is more closely related to frequently used statistical techniques such as logistic regression. Also, the odds ratio has the attractive property that, however you turn the table, it will always take on the same value or the inverse (1/odds) of that value in predicting someone's score after collecting additional information.

**Ordinal Association**

***For Seven by Two and Three by Three Table***

The selection 'Ordinal Association' will give you Kendall's Tau-a and Goodman and Kruskal's Gamma for testing ordinal associations, with their respective sample standard deviations and p-values. Tau-a is the difference between the number of concordant and discordant pairs divided by the total number of pairs; Gamma is the difference between the number of concordant and discordant pairs divided by the sum of concordant and discordant pairs. Gamma usually gives a higher value than Tau and is (for other reasons as well) usually considered to be a more satisfactory measure of ordinal association. The p-values are supposed to approach the exact p-value for an ordinal association asymptotically, and the program shows that they generally do that reasonably well. But, beware of small numbers: the p-values for the gamma and Tau become too optimistic!

The Gamma is calculated in a two by two table by way of the Yule's Q.

Testing the program showed that calculation of the standard errors of Gamma and Tau (to an even higher degree) is cumbersome if large numbers of cases are involved. If no p-value is given for the Tau, the p-value for the Gamma is also valid for the Tau. If calculations are impossible, the NaN result is given.

## T-test Proportions

### *For two by Two Tables*

In this module two proportions/percentages with their respective standard deviations and standard errors are at the center of attention. The two proportions concerned are first, the proportion of cases in column one which is located in row one of a two by two table, and second, the proportion of cases in column two which is located in row one. These same two proportions are at the center of interest in the NNT procedure.

Following some statistics about the two proportions the difference between the proportions is calculated, the standard error of this difference and the Confidence Interval of the difference. In the case of proportional data, these statistics can be obtained directly from the proportions themselves.

Lastly, the t-test is presented. The t-test gives the probability that the difference between the proportions has been caused by chance fluctuation. The t-test given is one-sided, in other words, it is assumed that before doing the test you had a hypothesis that one proportion of the two proportions was bigger than the other proportion. If you did not have such a prior hypothesis, and you only aim to test for a possible difference between the proportions, you need to do a double-sided test; in this case you should multiply the p-value by two.

The t-test is basically not valid for testing the difference between two proportions. However, the t-test in proportions has been extensively studied, has been found to be robust, and is widely and successfully used in proportional data. With one exception: if one of the proportions is very close to zero, one or minus one, you will do better with Fisher's exact test.

### *Intracorrelation/Kappa*

This module does intra-correlation calculations for dichotomous or binary yes/no type outcome variables according to the method proposed by Fleiss (1982) and including an addition to consider multi-level effects as proposed by Donner & Klar (1994). The intra-correlation coefficient is used for a number of purposes, two of which are discussed here. First the intra-correlation coefficient is used as an alternative to the kappa measure of agreement in case of multiple raters or judges considering the presence or absence of a trait on a larger number of items (objects) or individuals (subjects). High kappa means that there is a high level of agreement between the judges with regard to the presence of the trait. In the table each row pertains to the scoring of one judge, the first column shows the number of individuals having been scored 'positive', the second column the number of individuals having been scored 'negative'.

Second the intra-correlation is used as a measure of clustering in data which is collected using a multistage, multilevel, procedure of data collection. This is the case if, for example, a number of schools are selected randomly and in each school a number of pupils is sampled for study. The analysis is taking place at the pupil level. If there is intra-correlation the standard errors of statistics at the pupil level are estimated too narrow, tests become statistically significant too quickly and confidence intervals will be too small. The intra-correlation coefficient gives you a view as to what extent the observations at the individual level are influenced by clustering of observations in higher level groups, which is the case if, for example, schools are particularly good, and others particularly bad, at the trait measured with the dependent variable. If the intra-correlation coefficient equals 0 the schools are not different with regard to the independent variable, all the pupils could have been sampled from a single school and the result of the analysis would have been the same. The number of pupils is the correct sample size. If the intra-correlation coefficient equals 1 the schools are totally different and pupil performance is totally influenced by the school, effective sample size is the number of schools, and not the number of pupils. The method by Fleiss can be seen as the case of a single proportion, the proportion of pupils that passed a test. Each row in the table pertains to the result of one school, the first column shows the number of pupils having been scored 'positive' the second column the number of pupils having been scored 'negative'. It should be noted that the fast developing sample-resample, bootstrapping, methodology is a powerful, but unfortunately still complex, alternative to the use of the intra-correlation coefficient in clustered data.

The procedure calculates the intra-correlation coefficient, the significance of the intra-correlation coefficient, the standard error for the overall proportion when there is no intra-correlation, the standard error when there is full intra-correlation and the corrected standard error given the observed level of intra-correlation. On the basis of these three standard errors three confidence intervals are calculated.

## Number Needed to Treat (NNT)

### *For Two by Two Table*

Number Needed to Treat (NNT) is a measure which is becoming increasingly popular in the medical field. This measure is the reciprocal of the absolute risk-difference (ard=|proportion1-proportion2|) and expresses the number of persons to be treated to 'cure' one person.

The measure has some very appealing properties in interpretation, particularly in combination with cost calculation. An example: if no treatment is given 20% die, with treatment 15% die. NNT=20 (1/|0.2-0.15|). We need to treat 20 people to save one life. But now we develop a preventive program in a completely different area of health care and succeed in bringing the mortality down from 45% to 44.5%. NNT=200 (1/|0.45-0.445|). We need to apply our preventive program to at least 200 people to save one life. This does not seem very effective compared with treatment.

However, the cost of treatment is $ 200 per person, prevention costs $ 10 per person. The cost per life saved equals $ 4000 (20*200) for treatment against $ 2000 (200*10) for prevention. Prevention is highly cost effective and given a limited budget it should get precedence over treatment.

This way one can do quite a number of nice comparisons. A paper by Schulzer and Mancini gives some examples. In the program, confidence intervals for the NNT are calculated according to two methods. First the method suggested by Schulzer and Mancini, based on the Geometric distribution, and second the method suggested by Cook and Sacket, based on inverting the confidence interval of the difference between two means. The method suggested by Cook and Sackett is more often used in practice. The method suggested by Schulzer and Mancini is rather more interesting theoretically. Please note that whatever method is used, confidence intervals for the NNT are nonsensical if the difference between the two means is not statistically significant, i.e., if the probability of the t-value is more than 0.025 (in the case of a 95% confidence interval). The confidence interval for the NNT should NEVER be used for hypothesis testing. It is there for your information only. Use the t-test for hypothesis testing.

**Agreement Models**

Most models in tables are intended to test for statistical independence between the row and the column variable. They ask the question if knowledge of the row variable predicts someone's score on the column variable, and vice versa. For example, does someone's sex 'predict' his or her income, or does someone's schooling 'predict' his or her occupation? In these cases, independence would mean that sex does not predict income, and that schooling does not predict occupation.

However, one can also look at the pattern of the observations: the way they are distributed in a table. Examples of such models are migration or mobility models, in which we study the possible difference in the geographical or social location of individuals between two points in time, and agreement models, in which we compare the responses of different individuals on the same issue. All these models assume that observations are disproportionally more frequently located on the main diagonal, which is equivalent to the hypothesis that people did not migrate, were not mobile and agree. In other words, people tend to have the same score on two occasions and will be located on the main diagonal in a table (the main diagonal in a table is usually from the upper left, the 1,1 cell, to the lower right corner. In SISA tables the main diagonal is colored yellow). The basic migration/mobility/agreement model tests the hypothesis (H1) that the observations are disproportionally present on the diagonal as opposed to the outer, non-diagonal cells. This hypothesis is tested against the (H0) hypothesis that the observations are randomly distributed.

Two procedures are implemented in here. The first, an exact model, tests the likelihood that the observations are less frequently in the outer non-diagonal cells than can be expected on the basis of chance alone. The second procedure is Kappa, the measure most often used in agreement models. Kappa does a similar test and also gives a quantitative description of the strength of the relationship. These two measures will be discussed in sections under separate headings.

It should be noted that usually the theory underlying the migration/agreement models is very powerful and it occurs only rarely that the models are not statistically significant. The analysis should therefore serve only as a starting-point for further study. Examples of appropriate questions are: do people move more often to the upper than to the lower triangle, or are people more likely to move to cells closer to the origin cells than to cells which are further away. Agresti (1990) and Fleiss (1980) discuss the issues and give some examples.

## Kappa

### *Two Measures are Presented*

Kappa is a measure of agreement and takes on the value zero when there are no more cells on the diagonal of an agreement table than can be expected on the basis of chance. Kappa takes on the value 1 if there is perfect agreement, i.e. if all observations are on the diagonal. It is considered that Kappa values lower than 0.4 represent poor agreement between row and column variable, values between 0.4 and 0.75 fair to good agreement, and values higher than 0.75 excellent agreement.

Bowker Chi-square tests to see if there is a difference in the scoring pattern between the upper and the lower triangle (excluding the diagonal). If the Bowker Chi-square is statistically significant there is a difference: in other words, the pattern of scoring in the upper triangle is not the same as the lower triangle. Note that the pattern of scoring between the two triangles is dependent on two factors. First, whether there is a 'true' difference in the pattern of scoring. Second, the level of marginal heterogeneity. Marginal heterogeneity means that the marginals are different; this increases the Bowker Chi-square. The Bowker Chi-square is the same as the McNemar Chi-square in a two by two table.

## References

Agresti A. (1990), "Categorical Data Analysis", New York & Chichester, John Wiley and Sons.

Agresti A. (1992), "A Survey of Exact Inference for Contingency Tables", Statistical Science, 7(1):131-177.

Cook R.J., Sackett D.L. (1995) , "The Number Needed to Treat: A Clinically Useful Measure of Treatment Effect", *British Medical Journal*, 310:452-454.

4. Donner A., Klar N. (1994), "Methods for Comparing Event Rates in Intervention Studies when the Unit of Allocation is a Cluster", *American Journal of Epidemiology*, 140(3):279-289.

Fliess J.L. (1981), "Statistical Methods for Rates and Proportions", New York & Chichester, John Wiley and Sons.

Fleiss J.L. (1982), "Statistical Methods for Rates and Proportions", 2nd edition. New York [etc.], John Wiley.

Schultzer M., Mancini G.B.J. (1996), " 'Unqualified Success' and 'Unmitigated Failure': Numbers-Needed-to-Treat-Related Concepts for Assessing Treatment Efficacy in the Presence of Treatment induced Adverse Effects", *International Journal of Epidemiology*, 25(4):704-712.

# 14

# Geotrig

### Introduction

GEOTRIG is a collection of geologically-related geometric and trigonometric problem solvers for windows.

We can calculate the following by using this tool.

- Height
- 3-point Problem
- True Dip
- Apparent Dip
- Vertical Exaggeration
- Map Thickness(from Dist)
- Drilled Thickness
- Map Thickness(from Xyz)

### Height

The height estimator program is used to calculate the height of an object based on the distance from the object and the angle between the viewer and the object.

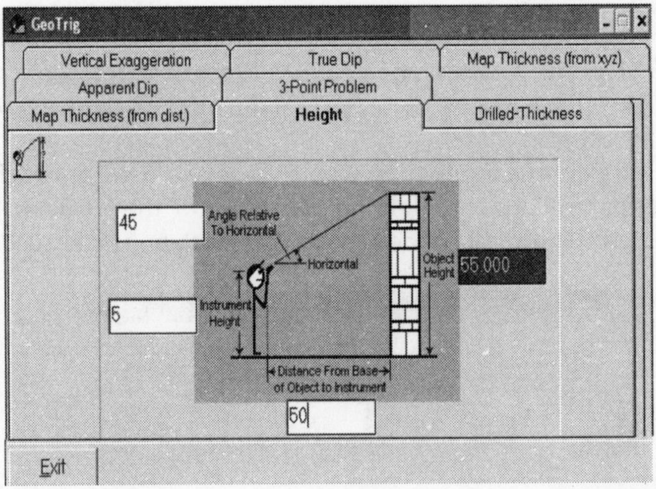


## 3-point Problem

This program calculates the strike and dip of a plane given three points along the plane.

*Note:* All points must be in the same units. For example, this program will not produce a correct answer if the easting and northings are in UTM's while the elevations are in feet.

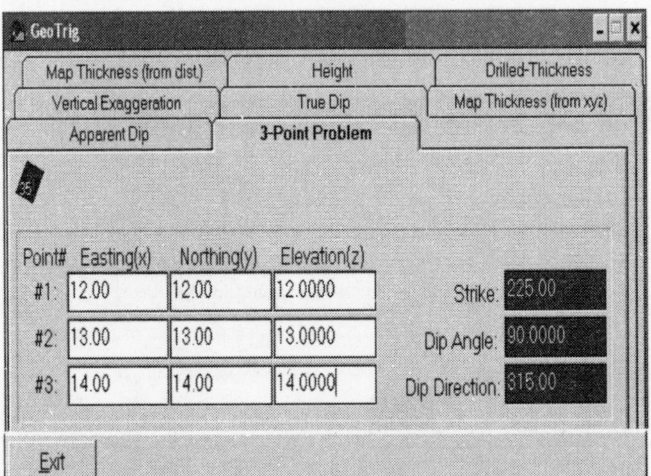

## True Dip

The True Dip Calculator calculates the true dip amount and dip direction based on two apparent dip amounts and apparent dip directions.

An example application would involve a roadcut in which an apparent dip is visible on each side of the roadcut. The apparent dip direction is defined by the orientation of the roadcut.

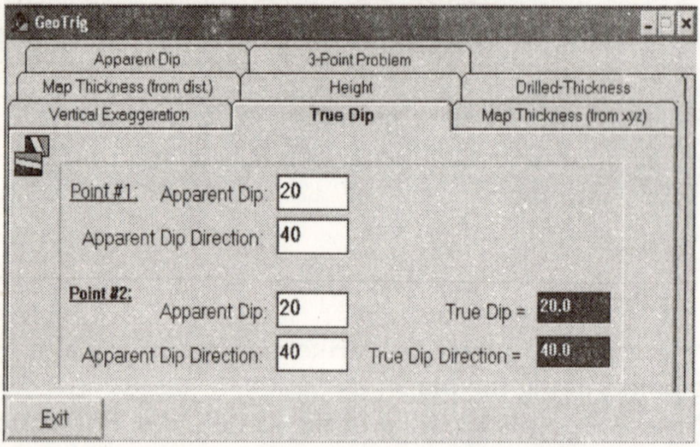


## Apparent Dip

The Apparent Dip calculator computes the apparent dip angle of a plane given the true dip angle the true dip angle direction and the apparent dip angle direction .this program is useful

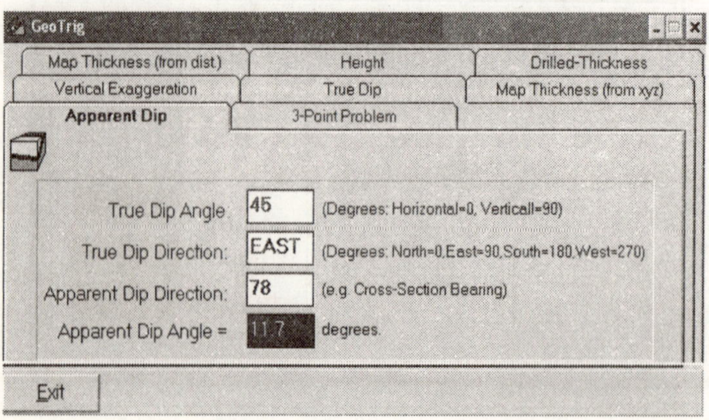

for applications such as cross-section construction in which the orientation of the cross-section is not necessarily equal to the dip direction.

## Vertical Exaggeration

The vertical Exaggeration calculator is used to calculate the vertical exaggeration factor and exaggerated dip angles when constructing cross-sections.

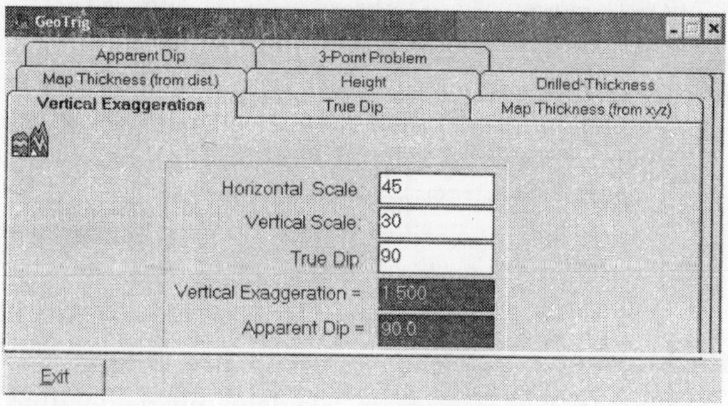


## Map Thickness (From Dist)

The Map Thickness program calculates the true thickness of a geologic unit based on the strike and dip of the formation and the upper and lower contacts.

*Note:* The dip-direction and dip must be entered in degrees.

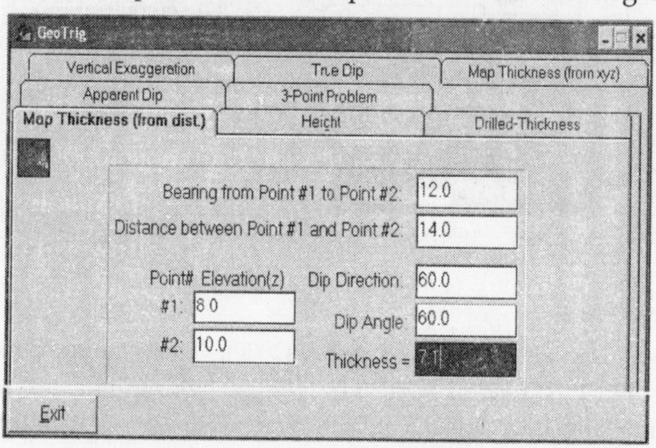

## Map Thickness (From Xyz)

The Map Thickness program calculates the true thickness of a geologic unit based on the strike and dip of the formation and the upper and lower contacts.

*Note:* The dip direction and dip must be entered in degrees.

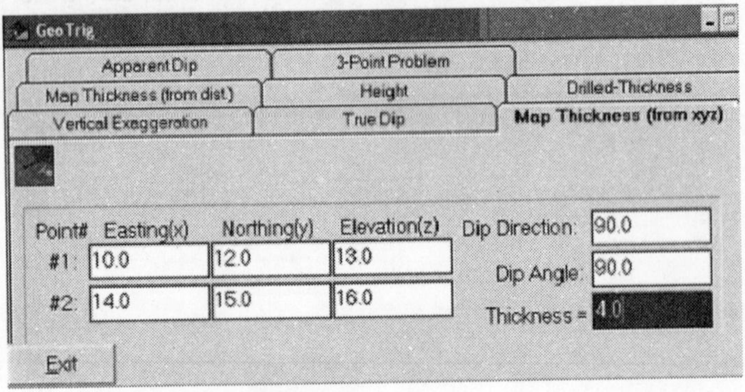


## Drilled-thickness

The Drilled-Thickness program calculates any field within the true thickness formula. Enter depths as absolute depths or elevations relative to sea level. Press the "=" button to calculate a value based on the other variables.

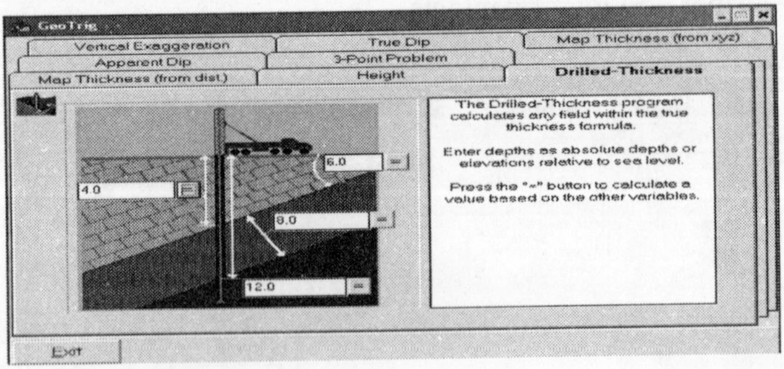


## References

Jiawei Han and Michiline Kamber (2000), "Data Mining–Concepts and Techniques", Morgan Kaufmman Publishers.

John Wang, Encyclopedia of Data Warehousing and Data Mining.

# 15

# MA (Mortality Analysis)

## Input

Input for each of the two input fields consists of rows of age categories, which at least contain an indicator of the age concerned for each category, the size of the population for that category, the total number of death in each age category, the number of death in an age category for a specific cause of death-k, the average proportion of time the death in an age category lived in that age category a, the proportion of the death of cause k. The age indicator gives the age up to the highest age concerned in the category. Thus, 0 contains the age group 0, 4 contains the age groups 1 up to and including age 4, 9 contains the ages 5 up to and including age 9, etc.

In the last category you give the age from, thus 85 means death aged 85 and older. Total number of death is smaller than the number of people in the population; number death due to a specific cause is smaller than the total number of death. Proportion lived by the death in an age category is a small positive number in between the values zero and one. The data is default read row-wise, the program considers that each row of data concerns an age category. The data can also be read "free", the program reads the data and tries to make sense of it. You can select between row-wise and free in the input options tab sheet.

You can cut and paste the data into the input field from a spreadsheet or word processor or type it into the input field manually. You can also read data from a *.txt file into the visible -current- population field using the open option in the file menu. There are a number of ready-made data sets available under the "read" button in the toolbar.

The program will ignore lines of text, which contain the words "Comment" or "comment" and lines that do not contain a number. Lines which contain the word "Title" or "title" will be read into the title array and these lines will appear in appropriate places in the output.

**Mortality**

The program will try to read a number from that line. Lines that contain the words "variance": the program will try to read a number from that line too. Beware to not include non-numerical symbols such as "e" or "E" in a line containing a number (i.e. variance), that will cause confusion.

Please be careful with continental European style decimal commas for the fractions, they are not accepted as valid, should be decimal dots. Any character that does not have a numerical function will be considered to be a separator between two numbers. There is a maximum of 150 age categories.

Characters with a numerical function are: '0'..'9','.','e','E','-','+'. All other characters are considered to be non-numerical. The tab setting sometimes causes the data in the input box to look strange. That is not serious.

**Analyze Options**

Method for discounting is discussed on another page. Tick one of the analyze options to determine which method you want to use after having read the discussion.

Include ai considers fraction of life lived in the age category of death in the calculation of the YPLL and LYPLL. The default option is "Yes". In the case of "No" it is considered that the death all die at the beginning of each period, thus, using the "No" setting the death aged 14 all die on exactly their 14th birthday. In the case of the "Yes" setting they die on average at the a-th fraction into their 14th life year, or, in general, into the age category concerned. Customarily this fraction is considered in calculating the YPLL, but not in calculating the LYPLL. Note that for the (L)YPLL all causes the first fraction in column 5 is used, for the (L)YPLL due to a specific cause k the second fraction in column 6 is used.

Give the annual discount rate into the box "discount at". Default set at 1.5% per annum. If you want to only partially eliminate k as a cause of death give the elimination percentage into the box "eliminate k at". Default set at 100%, or full elimination, of cause k. Show determines which tables are presented in the output. Please note that also under the output tab sheet preferences with regard to the output can be set.

Show wi gives you the weight or value of each additional life year from a particular age onwards. It gives the discounted weights in a single quite long table and the.

## CMF

The Comparative Mortality Figure (CMF) is primarily used to compare two directly standardized rates obtained by standardizing the mortality rates of two different populations on a single standard. Direct standardization is used in calculating the two rates. Calculations for the CMF come from the book by Breslow and Day. For the CMF the data is compared in numbers per 100.000 (or some other denominator) of the population. This number can be set on the General Options tab sheet. Note that the program will also calculate the CMF in case age specific mortality is found in the standard population. In this particular case the standard population death rates are standardized to its own population. The program will also calculate the CMF if it finds a "mortality" number in the standard population data field, it considers that this number is the total number of death in the standard population. In principle this number of death can be based on any rate standardized to the population in the population field concerned. The program will automatically put a number of deaths based on the standardized rate in the standard population input field if you request the program to do that.

This will enable you to compare the standard rate from an analysis with the standardized rate from a subsequent analysis.

**Compare Options**

This options page allows you to set instructions for how the compare analysis is done. If the "use cause k" option is not ticked the total number of death is used in comparing the two populations; if ticked the number of death due to cause k. is used. If a number of death due to cause k is not found for one or both of the populations the total number of death is used for the population concerned whether the box is ticked or not. If you tick "explain" you get a very basic explanation of what you find in the output. If you tick "apply age limits" the compare analysis is only done for the age groups specified in the general options page. If you want tests of statistical significance for the risk-ratio, CMF, SMR, or the difference in life expectancy, tick the "statistical significance" box. Tick "show CMF" to get the CMF analysis. To make a CMF analysis possible the program has to find age specific mortality in the index population.

Tick "Rate in Standard's Field" if you want the directly standardized rate of an analysis and it's variance to be written to the population field of the standard population. To the standard population field is written the number of death that would occur in the standard population if it had the same age specific mortality as the index population. The accompanying variance is based on the size and structure of the index population and re-weighted to consider the size of the standard population. After replacing the index population with another index population then after calculating the standardized rate for the second population the program will take the ratio (CMF) of the standardized rates of the first and the second population. For example, if you want to compare Virginia with Iowa, or Italy with Spain, first calculate the standardized rates for Virginia or Italy using the US or EU standard populations respectively, save the standardized rates and their variances to the standard population's input field, then standardize the data for Iowa or Spain and the program will automatically take the ratio of the new and the previous standardized rate.

Tick "show SMR" to get the SMR analysis. To make an SMR analysis possible the program has to find age specific mortality in the standard population.

Tick "compare life expectancies" to compare the life expectancies of the two populations. First, the life expectancies are calculated on the full data, which will be different for the two populations if the age distributions differ. Note that this difference can be a cause of a difference in life expectancy, whereby the life expectancy is particularly sensitive to differences in the age structure of the oldest age groups. If the "statistical significance" box is ticked the statistical significance of the difference between life expectancies is shown; otherwise the confidence interval of the difference between the life expectancies is shown. If the "use cause k" option is ticked the life expectancies excluding death from cause k are compared, if no data on cause k is available the instruction is ignored for one or both of the populations. If the populations have a different age structure, then after the two populations have been given the same (shorter) age structure the difference in life expectancy is calculated again. In this latter case, if the "use cause k" option is ticked the analysis is not done.

**Mortality Adjusted YPLL**

An important methodological problem with the YPLL is the fact that this measure does not consider competing causes of death. If the death of a group of people is prevented the fact that these people can die from other causes before the upper cut-off point in calculating the YPLL is reached, is not considered. Particularly in the case of populations with high mortality this can lead to an overestimation of the importance of preventing a particular cause of death. For this situation this SISA program introduces the mortality adjusted YPLL, were it is considered that survivors from a removed cause of death k have a certain probability of dying from competing causes in future years.

Note that the LYPLL, which is based on the life-table and not on the difference between age of death and a future cut-off point, does consider compete.

## Direct Standardization

Direct standardization is the case were the age specific mortality rates from the index, which is mostly the smaller population in which we are interested, is multiplied with the age structure of a standard. The results is the standardized number of death relative to a certain fixed denominator, mostly 100000. This denominator number can be set on the General Options tab sheet. You can compare the standardized rate with another standardized rate that has been standardized in the same way. This other rate can be:

(1) data from another population.

(2) data from the same population from different time periods; or even .

(3) data from different groups in the same population. The two rates can be compared directly or the CMF, the ratio of the two rates, can be used. The standard can be theoretical, such as the world standard or the US 2000 standard, but often the age distribution of a larger existing population is used.

Age specific death rates for the standard population are not required to do direct standardization. The age standardized rate and its variance, after being re-weighted to be representative for the standard population, can be written to the standard population input field for subsequent analysis using the "Rate in Standard's Field" tick box in the compare options tabsheet causes of death.

## Discounting

Discounting is used to weigh years in the near future as more important compared with years in the far away future. Mostly all future years of life are weighed equally in calculating the YPLL and the LYPLL; for example, no difference is made between the loss of the life years 25-29 compared with the life years 60-64, for an individual who dies at 24. Particularly in the case of peri-natal and infant death this has the consequence that a large number of years of lost life are accumulated, many in the far away future. It is usual to discount financial/ money data at or slightly above the rate of inflation as time progresses. So if you use the data to do a cost benefit analysis discounting seems appropriate (at about 5%). Discounting of life is considered much more problemaic and there is a philosophy that it is incorrect to consider future life-years of less value an current life-years. This is certainly not the case for many individuals; the immediate gratification of smoking a cigarette mostly weighs more heavily compared with the possibility of a future early death. However, at the level of life in a society discounting might not be right and it is considered that no discounting or only a modest level of discounting is appropriate (at about 1.5%). Health economists in the U.S. advice to discount at 3%.

**YPLL and LYPLL**

The YPLL measures for a group of individuals the total number of years these people would have additionally lived up to some point in the future, would they not have died. Mostly, as the age up to which life is "gained", the life expectancy for a population or the age of productivity, from 15 to 65 or 70, are chosen. If the life expectancy is used as the cut-off point the terminology Lifetime Years of Potential Life Lost (LYPLL) is used, in the case of an age limit being used the term YPLL is used. Sometimes the YPLL is also named as the PYLL, Potential Years of Life Lost. It concerns exactly the same concept.

An important methodological problem with the YPLL, but not the LYPLL, is the fact that this measure does not consider competing causes of death. If the death of a group of people is prevented the fact that these people can die from other causes before the upper cut-off point in calculating the YPLL is reached, is not considered. Particularly in the case of populations with high mortality this can lead to an overestimation of the importance of preventing a particular cause of death. For this situation this SISA program introduces the mortality adjusted YPLL, were it is considered that survivors from a removed cause of death k have a certain probability of dying from competing causes in future years. Another methodological problem is that the YPLL is highly sensitive to population age structure and findings regarding the costs of a disease are difficult to generalize from one population to another.

The life table describes the process of mortality in a population. The life table can be considered to be an old and distinguished predecessor of methods such as Kaplan-Meyer or Cox-Regression. A life table is a hypothetical construct with age specific death rates, the chance to die in a single year in a particular age category, as input (the 'M' column); and remaining years of life left, or life expectancy, at various ages as an important output (the 'e' column). What the life table represents is what a cohort of denominator (mostly a 100,000 is used) babies would experience in terms of mortality and age structure had they have the age specific death rates, which are based on the current mortality experience of a population, as given in the 'M' column. There are various interesting things one can do. The q column gives the probability for a person who is born into an age category to die in that category. Some simple methods applied to the I column can be used to determine the probability to survive from one age up to another age, this column is for example used to calculate the mortality adjusted YPLL. Lastly, life table analysis does not have to be limited to demography or epidemiology. It can be used in estimating the life expectancy after medical operations or the life expectancy of televisions or other industrial products. Similarly, death does not necessarily have to be the outcome studied, however, few examples exist were something else is used. You can compare two life tables using the compare mode.

**Fieller**

The Fieller Confidence Interval has two applications:

(1) The Fieller estimate is a method to estimate the approximate confidence interval around an Standardize Mortality Ratio (SMR) when there is error in both the observed and the expected value and the number of cases is relatively large. For large numbers, the Fieller provides a good method to approximate the results of the exact Binomial/Incomplete Beta method, which

is also presented in the module. The Incomplete Beta method is the more suitable exact method for estimating the confidence interval around an SMR with error in both the observed and the expected values, but the method may not work well for a very large number of observations.

(2) The Fieller method makes it possible to take covariance between the observation and the expectation into account. This would be relevant if the observations are a subset of the data on the basis of which the expectation was calculated. For example, the SMR is often calculated by applying data of the national population to the local population. The mortality in Hampshire could be compared with the national mortality by using an expectation calculated by applying the national age-specific death rates (the standard) to the population of Hampshire (the index). A major crash on the motorway in Hampshire would show up in both the observation of the number of deaths in Hampshire and in the national death rates, which are used to calculate the expectation. Silcocks (1994) proposes the correlation 'q' parameter for the Fieller in such a case to be: q=Sum(d(i)*n(i)/N(i))/d-tot whereby, d(i) number of deaths in the index population in the i-th age band, n(i) number of individuals in the i-th age band of the index population which are part of the standard population, N(i) number of individuals in the i-th age band in the standard population, d-tot, total number of deaths in the index population.

The Fieller will give an estimate only if the expected value is larger than one. Thus, real cases or a mean of real cases is considered and not a proportion.

**Mortality Adjusted YPLL**

An important methodological problem with the YPLL is the fact that this measure does not consider competing causes of death. If the death of a group of people is prevented the fact that these people can die from other causes before the upper cut-off point in calculating the YPLL is reached, is not considered. Particularly in the case of populations with high mortality this can lead to an overestimation of the importance of preventing a particular cause of death. For this situation this SISA program introduces the mortality adjusted YPLL, were it is considered that survivors from a removed cause of death k have a certain probability of dying from competing causes in future years.

Note that the LYPLL, which is based on the life-table and not on the difference between age of death and a future cut-off point, does consider competing causes of death.

### *Output Options*

Data used gives for both compare and analyze the data that is used in the output. It concerns the first table shown in the output.

Column numbers give the column number above the output data. These are not always consecutive; this is because the column numbers indicate the position in which the data is stored in the computer.

The two width boxes set the way the data is presented in the output field. This might be handy in case you have a low resolution monitor or if you want to neatly print the data. To effectuate a different tab setting the page has to be reset using the reset button in the toolbar, you will loose any output that is already on the page.

### PGLE

The spreadsheet calculates the Potential Gains in Life Expectancy (PGLE) after removing cause k, considering competing causes of death and following the examples by Chiang (1991). It gives the increase in the life expectancy should people no longer die from a particular cause of death. The PGLE is actuarially "correct", it allows for easy comparison between populations, and it does consider competing causes of death. However, gains in life expectancy are difficult to apply in a wider macro economic analysis.

**General Options**

Denominator sets the radix (n) for a number of calculations such as numbers of person years per n population lost in the case of the YPLL and what happens to a birth cohort sized n in the case of the life table or the number death per n of the population etc.

**Age Limits**

Default is from age 15 included up to but not including age 65. Set to any other value. Age limits are used in calculating the YPLL. You can limit comparing two populations to the age groups included in the age limits by ticking the "apply age limits" tick box in the compare options tab sheet.

By clicking the "show global parameters" button you get an overview of the value of all kinds of variables. This button is there for the programmers to check the program but it might also be handy for the user. If you believe that something is not right in the results of your analysis and that the program is the cause of the problem, this is the button to push for a first inspection of what the program is doing.

**Confidence Intervals**

Allows you to set the width of the confidence interval. Usually you would select a 95% confidence interval; this means that in 95% of research projects such as yours the sample mean will be within the stated interval. The alpha error is than 5%.

Default the, according to SISA; most appropriate confidence interval will be given for the various statistics given the situation. If you tick the "show confidence intervals" box you get many more.

**SMR**

SMR basically compares the mortality observed in the index-population with the mortality that could be expected, if the index-population had an age specific mortality pattern, which is comparable with the age specific mortality of the standard population. The SMR uses indirect standardization. Contrary to the CMF, the SMR reports the data in real empirical numbers, the number of death observed is divided by the number of death expected if the population studied -the index- would have had the same age specific death rates as the standard, the population we compare our data with. For calculating the SMR it is not necessary to have the age specific mortality figures for the index population, the age structure and the total number of death is adequate. If you only have the age structure for the index population in the input field you can enter the total number of death for the index population in the separate data box.

Exact confidence intervals are given when the number of cases is relatively low and approximations are given when the number of cases is larger. Poisson based confidence intervals are given considering error free expectations, this would be the case if the standard would be a hypothetical mortality schedule. We do not know of the existence of such a schedule. Other confidence intervals relate to the situation that the standard is an empirical population with observed mortality, for example, the mean population for the U.S. for the year 2000 and the observed numbers of death per five year age category in that year. Lastly, if the program believes that the index population might be a sub-population of the standard population the Fieller confidence interval is given which considers this case. Note that in the sub-population scenario the expectation is never error-free.

**Standard (-population)**

The standard concerns the data of the population to which you compare your specific population. Sometimes it concerns a hypothetical population, such as the U.S. standard 2000, and other times a larger population, the actual U.S. population on the 1st of July 2000. However, a standard population might sometimes be relatively small, for example, if we would want to directly compare Los Angeles with San Francisco. However, in this latter case we might prefer to use a method whereby we first compare both cities with a larger or a hypothetical standard population and then compare the standardized death rates of the two cities using the CMF. A discussion on the statistics of this second comparison can be found in Breslow and Day (1980). In the compare procedure the standard is presumed to be the population which is not in the visible field.

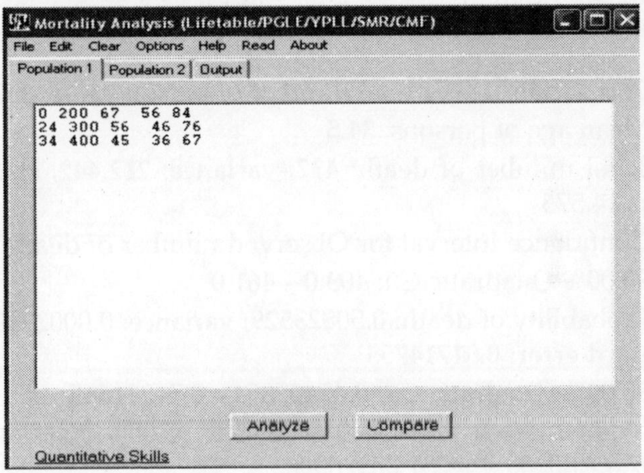


*Data read from Population 2*

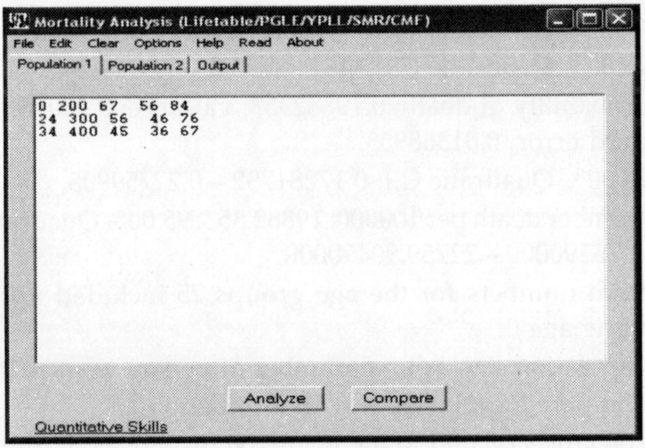


*** Lifetable Analysis ***
*** YPLL Analysis ***
*** Lifetable Analysis ***
*** YPLL Analysis ***

**The Given Data**

| # | *age* | *total D* | *Death.k* | *popul.* | *a(i)* | *a(i.k)* | *"age"* | *#.yr* |
|---|---|---|---|---|---|---|---|---|
| 1 | 0 | 67.00 | 45 | 300.0 | 78.000 | 0.100 | 0-0 | 1 |
| 2 | 24 | 98.00 | 79 | 200.0 | 76.000 | 0.500 | 1-24 | 24 |
| 3 | 34 | 267.00 | 45 | 350.0 | 67.000 | 0.500 | 25+ | 0 |

Population size or total number of person years: 850.0

Mean age of persons: 34.5

Total number of death: 432; variance: 212.442; standard error: 14.575

Confidence Interval for Observed number of death:

95.00% Quadratic C.I: 403.0 – 461.0

Probability of death: 0.50823529; variance: 0.00029403786; standard error: 0.01714753

95.00% Quadratic C.I: 0.47407854 – 0.54231665

Number death per 100000: 50823.529; 95.00% Quadratic C.I: 47407.85380000 – 54231.66520000.

Death caused by k:

Total number of death: 169; variance: 135.399; standard error: 11.636.

Confidence Interval for Observed number of death:

95.00% Quadratic C.I: 146.9 – 193.5.

Probability of death: 0.19882353; variance: 0.00018740322; standard error: 0.01368953.

95.00% Quadratic C.I: 0.17281732 – 0.22759905.

Number death per 100000: 19882.353; 95.00% Quadratic C.I: 17281.73190000 – 22759.90490000.

Total numbers for the age groups 25 included upto and including age 0:

Population size or total number of person years: 0.0

Compare Population 1: with Population 2:

The tables related to the below be display as output

***Statistics for population 1-***

***Statistics for population 2-***

***Direct standardization ****

-Population 1- is the index

-Population 2- is the index
***Indirect standardization****
-Population 1- is the index
-Population 2- is the index

## References

Breslow NE, Day NE. (1980), "Statistical Methods in Cancer Research", Vol. 2, The Design and Analysis of Cohort Studies. Lyon: International Agency for Research on Cancer.

Chiang C.L. (1968), "The Life Table and its Construction. In: Chiang C.L. Introduction to stochastic processes in Biostatistics", New York [etc.], John Wiley.

Chiang C.L. (1991), "Competing risks in mortality analysis", Annual Revue of Public Health, 12:281-307.

Fay M.P., Feuer E.J. (1997), "Confidence Intervals for Directly Standardized Rates: A Method based on the Gamma Distribution", Statistics in Medicine, 16:791-801.

Feinlieb M, Zarate A.O. (1992), "Reconsidering Age Adjustment Procedures", Vital and Health Statistics Reports, Series 4, No. 29. Centers for Disease Control and Prevention NCHS.

Fleiss J.L. (1982), "Statistical Methods for Rates and Proportions", 2nd edition. New York [etc.], John Wiley.

Gardner J.W., Sanborn J.S. (1990), "Years of Potential Life Lost-What does it measure?", Epidemiology, 1:322-329.

Lai D., Hardy R.J. (1999), "Potential Gains in Life Expectancy or Years of Potential Life Lost: Impact of Competing Risks of Death", *International Journal of Epidemiology*, 28:894-898.

Liddell F.D. (1984), "Simple exact Analysis of the Standardised Mortality Ratio", *Journal of Epidemiology and Community Health*, 38:85-88.

Newcombe R.G. (1998), "Two Sided Confidence Intervals for the Single Proportion: Comparison of Seven Methods", Statistics in Medicine, 17:857-87.

Silcocks P. (1994), "Estimating Confidence Limits on a Standardised Mortality Ratio when the Expected Number is not Error Free", *Journal of Epidemiology and Community Health*, 48:313-317.

Torgerson R.J., Raftery J. (1999), Economic Notes: *Discounting British Medical Journal*, 31.

# 16

## Magnetic

### The program, MAGNETIC.EXE(v.8.0.10)

The program is version 8.0.10 of MAGNETIC.EXE, by Robert Detenbeck, Professor Emeritus of Physics, University of Vermont, Burlington, VT 05405 [rdetenbe@uvm.edu]. It was written in Borland Delphi (v 1.0), and will run under Windows 3.1/95/98. The minimum configuration for satisfactory operation is a 486-DX/33 PC with 8 MB of memory, and a VGA monitor.



The original version of this program was written many years ago for use in a geophysics course for college sophomores, taught by Dr. Barry Doolan of the Department of Geology and Dr.Robert Detenbeck of the Department of Physics. The program permits students to compare the predictions of their own models, for magnetic anomalies over mid-ocean spreading ridges, with real experimental data. The geophysical situation is fascinating. Magnetic stripes on the ocean floor serve as a tape recorder of the reversals of the earth's magnetic field. The physics and geology are not hard to explain to students. However, calculations of the predictions of models are tedious without the help of a programmable computer, and discourage students from making models of their own and playing "what if..." games. Even a modest PC makes short work of the calculations, permitting students to test models and tinker with their details.

Even so, in early versions of the program, collecting the numbers required to specify a model tried the patience and organizational abilities of many students, sometimes to the point of tears.Successive versions of the program, rewritten in Power Basic, Turbo Pascal, and now Delphi, have become easier and easier to use.

Version 8.0, presented here, includes several easy-to-use editors designed especially for tinkering with models of mid-ocean spreading ridges. Hopefully it will increase the reward/ effort ratio for students.

This manual was rewritten for version 8.0.10. In general, the last decimal place changes with program changes too unimportant to be mentioned in the manual, so this manual should serve well with, for example, version 8.0.9. A change to version 8.1x would suggest that a manual for version 8.0x may be slightly out of date, but the program changes will still be minor. Version 9.0.0 of the program would involve major changes, such as altered formats for the data files, etc.

## Glossary

### *Typographic Conventions*

Underlined words refer to other Glossary entries. A capitalized word generally refers to a specific datum or set of data used by the program(e.g., see Traverse). Italics may be for emphasis, or to point out that a word is used within its own definition.

#### *Anomaly*

The geomagnetic field largely that of a magnetic dipole, varies in magnitude and direction from place to place. These variations on a global scale may be accompanied by smaller, localized variations due to nearby magnetic materials. The small, local variations are called *magnetic anomalies*. The most interesting ones, for the purposes of this program, are caused by magnetized blocks of cooled magma near spreading ridges on the ocean floor.

*Block*

A magnetized prismatic cylinder of rock on the ocean floor, with an infinite length parallel to t he spreading ridge. The magnetization of the block reflects the orientation of the earth's magnetic field at the time the block cooled through the Curie point of its ferromagnetic constituents. This is related to its distance from the ridge by the Spreading Rate of that ridge. Additional simplifying assumptions are built into the program, hopefully with no important loss of Generality.

(1) Blocks are distributed symmetrically across the ridge.

(2) Each block has a uniform magnetization.

(3) Each block has a single thickness.

(4) A ridge's spreading rate is constant in time.

*Blocks-model*

The ocean floor is modeled as a layer of magnetized prismatic cylinders (blocks), of infinite length parallel to the ridge, and therefore perpendicular to the Traverse. Each block has a location, a shape, a permanent magnetization and an age. The age of a block is related to its location and the Spreading Rate of the ridge. Since each block was created and magnetized during a particular period in the history of the Earth's magnetic field, a Blocks-Model assumes a corresponding geomagnetic history.

*Components*

The magnetic anomalies are produced by magnetized blocks on the sea floor, and are much smaller than the local geomagnetic field. A traverse may measure one or more of the components (see Coordinates), or the total field, depending on the types of instrumentation in use. Total Anomaly: This maximum measurable anomaly is the component of the blocks' field along the direction of the local geomagnetic field.

Vertical Anomaly. This is the projection of the Total Anomaly on the vertical direction. Within the program it is the Z *component*, positive downwards.

Horizontal Anomaly this is the projection of the Total Anomaly on the horizontal. X Component of the Anomaly this is the projection of the Total Anomaly on the horizontal traverse direction.

The positive X direction is the direction of the traverse.

Y Component this is the horizontal direction along t he ridge. In the approximation that the ridge is infinitely long, compared with the depth, there is no Y *component*.

*Model*

A *Model* is stored in a file whose name is of the form NAME.BLK. In addition to the name of its file, the Model should have a more detailed Title that will be displayed within the program. Because each Model is associated with a particular Traverse and a particular Blocks- Model of the ocean floor, the Title should suggest these associations.

*Normal*

As ferromagnetic rocks are formed at the spreading ridge and cool through the Curie point, they acquire a magnetization parallel to the geomagnetic field. By definition the present orientation of the geomagnetic field, in which the inclination in the Northern hemisphere is downward (positive), is *Normal*. During the long time period between reversals of the geomagnetic field, when one Block is formed, the wanderings of the magnetic poles are assumed to average out. The average magnetizing field is assumed to be that of a magnetic dipole aligned long the earth's axis. The Magnetization Declination of a Block will therefore be either 0(*Normal*) or 180 degrees (Reversed) and the Magnetization Inclination of each block can be calculated from its geographic latitude, the average Latitude of the Traverse.

*Reversed*

This adjective describes a permanently magnetized Block which was formed when the geomagnetic field corresponded to a dipole with a polarity reversed from that found today. See Normal.

*Spreading Rate*

At a mid ocean spreading ridge, new material is brought up from below in the form of molten rock, which cools to form new ocean floor. The resulting new ocean floor flows away from the ridge at a rate called the *spreading rate* of that ridge. Different ridges may have different spreading rates, but this program assumes that each ridge's spreading rate was const ant during the period in which the ocean floor beneath a traverse was laid down. The *Spreading Rate* of the Model is the value of this constant, of the order of 1 cm/yr (equivalent to 10 km/m.y.).

*Traverse*

In common usage, the *traverse* is the trip along which measurements are made. Here the capitalized word, *Traverse,* is used to mean a collection of the local geographic parameters, describing the location and direction of the trip and the terrestrial magnetic field, where the magnetic anomaly is to be measured. These parameters are common to the whole trip, as opposed to the description of the ocean floor block-by-block. They include the average latitude of the traverse (the longitude is no t required), the direct ion of the traverse, the altitude of the traverse (in case the measurement is by airplane), and the local inclination and declination of the Earth's magnetic field (the magnitude is not required). The horizontal direction of the traverse is perpendicular to that of the horizontal ridge. These two directions and the vertical define the coordinate system used in the program. See components and/or coordinates.

**Files**

The program file, MAGNETIC.EXE, and others listed below are produced by running the self-expanding, compressed file, MAGFILES.EXE with the select ion of a target directory.

### *Magnetic.exe*

This file is the main program, which can calculate a predicted magnetic anomaly from a complete Model of the situation.

### *Magnetic.hlp*

This is the help file for MAGNETIC.EXE. *.DAT These files contain graphs of data, to which the predicted magnetic anomaly can be compared. Usually a .DAT file contains a set of experimental data, recorded along a particular straight-line traverse across a region containing a mid ocean spreading ridge. Comments at the Beginning of the file should give the appropriate literature reference and description of the traverse. For some discussion of the .DAT files provided with the program files.

**Comparisons with Experiments**

The file will be an ASCII text file, of the form—

- Line 0: Title, identifying component and *brief* source description.
- Lines 1 to n: Comment lines, whose first character is a "*", followed by text. These are usually used for a more complete identification of the literature source.
- Lines n+1 to n+N: N data sets of t he form,

Column 1 (1 or more spaces) column 2 (1 space) columns 3, where column 1 is the location X in km along the traverse, column 2 is the anomalous magnetic field in n T, and column 3 is either blank or "u" or "d". If there are no gaps in the data, the third column is blank. If there is a gap, the next data point after the gap will have a "u" in column 3, signifying that the plotting pen is to appro ach that point with pen up. The next data point would have a "d", signifying pen-down from that point on.

The MAGNETIC program can also save a calculated anomaly graph as a .DAT file.

*.BLK. These files contain Models of the geophysical situation. Each Model includes a particular Traverse and a particular Blocks-Model of the ocean floor beneath it. The .BLK file contains numerical quantities describing the Traverse and

the Blocks-Model, sufficient to permit calculation of a predicted magnetic anomaly along the Traverse. The form of the file follows.

- Title: A brief, descriptive Title for the Model.
- Number of Blocks: Integer M, the number of blocks in the Model, must be even, because each block is mirrored on the other side of the spreading center. Only M/2 blocks are independent.
- Spreading Rate: Real decimal number, in cm/yr. One cm/yr produces a motion of 10 km in one million years.
- Latitude: Real decimal number, in degrees. The average geographic latitude of the traverse, positive in the Northern hemisphere.
- Direction of Traverse: Real decimal number, in degrees. The azimuthal angle of the traverse direction in the horizontal plane. Positive angles are East of geographic North.
- Declination of local geomagnetic field: Real decimal number, in degrees. The azimuthal angle of the horizontal component o f the local geomagnetic field, measured from geographic North. Positive angles are East of North.
- Inclination of local geomagnetic field: Real decimal number, in degrees. The angle of the local geomagnetic field, measured from the horizontal. Positive angles are downward.
- Altitude of Traverse: Real decimal number, in km. The altitude of the traverse, measured from sea level. Positive numbers are above sea level.
- BLOCK #1: Each block has five lines of data. The members of a pair of numbers on one line (e.g., X1, Z1) are separated by one or more spaces.

1. Name of Block: a brief textual description.
2. X1, Z1: X and Z coordinates of the top, left (minimum X) corner of Block #1 (has lowest values of X). Real decimal values are in km.

3. X2, Z2: X and Z coordinate of the top, right (maximum X) corner of Block #1.
4. Thickness, Magnetization: Thickness of Block #1 in km, and Magnetization of Block #1 in A/m, both real decimal values.
5. Azimuth and Dip of Block's remanent magnetization. Real decimal angles in degrees. Positive azimuth angles are East of North. Positive Dip angles are downward.

- Block #2: ...

  ...

- Block #M:

  Sample.BLK

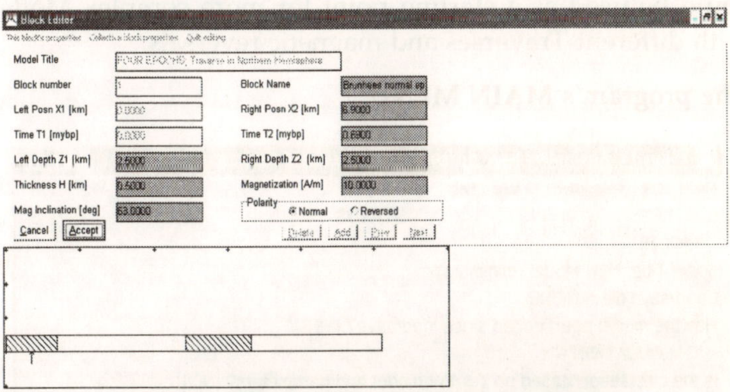


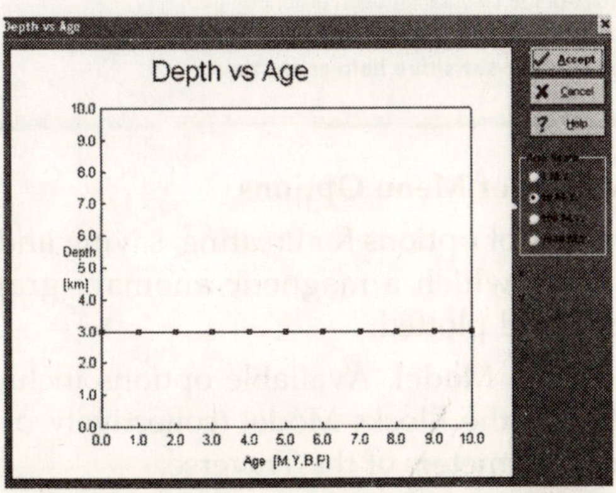

This sample .BLK file is a read-only file, provided with t he program. It contains parameters for a traverse at 45 degrees N latitude, with a Block-Model of four epochs and a spreading rate o f 1 cm/yr. It is commented, item-by-item, to help clarify the nature of a .BLK file. The comments can be viewed with an ASCII text editor, such as NOTEPAD.EXE or WORDPAD.EXE. When it is loaded into the program, MAGNETIC.EXE, the comments are ignored, and it can be edited by altering the Traverse, and adding to the blocks to create more complex models.

### Heirtzlr.BLK

This sample .BLK file is a read-only file, provided with the program. It contains a Block- Model proposed in a historically important paper by Heirtzler et al: JGR, v73, pp2119-2136. It could be used as a starting point for more complex Models with different Traverses and magnetic reversals.

### The program's MAIN MENU

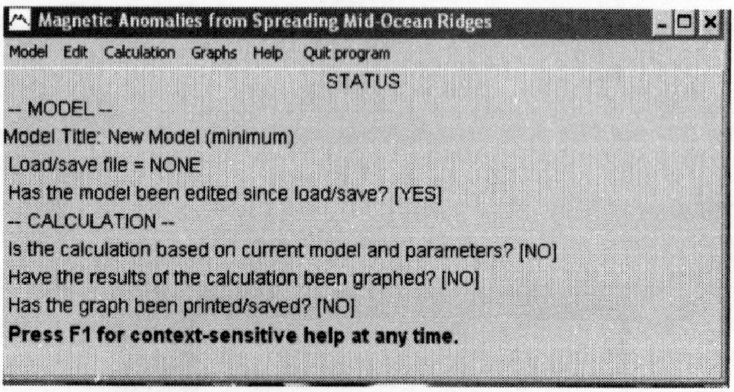


### Quick Summary of Menu Options

- Model: A set of options for creating, saving and loading a Model from which a magnetic anomaly graph can be calculated and plotted.
- Edit: Edit the Model. Available options include editing properties of the Blocks-Model (collectively or block-by-block) or parameters of the Traverse.

- Calculation: A set of options for setting up and/or beginning the calculation of the magnetic anomaly graph predicted by a particular Model. If the user wishes to deviate from the default parameters of the calculation (e.g., resolution, accuracy, calculation-time), some mathematical parameters of the calculation must be provided in addition to the Model.
- Graphs: Two kinds of graphs can be displayed, overlaid if desired. The first is a graph of the calculated magnetic anomaly, or any one of its components as a function of position along the specified traverse. The second is usually a graph of experimental data from an external file.
- Help: Display information and help concerning the program.
- Quit: End the program.

Details of menu options follow.

*Model*

A set of options for creating, editing, saving and loading a Model, from which a magnetic anomaly graph can be calculated and plotted.

**Load Model File:** Selecting this option initiates an Open-File Dialog, in which the user selects the name of an existing .BLK file, containing an already created Model. At the conclusion of a successful dialog, the selected Model will have been loaded into memory.

The Model in memory can be used as the basis for calculating a set of predicted magnetic anomalies, or it can be edited to produce a different Model.

**Save Model File:** Selecting this o patio n initiate a Save-File Dialog, in which the user select s the name of a new .BLK file in which to save the current Model. At the conclusion of a successful dialog, the selected Model will have been saved in a file, but will still be retained in memory.

**New Model:** This selection creates in memory a Minimum Model of two blocks with nominal parameter values. The Minimum Model can then be edited by t he user to produce any desired Model.

**Edit**

Edit either the Blocks Model or the Traverse by selecting the appropriate option. Edit Blocks in model. The Block Editor window includes five parts.

1. Title bar labeled "Block Editor";
2. Menu of possible modes for Block Editor;
   - This block's properties
   - Collective block properties
   - Quit editing
   - The default *Initial Mode* (See below);
3. Properties of the selected block;
4. Some control buttons; and a
5. Graphical display of the right half (X>0) of the Blocks-Model, with an arrow indicating that Block #1 (at X=0) has been selected. Normal magnetized blocks are shaded; Reversed blocks are not. Tick marks in the X direction (along the traverse) are separated by horizontal intervals of 10 km, with zero at the left and +X toward the right. Tick marks for depth (Z) are separated by 1 km, with zero at the top and +Z downward. Note that only blocks with X>0 need be edited; the other half of the model is assumed to be a mirror image.

In its *Initial Mode* the Block Editor displays data for the selected block, indicated by the arrow, in dimmed form. The choice of selected block *in this mode only* can be cont rolled by:

(a) Clicking on the [Next] or [Prev] buttons,
(b) By pressing the [>] or [<] keys, or
(c) Moving the mouse to the desired block and clicking on it.

The two other buttons available in this mode [Delete] the selected block, or [Add] a block at the right end, left end or interior of the selected block.

To change properties of the selected block, choose the menu item, [This block's properties], and edit the highlighted quantities.

This block's properties Change any of the highlighted properties. Note that some entries will be automatically cross-calculated to maintain consistency.

When you are satisfied, click the [Accept] button to record the changes in memory. If things get messed up, press [Cancel] to discard your changes. These are available for editing.

- Left Position X1 [km]: The horizontal distance from the spreading ridge to the nearer vertical edge of the block. For Block #1 it must be 0. For other blocks changing X1 of Block #N will automatically produce appropriate changes in the age T1 of Block #N, and in X2 and T2 of Block #N-1.
- Time T1 [mybp]: The age of the newest edge of the selected block, which is related to X1 by the Spreading Rate of the ridge (see Collective block properties). At a Spreading Rate of one cm/yr, a position change of 10 km corresponds to one million years change in age. The program automatically maintains consistency among X1, T1 of Block #N and X2, T2 of Block#N-1.
- Right Position X2 [km]: The horizontal position of the older vertical edge of the block.

  See X1 above.
- Time T2 [mybp]: The age corresponding to T2.
- Left Depth Z1 [km]: The depth to the edge of the block nearer to the ridge. The depth Z is measured positive downwards from sea level. If the traverse is not made at sea level, see Traverse in Model.
- Right Depth Z2 [km]: The depth to the older edge of the block.
- Thickness H [km]: The thickness of the block, which is assumed to be uniform across the block. The cross-sect ion of a block is taken to be a parallelogram with vertical edges, having corners at (X1,Z1), (X2,Z2), (X2,Z2+H), (X1,Z1+H).
- Magnetization [A/m]: The strength of the block's magnetization, assumed constant throughout the block.

- Magnetization Inclination [deg]: The Dip angle between the block's magnetization vector and the horizontal. A positive angle corresponds to a downward direction. Thus, a Normal block would have a positive Magnetization Inclination angle in the Northern hemisphere. You should initially adopt an axially-centered-dipole model for the earth's time-averaged field during each magnetic epoch or event. In that case the Magnetization Inclination can be calculated from the geographic Latitude of the Traverse (see Edit Traverse in model and Collective block properties below), and the Magnetization Declination will be 0 or 180 degrees. Later you might want to play around with the Inclinations to see how much they matter.
- Polarity: Switching from Normal to Reversed Polarity changes the sign of the Magnetization Inclination and switches the Magnetization Declination between 0 and 180 degrees.
- Magnetization Declination: This was omitted for lack of room. See Polarity, above. Collective block properties.
- Title of model: This is the t title of your Model, including both the Block-Model and the Traverse. You may want to change it after each set of changes to the Model. It is not the same as the name of the .BLK file.
- Spreading/Inclination/Thickness: Selecting this option brings up a window with three check boxes. Only those you check will be changed. You can:

1. Set a new Spreading Rate, which is always assumed to have the same value for the whole set of blocks at one ridge. It is useful to remember that 1 cm/yr corresponds to 10 km/million yrs.
2. Make every block have the same angle of Magnetization Inclination, as is appropriate for an axial-dipole model for the earth's magnetizing field. For a central axial dipole field, the Inclination angle, I, is related to the geographic Latitude, L, by the equation, tan (I) = 2 * tan (L).

3. Make every block have the same thickness. Simplicity might recommend this. What happens t o the anomalies if you double the magnetization of each block and simultaneously halve Its thickness?

- Depth vs. Age: This opt ion permits you to assign a functional relationship between the age of a block and its depth, as might be suggested by theories of ocean-floor cooling. Just drag the little squares around with the mouse to define a depth-vs.-age function for all of the blocks.
- Magnetization vs. Age: This option permits you to assign a functional relationship between the age of a block and the strength of its remnant magnetization. Just drag the little squares around with the mouse to define a magnetization-vs.-age function for all of the blocks.
- Reverse all blocks: This selection is useful in converting a Model from the Southern to the Northern hemisphere and vice versa, without editing the blocks one at a time.

Quit Editing

Leave the Block-Editor window, retaining all changes, and return to the startup window, containing the Main Menu.

*Edit Traverse in Model*

The frame in the Traverse Editor window surrounds seven editable, highlighted parameters which describe the Traverse.

**Title of Model**: This is actually a property of the entire Model, not just the Traverse. It can also be edited as a collective property of all the Blocks; therefore, this access to the Model Title is redundant. The name of the currently loaded Model (.BLK) File is listed above the frame, just for information.

**Spreading Rate of Ridge** [cm/yr]: Each ridge, across which a traverse is made while measuring magnetic anomalies, is assumed to have a Spreading Rate, the constant speed at which new crust moves away from that ridge. The program does not deal with time-varying spreading rates. The value of the

Spreading Rate can also be edited as a collective property of all the Blocks.

**Latitude of Traverse** [deg +N]: This is the average geographic latitude of the Traverse. If the geomagnetic field were due to an axial, centered dipole, one could calculate the direction of the field from this value and whether the dipole was normal or reversed. Because the magnetization of each Block took place over a long time, an axial-centered-dipole field is an appropriate assumption for t he direct ion of the average magnetization.

**Direction of Traverse** [deg +E]: The Traverse is assumed to follow a straight-line horizontal path, perpendicular to the line of the ridge. This defines t he direction of the X axis in the program. The azimuthal angle of this path from geographic North, taking positive angles to go from North toward East, thus suffices to specify the directions of both the Traverse and the ridge (horizontal Y axis in the program). See components.

**Declination of Earth Field** [deg +E]: The magnetic field produced by the magnetized sea floor is a very small field, that must be added vector ally to the much larger, present-day geomagnetic field. In such cases t he component of the small field perpendicular to the large field affects the sum only in second order. The measurable anomaly is due only to the component of the small field parallel to the present-day geomagnetic field. Therefore, after calculating the magnetic field of the ocean floor at the observation site, the program projects that field onto the direction of the local earth field. The projected field, or one of its components, will be the measurable anomaly. In order to calculate the required projection, the program must be given the direction (but not the magnitude) of the present-day geomagnetic field. That direction is specified by the declination (angle between the horizontal component o f the earth's field and geographic north) and the inclination (see immediately below).

**Inclination of Earth Field** [deg +Dn]: The inclination is the angle in degrees of the geomagnetic field below the horizontal. It is one of two angles required to specify the direction of the field (see immediately above).

**Altitude of Traverse** [km +Up]: This value would be positive in an airplane traverse, negative in a submarine. It is added to the depth of the ocean floor to get the total vertical distance between the magnetic sources and the measuring site.

### *Calculation*

A set of options for setting up and beginning the calculation of the magnetic anomaly graph predicted by a particular Model. In addition to the Model itself, certain mathematical parameters of the calculation must be provided.

**Default parameters:** This option selects reasonable default values for the mathematical parameters, listed below and used in calculating magnetic field anomalies. The first two parameters can be used to match the range of the calculation to the range of the expected external data.

1. Start of calculation (start of traverse): X = -250 km.
2. End of calculation (end of traverse): X = +250 km.

The last two parameters permit tradeoffs between speed and accuracy of the calculation.

3. Number of intervals at which to calculate along traverse: 600.
4. Distance beyond which to neglect field of one block: 250 km.

**User-edited parameters:** The parameters are those listed above. On a slow computer the user may wish to use smaller values: number of X intervals=200 , and cutoff distance=100 km.

**Calculate field anomalies:** This option tells the program to calculate and store in memory graphs of all the common components of the magnetic anomalies generated by the ocean floor. The selection of which one to graph, for comparison with an experiment, is made when the graph is displayed.

### *Graphs*

Two kinds of graphs can be displayed, simultaneously if desired. The first is a graph of the calculated magnetic anomaly, or any one of its components, as a function of position along the specified traverse. The second is usually a graph of experimental data from an external file. The external file's name will have the extension .DAT. However, note that a displayed graph can also be saved as a .DAT file. Thus the second graph could be the results o f a different calculation.

### *Help*

There are three choices.

1. Display information about the program, MAGNETIC. EXE.
2. Display information about the series, TEACHER'S TOYS.
3. Display the Contents of this Help file.

### Quit

End the program.

### Graphs Menu

This menu works just like the MAIN MENU, but deals only with the window on which graphs of the magnetic anomalies are displayed. One can select which of the calculated anomaly components to display for comparison with a file of external (experimental) data. One can adjust the axis scales for optimum viewing. The graphs can be saved in a file or printed on a printer. Two kinds of graphs can be displayed, simultaneously if desired. The first is a graph of the calculated magnetic anomaly, or any one of its components, as a function of position along the specified traverse. The second is usually a graph of experiment al data from an external file. The external file's name will have the extension .DAT. However, note that a displayed graph can also be saved as a .DAT file. Thus the second graph could be the results o f a different calculation.

### *Calculated Anomaly*

This menu option gives a choice among components of the calculated magnetic anomaly. The choices are–

Plot Total Anomaly.

Plot the changes in the total magnetic field.

Plot Horizontal Anomaly.

Plot the changes in the horizontal component of the field.

Plot Vertical Anomaly.

Plot the changes in the vertical component of the field.

Plot X-Anomaly.

Plot the changes in the X component of the field.

Clear Graph.

Erase the plot of magnetic anomalies.

### *External Data*

The external data loaded and plotted with this option would normally be experimental data from a real traverse described in the literature. Such data would be found in an ASCII text file, with the extension .DAT, and with the following form

- Line 0: Title, identifying component and brief source description.
- Lines 1 to n: Comment lines, whose first character is a "*", followed by text. These are usually used for a more complete identification of the literature source.
- Lines n+1 to n+N: N data sets of t he form, column 1 (1 or more spaces) column2 (1 space) column 3, where column 1 is the location X in km along the traverse, column 2 is the anomalous magnetic field in nT, and column 3 is either blank or "u" or "d". If there are no gaps in the data, the third column is blank. If there is a gap, the next data point after the gap will have a "u" in column 3, signifying that the plotting pen is to appro ach that point with pen up. The next data point would have a "d", signifying pen-down from that point on. Select external data (.DAT file):

This initiates a file-opening dialog. The selected data file is then read into memory, and the comment lines, 1-n above) are displayed to the user. The data are not displayed on the graph until the user selects t hat option.

**Add external data to graph in Black:** The data will be plotted in black, overlaying the previous graph contents. Red is nicer on the screen, but black prints more clearly than red on a black-and-white printer.

**Add external data to graph in Red:** The data will be plotted in red, overlaying the previous graph contents. Red is nicer on the screen, but black prints more clearly than red on a black-and-white printer.

**Remove external data from graph:** Erase the graph and then redraw only the calculated data. The external data remain in memory, to be replotted if appropriate, until they are overwritten.

Note that the calculated component of the graph can be saved in the form of a .DAT file (see Save Graph). This feature can be used to compare two slightly different calculations or even three if the user is clever with the red and black overlays.

*Axis Scales*

The user is offered a choice of accepting default values for the axis scaling, or manually entering appropriate values. The adjustable scaling parameters are—

- Minimum on X axis [km]: Default value =!250. Minimum acceptable value = !250.
- Maximum on X axis [km]: Default value =+250. Maximum acceptable value +250.
- Maximum Field Amplitude [+/-][nT]: Default value = 500. The Field Axis is symmetrically placed about zero.

The limitation, |X|<=250 km, is due to the arbitrary decision to mark the X axis at 10 km intervals. An adjustable interval would permit a longer axis, but would require cluttering the axis with labels. The listings of Component and Model at the bottom of the manual-scaling page are for information only, and are not editable.

*Save Graph*

Save graph to .DAT file:

The user will select a file name, of the form NAME.DAT, and the calculated graph will be saved in that file. The user will be offered a chance to add information to the comments section of the NAME.DAT file (see External Data).

**Print graph on printer:** Selecting this option causes the page to be printed graphically in the usual manner on the Windows printer.

**Adjust printer:** This option is redundant, because selecting the previous option brings up a "Setup Printer" button before printing.

**Help**

Display the Help file for the GRAPHS MENU.

**Quit Graphing**

Return to the MAIN MENU.

**Comparisons with Experiments**

The *simplest* way to compare the results of calculations with experimental data in the literature is compare it *visually* with a graph of experimental results from the literature. This takes advantage of the human mind's ability to recognize similar patterns, even if the scales of two graphs do not match. The program's attached collection of files includes a few samples of experimental data from traverses important in the early history of the idea of magnetic stripes near spreading centers. Such a .DAT file can be plotted on the screen, with the same scale and overlaying a plot of the predictions of a Model, Two different methods have been used for producing .DAT files from the literature.

1. A tablet digitizer recorded data pairs of the form (location, anomaly) from the printed graph. It also recorded the locations of calibration points having the same scale factors. The experimental data were rescaled somewhat subjectively, using simple computer programs and some subjective judgments.
2. A Paper Port One Touch raster scanner converted the figure in the literature into a Windows bitmap. The bitmap was cropped into appropriate pieces; the piece with the calibration marks would of course have the same scale as the data from that figure. The bitmaps

were cleaned up to remove flyspecks and smudges. The clean results permitted a simple scanning program to read the graph from the bitmap, along with the calibration points, and produce a .DAT file. The zero of each anomaly scale was arbitrarily set to give an average anomaly of zero, as Gauss's law would suggest for a sufficiently long traverse over magnetic dipoles. Accuracy is difficult to guarantee, since each reproduction process has potential problems. For example, at one time it was found, by copying a standard grid, that many photocopiers had regions of nonlinearity (i.e., varying magnification). A fair estimate for the .DAT files included with the program would seem to be +/- 10 km near 100 km from the ridge, and +/- 10% in anomaly amplitude. It would certainly not be appropriate, for example, to use these crude data samples to study time-varying spreading rates.

Many of the traverse parameters are left for students to provide from handbooks and other references, if not in the original literature. Leaving opportunities for all sorts of "what if" variations in the program may, unfortunately, give the impression that all the traverse parameters are equally important; they are not.

For example, the latitude of the traverse can be of crucial importance, but the depth to the ridge is not. The major effects of an increase in depth are a decrease in anomaly amplitude and a smoothing of the pattern. The decrease in amplitude can be compensated by an increase in the magnetization of each rock. The program permits the user to try out this idea. Conversely, it does not provide a good means of estimating depth to the ridge or absolute magnetization. The most important things to match in the experimental patterns are the magnetic field reversals and the average spreading rate.

**References**

Version 8.00 of MAGNETIC.EXE, Copyright, 1999 by Robert Detenbeck, Professor, Emeritus of Physics, University of Vermont, Burlington, VT 05405 rdetenbe@uvm.edu.

# 17

# Magnum Opus

## Introduction

**Magnum Opus** delivers the power of the most recent advances in pattern discovery technology. With unrivalled flexibility and ease-of-use, it finds new and unanticipated patterns from data. Use **Magnum Opus** to unlock the wealth of information implicit within your data. **Magnum Opus** supports **Association rules. Magnum Opus** is the only system that supports statistically sound pattern discovery.

*Some Important Features*

- **Magnum Opus** is **easy to use** and does not presume advanced knowledge of statistics or machine learning.
- **Magnum Opus** patterns are expressed in forms that are **simple to understand.**
- **Magnum Opus** finds patterns from both transaction data and attribute-value data.
- **Magnum Opus** has been designed to analyze **substantial databases** containing millions of records.
- **Magnum Opus** is **fast**. It has **linear compute time**. If the amount of data is doubled then the compute time will approximately double[†].
- **Magnum Opus** is **flexible**. The different search options support a wide range of differing analytic objectives.

**Magnum Opus** can be applied to two distinct types of data:

**Transaction Data & Attribute-value Data**

### *Transaction Data*

Transaction data consists of collections of items. A typical example is **market basket data,** where each transaction is the collection of items purchased by a customer in a single transaction. Transaction data can be imported from two different file types, **identifier-item files** and **item list files.**

### *Attribute-value Data*

Attribute-value data is a collection of cases, each described by a number of attributes. A typical example is a **customer database**. In this example, the cases are customers. Each set of attribute-value data must be described by two files, a **names file** and a **data file.**

**Magnum Opus** finds two forms of pattern: **Rules and Item sets.**

A **rule** has two parts, a Left Hand Side (LHS) and a Right Hand Side (RHS). Each rule indicates the relationship in the data between examples that have the LHS attribute values or items and those that have the RHS attribute values or items.

A **Magnum Opus item set** is a set of attribute values or items. The search options enable the user to control the types of item set that are found. By default, **Magnum Opus** finds item sets that maximize advantage.

A **Magnum Opus item set** supports only search by **Leverage and coverage.**

### *A Number of Values are Listed with each Rule*

**Coverage:** The coverage of a **rule** is the number of cases in the data that are covered by the Left Hand Side of the rule. The coverage of an **item set** is the number of cases in the data that are covered by the attribute values or items specified in the item set.

**Support:** The support of a **rule** is the number of cases in the data that are covered by both the Left Hand Side and the Right Hand Side of the rule.

**Strength:** The strength of a **rule** is the proportion of examples covered by the LHS of the rule that are also covered by the RHS. It indicates the probability that a case will satisfy the RHS if it satisfies the LHS.

**Lift:** The lift of a **rule** is the strength divided by the RHS coverage proportion. This indicates how much more frequent is the RHS if the LHS occurs than normal.

**Leverage:** The leverage of a **rule** is the number of additional cases covered by both the LHS and RHS above those expected if the LHS and RHS were independent of each other. This is a measure of the importance of the rule that reflects both the strength and the coverage of the rule. The leverage of an **item set** is the number of additional cases covered by the item set above the maximum expected if any disjoint subsets of the item set were independent of each other.

### *Filtering Out Unsound, Insignificant, Unproductive and Redundant Rules*

During search **Magnum Opus** can automatically filter out rules and item sets that are likely to be of little interest. The filter mode controls which such rules and item sets are filtered out. The four options are **Filter-out None, Filter-out Redundant, Filter-out Unproductive, Filter-out Insignificant** and **Filter-out Unsound.**

**Redundant:** A rule is **redundant** if there is another rule with the same Right-Hand-Side and a subset of the Left-Hand-Side that covers exactly the same cases from the data set. If a rule is **redundant** then it will have the same support, strength, lift, and leverage as the rule with respect to which it is redundant.

**Unproductive:** A rule is **unproductive** if there is another rule with the same Right-Hand-Side and a subset of the Left-Hand-Side that has equal or higher strength. If a rule is **unproductive** then it will have the same or worse support, strength, lift, and leverage as the rule with respect to which it is unproductive.

**Insignificant:** A rule is **insignificant** if its strength is not significantly greater than that of all of its immediate generalizations and a default rule. An immediate generalization is formed by deleting a single condition from the LHS of a rule. A default rule is formed by deleting all conditions from the LHS of a rule. A Fisher exact test is used to test for significance. The critical value for the significance test can be chosen by the user and defaults to 0.01.

Filtering out **insignificant rules** will remove many rules that result from adding another value to the Left-Hand-Side of another rule without substantially increasing its strength.

**Unsound:** The test for whether a rule or item set is **unsound** takes account of the number of rules or item sets considered in a search and adjusts the test for insignificance to take account thereof. It determines the number of patterns in the search space for each size of the LHS or item set. It then divides the critical value used for each pattern size by the number of possible patterns for that size times the number of sizes allowed.

**Preliminaries**

**Magnum Opus** detects patterns within data. The data is imported into the system from a text file. Users typically extract data from a database into a text file for use with the system. There is considerable flexibility in the formats that may be employed. The user selects settings that control a search for patterns in the data. The user can choose the type of pattern to be found and between alternative measures of the relative value of a pattern. The user also specifies the maximum number of patterns to be found and any further restrictions on the patterns to be considered.

Within the restrictions specified by the user, **Magnum Opus** finds the patterns with the highest values on the specified measure. **Magnum Opus** will only find fewer than the specified number of patterns if the search is terminated by the user or there are fewer than the specified number that satisfy the user specified constraints. The patterns found are recorded in an output file and may optionally be exported to a comma separated value file suitable for input into a spreadsheet for further analysis.

### *A Simple Example*

We start with a simple invented example of analyzing the purchasing habits of a customer of a fictitious grocery store. The customer has visited the store on ten occasions, each time buying a different selection of goods. The following item-list file records the customer's purchasing behavior. Each line represents the items bought on a single visit.

Plums, lettuce, tomatoes

Celery, confectionery

Apples, carrots, tomatoes, potatoes

Potatoes

Confectionery

Carrots

Apples, oranges, lettuce, tomatoes

Peaches, oranges, celery, potatoes, confectionery

Oranges, lettuce, carrots, tomatoes

Apples, bananas, plums, carrots, tomatoes, onions

These can be processed by Magnum Opus to find rules such as the following five.

apples -> tomatoes [Coverage=0.300 (3); Support=0.300 (3); Strength=1.000; Lift=2.00; Leverage=0.1500 (1.5)].

lettuce -> tomatoes [Coverage=0.300 (3); Support=0.300 (3); Strength=1.000; Lift=2.00; Leverage=0.1500 (1.5)].

tomatoes -> apples [Coverage=0.500 (5); Support=0.300 (3); Strength=0.600; Lift=2.00; Leverage=0.1500 (1.5)].

tomatoes -> lettuce [Coverage=0.500 (5); Support=0.300 (3); Strength=0.600; Lift=2.00; Leverage=0.1500 (1.5)].

tomatoes & oranges -> lettuce [Coverage=0.200 (2); Support=0.200 (2); Strength=1.000; Lift=3.33; Leverage=0.1400 (1.4)].

Each rule presents a list of items to the left of the arrow that are associated with the single item to the right of the arrow. Then a number of relevant statistics are presented that describe the nature of the association. Thus, the first two of these rules indicate that whenever either apples or lettuce are purchased, tomatoes are also purchased. The third and fourth rules indicate that both apples and lettuce are more likely to be purchased if tomatoes are purchased. The final rule shows that whenever both tomatoes and oranges are purchased, lettuce is also purchased.

This is a very simplistic example. In practice it would be foolish to draw strong conclusions from such limited data. Indeed, Magnum Opus includes facilities for assessing the strength of evidence in support of a rule, and these mechanisms would reject all the above rules as having insufficient support. This example is intended to illustrate the type of analysis that Magnum Opus performs, albeit, normally on much larger volumes of more complex data.

### *A Worked Example*

We now provide a fully worked example of an extended variant of the above scenario. The data is now extended to include all customers of the store for a given period, resulting in 1000 transactions. The data is contained in the example file distributed with **Magnum Opus** called tutorial.itl.

There are two versions of **Magnum Opus**. The command line version runs on both Sun Solaris and Linux systems. The interactive version runs under Windows. In the following and subsequent examples, we provide both a command line for executing the example on the command line system and a step-through of the process for running it on the interactive system. We present the output from the interactive system, which may vary in minor respects from that of the command line system.

In the first example, we run **Magnum Opus** with its default settings, except that we limit the number of rules produced to five only.

**Command line**: mol item-list-file = tutorial.itl maximum-results = 5.

**Interactive system**. First, run **Magnum Opus**. From the File Menu select Import Data. The system will display a dialog for selecting a file to open. If necessary, navigate to the Example Files folder within the folder into which you installed the software. Select the file tutorial.itl. The system will now display the following dialog box.

**Searching by strength: Magnum Opus** is different to most pattern discovery systems. One important difference is that it allows the user to specify both how many patterns to find and what measure should be used to judge how interesting a pattern is. Any of the measures coverage, support, strength, lift or advantage can be used for this purpose. The first example found the five rules with the highest advantage.

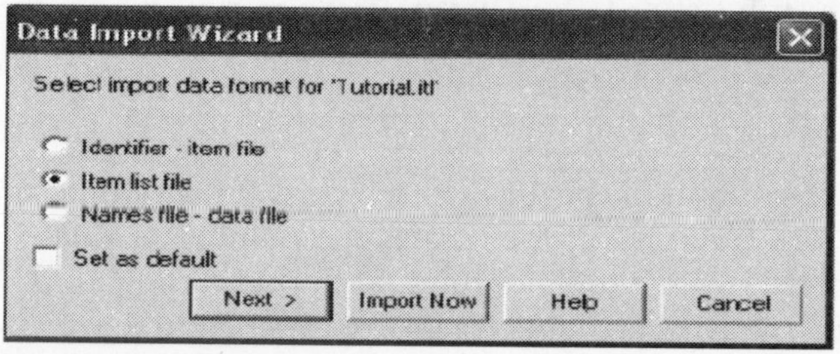


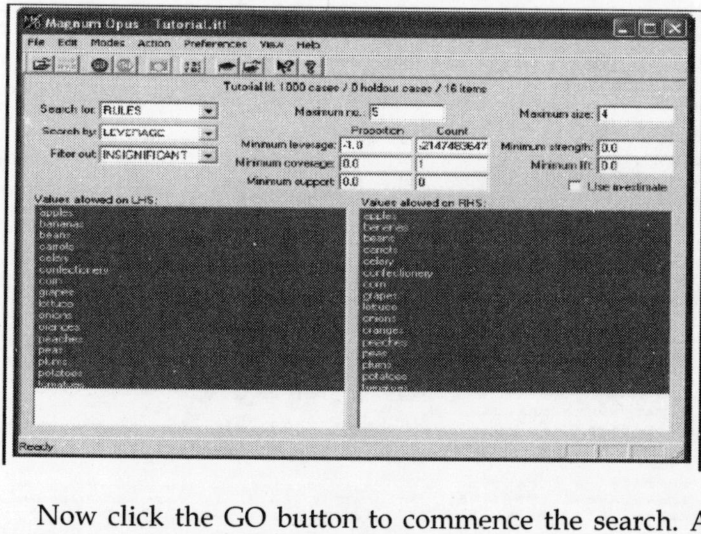


Now click the GO button to commence the search. As previously, a dialog will be displayed that allows you to select the file into which the results will be stored. Specify a file name and navigate to the folder in which you want it stored. Then click on the save button. The system will perform the search, saving the results in the specified file and then open the file for inspection.

```
Output:
Magnum Opus - The leader in pattern discovery technology.
Version 4.0
Copyright (c) 1999-2006 G. I. Webb & Associates Pty Ltd.

Data file: Tutorial.itl

1000 cases / 0 holdout cases / 16 items

Thu Sep 14 12:31:39 2006

Search for rules
Search by leverage
Filter out rules that are insignificant, critical value=0.05

Maximum number of attributes on LHS = 4
Maximum number of rules = 5
Minimum leverage = -1.0
```

The output file begins with a record of the settings used to produce the rules. It then states the number of rules found, followed by each of those rules. Each rule is composed of two parts. The left-hand-side (LHS) appears before the arrow and

```
Minimum leverage count = -2147483647
Minimum coverage = 0.0
Minimum coverage count = 1
Minimum support = 0.0
Minimum support count = 0
Minimum lift = 0.0
Minimum strength = 0.0

All values allowed on LHS

All values allowed on RHS

Found 5 rules

tomatoes -> lettuce
[Coverage=0.263 (263); Support=0.111 (111); Strength=0.422;
Lift=1.94; Leverage=0.0539 (53.9); p=2.35E-019]

lettuce -> tomatoes
[Coverage=0.217 (217); Support=0.111 (111); Strength=0.512;
Lift=1.94; Leverage=0.0539 (53.9); p=2.35E-019]

tomatoes -> carrots
[Coverage=0.263 (263); Support=0.085 (85); Strength=0.323;
Lift=1.85; Leverage=0.0390 (39.0); p=1.83E-012]

carrots -> tomatoes
[Coverage=0.175 (175); Support=0.085 (85); Strength=0.486;
Lift=1.85; Leverage=0.0390 (39.0); p=1.83E-012]

onions -> potatoes
[Coverage=0.189 (189); Support=0.082 (82); Strength=0.434;
Lift=1.53; Leverage=0.0285 (28.5); p=5.30E-007]
```

right-hand-side (RHS) appears after the arrow. Then a number of statistics are presented that describe the relationship between the LHS and RHS.

The first rule describes an association between tomatoes and lettuce. The following measures are presented that describe the association.

**Coverage:** The coverage of the rule is the number of cases that contain the LHS. In this Data 263 cases contain tomatoes, which is 0.263 of the 1000 cases in the Data.

**Support:** The Support of the rule is the number of cases that contain both the LHS and The RHS. In this data there are 111 cases that contain both tomatoes and Lettuce, which represents 0.111 of the total data.

**Lift:** The lift is the strength divided by the strength that would be expected if there were no relationship between the LHS and RHS. Higher values suggest stronger positive relationships. Lower values suggest stronger negative relationship.

**Advantage:** The advantage is the support minus the support that would be expected if LHS and RHS were unrelated to one another. A positive value suggests a Positive relationship and a negative value suggest a negative relationship.

**P:** The result of a statistical evaluation of the significance of the rule. The lower This value the less likely that this rule is a spurious outcome resulting from Adding an irrelevant value into the LHS.

### Searching by Strength

**Magnum Opus** is different to most pattern discovery systems. One important difference is that it allows the user to specify both how many patterns to find and what measure should be used to judge how interesting a pattern is. Any of the measures coverage, support, strength, lift or advantage can be used for this purpose.

The first example found the five rules with the highest advantage. High advantage rules have a strong positive association between the LHS and RHS and maximize the number of times more frequently the RHS occurs in the context of the LHS than would be expected if they were not associated with one another. The two other measures that are most frequently used are strength and lift. For our next example, we will rerun the previous analysis using strength as the measure by which to search.

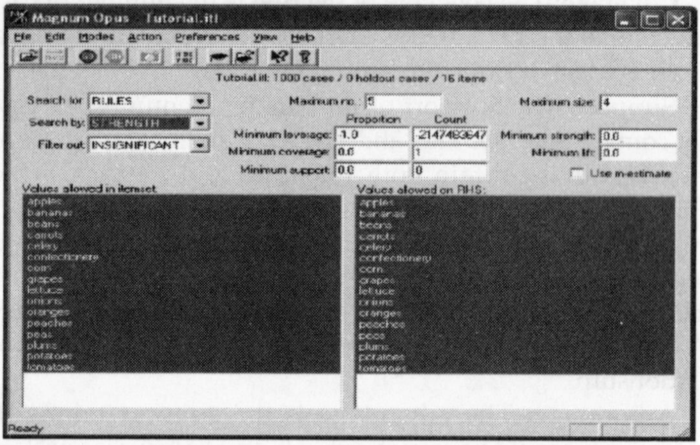


Now click the GO button to commence the search. As previously, a dialog will be displayed that allows you to select the file into which the results will be stored. Specify a file name and navigate to the folder in which you want it stored. Then click on the save button. The system will perform the search, saving the results in the specified file and then open the file for inspection.

**Output:**
```
Magnum Opus - The leader in pattern discovery technology.
Version 4.0
Copyright (c) 1999-2006 G. I. Webb & Associates Pty Ltd.

Data file: Tutorial.itl

1000 cases / 0 holdout cases / 16 items

Thu Sep 14 12:39:16 2006

Search for rules
Search by strength
Filter out rules that are insignificant, critical value=0.05

Maximum number of attributes on LHS = 4
Maximum number of rules = 5
Minimum leverage = -1.0
```

```
Minimum leverage count = -2147483647
Minimum coverage = 0.0
Minimum coverage count = 1
Minimum support = 0.0
Minimum support count = 0
Minimum lift = 0.0
Minimum strength = 0.0

All values allowed on LHS

All values allowed on RHS

Found 5 rules

bananas & lettuce & peaches -> apples
[Coverage=0.004 (4); Support=0.004 (4); Strength=1.000;
Lift=4.52; Leverage=0.0031 (3.1); p=0.0260]

bananas & plums & lettuce -> potatoes
[Coverage=0.004 (4); Support=0.004 (4); Strength=1.000;
Lift=3.53; Leverage=0.0029 (2.9); p=0.0385]

lettuce & confectionery & carrots & oranges -> beans
[Coverage=0.002 (2); Support=0.002 (2); Strength=1.000;
Lift=14.49; Leverage=0.0019 (1.9); p=0.0476]

plums & onions & peas -> bananas
[Coverage=0.002 (2); Support=0.002 (2); Strength=1.000;
Lift=7.87; Leverage=0.0017 (1.7); p=0.0452]

lettuce & oranges & onions -> potatoes
[Coverage=0.008 (8); Support=0.007 (7); Strength=0.875;
Lift=3.09; Leverage=0.0047 (4.7); p=0.0369]
```

## Searching by Lift

A search by strength with an m-estimate will tend to find strongly predictive rules. These are rules for which the RHS is very likely whenever the LHS occurs. However sometimes rather than highly predictive rules, it is desirable to find rules that 'beat the odds'. LIFT measures the how much the rules increases the probability of the RHS relative to the default.

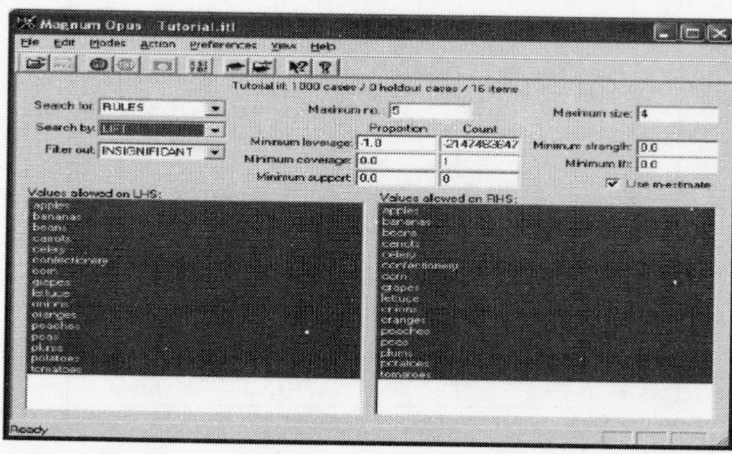

Now click the GO button to commence the search. As previously, a dialog will be displayed that allows you to select the file into which the results will be stored. Specify a file name and navigate to the folder in which you want it stored. Then click on the save button. The system will perform the search,

```
Output:
Magnum Opus - The leader in pattern discovery technology.
Version 4.0
Copyright (c) 1999-2006 G. I. Webb & Associates Pty Ltd.

Data file: Tutorial.itl

1000 cases / 0 holdout cases / 16 items

Fri Sep 22 22:15:30 2006

Search for rules
Search by lift
Filter out rules that are insignificant, critical value=0.05

Maximum number of attributes on LHS = 4
Maximum number of rules = 5
Minimum leverage = -1.0
```

```
Minimum leverage count = -2147483647
Minimum coverage = 0.0
Minimum coverage count = 1
Minimum support = 0.0
Minimum support count = 0
Minimum lift = 0.0
Minimum strength = 0.0

Use m-estimate, m = 2

All values allowed on LHS

All values allowed on RHS

Found 5 rules

lettuce & confectionery & carrots & oranges -> beans
[Coverage=0.002 (2); Support=0.002 (2); Strength
estimate=0.534; Lift estimate=7.75; Leverage=0.0019 (1.9);
p=0.0476]

plums & potatoes & grapes -> beans
[Coverage=0.003 (3); Support=0.002 (2); Strength
estimate=0.428; Lift estimate=6.20; Leverage=0.0018 (1.8);
p=0.0474]

apples & peaches & onions -> peas
[Coverage=0.007 (7); Support=0.004 (4); Strength
estimate=0.463; Lift estimate=5.45; Leverage=0.0034 (3.4);
p=0.0307]

bananas & beans -> corn
[Coverage=0.010 (10); Support=0.003 (3); Strength
estimate=0.259; Lift estimate=4.80; Leverage=0.0025 (2.5);
p=0.0357]

plums & onions & peas -> bananas
[Coverage=0.002 (2); Support=0.002 (2); Strength
estimate=0.564; Lift estimate=4.44; Leverage=0.0017 (1.7);
p=0.0452]
```

saving the results in the specified file and then open the file for inspection.

**Attribute Value Data**

So far, we have considered only data in the form of list of items. Many data are recorded in tabular format, with columns representing attributes or fields and each row representing a distinct entity.

The cell contains values of the respective attributes or fields for the given entity. Magnum opus supports such data, which must be listed in a data file. A delimiter characters such as a TAB or COMMA separate the columns.

**Computation Time, Snapshots and any Time Results**

Magnum opus provides tremendous flexibility to the user. Many forms of analysis can be requested, and magnum opus always provides exact results. When a computation is taking a long time, it is often helpful to view the best results discovered so far. This allows you to both assess whether you are actually performing the correct analysis and whether the results already obtained satisfy the analytic requirement. A set of intermediate results created while computation is in progress is called snapshot.

**Conclusion**

Magnum Opus is a powerful and flexible tool .For many analytic tasks it can be successfully run simply using the default settings. However, advanced users can use the sophisticated controls to perform a wide variety of tasks. We recommend that new users start by using the default settings and only start using the other controls as they become familiar with the system.

# 18

## MARS (Multivariate Adaptive Regression Spines)

### Introduction

Welcome to MARS, the world first truly successful automated regression modeling tool. **Multivariate Adaptive Regression Spines** was developed in the early 1990s by world-renowned Stanford physicist and statistician Jerome Friedman, but has become widely known in the data mining and business intelligence worlds only recently through our seminars and the enthusiastic endorsement of leading data mining specialists. We expect that you will find MARS an essential component in your data analysis tool kit.

MARS is an innovative and flexible modeling tool that automates the building of accurate predictive models for continuous and binary dependent variables. It excels at finding optimal variable transformations and interactions, the complex data structure that often hides in high-dimensional data. In doing so, this new approach to regression modeling effectively uncovers **important data patterns** and relationships that are difficult, if not impossible, for other methods to reveal.

Although regression is one of the most widely used tools in statistical analysis, it is almost never used in data mining. Nevertheless, a well-crafted regression model can be ideal for predictive modeling and data mining because of the following important characteristics:

- A regression model predicts the outcome variable by forming a weighted sum of the predictor variables; thus, the predicted outcome changes in a smooth and regular fashion as the inputs change.
- This is in contrast to a decision tree where a small change in a predictor could either move a prediction to a different node in the tree or result in no change in the prediction at all.
- When scoring a database, regression models typically produce unique scores for each record. Decision trees assign the same score to all records arriving at a specific node; thus, the smaller the decision tree, the fewer the number of unique scores assigned.
- In a regression, it is often possible to .read. The effect of a predictor variable on the outcome by examining its slope coefficient; experienced modelers can often read the effects of interactions directly from the model itself. Developing a good regression model is usually an extremely time intensive activity requiring considerable modeling expertise, even for small databases. For the large databases common in data mining projects, model-building challenges have deterred data miners from using this otherwise very effective tool. However, with the advent of MARS, regression models can now be routinely and automatically developed for the most complex data structures.

Given a target variable and a set of candidate predictor variables, MARS automates all aspects of model development and model deployment, including:

- Variable selection: separating relevant from irrelevant predictor variables.
- Transforming predictor variables exhibiting a nonlinear relationship with the target.
- Determining interactions between predictor variables.
- Handling missing values with new nested variable techniques.

- Conducting extensive self-tests to protect against over fitting.
- MARS enables you to rapidly search through all possible models and to quickly identify the .optimal. Solution. Because the software can be exploited via intelligent default settings, for the first time analysts at all technical levels can easily access MARS. Innovations.
- MARS essentially builds flexible models by fitting piecewise linear regressions; that is, the nonlinearity of a model is approximated through the use of separate regression slopes in distinct intervals of the predictor variable space. An example of a piecewise linear regression is shown below.

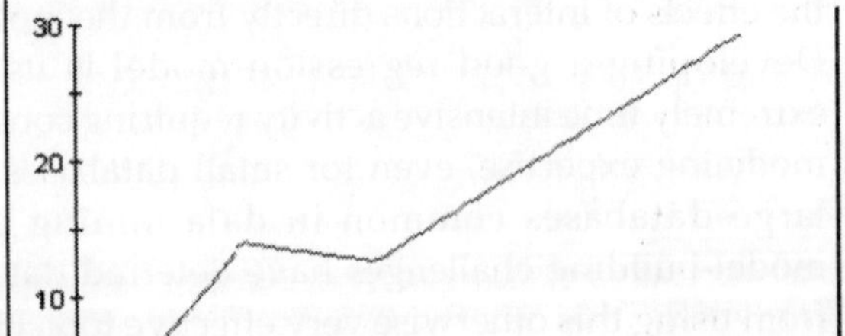


The slope of the regression line is allowed to change from one interval to the other as the two. Knot points are crossed. The variables to use and the end points of the intervals for each variable are found via a fast but very intensive search procedure.

In addition to searching variables one by one, MARS also searches for interactions between variables, allowing any degree of interaction to be considered.

The optimal MARS model is selected in a two-stage process. In the first stage, MARS constructs an overly large model by adding .basis functions. The formal mechanism by which variable intervals are defined. Basis functions represent either single variable transformations or multivariable interaction terms. As basis functions are added, the model becomes more flexible and more complex, and the process continues until a user specified maximum number of basis functions is reached.

In the second stage, basis functions are deleted in order of least contribution to the model until an optimal model is found. By allowing for any arbitrary shape for the function as well as for interactions, and by using this two-stage model selection method, MARS is capable of reliably tracking the very complex data structures that often hide in high dimensional data.

The MARS output contains an easy-to-deploy regression model that can be simply applied to new data from within MARS or exported as C-, SAS®- or XML/PMML-compatible code.

To facilitate interpretation of the model, the output includes interpretive summary reports as well as exportable two- and three-dimensional curve and surface plots.

The best way to learn about MARS is, to use it so let's start now!

**Interactive Example**

Let's now walk through a step-by-step example using data extracted from the March Current Population Survey of 1985. (These data are available in the Sample Data folder installed with MARS.) The target variable is the log of wage earned at the respondent's current job. The independent variables are years of education (ED), dummy variables for living in the South (South), race non-Caucasian and Non-Hispanic (NONWH), race Hispanic (HISP), female (FE), married (MARR), represented by a union (UNION), industry dummies for manufacturing and construction (MANUF, CONSTR), occupational dummies for managerial, sales, clerical, service and professional (MANAG, SALES, CLER, SERV, PROF), years of work experience (EX) and age in years (AGE).

Follow the five steps below to estimate a MARS model with main effects only:

(1) From the File menu, select Open. In the Open dialog, select files of type Systat (.syd) in the Files of Type drop down. Browse for CPS85B.syd and click OPEN.

(2) In the Variables tab of the Setup dialog, select LNWAGE as the target variable.

(3) Next select ED, SOUTH, NONWH, HISP, FE, MARR, EX, UNION, AGE, MANUF, CONSTR, MANAG, SALES, CLER, SERV, PROF as candidate predictors (total of 16 predictors).

(4) Specify SOUTH, NONWH, HISP, FE, MARR, UNION, MANUF, CONSTR,MANAG, SALES, CLER, SERV, and PROF as categorical variables in the Categorical column.

(5) Click Compute Model.

By default, MARS searches for a maximum of 15 basis functions in the first stage of the model building process and uses a degrees of freedom penalty of 3 in the second stage to prune the potentially over fit model. The other key default settings include minspan (minimum number of observations between knots) tuned automatically to the size of the data set (the literal parameter setting is 0) and maximum interactions equal to 1 (i.e., no interactions).

The constant is always entered into the model first as BF0. The next two basis functions, BF1 and BF2, are mirror image basis functions for ED with the knot located at education equal to 11 years. Similarly, the third and fourth basis functions are mirror image basis functions for EX with the knot at 12 years of work experience. Next, dummies for FE, UNION, SERV, MANAG and PROF and their complements are entered as BF5-BF14.

The final basis function entered, BF15, is the dummy for SOUTH. Note that the complement (South=0) is not entered because MARS reached the maximum allowed number of basis functions.

The final model selected the one with the lowest GCV score, keeps eight of the 15 basis functions added in the forward-stepping stage and has a GCV R-squared of 0.316.

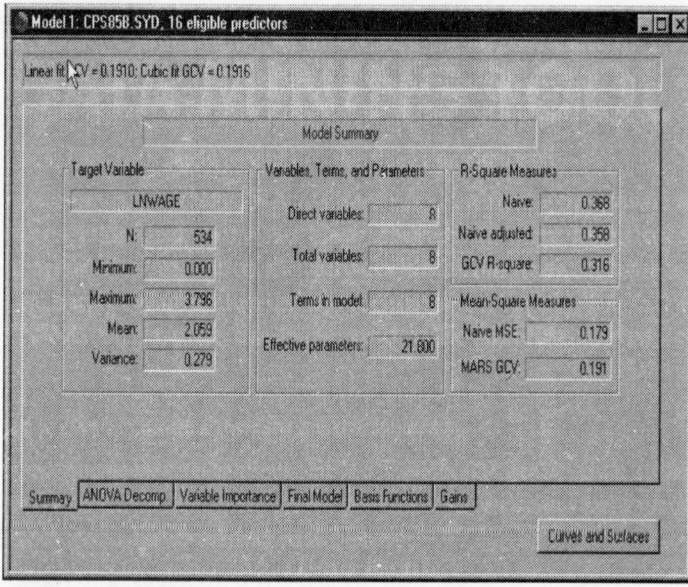


The set of final basis functions and the regression equation for this model are shown below:

BF1 = max(0, ED - 11.000);
BF4 = max(0, 12.000 - EX );
BF5 = ( FE = 0);
BF7 = (UNION = 0);
BF9 = (SERV = 0);
BF11 = (MANAG = 0);
BF13 = (PROF = 0);
BF15 = (SOUTH = 0);
Y = 2.202 + 0.071 * BF1-0.040 * BF4 + 0.197 * BF5-0.222 * BF7
+ 0.170 * BF9 - 0.239 * BF11-0.177 * BF13
+ 0.102 * BF15;

Only the upper portion of the set of mirror image basis functions for ED (BF1) is retained in the final model while the reverse is true for EX (BF4). The absence of mirror images indicates that there is a zero slope for the lower portion of ED and the upper portion of EX, as shown in the graphs below. Thus, education does not have a positive significant effect on wages until after 11 years whereas the effect of additional years of work experience ends at 12 years.

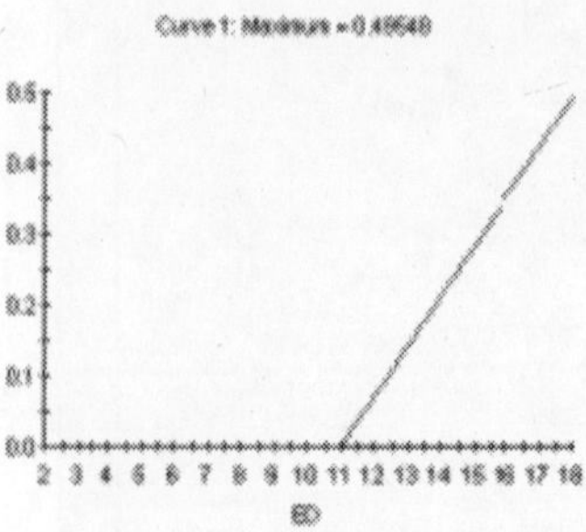


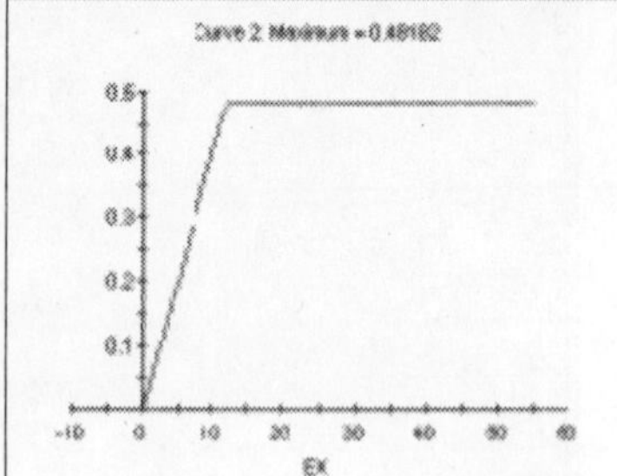


The remaining six basis functions in the model are the complementary basis functions created for dummy variables FE, UNION, SERV, MANAG, PROF and SOUTH. The Coefficients in the MARS model equation indicate whether each of these has a positive or negative effect on wages. For example, BF5, an indicator for not female, is positively related to wages with a coefficient of +0.197. Graphs are not created for categorical basis functions.

Let's now see if we can improve the model by allowing MARS to include two-way interactions:

(1) Open the Setup dialog again by selecting Set up Model from the Model menu (or

Clicking the Set up Model toolbar icon).

(2) In the Options and Limits dialog, increase Maximum Interactions to 2.

(3) Click Compute Model.

Interaction terms do not enter the model until BF9 and BF10; here, MARS has determined that adding an interaction between SERV and UNION=1 (a main effect already in the model) results in the greatest reduction in GCV. Note that UNION is interacted with SERV=1 (BF9) and its complement, SERV=0 (BF10).

The remaining two pairs of basis functions are also interaction terms. Interactions between a new pair of mirror image basis functions for ED with a knot at 12 and UNION=0 are entered as BF11 and BF12. Next, interactions between the (ED-11.000) + spine and the pair of MANUF dummies enter the model followed by an interaction between PROF and the complementary dummy for FE.

In the final model, the GCV R-squared is slightly higher and the number of basis functions remains the same as in the main effects model but now includes five interaction terms.

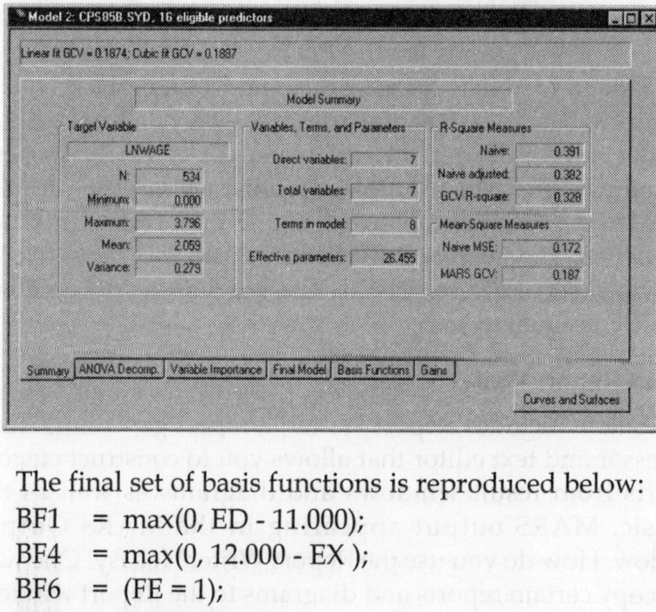


The final set of basis functions is reproduced below:

BF1 = max(0, ED - 11.000);
BF4 = max(0, 12.000 - EX );
BF6 = (FE = 1);
BF7 = (UNION = 0);
BF8 = (UNION = 1);
BF9 = (SERV = 0) * BF7;
BF11 = max(0, ED - 12.000) * BF8;
BF12 = max(0, 12.000 - ED ) * BF8;
BF13 = (MANUF = 0) * BF1;
BF15 = (PROF = 0) * BF6;
Y = 2.362 + 0.150 * BF1-0.044 * BF4-0.592 * BF7 + 0.231 * BF9
- 0.089 * BF11-0.119 * BF12-0.059 * BF13
- 0.216 * BF15;

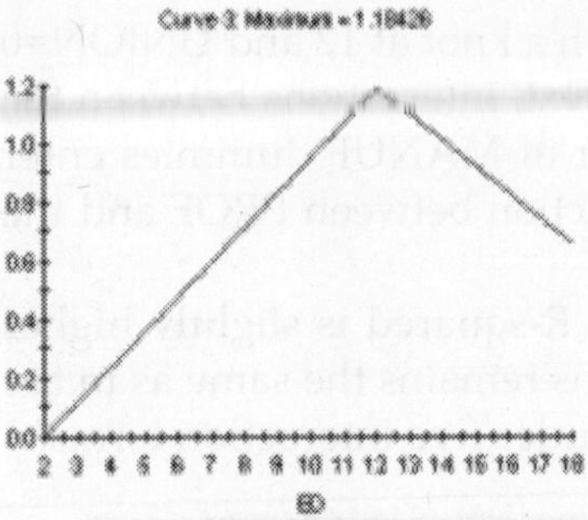


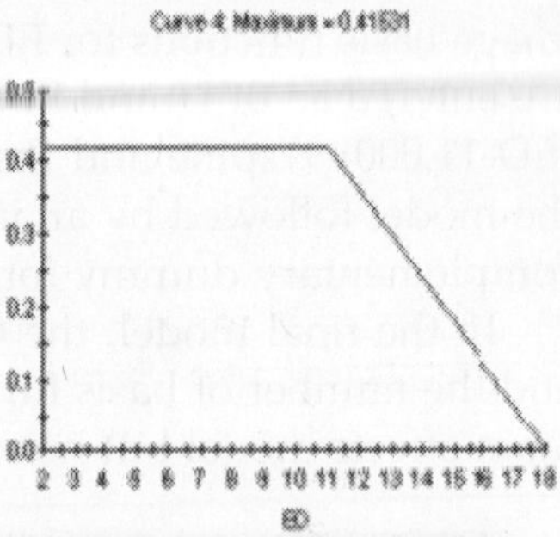


Look at the graphs for the ED interaction terms between UNION and MANUF. Because the interaction terms involve a categorical basis function, the graphs are only 2-D and display the effect on the dependent variable ONLY when the dummy condition is met. For example, the interaction graph for ED and MANUF shows the effect of ED on LNWAGE when MANUF=0. The small negative slope, -0.059, indicates that the positive effect of ED on LNWAGE is not quite as strong when MANUF is equal to zero.

## MARS Report Writer

MARS now includes Report Writer, a report generator, word processor and text editor that allows you to construct custom reports from result windows and diagrams as well as the .classic. MARS output appearing in the MARS Output window. How do you use the Report Writer? It easy! One way is to copy certain reports and diagrams to the Report window as you view the model in the results dialog or Selector windows.

Once a model has been built, a Model results dialog appears allowing you to explore the model and its performance with a variety of graphic reports and diagrams. Virtually any graph, table, grid display, or set of basis functions can be copied to the Report Writer. Simply right-click the item you wish to add to the Report Writer and it will appear at the bottom of the Report window.

MARS also produces .classic. Output for those users more comfortable with a text-based Summary of the MARS model and its performance. To add any (or all) of MARS classic output to the Report Writer window, highlight text in the classic output window, copy it to the Windows clipboard (**Ctrl+C**), switch to the Report Writer window and paste (**Ctrl+V**) at the point you want text inserted. This way you can combine those MARS elements you find most useful.either graphic in nature and originating in the Model results dialog, or textual in nature from the classic output.into a single custom Report.

**BFs 11 & 12. ED * UNION BF 13. ED * MANUF**

**Default Options**

In the Set Report Options dialog, the currently-selected reporting items and the **Automatic Report** checkbox can be saved as a default group of settings for future MARS sessions by clicking the **[Set Default]** button. These default options will then persist from session to session since they are saved in the MARS.INI file. You may recall these settings any time with the Use Default button.

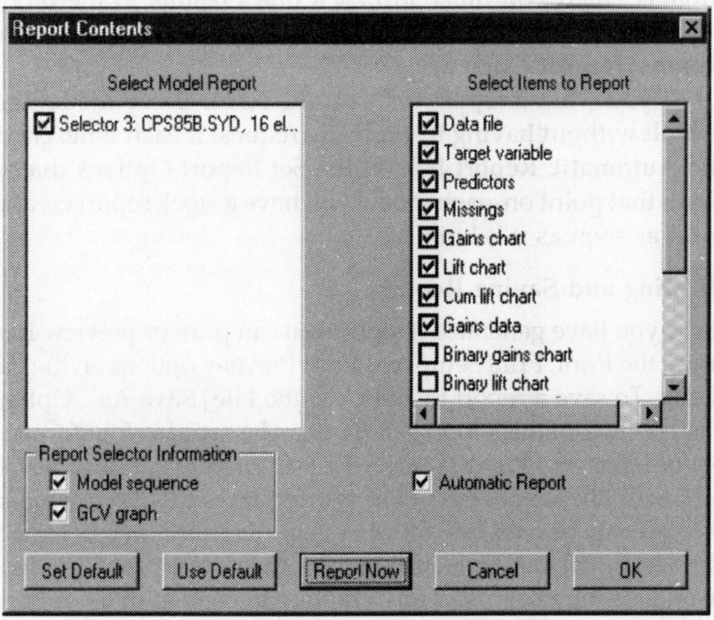

**Pre-configured Reports**

Additionally, MARS can produce a .stock report. with the click of a button. Select components of MARS output that are the most useful to you on the **Report | Set Report Options...** dialog. The stock report will be the same for all models in the session until you visit the Set Report Options dialog again. (In addition, the currently-open selectors are listed and individual ones can be excluded or added to the list that will appear in the report when **Report | Report All** is selected).

You can then generate a stock report for the currently active (i.e., foreground) Model results window or Selector by choosing **Report | Report Current**. If the active window is not a Model results window or Selector window, **Report Current** will be disabled. Furthermore, if you have several Selectors and their associated Model result windows open, you can generate a report for all the models (in the order in which they were built) by choosing **Report | Report All**. The **Report | Report All** and **Report | Summary** only work for Selectors (and their child Model results windows). If you have grown a series of .Best Models,. then you must add each one's results to the report separately by bringing it to the foreground and selecting **Report | Report Current**.

If you want a report to be produced for every model that is built without having to explicitly request it each time, check the **Automatic Report** box on the Set Report Options dialog. From that point on, each model will have a stock report created for it as soon as it is built.

**Printing and Saving Reports**

Once you have generated a report you can print or preview it by using the Print, Print Setup and Print Preview options on the File menu. To save a report to a file, use the **File | Save As...** Option. The contents of the Report Window can be saved in four formats: Salford Systems Report (.ssr), rich text format (.rtf), and text or text with line breaks (.txt). The .ssr format is the most compact but can only be read by Salford Systems modules such as MARS. Rich text (.rtf) can be read by most other word processors and maintains the integrity of any graphics imbedded in the report.

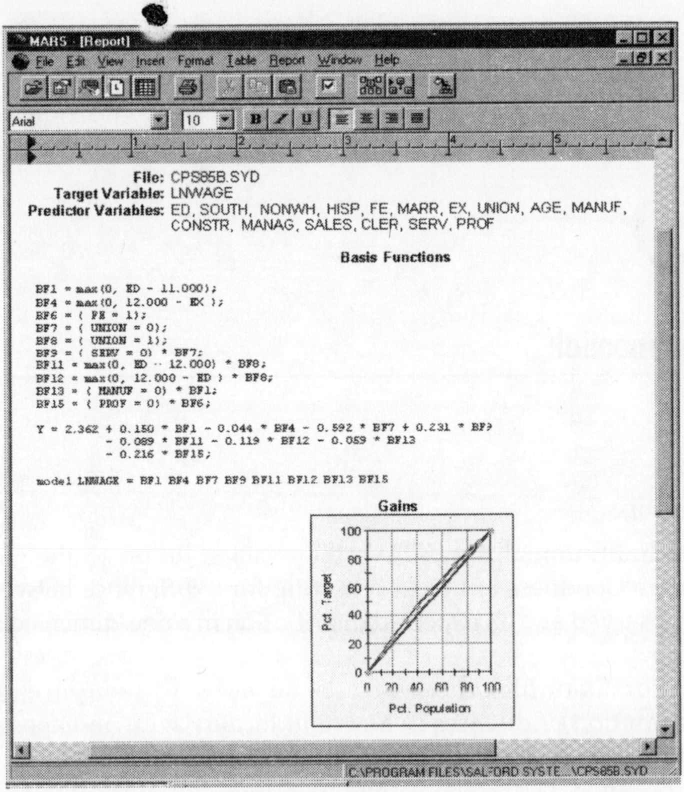


## References


Jiawei Han and Michiline Kamber (2000), "Data Mining–Concepts and Techniques", Morgan Kaufmman Publishers.

John Wang, "Encyclopedia of Data Warehousing and Data Mining".

# 19

# Multinomial

## Purpose

The multinomial program is the exact solution to the Chi-square Goodness of fit test of testing for a difference between an observed and an expected distribution in a one-dimensional array.

For example, the test can be used to compare the distribution of diseases in a certain locality with an expected distribution on the basis of national or international experiences using an ICD classification. In a two-category array the multinomial test provides a two-sided solution for the Binomial test.

For example, Multinomial {10 20 0.20 0.80} gives the two-sided probability (0.105) for the single sided Binomial {0.20 10 30} probability (0.061). The multinomial allows you to work with empty '0' observation cells although you must have an expectation about a cell.

## Input

The program recognizes two types of input. Observed values are integers in the range 0, 1 and >1. Non-integers that could potentially be an observed value are truncated to the nearest integer less than the given value. Expected values are proportions in the range >0 and <1. The sum of all the expected values should be 1.0, if this is not so the program gives you a warning. Note that the value 0, zero, nothing, can be an observed but not an expected value.

The program will consider that the number of expected values it finds is the number of valid categories to evaluate. In the case of too many observed values the program will ignore observed values, and the program will add zeros if there are too few observed values. The program will read the data in the order in which they are presented, the first observed value considered pertaining to the first category, same for the first expected value. You can cut and paste the data into the input field from a spreadsheet or type it into the input field manually. Please be careful with continental European style decimal commas, they are not accepted as valid, should be decimal dots.

Any character that does not have a numerical function will be considered to be a separator between two numbers. There is a maximum of 20,000 cases or 500 categories. However, the program will probably give up long before that. As for all exact procedures, sometimes a very large number of calculations are required to find a solution. The program will issue a warning if calculations might take too long for normal patience. Consider that sometimes it might take your computer a few hours to find a solution to your problem.

If you put (cut and paste) the following table into the input field and click "calculate":

10

50 30 5

.10 0.55

.20>.15

This will be part of the reply:

The (Two-sided) CUMULATIVE PROBABILITY for this or a larger difference: 0.0041541

**Output**

In the output field first a table of the data as read is presented, followed by a table of the data but now the observed data as a distribution of proportions and the expected proportions as expected numbers. Mean Absolute Difference, a measure of difference between the observed and the expected distribution follow this. Following this the Pearson (GFX) and the likelihood ratio (LRX) Chi-square are presented. These Chi-squares give you an approximate (two-sided) probability of the difference between the observed and the expected distribution having been caused by chance fluctuation. After this the point-probability, the likelihood of this very specific table is presented.

Next the number of calculations required for calculating the cumulative probability is presented. At this point the program issues a warning if the number of calculations required is very large. The cumulative probability is the most important statistic presented by the program.

It gives you the probability of this or a more extreme table having been produced on the basis of chance considering a certain expectation regarding the distribution. Additionally, it gives you the probability of a more extreme table and the mid-p probability. The mid-p probability is less conservative compared with the usual "the same and larger than" probability and is mostly closer to approximate statistics. The use of the mid-p value is not recommended.

The method of the sum of small p-values is used in the calculations and the probabilities are two-sided. The Chi-squares are also two-sided so both methods should produce the same probability, asymptotically.

**License**

This is free software. It can be freely distributed and installed. This program is provided to you by Quantitative Skills Research and Statistical Consultancy.

Although this program has been tested extensively, no program is ever bug or error free, and you should always check your results carefully. This software and the accompanying files are sold "as is" and without warranties as to performance or merchantability or fitness for a particular purpose. The entire risk arising out of use or performance of the software remains with you.

## Inputbox

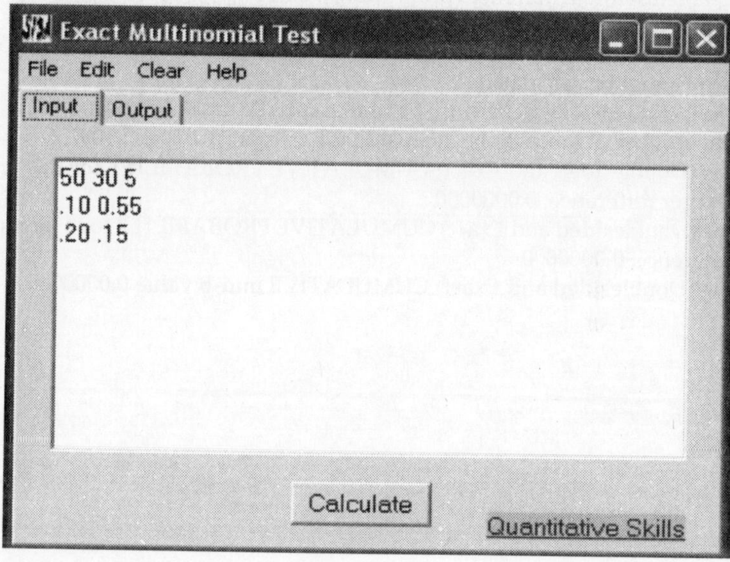


## Output

**The given Data (4 cells, 85 Cases)**

| # | *obs* | *exp* |
|---|---|---|
| 1 | 50 | 0.100 |
| 2 | 30 | 0.550 |
| 3 | 5 | 0.200 |
| 4 | 0 | 0.150 |
| Total | 85 | 1.000 |

**Rewritten**

| # | *obs* | *exp* |
|---|---|---|
| 1 | 0.588 | 8.5 |
| 2 | 0.353 | 46.8 |
| 3 | 0.059 | 17.0 |
| 4 | 0.000 | 12.7 |
| Total | 1.000 | 85.0 |

## Table Statistics

Mean Absolute Difference (proportions): 0.244
Mean Absolute Difference (values): 20.8
Pearson's Chi Square (df= 3): 229.840 (p= 0.00000)
LRX cannot be calculated
The Exact POINT PROBABILITY of this specific table: 0.0000000
The number of tables to be evaluated for an exact analysis : 109735
The (Doublesided and Exact) CUMULATIVE PROBABILITY for this or a larger difference: 0.0000000
The (Doublesided and Exact) CUMULATIVE PROBABILITY for a larger difference: 0.0000000
The (Doublesided and Exact) CUMULATIVE mid-p value 0.0000000.

# 20

## NLREG (Non Linear Regression Analysis)

**Introduction**

The goal of regression analysis is to determine the values of parameters for a function that cause the function to best fit a set of data observations that you provide In linear regression, the function is a linear (straight-line) equation For example, if we assume the value of an automobile decreases by a constant amount each year after its purchase, and for each mile it is driven, the following linear function would predict its value (the dependent variable on the left side of the equal sign) as a function of the two independent variables which are age and miles:

value = price + depage*age + depmiles*miles

where value, the dependent variable, is the value of the car, age is the age of the car, and miles is the number of miles that the car has been driven The regression analysis performed by NLREG will determine the best values of the three parameters, price, the estimated value when age is 0 (i.e., when the car was new), depage, the depreciation that takes place each year, and depmiles, the depreciation for each mile driven The values of depage and depmiles will be negative because the car loses value as age and miles increase.

For an analysis such as this car depreciation example, you must provide a data file containing the values of the dependent and independent variables for a set of observations In this example each observation data record would contain three numbers: value, age, and miles, collected from used car ads for the same model car The more observations you provide, the more accurate will be the estimate of the parameters The NLREG statements to perform this regression are shown below:

```
Variables value, age, miles;
Parameters price, depage, depmiles;
Function value = price + depage*age + depmiles*miles;
Data;
{data values go here}
```

Once the values of the parameters are determined by NLREG, you can use the formula to predict the value of a car based on its age and miles driven For example, if NLREG computed a value of 16000 for price, -1000 for depage, and -0.15 for depmiles, then the function,

value = 16000 – 1000*age – 0.15*miles

could be used to estimate the value of a car with a known age and number of miles.

If a perfect fit existed between the function and the actual data, the actual value of each car in your data file would exactly equal the predicted value Typically, however, this is not the case, and the difference between the actual value of the dependent variable and its predicted value for a particular observation is the error of the estimate which is known as the "deviation" or "residual" The goal of regression analysis is to determine the values of the parameters that minimize the sum of the squared residual values for the set of observations This is known as a "least squares" regression fit.

**Introduction to NLREG**

NLREG is a very powerful regression analysis program Using it you can perform multivariate, linear, polynomial, exponential, logistic, and general nonlinear regression What this means is that you specify the form of the function to be fitted to the data, and the function may include nonlinear terms such as variables raised to powers and library functions such as log, exponential, sine, etc For complex analyses, NLREG allows you to specify function models using conditional statements (IF, ELSE), looping (FOR, DO, WHILE), work variables, and arrays. NLREG uses a state-of-the-art regression algorithm that works as well, or better, than any you are likely to find in any other commercial statistical packages.

As an example of nonlinear regression, consider another depreciation problem. The value of a used airplane decreases for each year of its age Assuming the value of a plane falls by the same amount each year, a linear function relating value to age is:

value = p0 + p1*Age

Where p0 and p1 are the parameters whose values are to be determined.

However, it is a well-known fact that planes (and automobiles) lose more value the first year than the second, and more the second than the third, etc This means that a linear (straight-line) function cannot accurately model this situation A better, nonlinear, function is:

value = p0 + p1*exp(-p2*Age)

Where the 'exp' function is the value of e (2.7182818...) raised to a power This type of function is known as "negative exponential" and is appropriate for modeling a value whose

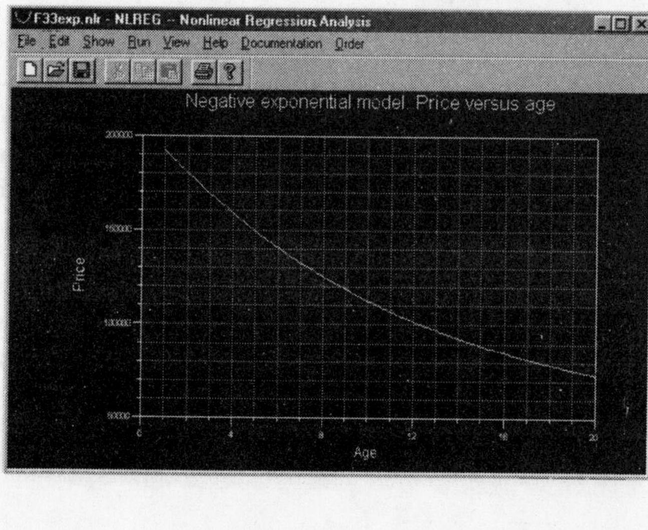

rate of decrease is proportional to the difference between the value and some base value. The F33YEAR.NLR example program file fits a linear function to the value of used airplanes The F33EXP.NLR example fits a negative exponential function to the same data Run both examples and compare the fitted functions See F33.NLR for an example of multiple regression using three independent variables Here is a plot produced by the f33exp.nlr function which shows a negative exponential function fitted to a set of data values:

Much of the convenience of NLREG comes from the fact that you can enter complicated functions using ordinary algebraic notation Examples of functions that can be handled with NLREG include:

| | |
|---|---|
| Linear | Y = p0 + p1*X |
| Quadratic | Y = p0 + p1*X + p2*X^2 |
| Multivariate | Y = p0 + p1*X + p2*Z + p3*X*Z |
| Exponential | Y = p0 + p1*exp(X) |
| Periodic | Y = p0 + p1*sin(p2*X) |
| Misc | Y = p0 + p1*Y + p2*exp(Y) + p3*sin(Z) |

In other words, the function is a general expression involving one dependent variable (on the left of the equal sign), one or more independent variables, and one or more parameters whose values are to be estimated.

Because of its generality, NLREG can perform all of the regressions handled by ordinary linear or multivariate regression programs as well as nonlinear regression However, in order to handle nonlinear functions, NLREG uses an iterative function optimization algorithm that is slower than the simple linear regression algorithm and has the potential for not converging to a solution.

### NLREG Program Files

The statements described in this section are placed in a program file A program file can be created using the editor built into NLREG or using any other editor of your choice However, the file must a simple text file (with carriage-return and line-feed characters separating lines) It may not be a formatted word-processor file NLREG program files should be given the extension ".NLR".

To execute a program file, either double click the name of the file, or start NLREG and then open the program file.

### *Comments*

The beginning of a comment is denoted with "//" (two consecutive slash characters). Everything from the "//" sequence to the end of the line is treated as a comment Comments may be on lines by themselves or on the ends of other statements You can also specify a comment by beginning the comment with the "/*" character sequence All characters following this are treated as comments up to the matching "*/" sequence The following lines illustrate both types of comments:

```
// Function to be fitted
y = a + b*x; // Simple linear equation
/*
 * This is a comment.
 */
z = y / 5;      /* This is a comment too */
```

### Required Statements

Every program file must contain the following statements: VARIABLES, PARAMETERS, FUNCTION, and DATA The DATA statement introduces the data for the analysis and must be the last statement in the file (data records may follow it) Other, optional, statements may be interspersed in the program file The following is an example of a complete program file:

```
title "Depreciation Example";
variables value, age, miles;
parameters base, depage, depmiles;
function value = base + depage*age + depmiles*miles;
data;
(data records follow).
```

### NLREG Statements

The following is a list of the valid NLREG statements that can be placed in a NLREG program file NLREG statements are not case sensitive Remember to end each statement with a semicolon.

#### Title

TITLE "string"; (optional)—Specifies a title line that is printed with the results of the analysis Note: the title string must be enclosed in quote signs and terminated with a semicolon For example:

TITLE "Fit quadratic function to data";

#### Variables

VARIABLES var1,var2,...; (required)—Specifies the names of the input variables whose values will be read from your data file The order of the variable names must match the order of the data values on each observation record You may define more variables than you actually use in the function specification A maximum of 200 variables may be specified The length of a variable name is limited to 10 characters Capitalize the variable names as you want them displayed in the results. The keyword "VARIABLE" may be used instead of "VARIABLES".

You may specify all of the variables on a single statement or you may use multiple VARIABLES statements If you use multiple statements, the order in which they appear in the program file must match the order of the variable values on each observation record The VARIABLES statement must precede the FUNCTION statement See F33.NLR for an example of multiple regression using three independent variables.

Here is an example of several VARIABLES statements:

Variables x,y;

Variable z;

#### Parameters

PARAMETERS param1[=initial1],param2[=initial2],...; (required)—Specifies the names of the parameters whose values are to be determined by NLREG NLREG is capable of handling up to 200 parameters The parameter names may not exceed 10 characters in length Do not specify any parameters that are not used in the analysis The PARAMETERS statement must precede the FUNCTION statement The keyword "PARAMETER" may be used instead of "PARAMETERS".

Here are examples of the PARAMETERS statement:

Parameters p0,p1;

Parameter Temperature=22;

Parameter Mass=1E-5;

The CONSTRAIN statement can be used to limit the range of values for parameters The SWEEP statement can be used to perform the regression analysis with a range of parameter initial values.

**Program Limits**

The following is a summary of the NLREG program limitations:

Maximum number of variables = 500
Maximum number of parameters = 500
Maximum number of work variables = 500
Maximum length of variable or parameter names = 30
Maximum length of a program statement = 800
Maximum length of data records = 2000

The maximum number of data observations that NLREG can handle is limited only by the available memory space provided by Windows However, if you have a large number of data records, you must use the form of the DATA statement that specifies a file name and place your data records in a separate file This is necessary because the editor built into NLREG can only handle up to 65,000 characters.

**Statement Syntax**

The syntax for NLREG statements follows the style of the C programming language Each statement must end with a semicolon character, you may place more than one statement on a line, and text strings and file names are enclosed in quote marks NLREG has the same arithmetic and logical operators as C, and brace characters ('{' and '}') are used to group statements.

The following keywords are reserved by NLREG and may not be used as the names of variables or parameters: angletype, break, confidence, connect, connect2, constant, constrain, covariance, data, do, domain, double, else, for, function, grid, if, iteration, model, noecho, nogrid, notitle, noxlabel, noylabel, nplot, output, plot, poutput, print, register, stop, sweep, title ,var, variable, variables, while, width, xlabel, xvar, xvar2, ylabel, yvar, yvar2.

**Variables and Parameters**

NLREG allows you to use four types of variables: input, computed, system, and constant.

Input variables are variables whose values are set by observations read from your data file. Input variables are declared using the VARIABLES statement For each step of the analysis NLREG cycles through each data observation and executes the statements in your NLREG program file Each execution begins by setting the input variables to the values for a specific observation If you want to transform input variables you should assign the transformed values to computed variables rather than modifying the values of input variables.

Computed variables are variables whose values are computed and assigned in the NLREG program file They are declared using the DOUBLE statement You can use computed variables to hold intermediate results of calculations or to hold transformed values of input variables Computed variables may hold single values (scalars), lists of items (vectors), or arrays of values You may assign initial values to computed variables when they are declared with the DOUBLE statement and you may modify the values during the course of execution.

System variables hold values calculated by NLREG during the execution of your program. There are three system variables:

- PREDICTED – the value of the dependent variable computed by executing your function using the current parameter and input variable values.
- RESIDUAL – the difference between predicted and actual value of the dependent variable of the function.

- OBS – the number of the observation record from your data file that is currently being executed, the first record is number 1 The PREDICTED and RESIDUAL variables only have defined values after the FUNCTION statement has been executed They are primarily useful in SPLOT and OUTPUT statements.

Symbolic constants are declared using the CONSTANT statement and assigned values with their declaration The values may not be altered after the declaration Symbolic constants may not appear on the left side of an equal sign; otherwise, they may be used wherever variables or constants may be used.

**Plots**

NLREG allows you to generate four types of plots as part of the analysis Any combination of these plot types may be requested and you can generate multiple scatter plots by including more than one SPLOT statement With the registered version of NLREG you can cause hard copy images of the plots to be printed. The plots are requested using the following statements:

PLOT – Generate a plot showing the computed value of the function superimposed on a scatter plot of the input data values NLREG evaluates the function using the computed values of the parameters at many data points over the domain and plots it as a smooth curve Because NLREG must evaluate the function at points between the observations the PLOT statement can only be used if your function has a single independent variable which is an input variable (not a computed variable) You may use symbolic constants in the function.

**Theory of Operation**

**Minimization Algorithm** NLREG uses a model/trust-region technique along with an adaptive choice of the model Hessian The algorithm is essentially a combination of Gauss-Newton and Levenberg-Marquardt methods; however, the adaptive algorithm often works much better than either of these methods alone.

The basis for the minimization technique used by NLREG is to compute the sum of the squared residuals for one set of parameter values and then slightly alter each parameter value and recompute the sum of squared residuals to see how the parameter value change affects the sum of the squared residuals By dividing the difference between the original and new sum of squared residual values by the amount the parameter was altered, NLREG is able to determine the approximate partial derivative with respect to the parameter This partial derivative is used by NLREG to decide how to alter the value of the parameter for the next iteration.

If the function being modeled is well behaved, and the starting value for the parameter is not too far from the optimum value, the procedure will eventually converge to the best estimate for the parameter This procedure is carried out simultaneously for all parameters and is, in fact, a minimization problem in n-dimensional space, where 'n' is the number of parameters.

For a much more detailed explanation of the regression algorithm used by NLREG see ACM Transactions on Mathematical Software 7,3 (Sept. 1981) "Dennis, J.E., Gay, D.M., and Welsch, R.E. – An adaptive nonlinear least-squares algorithm."

**Convergence Criterion**

NLREG has several convergence criteria that stop the iterative minimization procedure. The TOLERANCE statement can be used to alter the convergence tolerance value.

Two internal variables are used to determine when convergence has occurred. RFCTOL has a default value of 1E-10 and can be altered by use of the TOLERANCE statement AFCTOL has a default value of 1E-20 and is only altered by the TOLERANCE statement if the value specified is less than the default value. In the discussion which follows the "function value" is half the sum of the squared residuals computed using the current parameter estimates.

"Relative function convergence" is reported if the predicted maximum possible function reduction is at most RFCTOL*

ABS(F0) where F0 is the function value at the start of the current iteration, and if the last step attempted achieved no more than twice the predicted function decrease.

"Absolute function convergence" is reported if the function value is less than AFCTOL.

**Understanding the Results**

***Descriptive Statistics for Variables***

NLREG prints a variety of statistics at the end of each analysis. For each variable, NLREG lists the minimum value, the maximum value, the mean value, and the standard deviation. You should confirm that these values are within the ranges you expect.

***Parameter Estimates***

For each parameter, NLREG displays the initial parameter estimate (which you specified on the PARAMETER statement, or 1 by default), the final (maximum likelihood) estimate, the standard error of the estimated parameter value, the "t" statistic comparing the estimated parameter value with zero, and the significance of the t statistic Nine significant digits are displayed for the parameter estimates If you need to determine the parameters to greater precision, use the POUTPUT statement.

The final estimate parameter values are the results of the analysis. By substituting these values in the equation you specified to be fitted to the data, you will have a function that can be used to predict the value of the dependent variable based on a set of values for the independent variables For example, if the equation being fitted is

y = p0 + p1*x

and the final estimates are 1.5 for p0 and 3 for p1, then the equation

y = 1.5 + 3*x

is the best equation of this form that will predict the value of y based on the value of x.

t Statistic

The "t" statistic is computed by dividing the estimated value of the parameter by its standard error This statistic is a measure of the likelihood that the actual value of the parameter is not zero. The larger the absolute value of t, the less likely that the actual value of the parameter could be zero.

*Prob(t)*

The "Prob(t)" value is the probability of obtaining the estimated value of the parameter if the actual parameter value is zero The smaller the value of Prob(t), the more significant the parameter and the less likely that the actual parameter value is zero For example, assume the estimated value of a parameter is 1.0 and its standard error is 0.7 Then the t value would be 1.43 (1.0/0.7) If the computed Prob(t) value was 0.05 then this indicates that there is only a 0.05 (5%) chance that the actual value of the parameter could be zero If Prob(t) was 0.001 this indicates there is only 1 chance in 1000 that the parameter could be zero If Prob(t) was 0.92 this indicates that there is a 92% probability that the actual value of the parameter could be zero; this implies that the term of the regression equation containing the parameter can be eliminated without significantly affecting the accuracy of the regression.

**Understanding the Results**

***Descriptive Statistics for Variables***

NLREG prints a variety of statistics at the end of each analysis. For each variable, NLREG lists the minimum value, the maximum value, the mean value, and the standard deviation. You should confirm that these values are within the ranges you expect.

**Running NLREG**

Once NLREG has been installed, you can start it in either of two ways:

- Double click the icon representing the executable program (NLREG.EXE).
- Double click a NLREG analysis file which has the extension ".NLR" If you start the NLREG.EXE

program, it will begin with an empty workspace You can then either enter a new analysis program or click the open toolbar item to open an existing program file If you start NLREG by double clicking a program file, the program file will be loaded in the workspace when NLREG begins executing The sections that follow describe the statements that you can use in a program file.

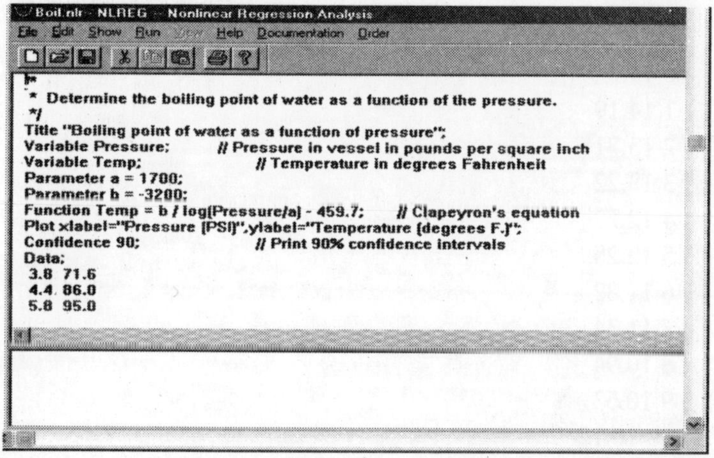


## Viewing the Results and Plots

When the analysis completes, the results of the analysis will be displayed The "Run" menu button will be grayed out and the "View" menu button will be enabled You can click "View" and select which view you wish to display If the analysis program specified one or more plots, you can display them by selecting the "Plot" option from the View list Select "Program source" from the View list to display and edit the current program file Anytime the program file is edited, the "Run" menu button will be reenabled and the "View" button will dim.

At this point, I suggest you pause in your reading and try running a NLREG example to get a feel for how it works Several example files with the extension ".NLR" are provided with the distribution LINEAR.NLR is a good one to start with followed by AIDS.NLR and TREND.NLR.

```
Title "Atmospheric pressure vs. altitude";
Variables altitude, pressure;
Parameter a = -4.4E-2;
Function pressure = 14.7*exp(a*altitude);
Plot xlabel="Altitude (thousands of feet)",ylabel="
Atmospheric pressure (PSI)";
Confidence;

Data;

0 14.7
1 14.19
2 13.71
3 13.22
4 12.72
5 12.25
6 11.82
7 11.34
8 10.94
9 10.53
10 10.12
15 8.3
18 7.35
20 6.8
25 5.5
30 4.4
36.09 3.2825
50 1.7
65.62 .802
```

```
1: Title "Atmospheric pressure vs. altitude";
2: Variables altitude, pressure;
3: Parameter a = -4.4E-2;
4: Function pressure = 14.7*exp(a*altitude);
5: Plot xlabel="Altitude (thousands of feet)", ylabel="
Atmospheric pressure (PSI)";
```

6: Confidence;
7: Data;

*Beginning computation...*

**Final Results**

Atmospheric pressure vs. altitude
Number of observations = 19
Maximum allowed number of iterations = 500
Convergence tolerance factor = 1.000000E-010
Stopped due to: Both parameter and relative function convergence.
Number of iterations performed = 4
Final sum of squared deviations = 6.4514166E-001
Final sum of deviations = 5.0755484E-001
Standard error of estimate = 0.189318
Average deviation = 0.156411
Maximum deviation for any observation = 0.388373
Proportion of variance explained (R^2) = 0.9981 (99.81%)
Adjusted coefficient of multiple determination (Ra^2) = 0.9981 (99.81%)
Durbin-Watson test for autocorrelation = 0.114
This Durbin-Watson value indicates autocorrelation or inappropriate function.
Analysis completed 4-Jan-1980 06:56 Runtime = 0.03 seconds.

**Descriptive Statistics for Variables**

| *Variable* | *Minimum value* | *Maximum value* | *Mean value* | *Standard dev.* |
|---|---|---|---|---|
| altitude | 0 | 65.62 | 16.56368 | 17.88034 |
| pressure | 0.802 | 14.7 | 9.140763 | 4.338967 |

**Calculated Parameter Values**

| *Parameter* | *Initial guess* | *Final estimate* | *Standard error* | *t* | *Prob(t)* |
|---|---|---|---|---|---|
| a | -0.044 | -0.039029244 | 0.000462987 | -84.30 | 0.00001 |

**90.000% Confidence Intervals**

| *Parameter* | *Lower limit* | *Best estimate* | *Upper limit* |
|---|---|---|---|
| a | -0.0398320817 | -0.039029244 | -0.0382264062 |

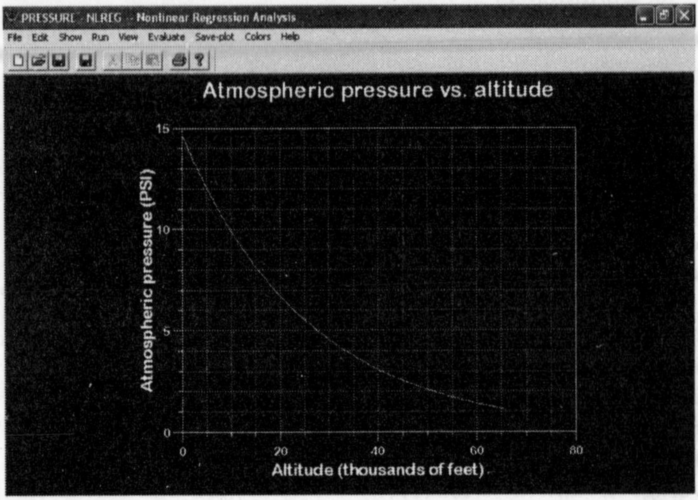
PRESSURE - NLREG - Nonlinear Regression Analysis
File Edit Show Run View Evaluate Save-plot Colors Help
Atmospheric pressure vs. altitude
Atmospheric pressure (PSI)
15
10
5
0
0
20
40
60
80
Altitude (thousands of feet)

# 21

# PAMCOMP (Person-years And Mortality computation Program)

## Introduction

PAMCOMP (*Person-years And Mortality computation Program-1.41*) is a free application for calculating person-years and standardized mortality ratios (SMR).The program was developed with Visual Basic 6.0 (SP5) and Visual C++ (SP5) and runs under Windows 95/98/2000/ME/NT and XP.

The calculation of person-years allows flexible stratification by sex, and self-defined and unrestricted calendar periods and age groups. Furthermore it is possible to lag person-years to account for latency periods. The SMR computation includes calculation of 90%, 95%, and 99% confidence intervals. Import and export filters for standard personal computer file formats (such as ASCII, dBase, MS-Excel, Paradox and MS-Access) to import cohort and reference data and to export distributions of person-years and deaths are available. In addition importing of external ODBC data sources is possible.

## User Interface

The main part of the graphical user interface consists of the navigator window and the output window.

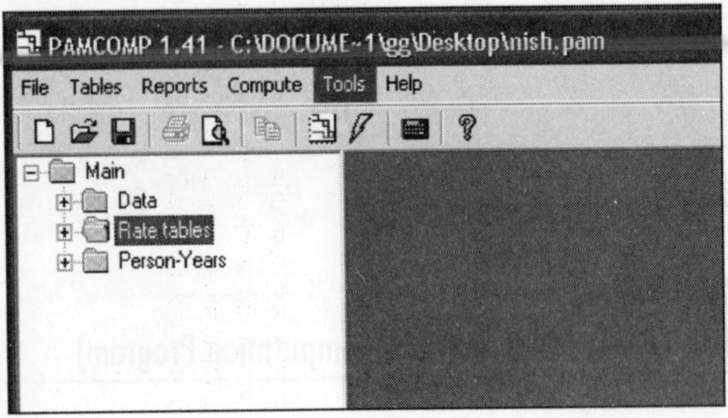


**Navigator window**

**Main**

| | | |
|---|---|---|
| ***Data*** | : | Here you can find your main file |
| ***Rate tables*** | : | Here you can find your rate files |
| ***Person-years*** | : | Here you can find the person-years output |

**Menus**

Menu File

| | | |
|---|---|---|
| ***New*** | : | Creates a new PAMCOMP file (*.Pam). |
| ***Open*** | : | Loads an existing PAMCOMP file. |
| ***Save*** | : | Saves the current PAMCOMP file. |
| ***Save as*** | : | Saves the current PAMCOMP file under a different name. |
| ***Exit*** | : | Exits PAMCOMP. |

**Menu Tables**

| | | |
|---|---|---|
| ***Main Table*** | : | Imports a main file to the current PAMCOMP file. |
| ***Rate Table*** | : | Imports a rate file to the current PAMCOMP file. |
| ***Copy*** | : | Copy results into the clipboard. |
| ***Save as*** | : | Saves the tables. |

**Menu Reports**

| | | |
|---|---|---|
| ***Save As*** | : | Saves the SMR report as ASCII or RTF-file. |
| ***Print*** | : | Prints the SMR report. |

**Menu Compute**

*Person-Years* : Computes the person-years.

**Menu Tools**

*SMR Calculator* : Launches the SMR Calculator.

*Options* : To set some options for the PAMCOMP software.

**Menu Help**

*Contents* : Displays the PAMCOMP help file.

*License* : Displays PAMCOMP license.

*About* : Displays version information as well as copyright information about PAMCOMP.

## What is A Main File?

The main file is the study file holds all interesting variables of the study cohort for calculating person years and standardized mortality ratios. For each cohort member there is one record which holds the following variables.

| *Variable* | *Description* |
|---|---|
| **Date-of-birth** | Date variable holding the date of birth. |
| **Entry-point-of-study** | Date variable holding entry point of study. |
| **Termination-point-of-study** | Date variable holding termination point of study. |
| **Date-of-hire** | Date variable holding date-of-hire (only for lagging). |
| **Sex** | Numeric variable holding sex status (optional). |
| **Death** | Numeric variable holding death status (only for SMR). |

## Creation of Main File

Main file can be created in MS-Excel, MS-Access, ODBC,SQL etc. Creation in excel is shown below.

| *DOB* | *EPS* | *TPS* | *DOH* | *ICD* | *SEX* |
|---|---|---|---|---|---|
| 01.01.1909 | 01.01.1981 | 06.01.1985 | 05.04.1929 | 0 | 1 |
| 01.01.1910 | 01.01.1981 | 08.01.1985 | 09.04.1924 | 162 | 2 |
| 01.01.1910 | 01.01.1981 | 20.04.1984 | 22.05.1960 | 162 | 2 |
| 01.01.1912 | 01.01.1981 | 04.01.1987 | 10.01.1955 | 0 | 1 |

After the creation of main table in excel sheet, the table is saved and then imported to the PAMCOMP like, go to Table/ Main table/add/excel 8.0.The table is shown below.

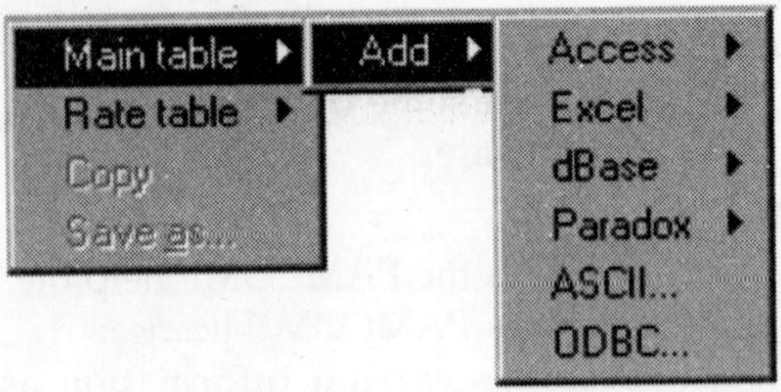


Adds the main table to the current PAMCOMP file.

**How to Compute Person Years?**

***Step1:*** Create a new PAMCOMP file with FILE | NEW.

***Step2:*** Add a main file with TABLES | MAIN TABLE | ADD.

***Step3:*** Go to COMPUTE | PERSON-YEARS. As shown below.

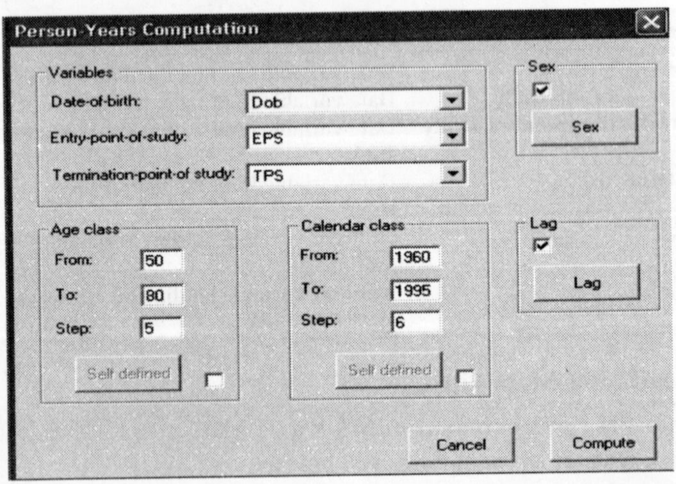


Now you must fill in the information PAMCOMP needs to compute person years.

***Date-of-birth:*** Date variable for the date-of-birth of each cohort member in the main file.

***Entry-point-of-study:*** Date variable for the entry-point-of study of each cohort member in the main file.

***Termination-point-of-study:*** Date variable for the termination-point-of-study for each cohort member in the main file.

*Age class:* Defines the age classes for the person-years computation.

*Calendar class:* Defines the calendar classes for the person-years computation.

*Sex:* Allows stratification by sex.

*Lag:* Allows to lag the person-years for a latency period.

*Step4:* Press the COMPUTE button and PAMCOMP will start to compute the person years.

## Age Class Definition

You can stratify the person-years by age. There are two possibilities.

### *Equal Interval Length*

If you want to have equal interval length (such as 5 years groups of age) you must fill in the fields. FROM, TO, STEP.

**Example:** FROM : 15
TO : 25
STEP : 5

This will produce two age classes: (15, 19)
(20, 24)

### *Unequal Interval Length*

If you want to have unequal interval length you must click on the checkbox on the lower right corner. This will enable the SELF DEFINED button. After clicking on this button a new dialog window will appear. Here you can input the age classes you want to have.

**Example:**

| Begin (incl.) | End (incl.) |
|---|---|
| 45 | 49 |
| 50 | 59 |

This will produce three classes: (45, 49)
(50, 59)

**Calendar Class Definition**

You can stratify the person-years by calendar year. There are two possibilities.

*Equal Interval Length*

If you want to have equal interval length (such as 5 years calendar classes) you must fill in the fields. FROM, TO, STEP.

**Example:** FROM : 1980
TO : 1990
STEP : 5

This will produce two calendar classes: (1JAN1980, 31DEC1984)
(1JAN1985, 31DEC1989)

*Unequal Interval Length*

If you want to have unequal interval length you must click on the checkbox on the lower right corner. This will enable the SELF DEFINED button. After clicking on this button new dialog window will appear. Here you can input the calendar classes you want to have.

**Example:** 1st January 31st December
1980 1984
1985 1994
1995 1999

This will produce three classes: (1JAN1980, 31DEC1984)
(1JAN1985, 31DEC1994)
(1JAN1995, 31DEC1999).

*Sex Stratification*

You can stratify by sex. You must click on the checkbox in the sex field. This will enable the SEX button. After clicking on this button a new dialog window will appear.

Firstly you have to choose the variable which holds the values for the gender. This variable must be of type integer. Secondly you have to insert the values for the sex separated by a comma.

**Example:** The values for the sex are Female=2
Male =1

Then you have to enter: 2, 1(or 1, 2).
All other values will be ignored.

**Lagging Person Years**

To lag for person years you must click on the checkbox in the lag field. This will enable the LAG button. After clicking on this button a new dialog window will appear.

First you have to choose the variable for date-of-hire which holds the date-of-hire for each cohort member in the main file. Second you have to insert the value for the lag years (a integer between 0 and 100).

**Example:** The following person was hired 1st January 1975. The entry-point-of-study was 1st January 1980 and the termination-point-of-study was 31st December 1995.

Without a lag this cohort member will contribute 15 person years.

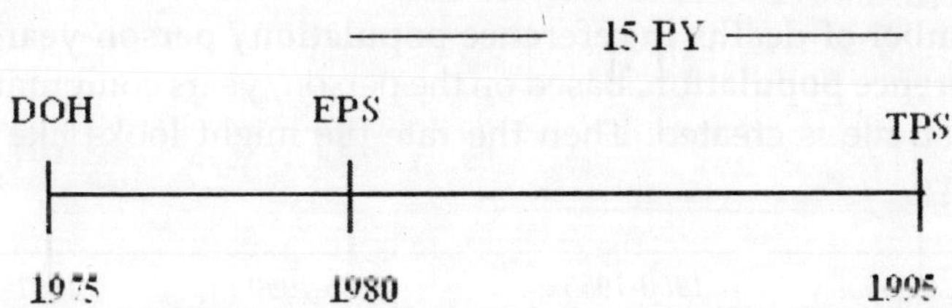


If you add a lag of 10 years the actual entry-point-of-study will change from 1st January 1980 to 1st January 1985 and this cohort member will now only contribute 10 person years.

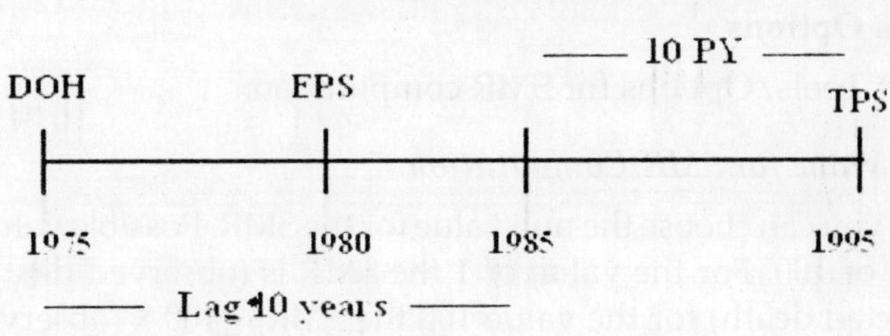


**Output Person-Years**

After person-years computation, you will find in the navigator window at MAIN | PERSON-YEARS either one or three person-year tables.

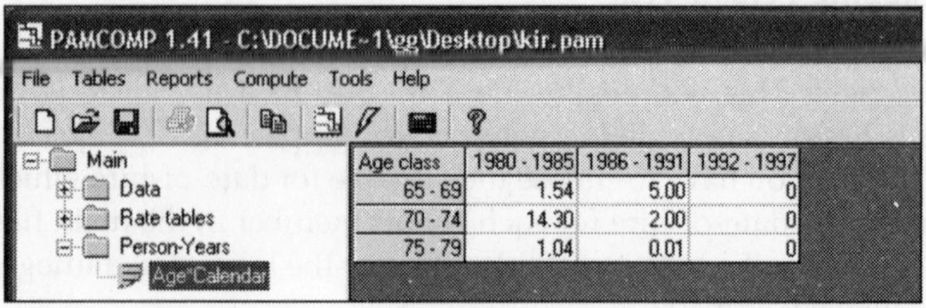


**What is a Rate File?**

The rate file holds the standard population reference rates for a specific cause of death. The rate file must have the same structure as the person-years table, i.e. the same number of age and calendar categories. The rate is defined as **Number of deaths in reference population / person-years in reference population.** Based on the person/years computation RATE file is created. Then the rate file might looks like the above.

| *Age/calendar* | *1980-1985* | *1986-1990* | *1991-1995* |
|---|---|---|---|
| 15-40 | 0.0089 | 0.0034 | 0.0167 |
| 40-50 | 0.0001 | 0.0021 | 0.0001 |
| 50-60 | 0.0012 | 0.0002 | 0.0008 |
| 60-85 | 0.0123 | 0.0223 | 0.0154 |

**Tools Options**

Select Tools/Options for SMR computation.

***Null Value for SMR Computation***

Here you can choose the null value for the SMR. Possible values are 1 or 100. For the value of 1 the SMR is (observed death/ expected death) for the value 100 the SMR is 100 x (observed death/expected death).

**TOOLS SMR Calculator**

With the SMR Calculator PAMCOMP gives you the ability to compute a SMR with confidence intervals by only knowing the observed and expected deaths. You have only to put in these numbers, and choose the different methods for calculating confidence intervals. Afterwards press the CALCULATE button.

It is also possible to print the result directly or save it as text (*.txt) or rich text format (*.rtf).

**Methods for Computing Confidence Intervals**

PAMCOMP is able to compute various confidence intervals for the SMR.

*Exact* : Computes exact confidence intervals.

*Byar* : Computes confidence intervals using the Byar approximation.

*Chi Square* : Computes confidence intervals using the Chi Square approximation.

*Square Root* : Computes confidence intervals using the Square Root approximation.

*Wald* : Computes confidence intervals using the Wald approximation.

Exact confidence intervals means that it is assumed that the observed deaths are distributed as a Poisson random variable. Because of the discrete nature of a Poisson distribution these confidence intervals are conservative. A good approximation for the exact method is the Byar approximation (which was used in previous version of PAMCOMP before v1.30). Chi Square, Square Root and Wald approximations are less accurate particularly for small observed deaths. Generally the confidence intervals can be constructed in that way that following holds:

CI_LOW = SMR x CI_L and CI_HIGH = SMR x CI_U

Where as CI_L and CI_ U appropriate multipliers.

Let be D the observed deaths and Z1-a/2 the 100(1- a/2) percentile of the normal distribution, i.e. for a=0.05 it is Z1-a/ 2=1.96 than the multipliers are:

**Exact** (see Sahai and Khurshid (1996) formulas 10.40 and 10.41)

$$CI\_L = SMR \times \frac{\lambda_L}{D}$$

*with* $\lambda_L$ *is solution of*

$$\sum_{i=D}^{\infty} \frac{\exp(-\lambda_L)\lambda_L^i}{i!} = \alpha / 2$$

$$CI\_U = SMR \times \frac{\lambda_U}{D}$$

*with* $\lambda_U$ *is solution of*

$$\sum_{i=0}^{D} \frac{\exp(-\lambda_U)\lambda_U^i}{i!} = \alpha / 2$$

**Byar approximation** (see Breslow and Day (1987) formula 2.13 or Sahai, H. and Khurshid, A. (1993) formulas 8.1 and 8.2).

$$CI\_L = SMR \times \left(1 - \frac{1}{9D} - \frac{Z_{1-\alpha/2}}{3\sqrt{D}}\right)^3$$

$$CI\_U = SMR \times \left(\frac{D+1}{D}\right)\left(1 - \frac{1}{9(D+1)} + \frac{Z_{1-\alpha/2}}{3\sqrt{D+1}}\right)^3$$

**Square Root** (see Breslow and Day (1987) formula 2.14 or Sahai, H. and Khurshid, A. (1993) formular 6.6)

$$CI\_L = SMR \times \left(1 - \frac{Z_{1-\alpha/2}}{2\sqrt{D}}\right)^2$$

$$CI\_U = SMR \times \left(\frac{D+1}{D}\right)\left(1 + \frac{Z_{1-\alpha/2}}{2\sqrt{D+1}}\right)^2$$

**Chi Square** (see Breslow and Day (1987) formula 2.15 or Sahai, H. and Khurshid, A. (1993) p. 864)

$$CI\_L = SMR \times \left[1 + \frac{1}{2D} Z_{1-\alpha/2}^2 \left[1 - \left(1 + \frac{4D}{Z_{1-\alpha/2}^2}\right)^{\frac{1}{2}}\right]\right]$$

$$CI\_U = SMR \times \left[1 + \frac{1}{2D} Z_{1-\alpha/2}^2 \left[1 + \left(1 + \frac{4D}{Z_{1-\alpha/2}^2}\right)^{\frac{1}{2}}\right]\right]$$

**Wald** (see Rothman and Greenland (1998) p. 236)

$$CI\_L = SMR \times \left[\exp\left(\frac{Z_{1-\alpha/2}}{\sqrt{D}}\right)\right]^{-1}$$

$$CI\_U = SMR \times \exp\left(\frac{Z_{1-\alpha/2}}{\sqrt{D}}\right)$$

## SMR Output

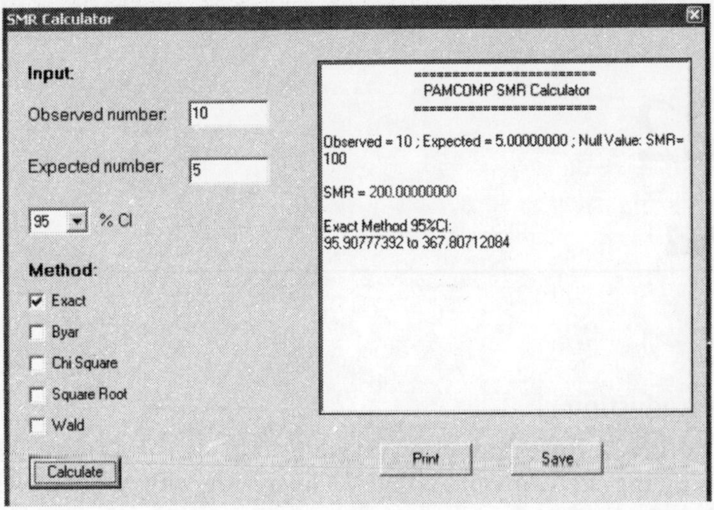
SMR Calculator
Input:
Observed number: 10
Expected number: 5
95 % CI
Method:
Exact
Byar
Chi Square
Square Root
Wald
Calculate
PAMCOMP SMR Calculator
Observed = 10 ; Expected = 5.00000000 ; Null Value: SMR= 100
SMR = 200.00000000
Exact Method 95%CI:
95.90777392 to 367.80712084
Print
Save

# 22

# Pnc2

## Introduction

The **PNC2 Rule Induction System** induces rules from data using the newly invented PNC2 Cluster Algorithm. The **PNC2 Rule Induction System** has a clean and useful user interface projects are set up within a few minutes.

## Basic Task of Data-based Modelling

The following figure illustrates the basic task of data-based modelling. Given is a system with an input vector **x** and the corresponding output y. The input vector consists out of one or several single input variables. The aim is to build up a model, which predicts the unknown output value given the input vector. A tuple P=(**x**,y) with the input vector and the output value is also called **data tuple**.

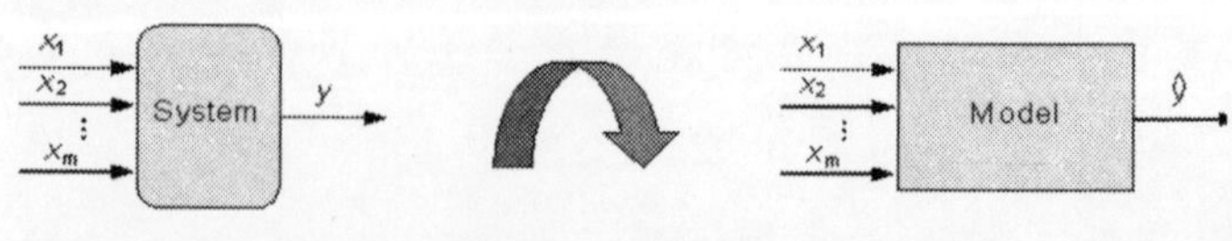


To build up a data-based model you first need to collect some data tuples from the real system by recording input and corresponding output values. Then the PNC2 cluster algorithm can be employed to find rules in your data.

With respect to the possible values there are three different types of variables. They are

**Nominal variables–**can only have symbolic values, that cannot be ordered with respect to a greater-less relation.

**Ordinal variables–**can only have symbolic values, but, in contrast to nominal variables, they can be ordered with respect to a greater-less relation.

**Learn and test data file format–**The learn and test data files have got to contain an **ASCII data matrix**. Each row corresponds to a data tuple and each column corresponds to a variable. The minimum number of tuples/rows in the learn data file is 10.

## Basic Idea of PNC2 Cluster Algorithm

The **PNC2 Cluster Algorithm** is a **supervised hierarchical agglomerative cluster algorithm.** This algorithm start treating each learn data tuple as an own cluster and then merge iteratively two clusters with each other until all clusters are merged into single cluster. In most hierarchical algorithms the clusters to be merged are chosen based on a distance or point density criterion.

### *Representation*

Each cluster is represented by an axis-parallel cuboid given in the input space and by an associated output value. The cuboid is build to include all the input vectors of the data tuples merged within the cluster. The cuboid corresponds to the premise and the associated output value is taken as the conclusion.

### *Agglomerative Clustering*

The agglomerative clustering is done as follows: First of all, each data tuple is considered as an own cluster by taking the data tuple's output as the cluster's output value and by building a trivial cuboid, that includes only the data tuple's input vectors. Only clusters with the same output value can be merged. Thus the clusters are assorted in groups according to their output values and it is tried to merge as many clusters as possible within each group. The clustering within a group is finished if there are no possible pairs of two clusters not tested anymore.

*Representation*

A data tuple is given, as described in What is it all about?, by an m dimensional input vector **x** and an associated output value y. A cluster is represented by an output value c and by an input space cuboid H. This cuboid has m single components that are defined as follows:

- **Nominal variables** can only have symbolic values, that cannot be ordered with respect to a greater-less relation. An example for a nominal variable is the color of an object, which can have the different symbols red, green and blue.
- **Ordinal variables** can only have symbolic values, but, in contrast to nominal variables, they can be ordered with respect to a greater-less relation. An example for an ordinal variable is a temperature that is measured with the qualitative terms cold, normal, warm and hot. Another example is the age of a person that is measured in years. Within the **PNC2 Rule Induction System,** ordinal variables with just a few different symbols, as the above example with the temperature, should be treated as nominal. But ordinal variables with many different symbols, as the above example with the age, should be treated as continuous.
- **Continuous variables** can have arbitrary real values-only limited by the precision of the measuring device. An example for a continuous variable is the temperature measured in centigrade.

The PNC2 Cluster Algorithm is primarily intended for classification tasks. However, it is also possible to handle regression tasks. Let us now see how to use the **PNC2 Rule Induction System** to learn a model and validate it using a separate test data set. The learn and test data files used are wine1.dat and wine2.dat.

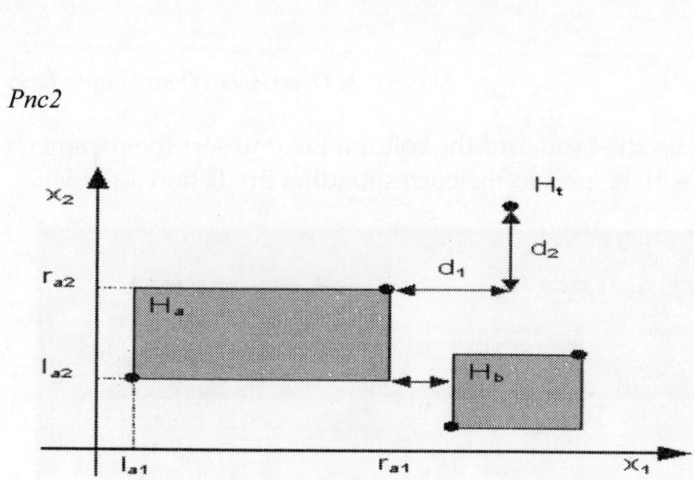


**Loading the Learn Data File**

Start the program. You will see just a single tab sheet named **BASIC**. Hit the **Load** button and select the file wine1.datThe file will be loaded, you will see the number of data tuples and variables, you will see that column 1 is selected as output and that the given problem is a classification task.

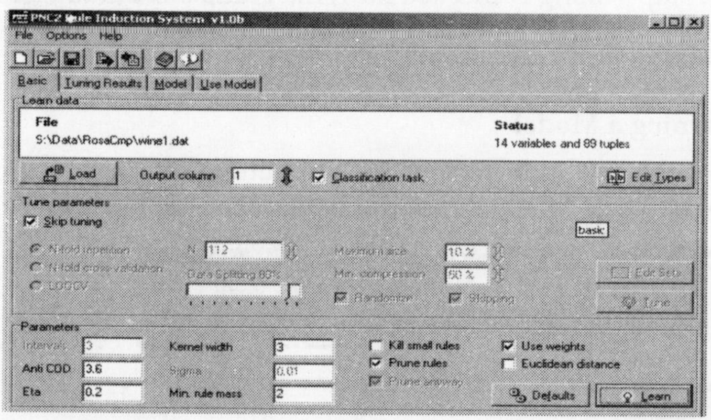


First, you have got to define some parameter sets. Hit the Edit Sets button. The Parameter Sets Dialog will pop up. Hit the button Go in the lower left corner to use the task wizard to automatically generate suitable parameter sets. Close the dialog by hitting Ok. Now the button Tune is enabled. Hit it. This will start the tuning process and open the new tab sheet Tuning results. Wait until the tuning is finished. Now click on the header of the column Error to sort the parameter sets with respect to the corresponding prediction accuracy.

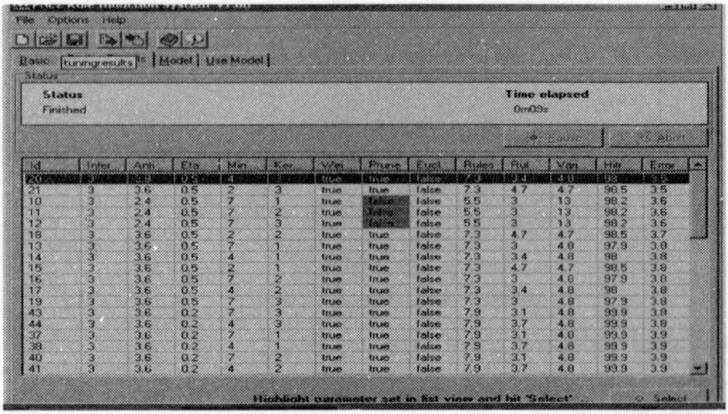


Select the best parameter set, as long as it is **not** colored red or yellow (light yellow is ok) by double clicking it. Now the program changes back to the tab sheet Basic. The check box Skip Tuning is checked now, the group box Parameters is enabled and the values of the selected parameter set have been copied to the corresponding edit fields.

## Learning a Model

Start the rule induction process by hitting the Learn button. The tab sheet Model appears and after the learning is finished

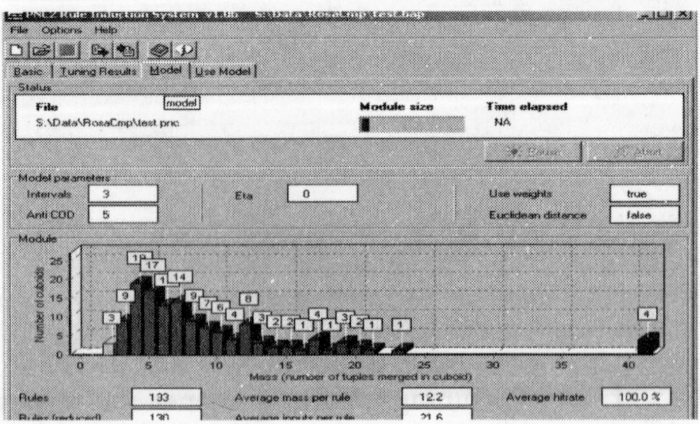

some model characteristics, like the number of rules induced, are shown. Also the tab sheet Use Model is visible now.

The Tabsheet USE MODEL is also shown.

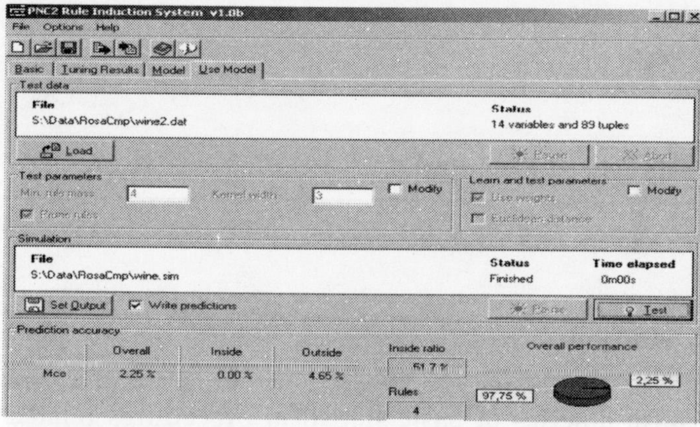

# 23

# SC (Statistics Calculator)

## Introduction

Statistics Calculator is an easy-to-use program designed to perform a series of basic statistical procedures related to distributions and probabilities. Most of the procedures are called inferential because data from a sample is used to infer to a population. The menu bar of Statistic Calculator contains eight choices. Exit, Distributions, Counts, Percents, Means, Correlation, Sampling & Help. These represent the basic types of operations that can be performed by the software.

## Exit

The Exit menu item is used to exit the software.

## Distribution

The Distributions menu item is the electronic equivalent of probability tables.Algorithms are included for the z, t, F, and chi-square distributions. This selection may be used to find probabilities and critical values for the four statistics.

## Count

The Counts menu item contains routines to analyze a contingency table of counts, compute Fisher's exact probability for two-by-two tables, use the binomial distribution to predict the probability of a specified outcome, and the poisson distribution to test the likelihood of observing a specified number of events.

**Percent**

The Percents menu item is used to compare two percents. Algorithms are included to compare proportions drawn from one or two samples. There is also a menu option to calculate confidence intervals around a per cent.

**Mean**

The Means menu item is used to calculate a mean and standard deviation of a sample, compare two means to each other, calculate a confidence interval around a mean, compare a sample mean to a population mean, compare two standard deviations to each other, and compare three or more standard deviations.

**Correlation**

The Correlation menu item is used to calculate correlation and simple linear regression statistics for paired data. Algorithms are included for ordinal and interval data.

**Sampling**

The Sampling menu item is used to determine the required sample size for a study. The software can be used for problems involving percents and means.

**Help**

The Help menu item is used to get this on-line help.

**Distribution**

***Normal Distribution***

It is used when the sample size is greater than 30. The menu offers three choices: 1) probability of a z value 2) critical z for a given probability, and 3) probability of a defined range.

*Probability of a z value*

When you have a z (standardized) value for a variable, you can determine the probability of that value.

***Example***

z-value: 1.96

Two-tailed probability = .0500

*Critical z for a given Probability*

This menu selection is used to determine the critical z value for a given probability.

*Probability of a Defined Range*

This menu selection will calculate the probability that the mean of a new sample would fall between two specified values.

***T Distribution***

The t distribution is used instead of the normal distribution when the sample size is small. The menu offers three choices: (1) probability of a t value, (2) critical t value for a given probability, and 3) probability of a defined range.

*Probability of a t Value*

If you have a t value and the degrees of freedom associated with the value, you can use this program to calculate the two-tailed probability of t.

***Example***

t-value: 2.228
df: 10

Two-tailed probability = .050

*Critical t Value for a given Probability*

It is used if you want to know what critical t value is required to achieve a given probability.

*Probability of a Defined Range*

You can use this program to calculate the probability that the mean of a new sample would fall between two values.

### F Distribution

The F-ratio is used to compare variances of two or more samples or populations. The menu offers two choices: (1) Probability of a F-ratio, (2) Critical F for a given probability

*Probability of a F-ratio*

If you have a F-ratio and the degrees of freedom associated with the numerator and denominator, you can use this program to calculate the probability.

**Example**

F-ratio: 2.774
Numerator degrees of freedom: 20
Denominator degrees of freedom: 10

---

Two-tailed probability = .0500

*Critical F for a given Probability*

If you know the critical alpha level and the degrees of freedom associated with the numerator and denominator, you can use this program to calculate the F-ratio.

### Chisquare Distribution

The chi-square statistic is used to compare the observed frequencies in a table to the expected frequencies. The menu has two choices: (1) Probability of a chi-square statistic (2) Critical chi-square for a given probability.

*Probability of a chi-square statistic*

If you have a chi-square value and the degrees of freedom associated with the value, you can use this program to calculate the probability of the chi-square statistic. It is the equivalent of computerized table of chi-square values.

**Example**

Chi-square value: 18.307
Degrees of freedom: 10

---

Probability = .050

*Critical chi-square for a given Probability*

If you have the critical alpha level and the degrees of freedom, you can use this program to calculate the probability of the chi-square statistic.

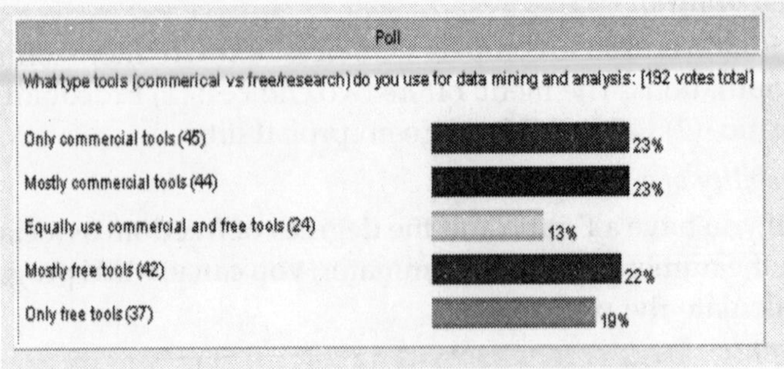


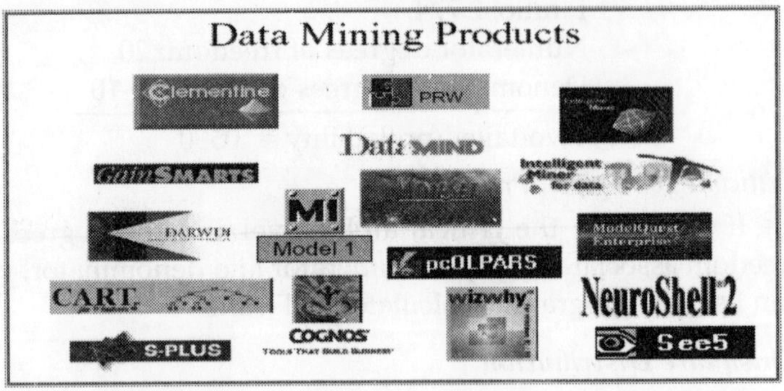


## Count

The Counts menu selection has four tests that can be performed for simple frequency data. The Counts menu has four selections:

- Chi-square test
- Fisher's exact test
- Binomial test
- Poisson distribution events test

### *Chi-square test*

The chi-square test is used to analyze a contingency table consisting of rows and columns to determine if the observed cell frequencies differ significantly from the expected frequencies.

### *Fisher's exact test*

Fisher's exact test is similar to the chi-square test except it is used only for tables with exactly two rows and two columns.

### *Binomial test*

The binomial test is used to calculate the probability of two mutually exclusive outcomes.

### *Poisson distribution events test*

The poisson distribution events test is used to describe the number of events that will occur in a specific period of time.

***Example***

Observed frequency: 25
Expected frequency: 39

Probability of 25 or fewer events = .0226

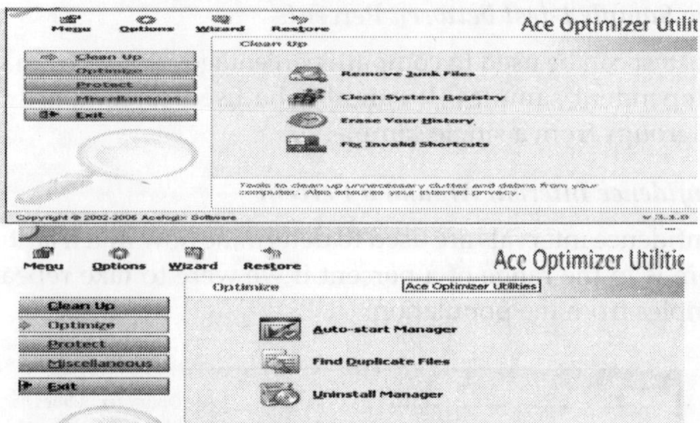


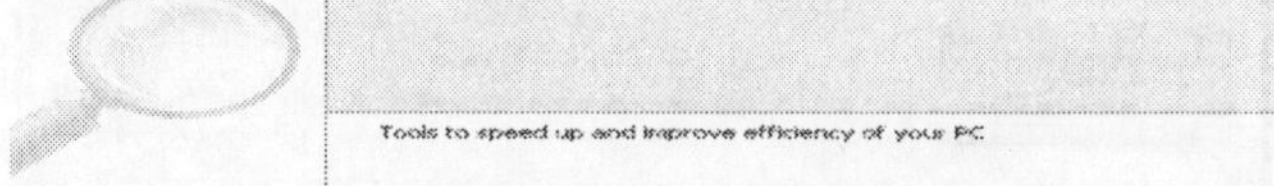


### Percent

Percents are understood by nearly everyone, and therefore, they are the most popular statistics cited in research. Researchers are often interested in comparing two percentages to determine whether there is a significant difference between them.The Percents menu has three selections:

- One sample t-test between percents
- Two sample t-test between percents
- Confidence interval around a percent

### *One sample t-test between Percents*

This test can be performed to determine whether respondents are more likely to prefer one alternative or another.

***Example***

Enter the first percent: 35.5
Enter the second percent: 22.4
Enter the sample size: 107

---

t-value = 1.808
Degrees of freedom = 106
Two-tailed probability = .074

### *Two Sample t-test between Percents*

This test can be used to compare percentages drawn from two independent samples. It can also be used to compare two subgroups from a single sample.

### *Confidence Interval Around a Percent*

Confidence intervals are used to determine how much latitude there is in the range of a percent if we were to take repeated samples from the population.

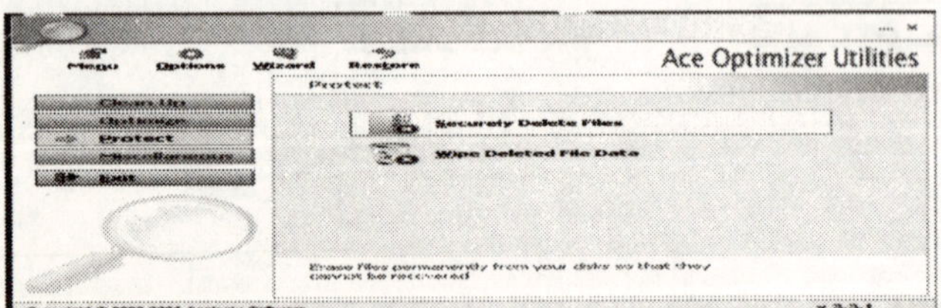


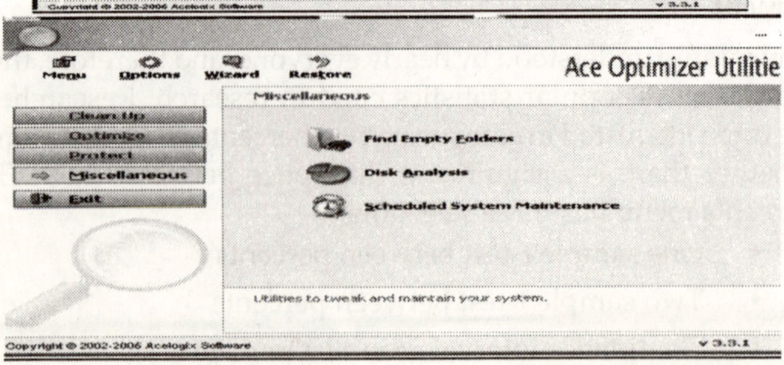

**Mean**

The Means menu has seven selections.

- Mean and standard deviation of a sample
- Matched pairs t-test between means
- Independent groups t-test between means
- Confidence intervals around a mean
- Compare a sample mean to a population mean
- Compare two standard deviations
- Compare three or more means

***Mean and Standard Deviation of a Sample***

This menu selection will let you enter data for a variable and calculate the mean, unbiased standard deviation, standard error of the mean, and median.

*Example*

A sample of ten was randomly chosen from a large population. The ten scores were:

20 22 54 32 41 43 47 51 45 35

Mean = 39.0

Unbiased standard deviation = 11.6

Standard error of the mean = 3.7

Median = 42.0

***Matched pairs t-test between Means***

The matched pairs t-test is used in situations where two measurements are taken for each respondent.

***Independent Groups t-test between Means***

This menu selection is used to determine if there is a difference between two means taken from different samples. If you know the mean, standard deviation and size of both samples, this program may be used to determine if there is a reliable difference between the means.

### *Confidence Interval Around a Mean*

You can calculate confidence intervals around a mean if you know the sample size and standard deviation.

### *Compare a Sample Mean to a Population Mean*

Occasionally, the mean of the population is known (perhaps from a previous census). After drawing a sample from the population, it might be helpful to compare the mean of your sample to the mean of the population.

### *Compare Two Standard Deviations*

The F-ratio is used to compare variances.In its simplest form, it is the variance of one group divided by the variance of another group.

### *Compare Three or More Means*

Analysis of variance (ANOVA) is used when testing for differences between three or more means.

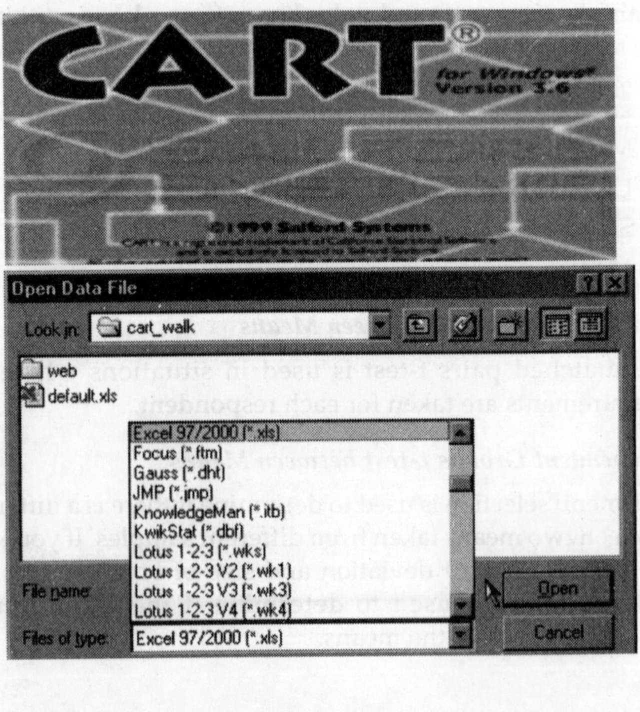

## Correlation

Simple regression is used to examine the relationship between one dependent and one independent variable.

In the regression equation, y is always the dependent variable and x is always the independent variable. Here are three equivalent ways to mathematically describe a linear regression model.

y = intercept + (slope · x) + error
y = constant + (coefficient · x) + error
y = a + bx + e

***Example***

| *IV* | *DV* |
|---|---|
| 4.2 | 27.1 |
| 6.1 | 30.4 |
| 3.9 | 25.0 |
| 5.7 | 29.7 |
| 7.3 | 40.1 |
| 5.9 | 28.8 |

Model: y = 10.079 + (3.700 · x) + error
Standard error of the estimate = 2.568
t-test for the significance of the slope = 4.095
Degrees of freedom = 4
Two-tailed probability = .0149
r-squared = .807

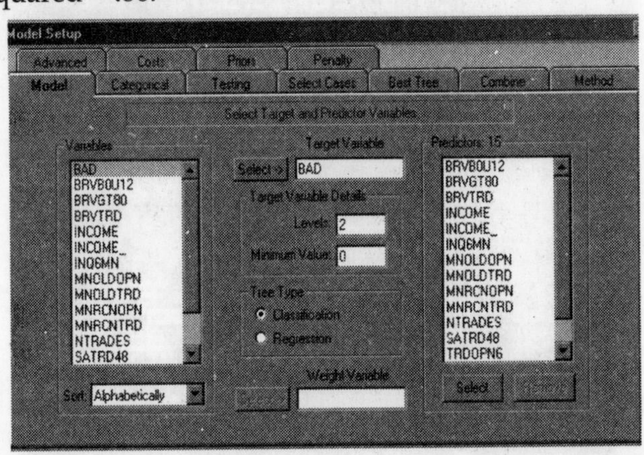

## Sampling

The formula to determine sample size depends upon whether the intended comparisons involve means or percents. The Sampling menu has two selections:

- Sample size for percents
- Sample size for means

### *Sample Size for Percents*

This menu selection is used to determine the required size of a sample for research questions involving percents.

***Example***

---

Best estimate of the population size: (left blank)
Best estimate of the rate in the population (%): 22
Maximum acceptable difference (%): 5
Desired confidence level (%): 95

---

Required sample size = 263

### *Sample Size for Means*

This menu selection is used to determine the required size of a sample for research questions involving means.

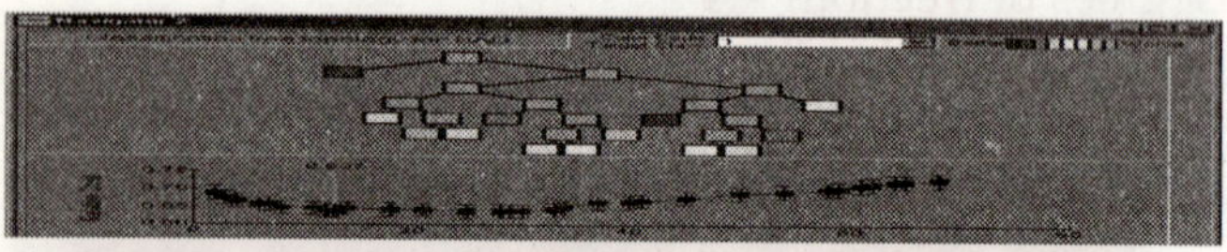

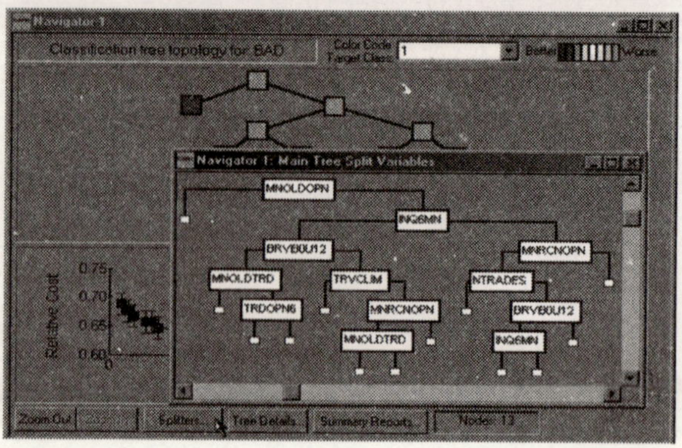

## References

Jiawei Han and Michiline Kamber (2000), *"Data Mining–Concepts and Techniques"*, Morgan Kaufmman Publishers.

John Wang, *"Encyclopedia of Data Warehousing and Data Mining"*.

# 24

## See5

### Introduction

Welcome to See5, a system that extracts informative patterns from data. The following sections show how to prepare data files for See5 and illustrate the options for using the system.

### Preparing Data for See5

We will illustrate See5 using a medical application—mining a database of thyroid assays from the Garvan Institute of Medical Research, Sydney, to construct diagnostic rules for hypothyroidism. Each case concerns a single referral and contains information on the source of the referral, assays requested, patient data, and referring physician's comments. Here are three examples:

***Attribute, Case 1, Case 2, Case 3 .....***

Age, 41, 23, 46
Sex, F, F, M
on thyroxine, F, F, F
query on thyroxine, F, F, F
on antithyroid medication, F, F, F
sick, F, F, F
pregnant, F, F, not applicable
thyroid surgery, F, F, F

I131 treatment, F, F, F
query hypothyroid, F, F, F
query hyperthyroid, F, F, F
lithium, F, F, F
tumor, F, F, F
goiter, F, F, F
hypopituitary, F, F, F
psych, F, F, F
TSH, 1.3, 4.1, 0.98
T3, 2.5, 2, unknown
TT4, 125, 102, 109
T4U, 1.14, unknown, 0.91
FTI, 109, unknown, unknown
referral source, SVHC, other, other
diagnosis, negative, negative, negative
ID, 3733, 1442, 2965

This is exactly the sort of task for which See5 was designed. Each case belongs to one of a small number of mutually exclusive classes (negative, primary, secondary, compensated). Properties of every case that *may* be relevant to its class are provided, although some cases may have unknown or non-applicable values for some attributes. There are 24 attributes in this example, but See5 can deal with any number of attributes.

See5's job is to find how to predict a case's class from the values of the other attributes. See5 does this by constructing a *classifier* that makes this prediction. As we will see, See5 can construct classifiers expressed as *decision trees* or as sets of *rules*.

### *Application Filestem*

Every See5 application has a short name called a filestem; we will use the filestem hypothyroid for this illustration. All files read or written by See5 for an application have names of the form filestem.extension, where filestem identifies the application and extension describes the contents of the file. The case of letters in both the filestem and extension is important—file names APP.DATA, app.data, and App.Data, are all different. It is important that the extensions are written exactly as shown, otherwise See5 will not recognize the files for your application.

*Names File*

Two files are essential for all See5 applications and there are three further optional files, each identified by its extension. The first essential file is the names file (e.g. hypothyroid.names) that describes the attributes and classes. There are two important subgroups of attributes:

- The value of an explicitly-defined attribute is given directly in the data. A *discrete* attribute has a value drawn from a set of nominal values, a *continuous* attribute has a numeric value, a *date* attribute holds a calendar date, a *time* attribute holds a clock time, a *timestamp* attribute holds a date and time, and a *label* attribute serves only to identify a particular case.
- The value of an implicitly-defined attribute is specified by a formula. (Most attributes are explicitly defined, so you may never need implicitly-defined attributes.)

The file hypothyroid.names looks like this:

```
diagnosis                          | the target attribute
age:                               continuous.
sex:                               M, F.
on thyroxine:                      f, t.
query on thyroxine:                f, t.
on antithyroid medication:         f, t.
sick:                              f, t.
pregnant:                          f, t.
thyroid surgery:                   f, t.
I131 treatment:                    f, t.
query hypothyroid:                 f, t.
query hyperthyroid:                f, t.
lithium:                           f, t.
tumor:                             f, t.
goitre:                            f, t.
hypopituitary:                     f, t.
psych:                             f, t.
```

```
TSH:                    continuous.
T3:                     continuous.
TT4:                    continuous.
T4U:                    continuous.
FTI:=                   TT4 / T4U.
referral source:        WEST, STMW, SVHC,
                        SVI, SVHD, other.
diagnosis:              primary, compensated,
                        secondary, negative.
ID:                     label.
```

**What's in a Name?**

Names, labels, classes, and discrete values are represented by arbitrary strings of characters, with some fine print:

- Tabs and spaces are permitted inside a name or value, but See5 collapses every sequence of these characters to a single space.
- Special characters (comma, colon, period, vertical bar '|') can appear in names and values, but must be prefixed by the escape character '\'. For example, the name "Filch, Grabbit, and Co." would be written as 'Filch\, Grabbit\, and Co\.'. (Colons in times and periods in numbers do not need to be escaped.)

Whitespace (blank lines, spaces, and tab characters) is ignored except inside a name or value and can be used to improve legibility. Unless it is escaped as above, the vertical bar '|' causes the remainder of the line to be ignored and is handy for including comments. This use of '|' should not occur inside a value.

**Specifying the Classes**

The first entry in the names file specifies the classes in one of three formats:

- A list of class names separated by commas, *e.g.* primary, compensated, secondary, negative.
- The name of a discrete attribute that contains the class value, *e.g.*: diagnosis.

- The name of a continuous target attribute followed by a colon and one or more thresholds in increasing order and separated by commas. If there are *t* thresholds *X1*, *X2*, ..., *Xt* then the values of the attribute are divided into *t+1* ranges:
  - less than or equal to *X1*.
  - greater than *X1* and less than or equal to *X2* . . .
  - greater than *Xt*.

  Each range defines a class, so there are *t+1* classes. For example, a hypothetical entry, age: 12, 19 would define three classes: age <= 12, 12 < age <= 19, and age > 19.

This first entry defining the classes is followed by definitions of the attributes in the order that they will be given for each case.

**Explicitly-defined Attributes**

The name of each explicitly-defined attribute is followed by a colon':' and a description of the values taken by the attribute. The attribute name is arbitrary, except that each attribute must have a distinct name, and case weight is reserved for setting weights for individual cases. There are eight possibilities for the description of attribute values:

***continuous***

The attribute takes numeric values.

***date***

The attribute's values are dates in the form YYYY/MM/DD or YYYY-MM-DD, e.g. 2005/09/30 or 2005-09-30.

***time***

The attribute's values are times in the form HH:MM:SS with values between 00:00:00 and 23:59:59.

***timestamp***

The attribute's values are times in the form YYYY/MM/DD HH:MM:SS or YYYY-MM-DD HH:MM:SS, e.g. 2005-09-30

15:04:00. (Note that there is a space separating the date and time.)

*a comma-separated list of names*

The attribute takes discrete values, and these are the allowable values. The values may be prefaced by [ordered] to indicate that they are given in a meaningful ordering, otherwise they will be taken as unordered. For instance, the values low, medium, high are ordered, while meat, poultry, fish, vegetables are not. The former might be declared as

grade: [ordered] low, medium, high.

If the attribute values have a natural order, it is better to declare them as such so that See5 can exploit the ordering. (**NB:** The target attribute should not be declared as ordered.)

*discrete N for some integer* N

The attribute has discrete, unordered values, but the values are assembled from the data itself; *N* is the maximum number of such values. This form can be handy for unordered discrete attributes with many values, but its use means that the data values cannot be checked. (**NB:** This form cannot be used for the target attribute.)

*ignore*

The values of the attribute should be ignored.

*label*

This attribute contains an identifying label for each case, such as an account number or an order code. The value of the attribute is ignored when classifiers are constructed, but is used when referring to individual cases. A label attribute can make it easier to locate errors in the data and to cross-reference results to individual cases. If there are two or more label attributes, only the last is used.

**Attributes Defined by Formulas**

The name of each implicitly-defined attribute is followed by ':=' and then a formula defining the attribute value. The formula is written in the usual way, using parentheses where needed, and may refer to any attribute defined up to this point. Constants in the formula can be numbers written in decimal notation, dates, times, and discrete attribute values enclosed in string quotes "".

The operators and functions that can be used in the formula are:

- +, -, *, /, % (mod), ^ (meaning 'raised to the power')
- >, >=, <, <=, =, <> or != (both meaning 'not equal')
- and, or
- sin(...), cos(...), tan(...), log(...), exp(...), int(...) (meaning 'integer part of')

The value of such an attribute is either continuous or true/false depending on the formula. For example, the attribute

FTI:= TT4 / T4U.

is continuous since its value is obtained by dividing one number by another. The value of a hypothetical attribute such as strange:= referral source = "WEST" or age > 40. would be either t or f since the value given by the formula is either true or false.

If the value of the formula cannot be determined for a particular case because one or more of the attributes appearing in the formula have unknown or non-applicable values, the value of the implicitly-defined attribute is unknown.

**Dates, Times, and Timestamps**

Dates are stored by See5 as the number of days since a particular starting point so some operations on dates make sense. Thus, if we have attributes,

```
1: date.
d2: date.
```

we could define

```
interval := d2 - d1.
gap := d1 <= d2-7.
d1-day-of-week := (d1 + 1) % 7 + 1.
```

interval then represents the number of days from d1 to d2 (non-inclusive) and gap would have a true/false value signaling whether d1 is at least a week before d2. The last definition is a slightly non-obvious way of determining the day of the week on which d1 falls, with values ranging from 1 (Monday) to 7 (Sunday).

Similarly, times are stored as the number of seconds since midnight. If the names file includes,

start: time.

finish: time.

elapsed := finish - start.

the value of elapsed is the number of seconds from start to finish.

Timestamps are a little more complex. A timestamp is rounded to the nearest minute, but limitations on the precision of floating-point numbers mean that the values stored for timestamps from more than thirty years ago are approximate. If the names file includes

departure: timestamp.

arrival: timestamp.

flight time := arrival - departure.

the value of flight time is the number of minutes from departure to arrival.

**Selecting the Attributes that can Appear in Classifiers**

An optional final entry in the names file affects the way that See5 constructs classifiers. This entry takes one of the forms

attributes included:

attributes excluded:

followed by a comma-separated list of attribute names. The first form restricts the attributes used in classifiers to those specifically named; the second form specifies that classifiers must not use any of the named attributes.

Excluding an attribute from classifiers is not the same as ignoring the attribute (see 'ignore' above). As an example, suppose that numeric attributes A and B are defined in the data, but background knowledge suggests that only their difference is important. The names file might then contain the following entries:

A: continuous.

B: continuous.

Diff := A - B.

attributes excluded: A, B.

In this example the attributes A and B could not be defined as ignore because the definition of Diff would then be invalid.

### Data File

The second essential file, the application's data file (e.g. hypothyroid.data) provides information on the *training* cases from which See5 will extract patterns. The entry for each case consists of one or more lines that give the values for all explicitly-defined attributes. If the classes are listed in the first line of the names file, the attribute values are followed by the case's class value. Values are separated by commas and the entry is optionally terminated by a period. Once again, anything on a line after a vertical bar ' | ' is ignored. (If the information for a case occupies more than one line, make sure that the line breaks occur after commas.)

For example, the first three cases from file hypothyroid.data are:

41,F,f,f,f,f,f,f,f,f,f,f,f,f,f,1.3,2.5,125,1.14,SVHC,negative,3733

23,F,f,f,f,f,f,f,f,f,f,f,f,f,f,4.1,2,102,?,other,negative,1442

46,M,f,f,f,f,N/A,f,f,f,f,f,f,f,f,0.98,?,109,0.91,other,negative,2965

**Don't forget the commas between values!** If you leave them out, See5 will not be able to process your data. Notice that '?' is used to denote a value that is missing or unknown. Similarly, 'N/A' denotes a value that is not applicable for a particular case. Also note that the cases do not contain values for the attribute FTI since its values are computed from other attribute values.

### Test and Cases Files (Optional)

Of course, the value of predictive patterns lies in their ability to make accurate predictions! It is difficult to judge the accuracy of a classifier by measuring how well it does on the cases used in its construction; the performance of the classifier on new cases is much more informative.

The third kind of file used by See5 consists of new test cases (e.g. hypothyroid.test) on which the classifier can be evaluated. This file is optional and, if used, has exactly the same format as the data file. Another optional file, the cases file (e.g. hypothyroid.cases), differs from a test file only in allowing the cases' classes to be unknown ('?'). The cases file is used primarily with the cross-referencing procedure and public source code, both of which are described later on.

**Costs File (Optional)**

The last kind of file, the costs file (e.g. hypothyroid.costs), is also optional and sets out differential misclassification costs. In some applications there is a much higher penalty for certain types of mistakes.

In this application, a prediction that hypothyroidism is not present could be very costly if in fact it is. On the other hand, predicting incorrectly that a patient is hypothyroid may be a less serious error. See5 allows different misclassification costs to be associated with each combination of real class and predicted class.

**User Interface**

It is difficult to see what is going on in an interface without actually using it. As a simple illustration, here is the main window of See5 after the hypothyroid application has been selected.

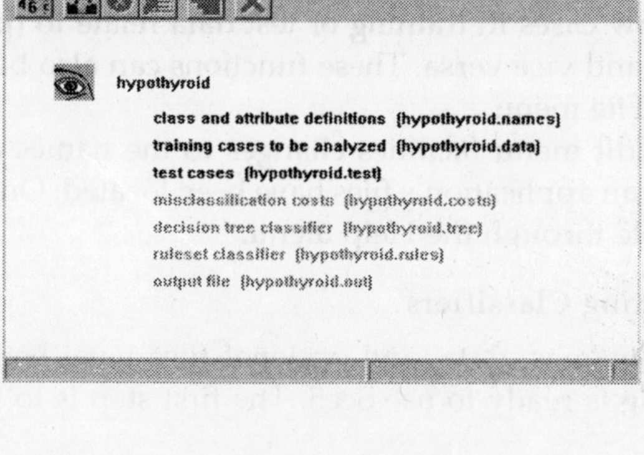

The main window of See5 has six buttons on its toolbar. From left to right, they are,

***Locate Data***

invokes a browser to find the files for your application, or to change the current application;

***Construct Classifier***

selects the type of classifier to be constructed and sets other options;

***Stop***

interrupts the classifier-generating process;

***Review Output***

re-displays the output from the last classifier construction (if any);

***Use Classifier***

interactively applies the current classifier to one or more cases; and shows how cases in training or test data relate to (parts of) a classifier and vice versa.

These functions can also be initiated from the File menu.

The Edit menu facilities changes to the names and costs files after an application's files have been located. On-line help is available through the Help menu

***Cross-Reference***

Shows how cases in training or test data relate to (parts of) a classifier and vice versa. These functions can also be initiated from the File menu.

The Edit menu facilities changes to the names and costs files after an application's files have been located. On-line help is available through the Help menu.

**Constructing Classifiers**

Once the names, data, and optional files have been set up, everything is ready to use See5. The first step is to locate the date using the Locate Data button on the toolbar. We will assume that the hypothyroid data above has been located in this manner. There are several options that affect the type of classifier that See5 produces and the way that it is constructed. The Construct Classifier button on the toolbar displays a dialog box that sets out th.lassifier construction options:

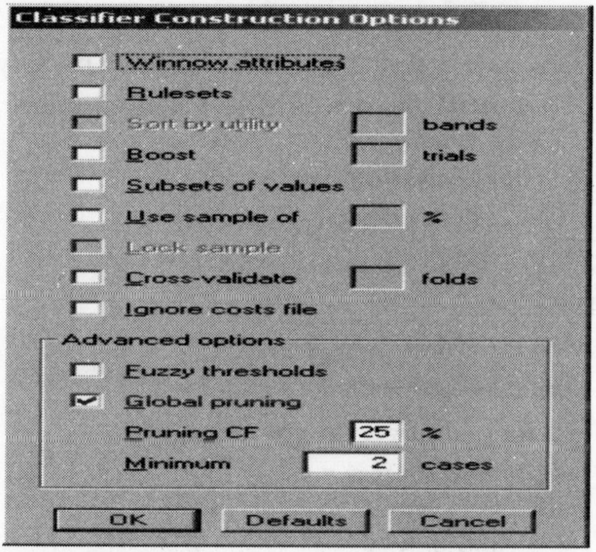


Many of the options have default values that should be satisfactory for most applications.

**Decision Trees**

When See5 is invoked with the default values of all options, it constructs a decision tree and generates output like this:

*See5 [Release 2.03]* Wed May 3 08:45:52 2006
Class specified by attribute 'diagnosis'
Read 2772 cases (24 attributes) from hypothyroid.data

***Decision Tree***

TSH <= 6: negative (2472/2)

TSH > 6:

:...FTI <= 65:

```
:...  thyroid surgery = t:
:     :.... FTI <= 36.1: negative (2.1)
:     :     FTI > 36.1: primary (2.1/0.1)
:     thyroid surgery = f:
:     :.... TT4 <= 61: primary (51/3.7)
:           TT4 > 61:
:           :...referral source in {WEST,SVHD}: primary (0)
:           referral source in {STMW,SVHC,SVI}: primary (4.9/
      0.8)
:           referral source = other:
:           :...TSH <= 22: negative (6.4/2.7)
:               TSH > 22: primary (5.8/0.8)
FTI > 65:
:...  on thyroxine = t: negative (37.7)
      on thyroxine = f:
      :...thyroid surgery = t: negative (6.8)
          thyroid surgery = f:
          :...TT4 > 153: negative (6/0.1)
              TT4 <= 153:
          :...TT4 <= 37: primary (2.5/0.2)
              TT4 > 37: compensated (174.6/24.8)
```

*Evaluation on training data (2772 cases)*

***Decision Tree***

| *Size* | *Errors* | | | |
|---|---|---|---|---|
| 12 | 7 (0.3%) | | << | |
| (a) | (b) | (c) | (d) | <-classified as |
| 60 | 3 | | | (a): class primary |
| | 153 | | 1 | (b): class compensated |
| | | 2 | | (c): class secondary |
| | 1 | 2552 | | (d): class negative |

*Evaluation on test data (1000 cases)*

***Decision Tree***

| *Size* | *Errors* | | | |
|---|---|---|---|---|
| 12 | 4 (0.4%) | << | | |
| (a) | (b) | (c) | (d) | <-classified as |
| 31 | | 1 | | (a): class primary |
| 1 | 39 | | | (b): class compensated |
| | | | | (c): class secondary |
| | 2 | 926 | | (d): class negative |

Time: 0.1 secs

The last section of the See5 output concerns the evaluation of the decision tree, first on the cases in hypothyroid.data from which it was constructed, and then on the new cases in hypothyroid.test. The size of the tree is its number of leaves and the column headed Errors shows the number and percentage of cases misclassified.

When there are no more than twenty classes, performance on the training cases is further analyzed in a *confusion matrix* that pinpoints the kinds of errors made. In this example, the decision tree misclassifies:

- three of the primary cases as compensated,
- one of the compensated cases as negative,
- both secondary cases as negative, and
- one negative case as compensated.

A similar report of performance is given for the optional test cases. A very simple *majority* classifier predicts that every new case belongs to the most common class in the training data. In this example, 2553 of the 2772 training cases belong to class negative so that a majority classifier would always opt for negative.

The 1000 test cases from file hypothyroid.test include 928 belonging to class negative, so a simple majority classifier would have an error rate of 7.2%. The decision tree has a lower error rate of 0.4% on the new cases, but notice that this is higher than its error rate on the training cases. If there are twenty or fewer classes, the confusion matrix for the test cases again shows the detailed breakdown of correct and incorrect classifications. The final line states the elapsed time for the run.

**Discrete Value Subsets**

By default, a test on a discrete attributes has a separate branch for each of its values that is present in the data. Tests with a high fan-out can have the undesirable side-effect of fragmenting the data during construction of the decision tree. See5 has a Subset option that can mitigate this fragmentation to some extent: attribute values are grouped into subsets and each subtree is associated with a subset rather than with a single value.

In the hypothyroid example, invoking this option merely simplifies part of the tree as referral source in {WEST,STMW,SVHC,SVI,SVHD}: primary (4.9/0.8) with no effect on classification performance on either the training or test data. Although it does not help much for this application, the Subset option is recommended when a dataset has important discrete attributes with more than four or five values.

**Rulesets**

Decision trees can sometimes be quite difficult to understand. An important feature of See5 is its ability to generate classifiers called *rulesets* that consist of unordered collections of (relatively) simple if-then rules. The Rulesets option causes classifiers to be expressed as rulesets rather than decision trees, here giving the following rules:

```
Rule 1: (31, lift 42.7)
        thyroid surgery = f
        TSH > 6
        TT4 <= 37
        -> class primary [0.970]
Rule 2: (63/6, lift 39.3)
        TSH > 6
        FTI <= 65
        -> class primary [0.892]
```

```
Rule 3: (270/116, lift 10.3)
        TSH > 6
        -> class compensated [0.570]
Rule 4: (2225/2, lift 1.1)
        TSH <= 6
        -> class negative [0.999]
Rule 5: (296, lift 1.1)
        on thyroxine = t
        FTI > 65
        -> class negative [0.997]
Rule 6: (240, lift 1.1)
        TT4 > 153
        -> class negative [0.996]
Rule 7: (29, lift 1.1)
        thyroid surgery = t
        FTI > 65
        -> class negative [0.968]
Default class: negative
```

*Each rule consists of*

- A rule number – this is quite arbitrary and serves only to identify the rule.
- Statistics ($n$, lift $x$) or ($n/m$, lift $x$) that summarize the performance of the rule. Similarly to a leaf, $n$ is the number of training cases covered by the rule and $m$, if it appears, shows how many of them do not belong to the class predicted by the rule. The rule's accuracy is estimated by the Laplace ratio $(n-m+1)/(n+2)$. The lift $x$ is the result of dividing the rule's estimated accuracy by the relative frequency of the predicted class in the training set.
- One or more conditions that must all be satisfied if the rule is to be applicable.
- A class predicted by the rule.

- A value between 0 and 1 that indicates the confidence with which this prediction is made.

**Boosting**

Another innovation incorporated in See5 is *adaptive boosting*, based on the work of Rob Schapire and Yoav Freund. The idea is to generate several classifiers (either decision trees or rulesets) rather than just one. When a new case is to be classified, each classifier votes for its predicted class and the votes are counted to determine the final class.

The Boost option with $x$ trials instructs See5 to construct up to $x$ classifiers in this manner. Naturally, constructing multiple classifiers requires more computation that building a single classifier—but the effort can pay dividends! Trials over numerous datasets, large and small, show that on average 10-classifier boosting reduces the error rate for test cases by about 25%.

Selecting the Boost option with 10 trials causes ten decision trees to be generated. The summary of the trees' individual and aggregated performance on the 1000 test cases is:

| *Trial* | *Decision Tree* | |
|---|---|---|
| | *Size* | *Errors* |
| 0 | 12 | 4 (0.4%) |
| 1 | 7 | 52 (5.2%) |
| 2 | 11 | 9 (0.9%) |
| 3 | 15 | 21 (2.1%) |
| 4 | 7 | 12 (1.2%) |
| 5 | 10 | 7 (0.7%) |
| 6 | 8 | 8 (0.8%) |
| 7 | 13 | 13 (1.3%) |
| 8 | 12 | 12 (1.2%) |
| 9 | 16 | 54 (5.4%) |
| boost | | 2 (0.2%) << |

The performance of the classifier constructed at each trial is summarized on a separate line, while the line labeled boost shows the result of voting all the classifiers. The decision tree constructed on Trial 0 is identical to that produced without the

Boost option. Some of the subsequent trees produced by paying more attention to certain cases have relatively high overall error rates. Nevertheless, when the trees are combined by voting, the final predictions have a lower error rate of 0.2% on the test cases.

**Winnowing Attributes**

The decision trees and rulesets constructed by See5 do not generally use all of the attributes. The hypothyroid application has 22 predictive attributes but only six of them appear in the tree and the ruleset. This ability to pick and choose among the predictors is an important advantage of tree-based modeling techniques.

When there are numerous alternatives for each test in the tree or ruleset, it is likely that at least one of them will appear to provide valuable predictive information. In applications like these it can be useful to pre-select a subset of the attributes that will be used to construct the decision tree or ruleset. The See5 mechanism to do this is called "winnowing" by analogy with the process for separating wheat from chaff.

Winnowing is not obviously relevant for the hypothyroid application since there are relatively few attributes. To illustrate the idea, however, here are the results when the Winnowing option is invoked:

*See5 [Release 2.03]* *Wed May 3 08:50:27 2006*

Options:

Winnow attributes

Class specified by attribute 'diagnosis'

Read 2772 cases (24 attributes) from hypothyroid.data

14 attributes winnowed

*Estimated importance of remaining attributes*

990% TSH

270% FTI

200% on thyroxine

30% thyroid surgery

```
        <1% age
        <1% T3
        <1% TT4
        <1% referral source
```

***Decision tree***

```
TSH <= 6: negative (2472/2)
TSH > 6:
:...FTI <= 65:
    :...thyroid surgery = t:
    :   :...FTI <= 36.1: negative (2.1)
    :   : FTI > 36.1: primary (2.1/0.1)
    :   thyroid surgery = f:
    :   :...TT4 <= 61: primary (51/3.7)
    :       TT4 > 61:
    :       :...referral source in {WEST,SVHD}: primary (0)
    :           referral source in {STMW,SVHC,SVI}: primary
    :           (4.9/0.8)
    :           referral source = other:
    :           :...TSH <= 22: negative (6.4/2.7)
    :               TSH > 22: primary (5.8/0.8)
    FTI > 65:
    :...on thyroxine = t: negative (37.7)
        on thyroxine = f:
        :...thyroid surgery = t: negative (6.8)
            thyroid surgery = f:
            :...TT4 > 153: negative (6/0.1)
                TT4 <= 153:
                :...TT4 <= 37: primary (2.5/0.2)
                    TT4 > 37: compensated (174.6/24.8)
```

*Evaluation on training data (2772 cases)*

**Decision Tree**

| *Size* | *Errors* | | | |
|---|---|---|---|---|
| 12 | 7(0.3%) | | << | |
| (a) | (b) | (c) | (d) | <-classified as |
| 60 | 3 | | | (a): class primary |
| | | 153 | 1 | (b): class compensated |
| | | | 2 | (c): class secondary |
| | | 1 | 2552 | (d): class negative |

*Evaluation on test data (1000 cases)*

**Decision Tree**

| *Size* | *Errors* | | | |
|---|---|---|---|---|
| 12 | 4 (0.4%) | | << | |
| (a) | (b) | (c) | (d) | <-classified as |
| 31 | | | 1 | (a): class primary |
| 1 | 39 | | | (b): class compensated |
| | | | | (c): class secondary |
| | | 2 | 926 | (d): class negative |

Time: 0.0 secs

After analyzing the training cases and before the decision tree is built, See5 winnows 14 of the 22 predictive attributes. This has the same effect as marking the attributes as excluded by an entry in the names file; winnowed attributes can still be used in the definition of other attributes. In this example, T4U is winnowed but is still available for use in the definition of FTI.

### Softening Thresholds

The top of our initial decision tree tests whether the value of the attribute TSH is less than or equal to, or greater than, 6. If the former holds, we go no further and predict that the case's class is-ve, while if it does not we look at other information before making a decision. Thresholds like this are sharp by default, so that a case with a hypothetical value of 5.99 for TSH is treated quite differently from one with a value of 6.01. See5 contains an option to 'soften' thresholds such as 6 above. When this is invoked, each threshold is broken into three ranges—let us denote them by a lower bound *lb*, an upper bound *ub*, and a central value *t*. If the attribute value in question is below *lb* or above *ub*, classification is carried out using the single branch corresponding to the '<=' or '>' result respectively. If the value lies between *lb* and *ub*, both branches of the tree are investigated and the results combined probabilistically. The values of *lb* and *ub* are determined by See5 based on an analysis of the apparent sensitivity of classification to small changes in the threshold. They need not be symmetric—a fuzzy threshold can be sharper on one side than on the other.

Invoking the Fuzzy thresholds option gives the following decision tree:

```
TSH <= 6 (6.05): negative (2472/2)
TSH >= 6.1 (6.05):
:...FTI <= 64 (65.35):
    :...thyroid surgery = t:
    :   :...FTI <= 24 (38.25): negative (2.1)
    :   :   FTI >= 52.5 (38.25): primary (2.1/0.1)
    :   thyroid surgery = f:
    :   :...TT4 <= 59 (61.5): primary (51/3.7)
    :       TT4 >= 63 (61.5):
    :       :...referral source in {WEST,SVHD}: primary (0)
    :           referral source in {STMW,SVHC,SVI}: primary
                (4.9/0.8)
    :           referral source = other:
    :           :...TSH <= 19 (22.5): negative (6.4/2.7)
    :               TSH >= 26 (22.5): primary (5.8/0.8)
```

```
FTI >= 66 (65.35):
:...on thyroxine = t: negative (37.7)
    on thyroxine = f:
    :...thyroid surgery = t: negative (6.8)
        thyroid surgery = f:
        :...TT4 >= 159 (153): negative (6/0.1)
            TT4 <= 146 (153):
            :...TT4 <= 14 (37.5): primary (2.5/0.2)
                TT4 >= 61 (37.5): compensated (174.6/24.8)
```

Each threshold is now of the form <= *lb* (*t*) or >= *ub* (*t*). In this example, most of the thresholds are still relatively tight, but notice the asymmetric threshold values for the test FTI <= 64. For this application, soft thresholds slightly improve the classifier's accuracy on both training and test data.

A final point: soft thresholds affect only decision tree classifiers—they do not change the interpretation of rulesets.

### Advanced Pruning Options

Three further options enable aspects of the classifier-generation process to be tweaked. These are best regarded as *advanced* options that should be used sparingly, so that this section can be skipped without much loss.

See5 constructs decision trees in two phases. A large tree is first grown to fit the data closely and is then 'pruned' by removing parts that are predicted to have a relatively high error rate. This pruning process is first applied to every subtree to decide whether it should be replaced by a leaf or sub-branch, and then a global stage looks at the performance of the tree as a whole.

Turning off the default Global pruning option disables this second pruning component and generally results in larger decision tees and rulesets. For the hypothyroid application, the tree increases in size from 12 to 13 leaves. Turning off global pruning can be beneficial for some applications, particularly when rulesets are generated.

The Pruning CF option affects the way that error rates are estimated and hence the severity of pruning; values smaller than the default (25%) cause more of the initial tree to be pruned, while larger values result in less pruning.

**Sampling from Large Datasets**

Even though See5 is relatively fast, building classifiers from large numbers of cases can take an inconveniently long time, especially when options such as boosting are employed. See5 incorporates a facility to extract a random sample from a dataset, construct a classifier from the sample, and then test the classifier on a disjoint collection of cases. By using a smaller set of training cases in this way, the process of generating a classifier is expedited, but at the cost of a possible reduction in the classifier's predictive performance.

In the hypothyroid example, using a sample of 60% would cause a classifier to be constructed from a randomly-selected 1663 of the 2772 cases in hypothyroid.data, then tested on the remaining 1109 cases.

By default, the random sample changes every time that a classifier is constructed, so that successive runs of See5 with sampling will usually produce different results. This re-sampling can be avoided by selecting the Lock sample option that uses the current sample for constructing subsequent classifiers. If this option is selected, the sample will change only when another application is loaded, the sample percentage is altered, the option is unselected, or See5 is restarted.

**Cross-validation Trials**

If the cases in hypothyroid.data and hypothyroid.test were to be shuffled and divided into a new 2772-case training set and a 1000-case test set, See5 might construct a different classifier with a lower or higher error rate on the test cases. One way to get a more reliable estimate of predictive accuracy is by *f-fold cross-validation*. The cases in the data file are divided into *f* blocks of roughly the same size and class distribution.

For each block in turn, a classifier is constructed from the cases in the remaining blocks and tested on the cases in the hold-out block. In this way, each case is used just once as a test case. The error rate of a classifier produced from all the cases is estimated as the ratio of the total number of errors on the hold-out cases to the total number of cases.

The Cross-validation option with *f* folds runs such a *f*-fold cross-validation. Suppose now that we select the Cross-validation option with 10 folds together with the Rulesets option. After giving details of the individual rulesets, the output shows a summary like this:

| *Fold* | *Rules* | |
|---|---|---|
| | *No* | *Errors* |
| 0 | 7 | 0.8% |
| 1 | 7 | 0.3% |
| 2 | 7 | 0.5% |
| 3 | 7 | 0.3% |
| 4 | 8 | 0.8% |
| 5 | 7 | 0.5% |
| 6 | 7 | 0.3% |
| 7 | 6 | 0.5% |
| 8 | 7 | 0.5% |
| 9 | 7 | 0.8% |
| Mean | 7.0 | 0.5% |
| SE | 0.1 | 0.1% |

This estimates the error rate of the rulesets produced from the 2772 cases in hypothyroid.data at 0.5%. The *SE* figures provide an estimate of the variability of these results.

The cross-validation procedure can be repeated for different random partitions of the cases into blocks. The average error rate from these distinct cross-validations is then an even more reliable estimate of the error rate of the single classifier produced from all the cases.

Since every cross-validation fold uses only part of the application's data, running a cross-validation does not cause a classifier to be saved. To save a classifier for later use, simply run See5 without employing cross-validation.

**Using Classifiers**

Once a classifier has been constructed, an *interactive interpreter* can be used to predict the classes to which new cases belong.

The Use Classifier button invokes the interpreter, using the most recent classifier for the current application, and prompts for information about the case to be classified. Since the values of all attributes may not be needed, the attribute values requested will depend on the case itself. When all the relevant information has been entered, the most likely class are shown, each with a confidence value. For example, this is the result of analyzing a case using the first decision tree above.

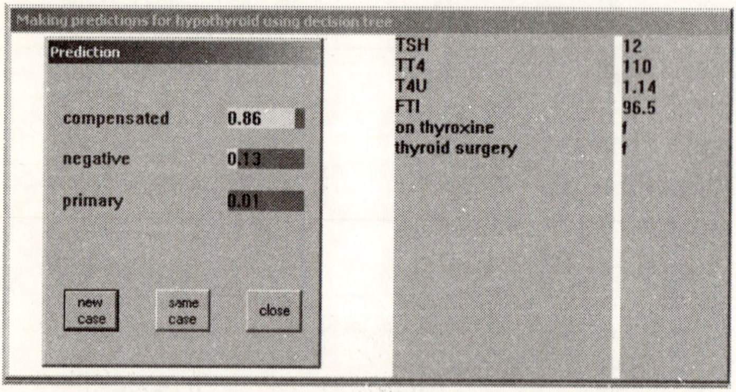


Classifiers can also be used in batch mode. The sample application provided in the public source code reads cases from a cases file and shows the predicted class and the confidence for each.

**Cross-Referencing Classifiers and Data**

See5 incorporates a unique facility that links data and the relevant sections of classifiers. We will illustrate this facility using the first decision tree for the hypothyroid application and the cases in hypothyroid.data from which it was constructed. The Cross-Reference button brings up a window showing the most recent classifier for the current application and how it relates to the cases in the data, test or cases file. The window is divided into two panes, with the classifier on the left and a list of cases on the right. The Reset button can be used at any time to restore the window to this initial state. Each case has a **[?]** tag, an identifying number or label, and the class predicted for the case. Clicking on the tag **[?]** in front of a case number or label displays that case:

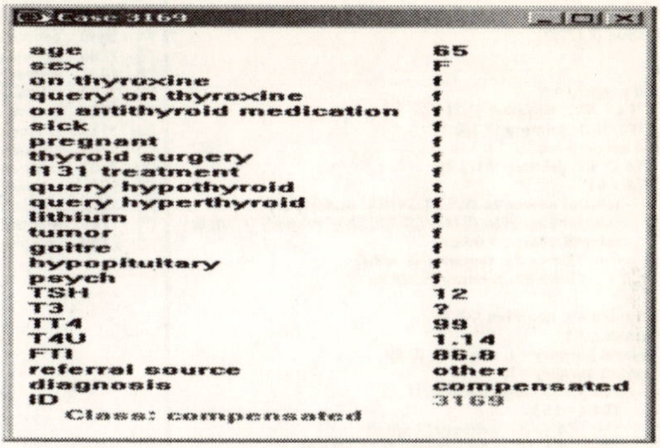


The values of label attributes and attributes excluded or ignored are displayed in a lighter tone to indicate that they play no part in classifying the case. Clicking on a case's label or number shows the part(s) of the classifier(s) relevant to that case. For instance, clicking on case **3169** shows the leaf to which this case is mapped:

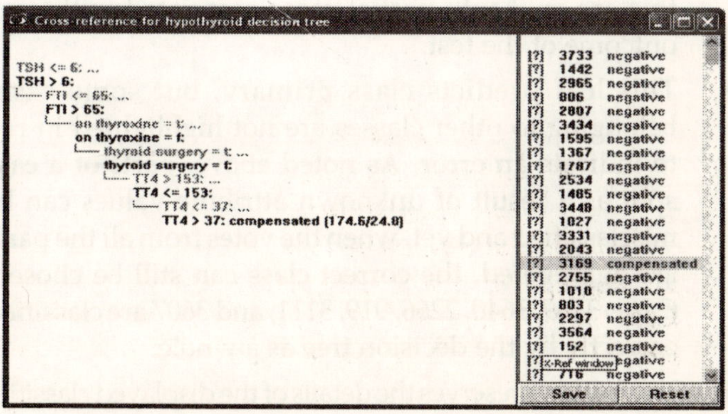


If a case has missing values for one or more attributes, if it is covered by several rules, or if boosted classifiers are used, more than one leaf or rule may be relevant to a case. In such situations, all relevant classifier parts are shown. Click on any leaf or rule, and all the cases that map to the leaf or rule are shown. For instance, clicking on Reset and then the leaf indicated shows all cases that are covered by that leaf:

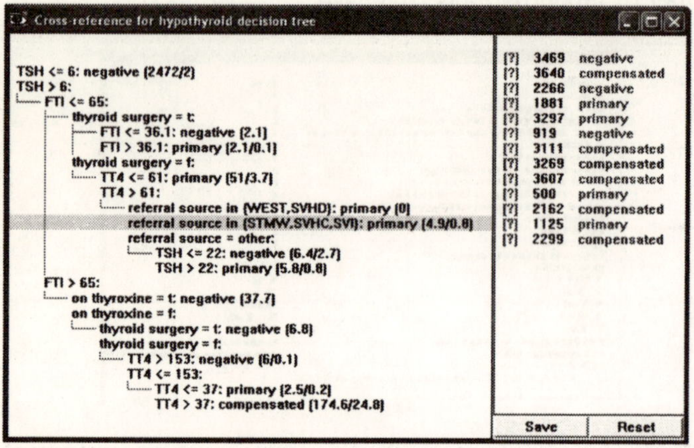


This last pane may be puzzling for two reasons:

- The case pane shows thirteen cases but the count shown at the leaf is 4.9. This happens because some of these thirteen cases have unknown values for the attributes tested on the path to this leaf . Cases like this are split into partial cases associated with each outcome of the test.
- This leaf predicts class primary, but some cases belonging to other classes are not highlighted in red to indicate an error. As noted above, parts of a case split as a result of unknown attribute values can be misclassified and yet, when the votes from all the parts are aggregated, the correct class can still be chosen. Cases 3469, 3640, 2266, 919, 3111, and 3607 are classified correctly by the decision tree as a whole.

The Save button preserves the details of the displayed classifier and case list as an ASCII file selected through a dialog box.

### Generating Classifiers in Batch Mode

The See5 distribution includes a program See5X that can be used to produce classifiers non-interactively. This console application resides in the same folder as See5 and is invoked from an MS-DOS Prompt window. The command to run the program is:

start/B See5X -f filestem parameters

where the parameters enable one or more options discussed above to be selected:

| | |
|---|---|
| -s | use the Subset option |
| -r | use the Ruleset option |
| -u bands | sort rules by their utility into bands |
| -b | use the Boosting option with 10 trials |
| -t trials | ditto with specified number of trials |
| -w | winnow attributes before constructing a classifier |
| -S x | use the Sampling option with x% |
| -I seed | set the sampling seed value |
| -X folds | carry out a cross-validation |
| -g | turn off the global tree pruning stage |
| -c CF | set the Pruning CF value |
| -m cases | set the Minimum cases |
| -p | use the Fuzzy thresholds option |
| -e | ignore any costs file |

If desired, output from See5 can be diverted to a file in the usual way.

**Linking to other Programs**

The classifiers generated by See5 are retained in files filestem.tree (for decision trees) and filestem.rules (for rulesets). Free C source code is available to read these classifier files and to make predictions with them, enabling you to use See5 classifiers in other programs. As an example, the source includes a program to read cases from a cases file, and to show how each is classified by boosted or single trees or rulesets.

**References**

See5 RuleQuest INC.

Witten, E. Frank (2000), "Data Mining-Practical Machine Learning Tools and Techniques with JAVA Implementations", Morgan Kaufmann Publishers.

# 25

## SSC (Sample Size Calculator)

### Introduction

It calculate sample size required for a given confidence interval for a given sample size. It can handle all finite populations. This sample size calculator is used for performing sample size calculations. This tool runs under Microsoft windows operating systems. This is used for studies of opinions and behaviour of groups. Sampling is the foundation of all research. Reliable sampling helps you make business decisions with confidence.

There are **two main components** in determining whom you will interview.

The first is deciding **what kind of people to interview**. Researchers often call this group the target population. If you conduct an employee attitude survey or an association membership survey, the population is obvious. If you are trying to determine the likely success of a product, the target population may be less obvious. Correctly determining the target population is critical. If you do not interview the right kinds of people, you will not successfully meet your goals.

The next step is to decide **how many people you need to interview**. Statisticians know that a small, representative sample will reflect opinions and behavior of the group from which it was drawn. The larger the sample, the more precisely it represents the target group. However, the rate of improvement in the precision decreases as your sample size increases. For example, to increase a sample from 250 to 1,000 only doubles the precision. You must make a decision about your sample size based on factors such as: time available, budget and necessary degree of precision.

**Sample Size Terminology**

There are three factors that determine the size of the confidence interval for a given confidence level. These are: sample size, percentage of sample that picked a particular answers and population size.

*Sample Size*

The larger your sample, the more sure you can be that their answers truly reflect the opinion of the population. This indicates that for a given confidence level, the larger your sample size, the smaller your confidence interval. However, the relationship is not linear (i.e., doubling the sample size does not halve the confidence interval).

*Percentage of Sample that Picked a Particular Answer*

Your accuracy also depends on the percentage of your sample that picks a particular answer. If 99% of your sample said "Yes" and 1% said "No" the chances of error are remote, irrespective of sample size. However, if the percentages are 51% and 49% the chances of error are much greater. It is easier to be sure of extreme answers than of middle-of-the-road ones.

The sample size needed for a given level of accuracy you must use the worst-case percentage (50%). You should also use this percentage if you want to determine a general level of accuracy for a sample you already have. To determine the confidence interval for a specific answer your sample has given, you can use the percentage picking that answer and get a smaller interval.

*Population Size*

How many people does your sample represent? This may be the number of people in a city you are studying, the number of people who buy new cars, etc. Often you may not know the exact population size. This is not a problem. The mathematics of probability proves the size of the population is irrelevant, unless the size of the sample exceeds a few percent of the total population you are examining. This means that a sample of 500 people is equally useful in examining the opinions of a state of 15,000,000 as it would a city of 100,000. For this reason, the population size is ignored when it is "large" or unknown. Population size is only likely to be a factor when you work with a relatively small and known group of people (e.g., the members of an association).

The confidence interval calculations assume you have a genuine random sample of the relevant population. If your sample is not truly random, you cannot rely on the intervals. Non-random samples usually result from some flaw in the sampling procedure. An example of such a flaw is to only call people during the day, and miss almost everyone who works. For most purposes, the non-working population cannot be assumed to accurately represent the entire (working and non-working) population.

### *Confidence Interval*

It is the plus-or-minus figure usually reported in newspaper or television opinion poll results. For example, if you use a confidence interval of 4 and 47% percent of your sample picks an answer you can be "sure" that if you had asked the question of the entire relevant population between 43% (47-4) and 51% (47+4) would have picked that answer.

### *Confidence Level*

It tells you how sure you can be. It is expressed as a percentage and represents how often the true percentage of the population who would pick an answer lies within the confidence interval. The 95% confidence level means you can be 95% certain; the 99% confidence level means you can be 99% certain. Most researchers use the 95% confidence level.

When you put the **confidence level** and the **confidence interval** together, you can say that you are 95% sure that the true percentage of the population is between 43% and 51%.

### *Correlation between Sample Size and Confidence Interval*

The wider the confidence interval you are willing to accept, the more certain you can be that the whole population's answers would be within that range. For example, if you asked a sample of 100 people in a city which brand of cola they preferred, and 60% said Brand A, you can be very certain that between 50% and 70% of all the people in the city actually do prefer that brand, but you cannot be sure that between 59% and 61% of the people in the city prefer the brand.

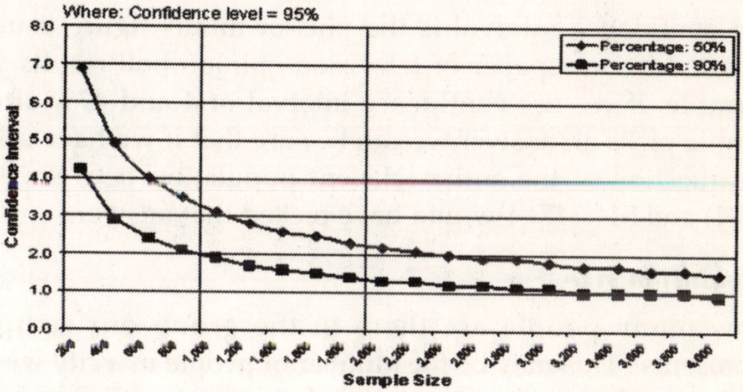


### *Sample Size Formula*

$$ss = \frac{Z^2 * (p) * (1-p)}{C^2}$$

where:
Z = Z value (e.g. 1.96 for 95% confidence level)
p = percentage picking a choice, expressed as decimal
(.5 used for sample size needed)
c = confidence interval, expressed as decimal
(e.g., .04 = ±4)

Correction for Finite Population

$$\text{new ss} = \frac{ss}{1 + \frac{ss-1}{pop}}$$

where: pop = population

## Features of Sample Size Calculator

### *Confidence Level*

The confidence level tells us how sure we can be.It is expressed as a percentage and represents how often the time percentage of the population who would pick an answer lies with in the confidence interval. The 95% confidence level means we can be 95% certain; the 99% confidence level means we can be 99% certain.Most researchers use 95% confidence level.

### *Confidence Interval*

The confidence interval is the plus-or-minus figure usually reported in newspaper or television opinion poll results. For **example,** if we use confidence interval of 4 and 47% of our sample picks an answer we can be sure that if we have asked the question of the entire relavent population between 43% (47-4) and 51%(47+4)would have picked that answer.

### *Population size*

How many people are there in the group our samples represents? This may be the number of people in a city we are studying, The number of people who buy new cars, etc.

Often we may not know the exact population size.This is not a problem. The mathematics of probability proves the size of population is irrelevant, unless the size of the sample exceeds a few percentage of the total population we are examining.This means that sample of 500 people is usually useful in examining the opinion of a state of 15,000,000 as it would a city of 1,00,000.For this reason,population size ignored when it is large are unknown .Population size is only likely to be a factor when we work with a relatively small and known group of people.

### *Sample Size*

The larger your sample ,the more 'sure' you can be that their answer truly reflect the population.This indicates that for a given confidence level,the larger your sample size the smaller confidence interval however the relationship is not linear htat is doubling the sample size does not halve the confidence interval. when determining the sample size needed for a given level of accuracy the worst case percentage (50%) is used .we should also use this percentage if we want to determine a general level of accuracy for a sample we already have to determine the confidence interval for a specific answer our sample has given we can use the percentage picking that answer and get a smaller interval.

### *Percentage*

Our accuracy also depends on the percentage of our sample that picks a particular answer.If 99% of our sample said "YES"and 1% said "NO" the chances of error remote, irrespective of sample size.However ,if the percentages are 51% and 49% the chances of error are much greater. It is easier to be sure of extreme answers than of middle-of -the-road ones. When determining the sample size needed for a given level of accuracy we must use the worst case percentage (50%). We should also use this percentage if we want to determine a general level of accuracy for sample we already have. To determine the confidence interval for a specific answer our sample has given, we can use the percentage picking that answer and get a smaller interval.

### References

Arrest Alan (2002), "Categorical Data Analysis", 2nd ed. and Wiley Series in Probability and Statistics.

John Wang, Encyclopedia of Data Warehousing and Data Mining.

# 26

# Tables

## Introduction

A windows program for the analysis of tables with up to 2*7 and 3*3 cells. The program allows for exact and approximate statistics to be calculated for traditional, ordinal and agreement tables. Fisher exact, Number Needed to Treat (NNT) proportional reduction in error statistics, Normal approximations, Four different chi-squares, Gamma, odds-ratio, T-tests and Kappa are among the many statistical procedures available.

## Demonstration

Now the following are the calculations that perform in the tables:

Here we have selected the **Fisher** calculation. The input for the **2*2** table is as shown below:

### 2*2 *Table*

The Fisher's Exact procedure calculates an exact probability value for the relationship between two dichotomous variables, as found in a two by two table. The program calculates the difference between the data observed and the data expected, considering the given marginal and the assumptions of the model of independence. It works in exactly the same way as the Chi-square test for independence; however, the Chi-square

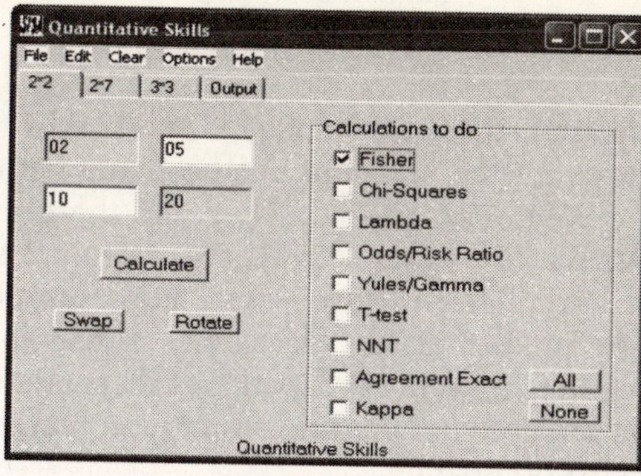


gives only an estimate of the true probability value, an estimate which might not be very accurate if the marginal is very uneven or if there is a small value (less then five) in one of the cells. In such cases the Fisher is a better choice than the Chi-square. However, in many cases the Chi-square is preferred because the Fisher is difficult to calculate.

Now the **output** for the **FISHER 2*2** calculation can be displayed as follows:

### *Fisher's Output*

Now the same process will be applied for the following statistical procedures. They are as follows:

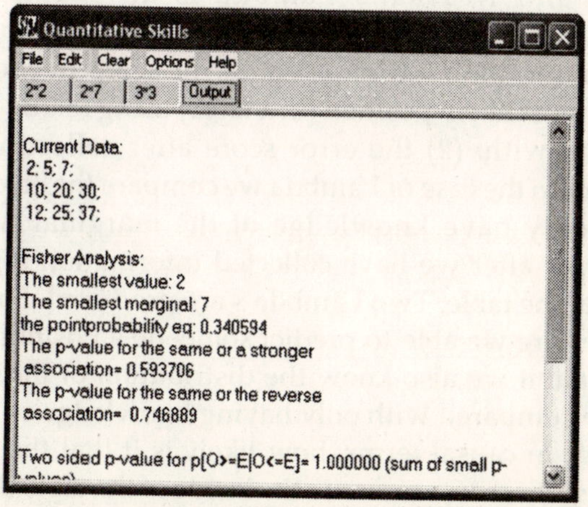

**Chi-Squares**

Chi-square is applied for all the tables. In all tables the Chi-square test tests for the model of independence between the row and the column marginal. They ask the question if knowledge of the row variable predicts someone's score on the column variable, and vice versa. For example, does someone's sex 'predict' his or her income, or does someone's schooling 'predict' his or her occupation? Independence is the situation that sex does not predict income, and that schooling does not predict occupation.

*The following chi-square tests are available*

Pearson's Goodness-of-Fit (in all tables) (preferred)

Maximum Likelihood (in all tables) (second best)

Mantel-Haenszel (in 2 by 2 table) (not often used)

Yates (in 2 by 2 table) (Pearson with continuity correction)

Empty rows are ignored and the table is reduced before analysis. An empty-zero–

cell is not ignored if it is located beside a valid cell.

***Lambda***

Goodman and Kruskal's Lambda is an example of a Proportional Reduction in Error (PRE) measure. PRE measures work by taking the ratio of: (1) an error score in predicting someone's most likely position (in a table) using relatively little information; with: (2) the error score after collecting more information. In the case of Lambda we compare the error made when we only have knowledge of the marginal with the reduced error after we have collected information regarding the inside of the table. Two Lambda's are produced. First, how much better are we able to predict someone's Position on the row marginal if we also know the distribution of individuals in the table compared with only having knowledge of the row marginal, or in causal terms, how likely is it that the column scores 'cause' the row scores via the inside of the table (Lambda A). Second, how much better are we able to predict someone's position on the column marginal if we also know the distribution of individuals in the table compared with only having knowledge of the column marginal, or in causal terms, how likely is it that the row scores 'cause' the column scores via the inside of the table (Lambda B). The program gives the proportional improvement in predicting someone's score after collecting additional information.

### Odds Ratio/ Risk Ratio

The **odds ratio** takes values between zero ('0') and infinity. One ('1') is the neutral value and means that there is no difference between the groups compared; close to zero or infinity means a large difference. An odds ratio larger than one means that group one has a larger proportion than group two, if the opposite is true the odds ratio will be smaller than one. If you swap the two proportions, the odds ratio will take on its inverse (1/OR) The odds ratio gives the ratio of the odds of suffering some fate. The odds themselves are also a ratio. To explain this we will take the example of traditional versus alternative surgery. If 10% of operations results in complications, then the odds of having complications if traditional surgery is used equals 0.11 (0.1/0.9, you have a 0.11 times higher chance of getting complications than of not getting complications). 12.5% of the operations using the alternative method result in complications, giving odds of 0.143 (0.125/0.875). The odds ratio equals 0.778 (0.11/0.143). You have a 0.778 times higher chance of getting complications than of not getting complications, in traditional as compared with alternative surgery. The inverse of the odds ratio equals 1.286. You have a 1.286 times higher chance of getting complications than of not getting complications, in alternative as compared with traditional surgery. This takes some getting used to, we admit, but it has its advantages. The odds ratio can be compared with the Risk Ratio. The risk ratio is easier to interpret than the odds ratio. However, in practice the odds ratio is used more often. This has to do with the fact that the odds ratio is more closely related to frequently used statistical techniques such as logistic regression. Also, the odds ratio has the attractive property that, however you turn the table, it will always take on the same value or the inverse (1/odds) of that value.

The **risk ratio** takes on values between zero ('0') and infinity. One ('1') is the neutral value and means that there is no difference between the groups compared, close to zero or infinity means a large difference between the two groups on the variable concerned. A risk ratio larger than one means that group one has a larger proportion than group two; if the opposite is true the risk ratio will be smaller than one. If you swap the two proportions, the risk ratio will take on its inverse (1/RR). The risk ratio gives you the percentage difference in classification between group one and group two. For example, the proportion of people suffering from complications after traditional surgery equals 0.10 (10%), while the proportion suffering from complications after alternative surgery equals 0.125 (12.5%). The risk ratio equals 0.8 (0.1/0.125); 20% ((1-0.8)*100) fewer patients treated by the traditional method suffer from complications. Another example: 8% of freezers produced without quality control have paint scratches. This percentage is reduced to 5% if quality control is introduced. The risk ratio equals 1.6 (8/5); 60% more freezers are damaged if there is no quality control. The risk ratio can be compared with the Odds Ratio. The risk ratio is easier to interpret than the odds ratio. However, in practice the odds ratio is used more often. This has to do with the fact that the odds ratio is closely related to frequently used statistical techniques such as logistic regression. Also, the odds ratio has the attractive property that, however you turn the table, it will always take on the same value or its reciprocal (1/odds ratio).

## Yules/Gamma

### *Yule's Q*

For Two by Two Table

Yule's Q is based on the odds ratio and a symmetric measure taking on values between-1 and+1.1 (one) implies perfect negative or positive association, 0 (zero) no association. In two by two tables Yule's Q is equal to Goodman and Kruskal's Gamma.

### *Yule's Y*

For Two by Two table
Yule's Y is based on the odds ratio and a symmetric measure taking on values between-1 and+1.1 (one) implies perfect negative or positive association, 0 (zero) no association.

Gamma is calculated in a two by two table by way of the Yule's Q.

### *T-test*

The t-test tells you how probable it is that a difference between two means has resulted from chance fluctuation. The t-test is considered not valid for data of an ordinal or dichotomous nature. However, the test is very often used in this type of data and is considered to produce conservative results if the assumption of normally distributed continuous variables is not met. Thus, if the t-test is significant in ordinal data then it is very likely that there is a significant difference between two means; if the t-test is not significant you do not know for sure if this lack of a statistically significant difference is a valid observation. The procedure also gives you some statistics related to the two columns. The measure tends to estimate associations more conservatively than Yule's Q. The measure has little substantive or theoretical meaning.

### Number Needed to Treat (NNT)

Number Needed to Treat (NNT) is a measure which is becoming increasingly popular in the medical field. This measure is the reciprocal of the absolute risk-difference (ard=|proportion1-proportion2|) and expresses the number of persons to be treated to 'cure' one person. The measure has some very appealing properties in interpretation, particularly in combination with cost calculation. An example: if no treatment is given 20% die, with treatment 15% die. NNT=20 (1/|0.2-0.15|). We need to treat 20 people to save one life. But now we develop a preventive program in a completely different area of health care and succeed in bringing the mortality down from 45% to 44.5%. NNT=200 (1/|0.45-0.445|). We need to apply our preventive program to at least 200 people to save one life. This does not seem very effective compared with treatment.

### Exact Agreement Test

This test is yet another derivative of Fisher's Exact Test. It generates all tables that are possible given the marginal, and cumulates the p-values of all tables that have the same number of off-diagonal observations as the table observed, or fewer. This exact test gives the probability of the exact number or a lesser number of observations of the marginal being there on the basis of chance. The test is equivalent to the single-sided Fisher in two by two tables. The p-value produced should be comparable with the Kappa p-value, and this does in fact usually seem to be the case.

#### *Kappa*

Two measures are presented. Kappa is a measure of agreement and takes on the value zero when there are no more cells on the diagonal of an agreement table than can be expected on the basis of chance. Kappa takes on the value 1 if there is perfect agreement, i.e. if all observations are on the diagonal. It is considered that Kappa values lower than 0.4 represent poor agreement between row and column variable, values between 0.4 and 0.75 fair to good agreement, and values higher than 0.75 excellent agreement.

#### 2*7 *Table*

Now the **Exact Test input** for the **2*7 table** is as shown:

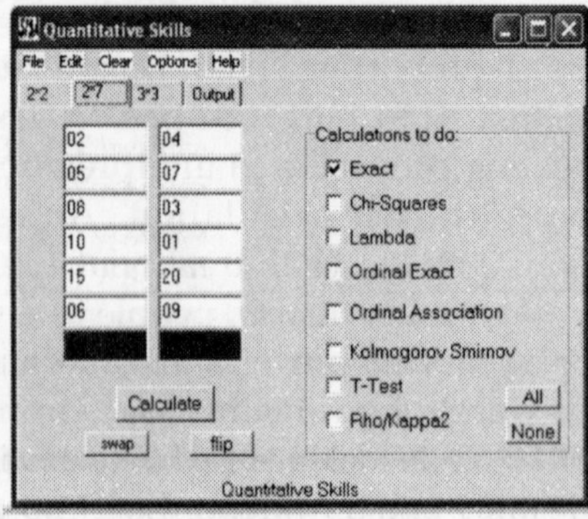

### *Exact Test*

The exact test is a generalization of the Fisher procedure and calculates an exact probability value for the relationship between two variables in larger tables. The procedure will handle smaller tables too and is similar to the Fisher in a 2*2 table (try it!). The program calculates the difference between the data observed and the data expected, considering the given marginal and the assumptions of the model of independence. It works in exactly the same way as the Chi-square test for independence; however, the Chi-square gives only an estimate of the true probability value, an estimate which might not be very accurate if the marginal is very uneven or if there is a small value (less then five) in one of the cells. In such cases the exact test is a better choice than the Chi-square. However, in many cases the Chi-square is preferred because the exact test is difficult to calculate. Two statistics are offered. The point probability of this unique single table, and the two-sided probability. For the two-sided probability the sums of small p-values method is used. All possible tables given the marginal are evaluated and the p-values of the more extreme tables are added up. See the Fisher help file for a more detailed discussion. The procedure is based on the evaluation of many thousands of tables. The number of tables to evaluate increases linearly with the number of cases and exponentially with the number of cells. Tables in which the number of cases is larger than 4000 in a 2*3 table, 2000 in a 2*4, 1000 in a 2*5 table, 500 in a 2*6 and 100 in a 2*7 table may take longer. The 7th row in the 2*7 table is marked red, full table only to be used in case of emergency. However, you can input large numbers of cases and you will get an answer, eventually. Also, the number of cases can be very much larger if the table has a very skewed marginal distribution. Agresti (1992) discusses a 2*5 table with 32,574 cases which SISA tables will work out in a couple of minutes. The maximum number of tables to evaluate is set at 2,147,483,646, which would take about 30 hours to do. Smaller tables can be used in the 2*7 and the 3*3 modules. The 2*7 module is more efficient for evaluating a 2*3 table than the 3*3 module.

Now the **output** for the **Exact Test** is as follows:

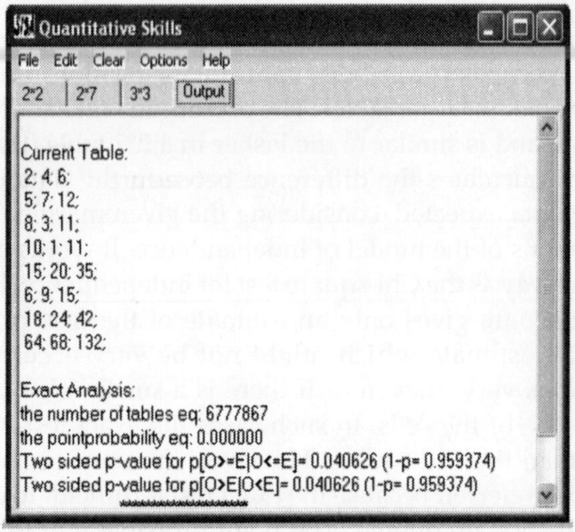


Now the same process is repeated for the **Chi-square, Lambda, Ordinal-Exact, Ordinal Association, Kolomogorov smirnov, T-Test,Rho/Kappa2.**

### *Ordinal Exact*

If you tick the Ordinal Exact box you get a p-value for the likelihood that there are tables with a higher number of concordant pairs than the number in the observed table. This is an exact test of ordinal association. This procedure is another derivative of the Fisher and works in the same way, by generating tables and estimating their likelihood. In a 2 by 2 table the cumulative ordinal exact value is equivalent to the single-sided Fisher. The procedure is based on the evaluation of thousands of tables to check how many concordant pairs they have. The number of tables to evaluate increases more or less linearly with the number of cases and exponentially with the number of cells. Tables in which the number of cases is larger than 3000 in a 2*3 table, 1500 in a 2*4, 750 in a 2*5 table, 300 in a 2*6 and 75 in a 2*7 table may take longer. The last entries in the 2*7 table are marked red, only to be used in case of emergency. However, you can input any number of cases in any number of cells, and you will get an answer, eventually. The maximum number of tables to evaluate is set at 2,147,483,646, which would take about 45 hours on a P100 computer. Note: because the ordinal integrity of the table must be maintained in the calculations the ordinal exact procedure is less efficient than the basic exact procedure.

### *Ordinal Association*

The selection 'Ordinal Association' will give you Kendall's Tau-a and Goodman and Kruskal's Gamma for testing ordinal associations, with their respective sample standard deviations and p-values. Tau-a is the difference between the number of concordant and discordant pairs divided by the total number of pairs; Gamma is the difference between the number of concordant and discordant pairs divided by the sum of concordant and discordant pairs. Gamma usually gives a higher value than Tau and is (for other reasons as well) usually considered to be a more satisfactory measure of ordinal association. The p-values are supposed to approach the exact p-value for an ordinal association asymptotically, and the program shows that they generally do that reasonably well. But, beware of small numbers: the p-values for the gamma and Tau become too optimistic!

### *Kolmogorov-Smirnov*

The Kolmogorov-Smirnov Test is not a test of association. This test gives the likelihood of two orders coming from different orderings or the same ordering. Have a look at this table:

Do you agree or disagree with the following statement (proportions between brackets) [cumulative proportions between square brackets].

| | *Males* | *Females* | *Difference* |
|---|---|---|---|
| Totally agree | 10 (0.12)[0.12] | 24 (0.26)[0.26] | 14 (0.14)[0.14] |
| Agree | 15 (0.18)[0.30] | 15 (0.17)[0.43] | 0 (0.01)[0.13] |
| Neither agree/dis | 19 (0.23)[0.53] | 21 (0.23)[0.66] | 2 (0.00)[0.13] |
| Disagree | 18 (0.21)[0.74] | 17 (0.19)[0.85] | 1 (0.02)[0.10] |
| Totally disagree | 22 (0.26)[1.00] | 14 (0.15)[1.00] | 8 (0.11)[0.00] |
| Total | 84 (1.00) | 91 (1.00) | 7 (0.00) |

### *T-test*

The t-test tells you how probable it is that a difference between two means has resulted from chance fluctuation. The t-test is considered not valid for data of an ordinal or dichotomous nature. However, the test is very often used in this type of data and is considered to produce conservative results if the assumption of normally distributed continuous variables is not met. Thus, if the t-test is significant in ordinal data then it is very likely that there is a significant difference between two means; if the t-test is not significant you do not know for sure if this lack of a statistically significant difference is a valid observation. The procedure also gives you some statistics related to the two columns. The measure tends to estimate associations more conservatively than Yule's Q. The measure has little substantive or theoretical meaning.

### *3*3 Table*

Now the **input** for the **Agreement Exact Test** for**3*3** is as shown

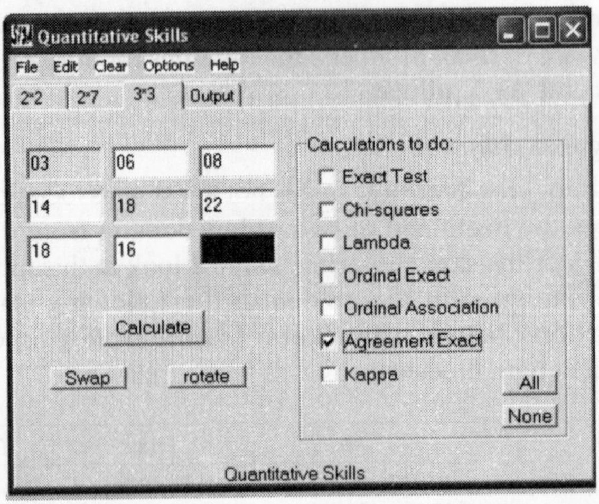


### Exact Agreement Test

This test is yet another derivative of Fisher's Exact Test. It generates all tables that are possible given the marginal, and cumulates the p-values of all tables that have the same number of off-diagonal observations as the table observed, or fewer. This exact test gives the probability of the exact number or a lesser number of observations of the marginal being there on the basis of chance. The test is equivalent to the single-sided Fisher in two by two tables. The p-value produced should be comparable with the Kappa p-value, and this does in fact usually seem to be the case.

The **output** for the **Exact Agreement Test** for **3*3** is as shown:

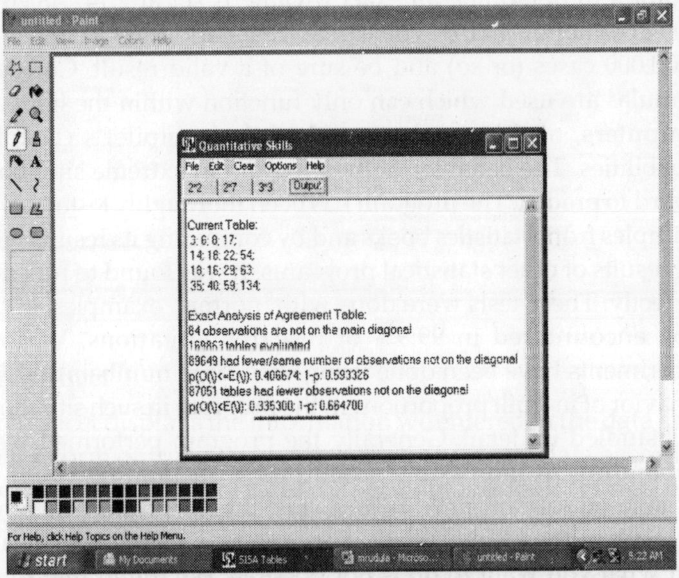


The same procedure is repeated for Exact test, Chi-square, Lambda, Ordinal-Exact, Ordinal Association, Agreement Exact, Kappa.

### *Kappa*

Two measures are presented: Kappa is a measure of agreement and takes on the value zero when there are no more cells on the diagonal of an agreement table than can be expected on the basis of chance. Kappa takes on the value 1 if there is perfect agreement, i.e. if all observations are on the diagonal. It is considered that Kappa values lower than 0.4 represent poor agreement between row and column variable, values between 0.4 and 0.75 fair to good agreement, and values higher than 0.75 excellent agreement.

### *Limitations*

This program has very few in-built limitations. In this-purchased-version of the program, the maximum number of cases per table is 2,147,483,646. For an exact analysis or a Fisher analysis the maximum number of cases is 1.000.000. The maximum number of tables to determine an exact p-value is set at 2,147,483,646. This does not mean that you can do calculations on a table with 1.000.000 cases (or so) and be sure of a valid result. Complex formulas are used which can only function within the limits of computers, of this program and of the compiler's (Delphi) capabilities. The behavior of the program in extreme situations is hard to predict. The program has been thoroughly tested using examples from statistics books and by comparing its results with the results of other statistical programs. It was found to function perfectly. These tests were done with 'normal' examples, of the type encountered in 99.9% of research situations. Various experiments have been done using very large numbers and the behavior of in-built proportions in the program in such situations was studied in detail. Generally the program performed well, responding to impossible situations with floating point or variable out-of-range errors and crashing, or producing either no result or the "NaN" result. Encountering such errors means that what you want to do is not possible. We found that these errors occur particularly frequently in cases in which you do not really need a statistics program to tell you that the p-value is very close to zero or one. Furthermore, sometimes many millions of calculations are required to produce the results of the exact procedures. On a P-100 it takes from 30 to 45 hours to evaluate the maximum of 2,147,483,646 tables. For some procedures (particularly the ordinal tests), if you have problems with out-of-range errors or very lengthy calculations, it may help if you try to order your data in a different way. The program's 'flip', 'swap' and 'rotate' buttons may be of assistance. Although this program has been tested extensively, no program is ever bug or error free, and you should always check your results carefully. You can check results by comparing different statistics: exact results with Chi-squares, p-values for Gamma with p-values for Tau, etc. However, even then there may be problems (though it is hard to imagine what they might be!) and no statistic can ever replace a healthy mind and a critical attitude in research. If you have a data set to analyze and you do not get the expected result, please report this to Quantitative Skills.

**About Input box**

The input boxes are the fill-in boxes that form a table on the left of the form. They assume integer input: whole positive numbers. The boxes should only contain numbers: no commas, decimal points or any other non-numeric characters. There is one exception: the letter E for a mantissa. In the table thus formed the 1,1 cell is in the upper left corner. The '**main diagonal**' is **colored yellow** and runs from the upper left to the lower right. The total number you can input is: 2,147,483,646 for most analyses and 1,000,000 for exact analyses. However, if you input such a large number, you should not expect with certainty to get a meaningful output. The **red boxes** are colored red to warn you of the fact that if you specify a full table an exact analysis might take a very long time. Empty rows are ignored in most statistical procedures and a reduced table is analyzed. Empty -zero- cells are not ignored if they are located beside a valid cell.

**Output Field**

In the output field the output of the analysis is presented. The statistics in the output are related to the first 'current table' above. Each time you change between procedures or change the input a new 'current table' is printed in the output field.

**References**

Agresti A. (1990), "Categorical Data Analysis", New York & Chichester, John Wiley and Sons.

Fliess J.L. (1981), "Statistical Methods for Rates and Proportions", New York & Chichester, John Wiley and Sons.

Agresti A. (1992), "A Survey of Exact Inference for Contingency Tables", Statistical Science, 7(1):131-177.

# 27

# Tanagra

## Introduction

**TANAGRA (1.4.13)** is free **DATA MINING software** for **academic and research purposes.** It proposes several data mining methods from exploratory data analysis, statistical learning, machine learning and databases area.

**TANAGRA** is more powerful, it contains some supervised learning but also other paradigms such as clustering, factorial analysis, parametric and nonparametric statistics, association rule, feature selection and construction algorithms.

**TANAGRA** is an "*open source project*" as every researcher can access to the source code, and add his own algorithms, as far as he agrees and conforms to the software distribution license.

## Components

**GUI**–Since its introduction by SPAD (DECISIA) at the beginning of the 90s, the modification of a chain of process as a "stream diagram" has been adopted by many software. Consciously or not, most of the "big" entreprises in DATA MINING industry have re-used this notion of visual programming to describe the successive operations applied on data.

**Data access**–The access and analysis of the data source are made at the defining of a new diagram. The data are put in memory after having been internally encoded. Fastness is an aim in the importing of data. Presently, only textiles with tab separator are imported, either the ones of UNIX origin or DOS. Variable names figure on the first line, their type (discrete or continuous) is deduced from the next line.

**Operators (components)**–The bottom frame contains the data-mining operators. All of them use data as input, perform analyses and produce results; nethertheless, only a few of them make predictions. In this case, one or more variables are added to the data, which would be transmitted to the following operator.

**Dataminingdiagram**–As with the other software of this domain, the Data Miner can define analysis by starting with data and adding operators one after each other. To experiment various assumptions, and compare the results obtained with, the user can explore several branches of the diagram. Choosing a tree structure (Tree view) facilitates the managing of diagrams, as much at a programming level than at an end-user level. Complex analyses can so be easily represented and achieved. On the other hand, there is not possibility to accomplish some merging in the analysis diagram, as with other graphical software. For example, it is not possible to automatically group various data sources.

**Results**–More often, Tamara operators produce HTML format output. Therefore, it is simple to export the results towards edition software, like EXCEL(C), for subsequent processing. Generally, output is composed from two parts: the decryption of the analysis parameters, and the results. Choosing HTML format has also the advantage of easily export results, to look at it after closing the software. As far print it.

When necessary, results can be displayed in a window, in which the user can interact. Therefore, it is for the "X-Y graph" operator, the user can use the mouse to select the variables used for horizontal and vertical axis, in order to understand better how points are distributed.

**Different Functions**

**Stream diagram**–Introduced by SPAD for data analyses in the early 90s-at this time people didn't talk about Data Mining yet-the stream diagram represents the sequence of operations applied on data by a graph where (1) the nodes (an operator, a component, etc.) symbolize the analysis performed on the data; (2) the links between nodes, the flow of processed data.

**Operator(s)**–The operator (component) is a key element, as it represents an operation done on the data. The first operator is always a connection to a dataset, a set of records-attributes. The importation wizard automatically places the connection at the top of the diagram.

**Four types** of results can be expected when adding the operators, each of them having parameters:

(a) analytical results, that describe the data or modeless them;

(b) a restriction or an enlargement of the set of active examples used for analyses;

(c) a restriction or an enlargement of the set of attributes used for analyses;

(d) the production of new attributes, added to the dataset.

**Operators Compatibilities**–Commonly, operators are linked to form a sequence in a diagram; there are two levels of controls: while adding the operator, or while executing the sequence.

Two categories of operators have some unusual comportment to take care of the specificities of their methods: supervised learning and Meta supervised learning. So that their way of working is: first to add a "meta" component to the diagram, which is a sort of support for single methods or even arcing ones, then to include the "learning" operator in it (discriminate analysis, induction tree, etc.). This way of doing allows multiplying the combinations, for example to proceed a boosting on a multi-layer perception, that is not really recommended, but it is possible anyway.

**Save formats**–Among other things, two were annoying in "old" Supine: (a) there was no possibility to keep track of the analyses you were working on; (b) and even if you had written it on some paper, you always had to re-create it by selecting the good commands in the same order. With the introduction of stream diagrams in order to describe the successive processes, these problems easily became out of date due to a new save format: now we can conserve the chain of analyses built, with the associated parameters (!); then, after having loaded the diagram, launch it again by a single mouse click. Only the diagram description-the program in other words-is saved, results are not in any way. Two formats can be used, they fulfill different requirements.

**Binary description of the stream diagram (*.bum)**–The data imported are included in the saved file with this format. The resulting file can only be exploited by TANAGRA. The main advantage is that, since the data are imported once and only once, loading in memory the diagram at the next execution is very quick. On the other hand, the main inconvenience is that the analyses composing the diagram are definitively defined on these imported data. So if data change, by adding some records for example, data must be imported again, and diagram must be redefined. So prefer to use this format if: (a) data should no longer change; (b) if loading time is an important factor in the context of your work. There are many advantages: (a) there is only a reference to the data in the saved file, so if they change, the next execution would work on the new version of data, and produce updated results; (b) the file respects the INI specification, so it is possible to define new diagrams, without opening Tanagra.

**Data source Concepts**–These components allow you to read a data source. They present two main characteristics: (1) it is necessarily located at the beginning of the stream diagram; (2) it is inserted automatically by a wizard, it is thus not visible in the components palette.

**Attribute Status: None**
**Available Components**

| *Component* | *Description* | *Parameters* | *Note* |
|---|---|---|---|
| Dataset | Download a raw table (examples vs. attributes), text file format with tab separator. Not sophisticated component, data cleansing is not supported (missing data,). | File name | The first row represents attributes name. The second row allows allows recognizing the type of attributes(continuous or discrete). The decimal separator depends on your Windows configuration. |

**Data visualization Concepts–**Data visualization components, restricted to active examples.

**Attribute Status: None**
**Data Visualization Components**

| *Component* | *Description* | *Parameters* | *Note* |
|---|---|---|---|
| View dataset | View dataset in a grid – read only. | | |
| Export dataset | Export current dataset into a text file. | Examples to export: all or active examples. Attributes to export: all or target only File name. | |
| Scatter Plot | Scatter plot, axis can be modified. | | No reports are generated |
| Correlation Scatter Plot | Correlation of attributes with two axes. | | **Attributes status** Target: 2 axis attributes. Input: continuous descriptors attribute. **Report :** None |
| View Multiple Scatter Plot | View values of discrete attributes on two axes. | | **Attributes status** Target: 2 axis attributes. Input: discrete descriptors attribute. **Report :** None |

**Descriptive statistics Concepts–**These components produce a statistical summary of the dataset.

**Attribute Status: None**
**Descriptive Statistics Components**

| *Component* | *Description* | *Parameters* | *Note* |
|---|---|---|---|
| Cross tabulation | Cross tabulation of attributes. | Sort results from attribute name or statistical indicators Attribute selection : (1) "target" = row, "input" = column, or (2) crossing of input attributes.- Threshold for cells highlight. | Discrete attributes only. |
| Linear correlation | Compute linear correlation of attributes. | Sort results from attribute name or statistical indicators. Attribute selection: (1) "target" = row, "input" = column, or (2) crossing of input attributes. | Continuous attributes only. |
| One-way ANOVA | One way analysis of variance | "Target": measurements "input": factors. Sort results. Other descriptive statistics. | "Target" must be continuous. "Input" must be discrete. |
| University discrete stat | Descriptive statistics for discrete attributes. | Select input attributes with "define status" component. Sort results. | Input must be discrete. |
| University continuous stat | Descriptive statistics for continuous attributes. | Select input attributes with "define status" component. - Sort results. | Input must be continuous. |
| Non-parametrical test (KW) | KRUSKAL et WALLIS non-parametrical population comparison. | Target: measurements input factors. | Target is continuous. Input is discrete. |

| | | |
|---|---|---|
| Group characterization | Group characterization, for instance, allow to describe group define by a clustering algorithm. | With "define status": target is discrete, input can be continuous or discrete. |

**Instance selection Concepts**–These components reduce the set of actives examples before an analysis. Examples are subdivided in active and inactive examples.

**Attribute Status: None**
**Instance Selection Components:**

| *Component* | *Description* | *Parameters* | *Note* |
|---|---|---|---|
| Sampling | Sampling. Stratified Sampling. | Size of sample: proportion or number of examples. | |
| Stratified Sampling | | Stratification attributes a discrete one. Stratification type: balanced or proportional. Size of the sample: proportion or number of examples. | A discrete attribute must be available in the dataset. |
| Recover examples | Permutation of the status of examples: actives become inactive, and conversely. | Set to be active: inactive or all examples. | |

**Feature selection Concepts**–These components modify, automatically or not, attributes status. They generally reduce "input" attributes set.

**Attributes status**–*Define Status* has a very particular function in the stream diagram. Others components work as other components.

**Feature Selection Components**

| *Component* | *Description* | *Parameters* | *Note* |
|---|---|---|---|
| Define status | Allow to define the status of attributes (target, input, illustrative) in the stream diagram. **This component is of primary importance in the stream diagram.** | 3 possible statuses: (a) target, (b) input, (c) illustrative. **An attribute can have several statuses,** in some clustering algorithms for instance. | It is the only component, which has a short cut in the toolbar. |

**Feature construction concepts–**These components produce new attribute, automatically or not, from available attributes.

**Attribute Status: Generally None**
**Feature Construction Components**

| *Component* | *Description* | *Parameters* | *Note* |
|---|---|---|---|
| Formula | Create a new attribute from algebraic formula. | Algebraic formula, constants, math operators such as log, | Continuous attributes only. |
| Alfred Disc | Equal-frequency binning discrimination | Number of intervals. | Continuous INPUT attributes only. |
| Equity Disc | Equal-width binning discrimination. | Number of intervals. | Continuous INPUT attributes only. |
| MDLPC | Fayyad and Iran's state-of-the art supervised university discrimination. | | Continuous INPUT attributes only are discredited, because this method is supervised, you have to specify a discrete TARGET attribute. |
| Standardize | Standardization of attributes. | Standardization function. | Continuous INPUT attributes only. |

**Regression Concepts**–These components perform regression analysis: predict values of a continuous attribute (endogenous) from others (exogenous).

**Attribute status**–Target attribute must be continous, input can be generally continuous or discrete.

**Regression Components**

| *Component* | *Description* | *Parameters* | *Note* |
|---|---|---|---|
| Multiple linear regression | Regression analysis, least square method. | | "Input" must be continuous. Constant is imposed. |

**Factorial analysis Concepts**–These components perform factorial analysis. They produce a description of examples in a reduced dimensionality.

**Attribute status**–Two or more descriptors (input). No target attribute.

**Available Components**

| *Component* | *Description* | *Parameters* | *Note* |
|---|---|---|---|
| Principal components analysis | Principal component analysis | Number of axis to produce | Only continuous descriptors |
| Multiple corresponden ce analysis | Multiple correspondence analyses. | Number of axis to produce. Threshold test value for attribute value visualization | Only discrete descriptors |

**Clustering Concepts**–These components perform clustering, they produce homogenous group by optimization of some criteria. They are also known as **unsupervised methods**.

**Attribute status**–"Input" attributes only, they are generally continuous.

**Clustering Components**

| *Component* | *Description* | *Parameters* | *Note* |
|---|---|---|---|
| K-Means | K-Means-Fogy and Mc Queen algorithms.<br>Several trials are performed. | Number of clusters.<br>Number of iterations.<br>Number of trials.<br>Data standardization.<br>Average computation during optimization process | |
| Coonan's SOM | Coonan's Self Organization Map. | Map: number of row.<br>Map : number of columns.<br>Data standardization.<br>Learning rate . | |
| LVQ | Coonan's Learning Vector Quantizes, a "supervised" clustering algorithm. | Number of cluster per class.<br>Learning rate.<br>Number of iterations.<br>Data standardization. | "Target" discrete attribute must be defined. |
| HAC | Hierarchical agglomerative clustering.<br>The tree is built into two steps: (1) use a "fast" clustering method. (K-Means, SOM), which produces many low-level clusters; (2) use these clusters for the endogamy construction.<br>This method allows applying HAC on dataset with many examples.<br>How to set the number of low-level clusters? It must be lower than the size of the dataset, a good compromise seems to be 15 – 20. | Clusters detection strategy.<br>Number of clusters.<br>Standardization or not of attributes for distance evaluation | Discrete TARGET must be defined; it comes from first clustering component such as K-MEANS or SOM. |

**Supervised learning Concepts–**These components implement a supervised algorithm.

**Attribute status–**Target attribute must be discrete; input can be continuous or discrete.

**Supervised Learning Components**

| *Component* | *Description* | *Parameters* | *Note* |
|---|---|---|---|
| Binary logistic regression | Maximum likelihood method, Liebenberg-Marquardt optimization algorithm. | | Target attribute must have two values. Input attributes must be continuous. Constant is imposed. |
| k-Nearest Neighbor (k-NN) | K-Nearest neighbor – Heterogeneous Value Difference Metric (HVDM), discrete descriptors can be used. | Number of neighbor | Input can be discrete and/or continuous. No attribute standardization is necessary. |
| Multi-layer perception | Multi-layer perception, back-propagation algorithm | **Neural network architecture.** Use hidden layer. Neuron in the hidden layer **Learning parameters.** Learning rate Size of pruning/validation set- Attribute standardization **Stopping rule** Max number of iterations. Threshold error rate. Error stagnation. Gap of error stagnation evaluation. | Input must be continuous. |
| Prototype-NN | Kernels (prototypes) are built off-line, with a clustering algorithm for instance. At each kernel, we affect a class membership. Therefore, for a new instance, we give it the class of the nearest prototype. | Attribute to define kernels Standardization of attributes | Input must be continuous. |
| ID3 | Quinlan's ID3 algorithm, with some minor modifications. | Min size of node to split. Min size of leaf to produce. Max depth of the tree. Max entropy gain for a splitting . | |

| | | | |
|---|---|---|---|
| Linear Discriminate Analysis | Linear discriminate analysis... | | **Input must be continuous. Be careful about co linearity.** |
| Naive Bays | Naive Bays algorithm. | | Input must be discrete. |
| Radial basis function | Radial basis function, off-line processing... | Attribute which defines kernels. Other parameters: see MLP. | Input attributes must be continuous. *I have some doubts about the actual implementation!* |

**Meta-spa learning Concepts**–These components integrate supervised learning algorithms. They can produce one or more instances of the supervised learning algorithm, and make them to cooperate.

These components must be used with "supervised learning" component. All kind of supervised learning algorithm can be combined.

**Attributes status**–supervised learning components.

**Meta-spa learning Components**

| *Component* | *Description* | *Parameters* | *Note* |
|---|---|---|---|
| Instance Spa Learning (Supervised Learning) | Instantiate a single supervised learning algorithm. | | Basic meta-spa learning. |
| Arcing [Arc-x4] | Run several learning process, with reweighed examples. | Number of classifiers. | |
| Boosting | Similar to Arcing. | Number of classifiers. | |
| Bagging | Run several learning process, examples are sampled with replication | Number of classifiers. | |

**Spa learning assessment Contents–**These components allow evaluating the performances (error rate) of the supervised learning algorithms.

**Attribute status–**None.

**Spa Learning Assessment Components**

| *Component* | *Description* | *Parameters* | *Note* |
|---|---|---|---|
| Train-Test | Divide the dataset into learning set and test set: the model is built of the first sample, and the error rate is computed on the second one. | Proportion of the dataset used for the training phase. Number of trials. | |
| Cross-validation | Cross-validation | Number of folds. Number of trials. | Several show that studies 5x2-fold co soften effective. |

**Association Concepts–**Operators to build association rules.

**Attribute status–**All attributes are "input", they are discrete.

**Association Components**

| *Component* | *Description* | *Parameters* | *Note* |
|---|---|---|---|
| A priori | Build association rule with from Agrawal's description. | Min Support. Min Confidence. Max rule length. Min lifts of rules. | This implementation is not very optimized: description. max table size is 250,000 examples. Be careful, calculations can be greedy in time and memory resources. |

**How to Work on Tanagra**

Here we show basic characteristics of TANAGRA user interface, through the analysis of the« **weather.txt » dataset.** In this Application, we use the following components:

| Tab | Operator (Component) | Function |
|---|---|---|
| Data visualization | View dataset | View the contents of the data file in a grid |
| Feature selection | Define status | Specify the attributes to use |
| Descriptive stats | Univariate continuous stat | Descriptive statistics for continuous attributes |
| Descriptive stats | Univariate discrete stat | Descriptive statistics for discrete attributes |
| Descriptive stats | Group characterization | Statistics for sub-populations |

### *Creating a New data-mining Diagram*

1. Choose *File/New…* in the main menu of TANAGRA.
2. Enter a title for the diagram: « TANAGRA Basics ».

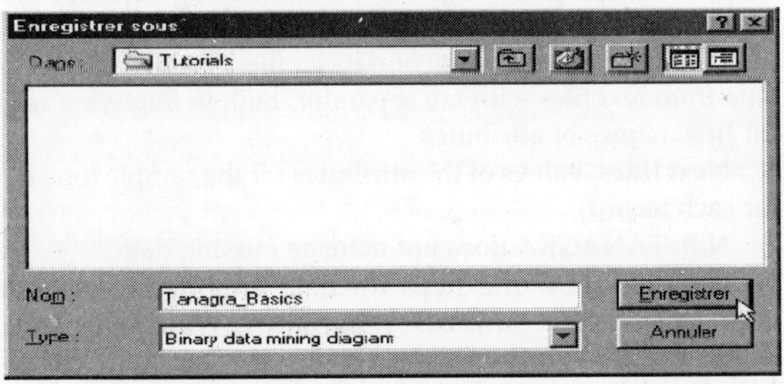


3. Enter the name of the associated file in which you will save your work

   (« TANAGRA_Basics.bdm »). Before click on button: to run through the hard disk and

   Place yourself in the directory « …\TANAGRA\ Tutorials ».
4. Select the text file containing the data you want to explore by clicking on this icon:

Choose the file "weather.txt", located in TANAGRA subdirectory Dataset.

5. Validate by clicking the OK button to start loading.

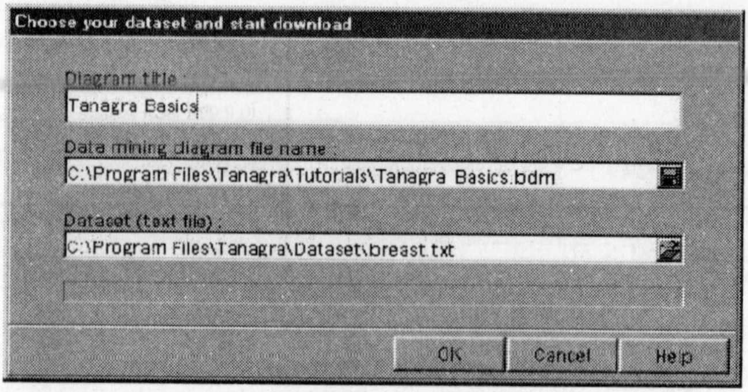


## How to Import the Database

While developing TANAGRA, the underlying objective was to give access to many data mining methods, and not to manage with the numerous formats of dataset files. **TANAGRA** loads data from text files with tab separator, built in following way: **1st line**: names of attributes

**Next lines**: values of the attributes for the sample (one line for each record).

**N.B**: TANAGRA does not manage missing data.

Here we show the steps for data importation from an Excel spreadsheet towards TANAGRA. We choose **Excel** as the original source of data; because it is generally easy to copy the data, you are working on, and paste it in an Excel sheet.

***Saving an Excel sheet to TANAGRA format:***

1. Launch Excel.
2. Enter the example data as in the following screenshot.
3. In the *File* menu, choose the "*Save as...*" command. A dialog box opens, in the "Type of file" list, choose « Text (separator: tabulation) ». Enter « weather.txt » as the name of the file.
4. Click on the Save button.
5. A dialog box advertises you that, in textile format, only one sheet can be saved at the same time. Click the OK button.

6. Another dialog box tells you that « weather.txt » can contain data that are incompatible with the text file format. Click on Yes.
7. The data are ready to be imported into TANAGRA. Close Excel.
8. You can visualize the file you have just saved under any text editor. Here is this file

   « weather.txt », opened in the Windows notepad.

### *Importing your Data in TANAGRA*

1. Choose *"File/New..."* in the main menu of TANAGRA.
2. Enter a title for the diagram: « TANAGRA: Importing Data ».
3. Enter the name of the associated file in which you will save your work.

   (« TANAGRA_ImportingData.bdm »). Before click on this button: to run through the hard disk and place yourself in the directory « ...\TANAGRA\Tutorials ».
4. Click on the icon to seek the file you have created "weather.txt".
4. Validate with OK to start data importation.

A new diagram is created, based on the file « weather.txt ». You can see the description of its contents in the right frame.

### *Important Precisions on Diagrams Saving Formats*

While creating a new diagram, we have used the extension "BDM" for the name of the diagram file (« TANAGRA_ImportingData.bdm »).

**BDM** (Binary Diagram) is the extension for a TANAGRA file containing, besides the diagram description, the imported dataset (here the data from the file « weather.txt »). So we loose the association to the original data textile, which can be modified or deleted without impacting the work we done under TANAGRA.

**TDM** (Text Diagram), the other TANAGRA file format for diagrams, is the one used if, besides the diagram description, you only want to save a **reference** to the data file. So that if you make any change in the data file (here « weather.txt »), you will have different results the next time you execute the sequences of operations in TANAGRA! But be careful not to delete the source file if you want to be able to reopen the diagram.

Adding an operator to the diagram in order to visualize data:

1. Add a **View dataset** component to the diagram. To do this, click on the DATA VISUALIZATION tab of the components palette. Drag and drop **View Dataset** from components palette to stream diagram, under the "Dataset" node (the node must appear to be selected).
2. Then click on the "View dataset" node to select it (if not yet), and right-click on it to activate the popup menu: choose the *View* command. Data are displayed in the right Frame.

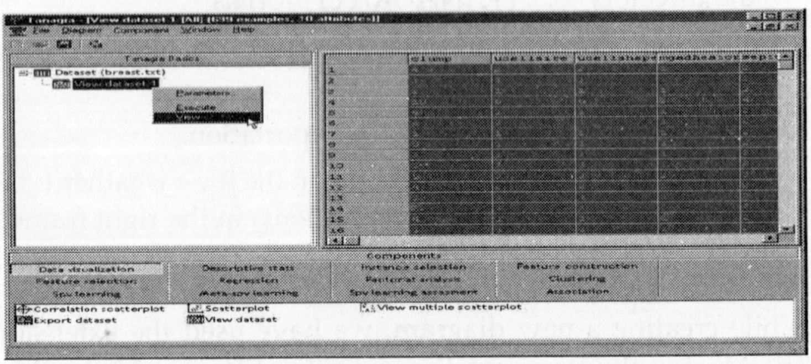


### *Use and Importance of the Define Status Operator*

In TANAGRA, you can build sequences of operations. However, almost all operators require, before executing it, that you have defined the attributes to use, and how to use them (View dataset that we have just used before, is an exception to this rule). To avoid repetition of status definition for each operator, TANAGRA centralizes this declaration in the **Define status** component.

1. Add a **Define Status** component (FEATURE SELECTION tab) to the diagram, under the « Dataset » node. (If, by error, you put it under the « View Dataset » node, you can delete it via the *Diagram / Delete component* menu).
2. Then click on the "Define status" node to select it, and activate its popup menu by clicking the mouse right button: choose the *Parameters....* Command.
3. In the dialog box that appears, choose some continuous variables (these marked with a C blue letter): click on them (in the left list), then press the arrow button. They will act as input, since it is the active tab. Validate with OK, the window closes.
4. Add a **University continuous stats** component (DESCRIPTIVE STATS tab) to the diagram, under the «Define status 1» node. In the popup menu, choose the *View* command. Descriptive statistics for the selected attributes are displayed in the right Frame.

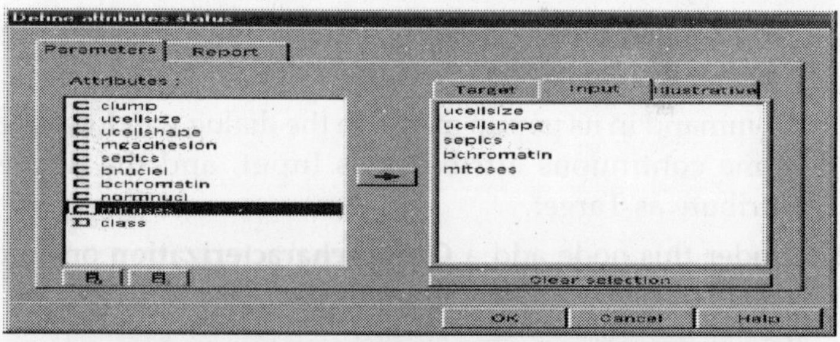

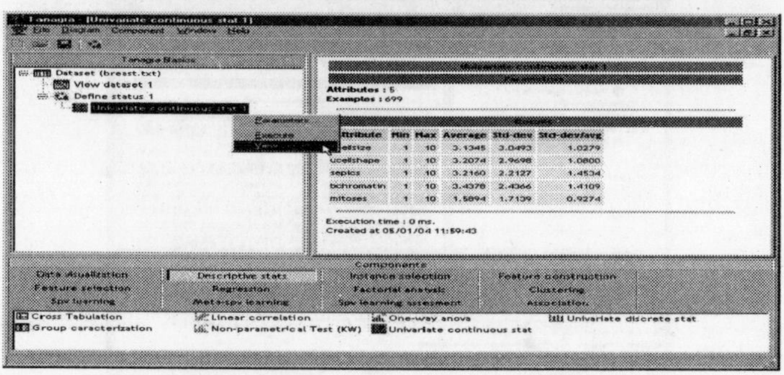

5. Add another **Define status** component to the « Dataset » node, and select the discrete Attribute «class».Add a **University discrete stats** operator under the node«Define status 2», and choose the *View* command as previously. Below is the result you should obtain.

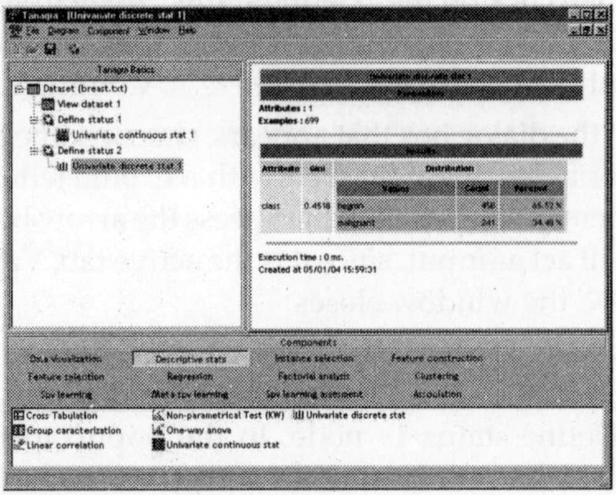


## Statistics for each sub-population

1. Add another **Define status** operator to the « Dataset » node. Choose the *Parameter.*

   Command in its popup menu. In the dialog window, select some continuous attributes as Input, and the discrete attribute as Target.

2. Under this node add a **Group characterization** operator, and choose *View* in its popup menu.

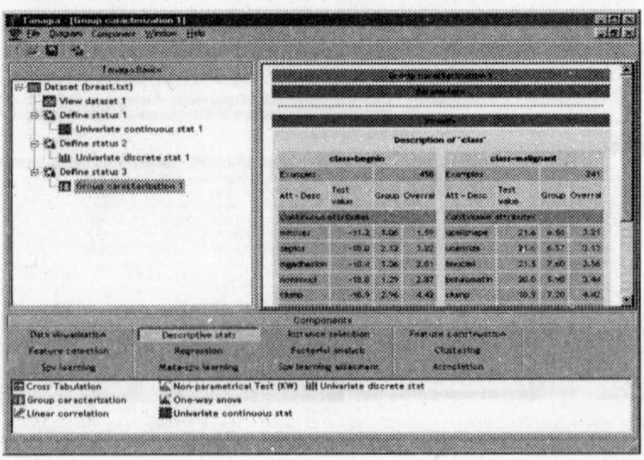

## Regression Analysis

Now we show how to perform a **regression analysis.** Our dataset consists in engine cars description. We want to predict "mpg" consumption from cars characteristics such as weight, horsepower, we use the following components:

| TAB | Operator (Component) | Comment |
|---|---|---|
| Data visualization | View dataset | View the dataset in a grid |
| Feature selection | Define status | Define attributes status |
| Regression | Multiple linear regression | Perform the regression analysis |

### *Loading the Dataset*

1. Choose *File/Open*... in the TANAGRA main menu.
2. Get « autompg.bdm » which is in the « Dataset » sub-directory.

### *Add a Component for Data Visualization*

1. Add **View dataset** to the diagram. Click on DATA VISUALIZATION components tab, select **View dataset** component. Drag this component over the diagram and drop on the "Dataset" node.
2. Select the "View dataset" component in the diagram (if it is not already selected) and right click to show the popup menu. Choose the *View* command, dataset will be visible in the right frame.

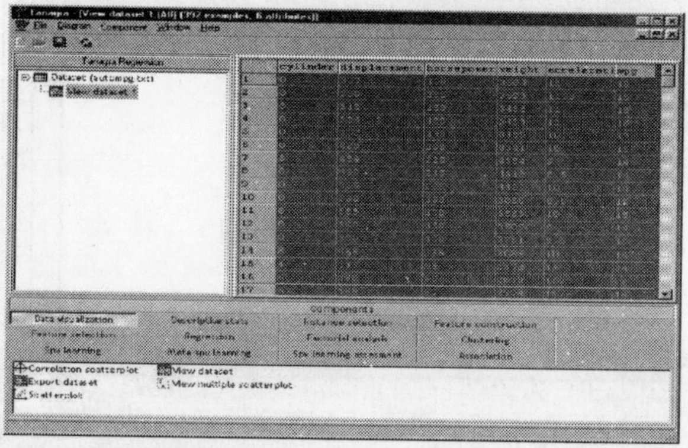

### *Define Status of Attributes for Regression*

1. Click on the "Dataset" component in the diagram and add a **Define Status** component with the shortcut in the tool bar. A dialog box appears automatically, you may define the status of each attribute.

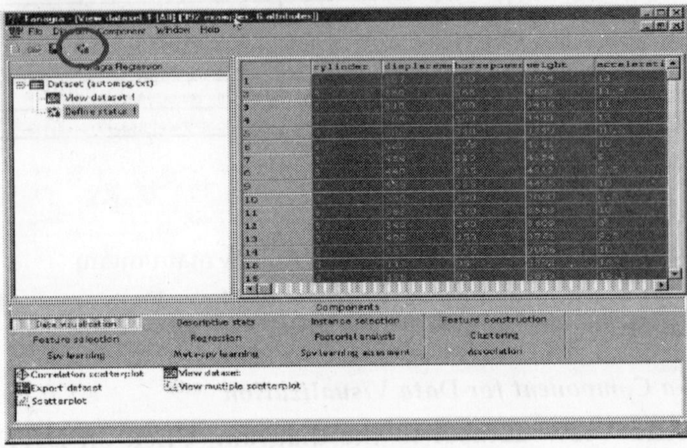


2. Ensure that "Input" tab is selected, choose the five first attributes of the list, and click on the arrow button to add them to the "Input" list. These attributes are "exogenous" attributes of the analysis.

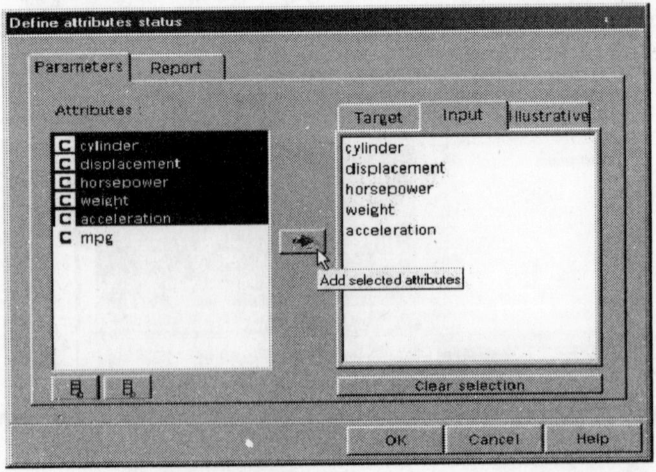

3. Activate the "Target" tab. Select "mpg" attribute and add this one to the target list. This Attribute is the "endogenous" attribute; we want to predict its values from exogenousones.

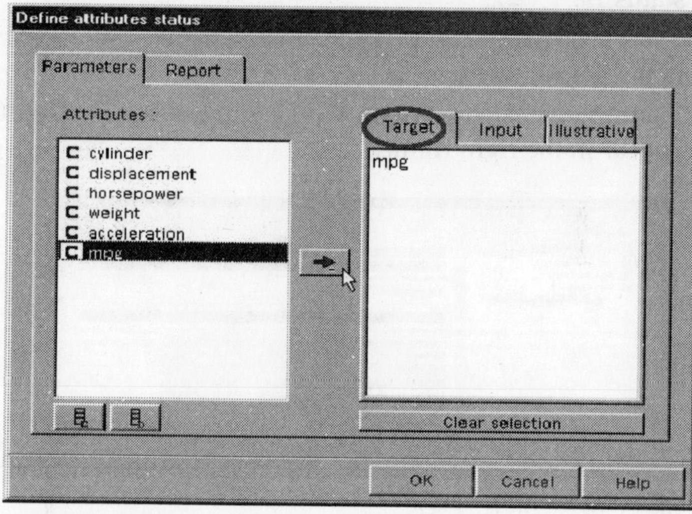


4. Click on the OK button to validate this selection and close this dialog box.
5. Double-click this **Define Status** component, you can verify on the right side of the window your attribute selection.

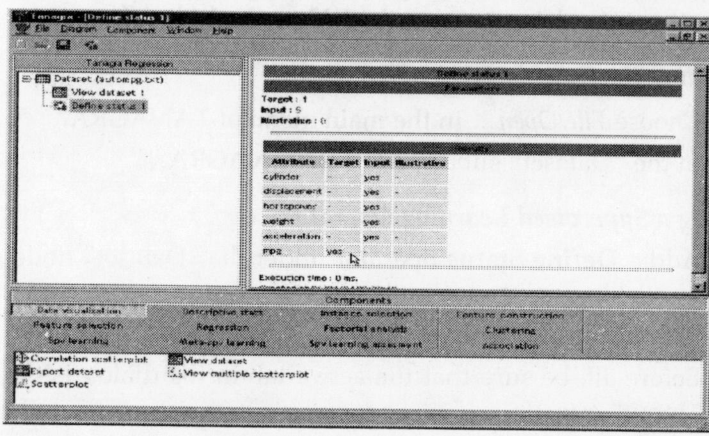

### *Perform the Regression Analysis*

1. Add **multiple linear regression components** (REGRESSION TAB) to the stream diagram, after the node «Define status 1».
2. There is no parameter to specify in this analysis, select *View* in the popup menu of

   "Multiple linear regression 1" to run the analysis. Results appear in the right frame.

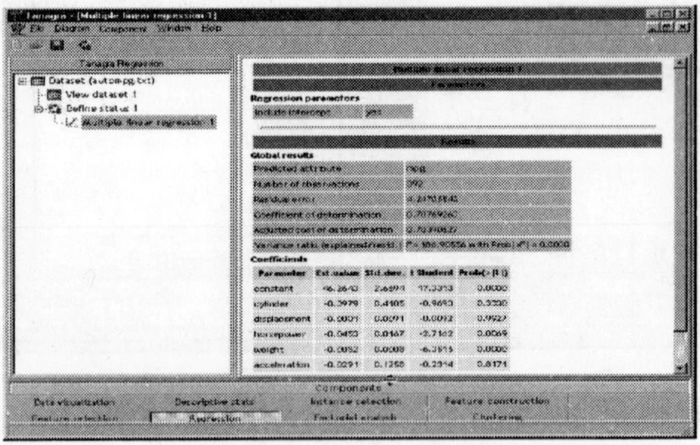

## Decision Tree Construction

Now we discussing how to apply a supervised learning method on your data; for this example. We are going to analyze the «weather.txt » dataset, using the ID3 method (decision tree).

### *Loading the Data in TANAGRA*

1. Choose *File/Open…* in the main menu of TANAGRA.
2. In the "Dataset" subdirectory of TANAGRA.

### *Using a Supervised Learning Operator*

1. Add a **Define Status** operator under the "Dataset" node, by clicking on its icon in the

   Shortcut toolbar.
2. Before all, be sure that the active tab in the dialog is the "Input" one.

3. In the same dialog box, activate the Target tab. Select the « class » attribute in the list and Click the arrow button.
4. Now you have defined the class attribute (« class » = Target), and the descriptors to do this (The others = Input).

   Click OK to validate and close this dialog box.

However, as TANAGRA always needs a meta-operator, a basic one exists that suits our Case, launching only one times the encapsulated method: the **Supervised Learning** operator. Add a **Supervised learning** component (META-SPV LEARNING tab) to the diagram, under the «Define status 1» node.

***Adding a Supervised Learning Component***

1. In the components palette, SPV LEARNING tab, drag with the mouse an **ID3** component on the « Supervised Learning » node you have added just before.

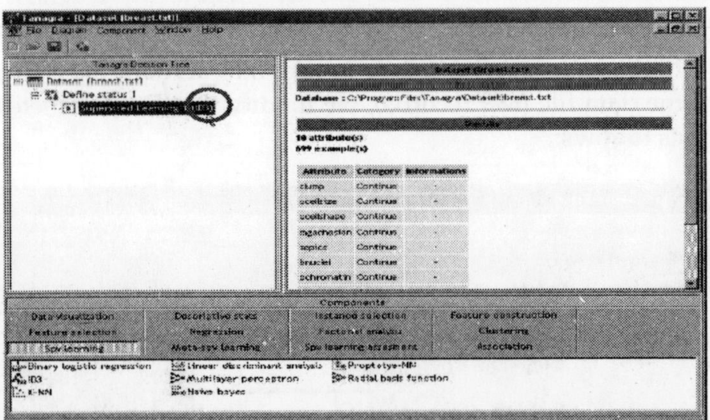

The operator is included in the Meta one, so we don't see another node under the Meta node, but we notice that the name of the method appears in the Meta node label.

***Defining the Method Parameter***

1. Activate the popup menu of the « Supervised learning (ID3) » node by right clicking on it .There is a new command

under the well-known *Parameters*: *Supervised parameters…* The first (*Parameters…*) applies to the meta-operator, the second (*Supervised parameters…)* Applies to the supervised learning operator. Choose this last one.

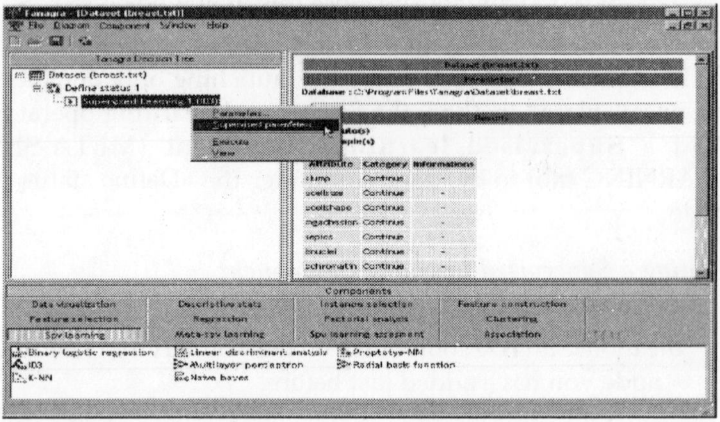


2. In the opening dialog box, to take into account the size of the data file (699 records), we modify the ID3 parameters as follows:

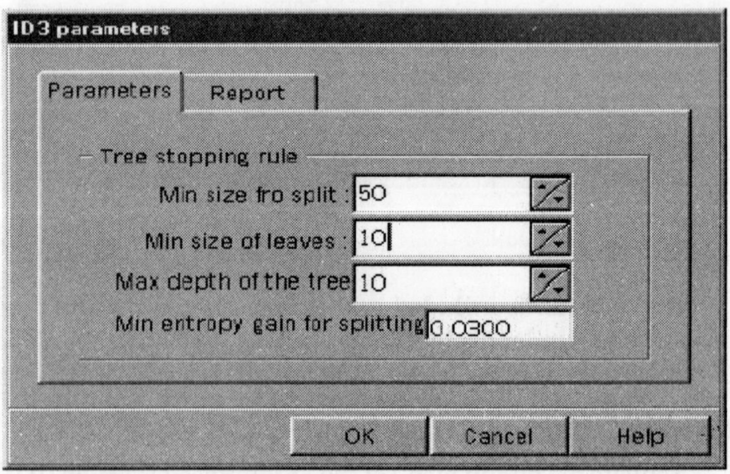


3. Click OK to validate.

## Executing the Learning Process

In the contextual menu of the Meta node, choose the *View* command. Results are displayed in the right frame.

## References

Hastie T., Tibshirani R., Friedman J. (2001) , "The Elements of Statistical Learning-Data Mining, Inference and Prediction", Ed. Springer.

Lebart L., Morineau A., Piron M. (2000), "Statistique Exploratoire Multidimensionnelle", Ed. Dunod.

Mitchell T. (1997), "Machine Learning", Ed. McGraw-Hill International Editions.

Saporta G. (2000), "Probabilités, Analyse des données et statistique", Ed. Technip.

Witten I., Frank E. (2000), "Data Mining-Practical Machine Learning Tools and Techniques with JAVA Implementations", Morgan Kaufmann Publishers.

# 28

# WinIDAMS

## Origin and a Short History of IDAMS

IDAMS was originally derived from the software package OSIRIS III.2 developed in the early seventies at the Institute for Social Research of the University of Michigan, U.S.A. It has been and is continuously enriched, modified and updated by the UNESCO Secretariat with the co-operation of experts from different countries.

## Introduction

IDAMS is a software package for the validation, manipulation and statistical analysis of data. It is organized as a collection of data management and analysis facilities accessible through a user interface and a common control language. Examples of the types of data that can be processed with IDAMS are: the answers to questions by respondents in a survey, information about books in a library, the personal characteristics and performance of students at a college, measurements from a scientific experiment. The common features of such data are that they consist of values of variables for each of a collection of objects/cases (e.g. in a sample survey, the questions correspond to the variables and the respondents to the cases).

IDAMS performs classical techniques such as table building, regression analysis, one-way analysis of variance, discriminant and cluster analysis and also some more advanced techniques such as principal components factor analysis and analysis of correspondences, partial order scoring, rank ordering of alternatives, segmentation and iterative typology.

In addition, WinIDAMS provides for interactive construction of multidimensional tables, interactive graphical Data Analysis Facilities

**Cluster analysis (CLUSFIND)**

Performs cluster analysis by partitioning a set of objects (cases or variables) into a set of clusters as determined by one of 6 algorithms, 2 based on partitioning around medoids, one based on fuzzy clustering and the other 3 based on hierarchical clustering.

**Linear regression (REGRESSN)**

Multiple linear regression analysis: standard and stepwise. Either a dataset or a correlation matrix may be used as input. Residuals can be printed with the Durbin-Watson statistic for their first-order autocorrelation, and they can also be output for **Interactive graphical exploration of data.** A separate component, GraphID, is available for exploring data through graphic displays. The basic display is in the form of multiple scatter plots for different pairs of variables. Additional information such as histograms and regression lines may be displayed on each plot. The plots may be manipulated in various ways. For example, selected cases can be marked in one plot and then highlighted in all the other plots. Parts of the display may be enlarged ("zoomed"). IDAMS matrices are displayed as three dimensional plots with rows and columns being represented by two of the axes and the third dimension being used to show the size of the statistic for each cell.

***Interactive Time Series Analysis***

Another separate component, TimeSID, provides a possibility for interactive analysis of time series. It contains analysis of trends, auto-correlations and cross-correlations, statistical and graphical analysis of time series values, tests of randomness and trends, forecasting for short terms, periodograms and estimation of spectral densities. Series can be transformed by calculating averages, arithmetic compositions, sequential differences, rates of change, smoothed by moving averages and decomposed using frequency filters.

**Data in IDAMS**

**IDAMS dataset-the Data file:** The data file input to IDAMS may be any character (ASCII) fixed format file, i.e. the values for a given variable occupy the same position (field) in the record for every case. Characteristics of this file are:

- 1-50 records per case;
- each case can contain up to 4096 characters;
- number of cases limited by the disk capacity and the internal representation of numbers;
- variables can be numeric (up to 9 characters) or alphabetic (up to 255 characters).

**IDAMS dataset-the Dictionary file:** The dictionary is used to describe the data:

- it may contain up to 1000 variables identified by a unique number between 1 and 9999;
- for each variable, it contains at minimum the variable's number, its type (numeric or alphabetic), and its location in the data record;
- for each variable, a variable name, two missing data codes, the number of decimal places and a reference number may also be specified;
- for qualitative variables, codes and corresponding labels may be included.

The pair of files consisting of a Dictionary file and the Data file it describes is known as an **IDAMS dataset.**

**IDAMS Commands and the "Setup" File**

With the exception of WinIDAMS interactive components, execution of an IDAMS program is launched by a setup. The setup contains information such as file specifications, program control statements, variable recoding instructions, etc., separated by IDAMS commands (starting with a $ character) which identify the kind of information being specified. The first IDAMS command in the Setup file always identifies the first program to be executed, e.g.

```
$RUN TABLES
$FILES
DICTIN = name of Dictionary file
DATAIN = name of Data file
$SETUP
control statements for TABLES program
$RECODE
variable recoding statements
```

**Standard IDAMS Features**

**Case selection.** By default all cases from a Data file will be processed in a program execution. To select a subset, a filter statement is included in the setup, e.g. INCLUDE V3=1 (include only those cases where variable 3 is equal to 1).

**Variable selection:** Variables are referenced by their numbers assigned in the dictionary. A set of variables is specified in a variable list following keywords such as VARS, CONVARS, OUTVARS. Such variable lists may also include R-variables constructed by the IDAMS Recode facility (see below), e.g. VARS=(V3-V6,V129,R100,R101).

**Transforming/recoding data:** A powerful Recode facility permits the recoding of variables and the construction of new variables. Recoding instructions are prepared by the user in the IDAMS Recode language. This includes the possibility of arithmetic computation as well as the use of several special functions for operations such as the grouping of values, the creation of "dummy" variables, etc. Conditional statements are also allowed. Examples of Recode statements for constructing 3 new variables R100, R101 and R102 are:

```
R100=V4+V5
R101=BRAC(V10,0-15=1,16-60=2,61-98=3,99=9)
IF(MDATA(V3,V4) OR V4 EQ 0) THEN V102=99 ELSE
R102=V3*100/V4
```

The R-variables thus constructed for each case can be used temporarily in the program being executed or can be saved in a dataset using the TRANS program.

**Weighting data:** When complex sampling procedures are used during data collection, it may be necessary to use different weights for cases during analysis. Such weights are usually stored as a variable in the Data file. The WEIGHT parameter is then used in the program control statements to invoke weighting, e.g. WEIGHT=V5.

**Overview of Steps to be Performed with WinIDAMS**

In this example, an IDAMS dictionary for the description of data collected by a questionnaire is prepared and data for a few respondents are entered. A set of IDAMS control statements (a "setup") is then prepared and used to produce frequency distributions of Age, Sex and Education (number of years) bracketed into 4 groups. The steps below are followed:

1. Create an application environment.
2. Prepare and store an IDAMS dictionary describing the variables in the data.
3. Enter the data (this step would be eliminated if the data were prepared outside WinIDAMS).
4. Prepare and store a "setup" of instructions specifying what is to be done with the data.
5. Execute the IDAMS program as given in the setup.

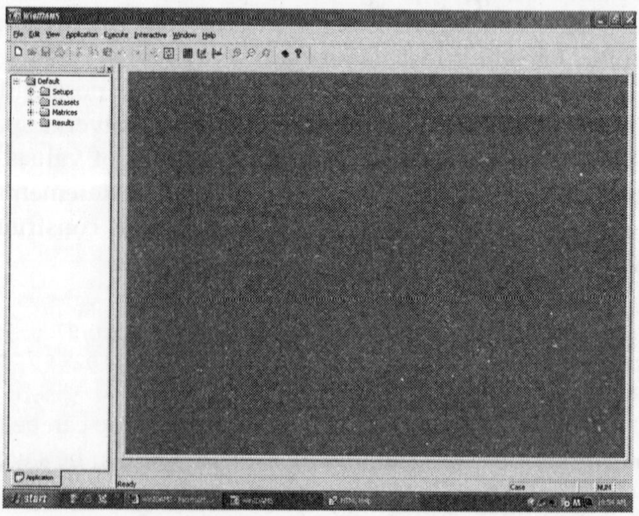

6. Review the results and modify the setup if necessary; then repeat from step 4.
7. Print the results.

To get started, first launch WinIDAMS. You will see the WinIDAMS Main window.

Press Ctrl/N or click on File/New. These commands open the New document dialogue:

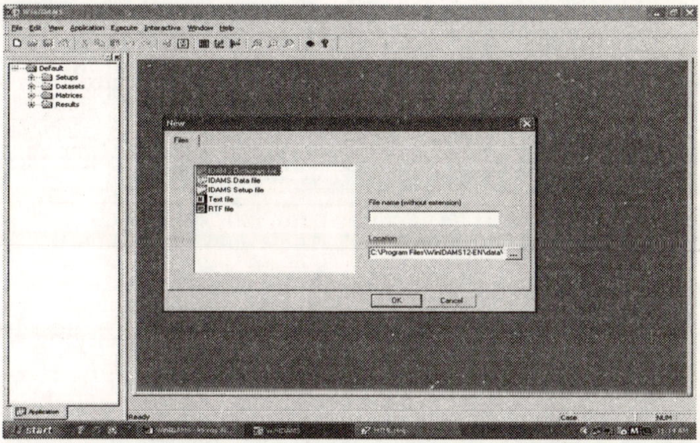


The dialogue displays the list of document types used in WinIDAMS. Choose "IDAMS Dictionary file", already selected by default.

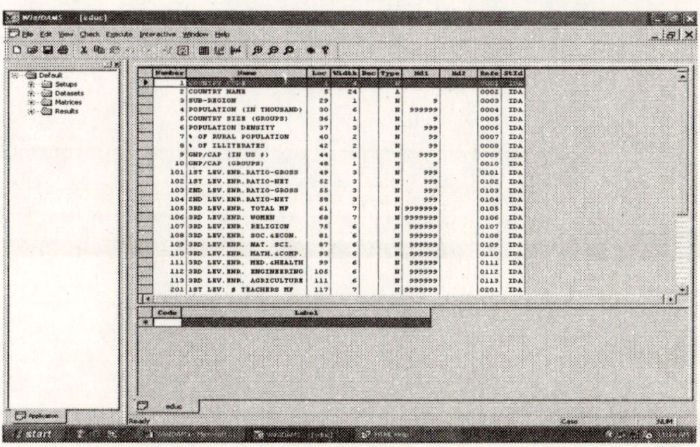

Enter the data by creating data file:

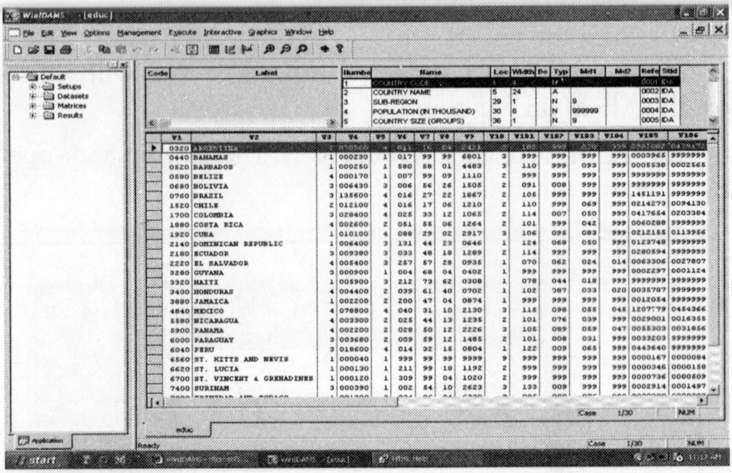


Prepare and store a "setup" of instructions specifying what is to be done with the data.

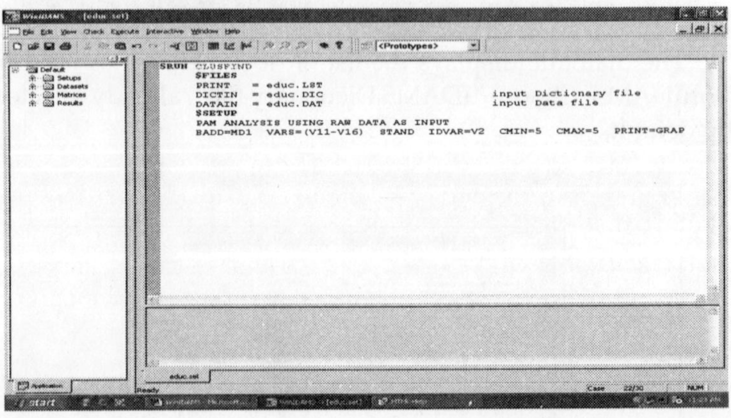


## Output

### *Multi Dimensional Table*

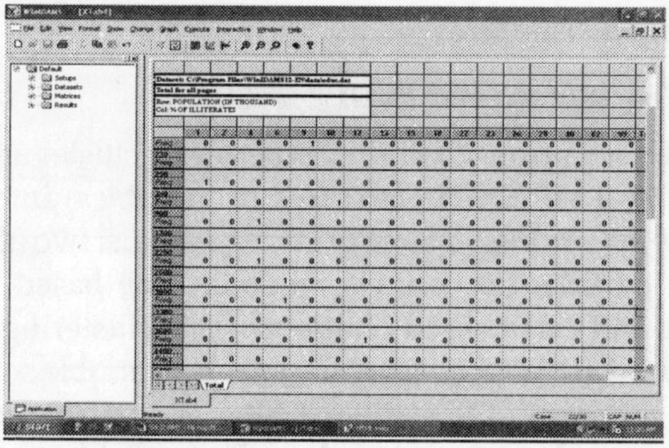

## Graphical Exploration

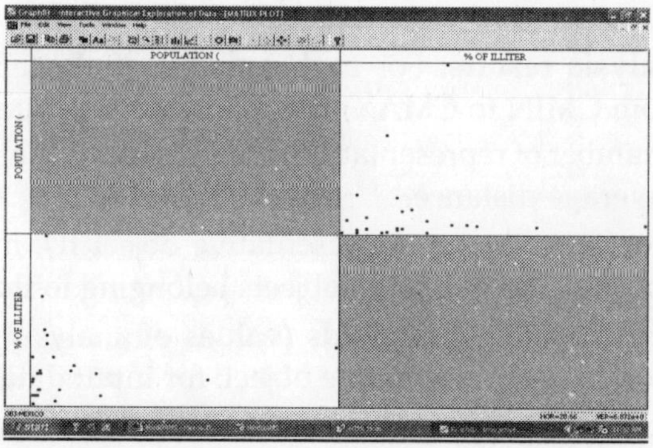


## Time Series Analysis

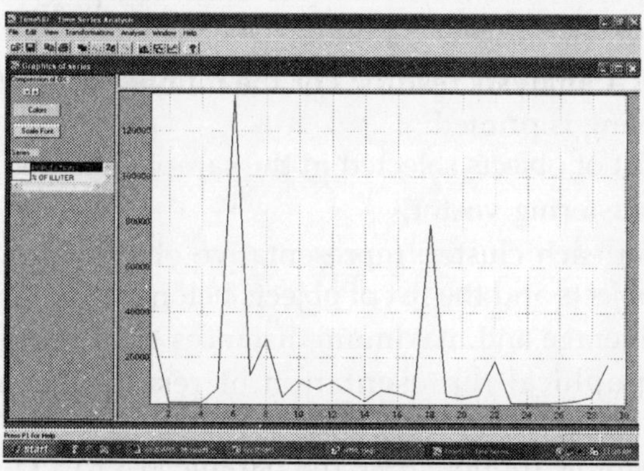

## Data Analysis Facilities

### *Cluster Analysis (CLUSFIND)*

**General Description:** CLUSFIND performs cluster analysis by partitioning a set of objects (cases or variables) into a set of clusters as determined by one of six algorithms: two algorithms based on partitioning around medoids, one based on fuzzy clustering and three based on hierarchical clustering.

**Standard IDAMS Features:** Case and variable selection. If raw data are input, the standard filter is available to select a subset of cases from the input data. The variables for analysis are specified in the parameter VARS.

### *Results*

**PAM analysis results:** For each number of clusters in turn (going from CMIN to CMAX) the following is printed:

- number of representative objects (clusters) and the final average distance,
- for each cluster: representative object ID, number of objects and the list of objects belonging to this cluster,
- coordinates of medoids (values of analysis variables for each representative object; for input dataset only),
- clustering vector (vector of numbers corresponding to the objects indicating to which cluster each object belongs) and clustering characteristics,
- graphical representation of results, i.e. a plot of silhouette for each cluster (optional - see the parameter PRINT).

**CLARA analysis results:** For the number of clusters tried the following is printed:

- list of objects selected in the sample retained,
- clustering vector,
- for each cluster: representative object ID, number of objects and the list of objects belonging to this cluster,
- average and maximum distances to each medoid,
- graphical representation of results, i.e. a plot of silhouette for each cluster belonging to the selected sample (optional-see the parameter PRINT).

### Input Dataset

The input raw dataset is a Data file described by an IDAMS dictionary. All variables used for analysis must be numeric; they may be integer or decimal valued. The case ID variable can be alphabetic. Variables used in PAM, CLARA, FANNY, AGNES or DIANA analysis should be interval scaled. Variables used in the MONA analysis should be binary (with 0 or 1 values). Note that CLUSFIND uses at most 8 characters of the variable name as provided in the dictionary.

### Setup Structure

```
$RUN CLUSFIND
$FILES
File specifications
$RECODE (optional with raw data input; unavailable
with matrix input)
Recode statements
$SETUP
1. Filter (optional; for raw data input only)
2. Label
3. Parameters
$DICT (conditional)
Dictionary for raw data input
$DATA (conditional)
Data for raw data input
$MATRIX (conditional)
Matrix for matrix input
Files:
FT09 input matrix (if $MATRIX not used and a matrix
input)
DICTxxxx input dictionary (if $DICT not used and
INPUT=RAWDATA)
DATAxxxx input data (if $DATA not used and INPUT=RAWDATA)
PRINT results (default IDAMS.LST)
```

### Program Control Statements

**Filter** (optional).

Selects a subset of cases to be used in the execution. Available only with raw data input.

*Example:* INCLUDE V8=5-10

**Label** (mandatory).

One line containing up to 80 characters to label the results.

*Example*: PARTITION AROUND MEDOIDS

**Parameters** (mandatory).

For selecting program options.

*Example:* ANALYSIS=PAM VARS= (V7-V12) IDVAR=V1 INPUT=RAWDATA/SIMILARITIES/DISSIMILARITIES/ CORRELATIONS

RAWD Input:

Data file described by an IDAMS dictionary.

**Parameters for input**

VARS= (variable list)

The variables to be used in this analysis. No default.

ANALYSIS=PAM/FANNY/CLARA/AGNES/DIANA/ MONA

Specifies the type of analysis to be performed.

PAM

Partition around medoids.

**Clar**

Partition around medoids (same as PAM), but for datasets of at least 100 cases. CLUSFIND will sample the cases and choose the best representative sample. Five samples of 40+2*CMAX cases are drawn (see CMAX parameter below). Only for raw data input.

CMIN=2 /n

For PAM the minimum number of clusters to try.

CMAX=n

For PAM, the maximum number of clusters to try.

For CLARA, the exact number of clusters to try.

Default: The larger of 20 and the value specified for CMIN.

PRINT= (DISSIMILARITIES, GRAPH, TRACE, VNAMES)

DISS

Print the dissimilarity matrix.

GRAP

Print the graphical representation of the results.

### *Example*

Clustering the first 100 cases into 5 groups using 6 quantitative variables V11-V16; variable values are standardized and Euclidean distance is used in calculations; clustering is done as partitioning around medoids; printing of graphics is requested; cases are identified by variable V2.

```
$RUN CLUSFIND
$FILES
PRINT = CLUS1.LST
DICTIN = MY.DIC input Dictionary file
DATAIN = MY.DAT input Data file
$SETUP
PAM ANALYSIS USING RAW DATA AS INPUT
BADD=MD1  VARS=(V11-V16)  STAND  IDVAR=V2  CMIN=5
CMAX=5 PRINT=GRAP
```

## Multidimensional Tables and their Graphical Presentation

### *Overview*

The interactive "Multidimensional Tables" component of WinIDAMS allows you to visualize and customize multidimensional tables with frequencies, row, column and total percentages, univariate statistics (sum, count, mean, maximum, minimum, variance, standard deviation) of additional variables, and bivariate statistics. Variables in rows and/or columns can either be nested (maximum 7 variables) or they can be put at the same level. Construction of a table can be repeated for each value of up to three "page" variables. Each page of the table can also be printed, or exported in free format (comma or tabulation character delimited) or in HTML format.

IDAMS datasets used as input must have the same name for the Dictionary and Data files with extensions .dic and .dat respectively.

Only one dataset can be used at a time, i.e. opening another dataset automatically closes the one being used.

## Graphical Exploration of Data

### *Overview*

GraphID is a component of WinIDAMS for interactive exploration of data through graphical visualization. It accepts two kinds of input:

- IDAMS datasets where the Dictionary and Data files must have the same name with extensions .dic and .dat respectively,
- IDAMS Matrix files where the extension must be .mat.

Only one dataset or one matrix file can be used at a time, i.e. opening of another file automatically closes the one being used.

## Time Series Analysis

### *Overview*

TimeSID is a component of WinIDAMS for time series analysis. It uses IDAMS datasets as input where the dictionary and data files must have the same name with extensions .dic and .dat respectively.

Only one dataset can be used at a time, i.e. opening of another dataset automatically closes the one being used.

## References

Kaufman, L., and Rousseeuw, P.J. (1990), "Finding Groups in Data: An Introduction to Cluster Analysis", John Wiley & Sons, Inc., New York.

Rousseeuw, P.J., Silhouettes (1987), "A Graphical Aid to the Interpretation and Validation of Cluster Analysis", *Journal of Computational and Applied Mathematics,* 20sss..